Activism under Fire

RECENT TITLES IN

Global and Comparative Ethnography
Edited by Javier Auyero

Violence at the Urban Margins
Edited by Javier Auyero, Philippe Bourgois, and Nancy Scheper-Hughes

Concrete Jungles
By Rivke Jaffe

Soybeans and Power
By Pablo Lapegna

Occupying Schools, Occupying Land
By Rebecca Tarlau

Privilege at Play
By Hugo Cerón-Anaya

Narrow Fairways
By Patrick Inglis

Lives on the Line
By Jeffrey J. Sallaz

The Ambivalent State
By Javier Auyero and Katherine Sobering

Beyond the Case
Edited by Corey M. Abramson and Neil Gong

Burning Matters
By Peter C. Little

Delivery as Dispossession
By Zachary Levenson

Activism under Fire
By Anjuli Fahlberg

Activism under Fire

The Politics of Non-Violence in Rio de Janeiro's Gang Territories

ANJULI FAHLBERG

OXFORD
UNIVERSITY PRESS

OXFORD
UNIVERSITY PRESS

Oxford University Press is a department of the University of Oxford. It furthers the University's objective of excellence in research, scholarship, and education by publishing worldwide. Oxford is a registered trade mark of Oxford University Press in the UK and certain other countries.

Published in the United States of America by Oxford University Press
198 Madison Avenue, New York, NY 10016, United States of America.

Library of Congress Cataloging-in-Publication Data
Names: Fahlberg, Anjuli, author.
Title: Activism under fire : the politics of non-violence in Rio de
Janeiro's gang territories / Anjuli Fahlberg.
Description: New York, NY : Oxford University Press, [2023] |
Series: Global and comparative ethnography | Includes bibliographical references and index.
Identifiers: LCCN 2022062187 (print) | LCCN 2022062188 (ebook) |
ISBN 9780197519332 (paperback) | ISBN 9780197519325 (hardback) |
ISBN 9780197519356 (epub) | ISBN 9780197519363
Subjects: LCSH: Slums—Brazil—Rio de Janeiro. | Gangs—Brazil—Rio de Janeiro. |
Violence—Brazil—Rio de Janeiro. | Nonviolence—Brazil—Rio de Janeiro. |
Urban poor—Brazil—Rio de Janeiro. | Marginality, Social—Brazil—Rio de Janeiro.
Classification: LCC HV4075 .R53 F345 2023 (print) | LCC HV4075 .R53 (ebook) |
DDC 307.3/364098153—dc23/eng/20230303
LC record available at https://lccn.loc.gov/2022062187
LC ebook record available at https://lccn.loc.gov/2022062188

DOI: 10.1093/oso/9780197519325.001.0001

Paperback printed by Sheridan Books, Inc., United States of America
Hardback printed by Bridgeport National Bindery, Inc., United States of America

Contents

Acknowledgments   vii
Survivors   xiii

Introduction—Conflict Activism in Rio de Janeiro's Gang Territories   1

1. Cidade de Deus: A Contested Territory   33

2. Milking the Resource Matrix: Democracy, Development, and
   Digital Devices   76

3. Violent Clientelism and Gendered Governance   113

4. Political Upcycling: Anti-Violence Protest through Education,
   Culture, and Racial Solidarity   149

5. Ties that Strengthen, Ties that Bind: Favela Activists in Urban
   Politics and Transnational Movements   196

Conclusion—Seek and Ye Shall Find: Looking for Non-Violence in
   Conflict Zones   234

Appendix—Ethnographic Reflections: Participatory Action Research in
   Areas of Violence   247
Notes   259
Bibliography   265
Index   283

Acknowledgments

"Daughter, when are you coming back?" Esther asked me one day over WhatsApp, a question she asked me at least once a month since I had last visited Cidade de Deus. I had returned to the United States just before the COVID-19 pandemic hit, and shortly after travel to Brazil became too risky. But I remained involved in the neighborhood through a series of research projects we conducted online, and I am still in regular contact with Esther and her family, who so generously hosted me and welcomed me into their family throughout my time researching Cidade de Deus. However, it has been a while since I last sat on Esther's couch sipping coffee, laughing along as her sister Maria Rita joked about the latest home remedy Esther had concocted for her swollen legs, flinching at Maria Rita's near-death escape from a shootout, and debating with Esther's son Leonardo about the different forms of politics in Cidade de Deus. Theirs was a home filled with love, laughter, and incredible hearts and minds. Esther, Maria Rita, Leonardo, Esther's younger son André, and all in Esther's large kinship network went out of their way to make me feel at home, help me understand their neighborhood, and ensure that I was well cared for, safe, and productive while I was in the field.

Living with Esther's family in Cidade de Deus, hearing about the trials and battles of the neighborhood's residents, learning from dozens of incredible activists, and writing about their stories and strategies has been an amazing journey. What began as a sociological investigation into how people organize in contexts of violence and repression became an opportunity to spend time with some of the people I most respect and care for, whose lives are filled with more challenges and more victories than could possibly fit in this book. The challenges they face are enormous, and the victories they achieve may sometimes seem small, but they serve as a reminder of the humanity, the interpersonal networks of support, and the deep commitments to making change in areas that the state and society have relegated to its most vulnerable and dangerous margins.

Words cannot express how grateful I am to the many people I met in Cidade de Deus who allowed me to hear their stories, visit them in their homes, participate in their meetings, and eventually join them in the fight for improvements to their community. I would not have been able to conduct this research without their willingness to let me into their organizations and events, their invitations to accompany them to new sites of action, and their openness about their ideas, struggles, inspirations, and fears.

In order to protect their identities, I thank them by their pseudonyms. Thank you to Esther, Maria Rita, Leonardo, André, Solange, Rosangela, Sonia, Natalia, Isabella, Carmen, Geovana, Luz, Clara, Camilla, Jefferson, João Paulo, and dozens of other Cidade de Deus residents and activists whose stories are part of this book. Thank you for the work you do to make this world a better place, for shining light in dark spaces, and for giving us another reason to hope that, even in the harshest environments, life and love can continue to thrive. Your insights, enthusiasm, suggestions, critiques, support, care, guidance, and the many close bonds we established in my years of learning, researching, and writing are ultimately what have kept me going and have made this project so worthwhile.

In addition to the activist community in Cidade de Deus, I received incredible guidance and support from many people at Northeastern University as I completed my PhD in Sociology. Liza Weinstein, the chair of my dissertation committee, has been an endless source of support, while also motivating me to improve my work. She constantly challenged me to ask, "Where is the puzzle here?" and to push the limits of sociological theory. Gordana Rabrenovic was my rock in some of the hardest years of my academic career, reassuring me that things would work out, even if not in the ways I had originally planned. In addition to being a very good friend, Thomas Vicino fought for me relentlessly, helping me find funding for my research, teaching me how to write academic articles and present at conferences, and otherwise training me on the "hidden curriculum" of the academy. Valentine Moghadam was the first to expose me to studies of social movements and help me appreciate the many ways that activists, and women in particular, have become fearless leaders of social change. Diane Davis, at Harvard University's Graduate School of Design, challenged me to think broadly and deeply about Cidade de Deus, to place it in conversation with larger questions about urban violence and politics, and to reflect critically on my findings.

Many others in the Department of Sociology and Anthropology at Northeastern University have been critical to my success. Sarah Faude, Edgar Benitez, Sam Maron, Yingchan Zhang, Anna Revette, Elicia Cousins, Marhabo Sarapova, Mollie Pepper, Camilla Gaiaschi, Steve Vallas, Kathrin

Zippel, Linda Blum, Doreen Lee, Ineke Marshall, Jack Greene, Chris Chambers, Phil Brown, and many more have offered me guidance, support, reflections on drafts, new ideas, or simply the space to vent or brainstorm aloud. Thank you also to Sara Wylie for teaching me about Community Based Participatory Research and encouraging me to apply these principles in my own research. Many other Northeastern faculty and students were also very helpful, including Dietmar Offenhuber, Carlos Cuevas, Lori Lefkowitz, and Erika Boeckler.

I thank the Department of Sociology and Anthropology, the Dean's Office, the Office of the President, and the Office of the Provost at Northeastern University for their generous support of my scholarship through multiple grants and fellowships. These included the Outstanding Graduate Student Research Award, the Graduate Thesis/Dissertation Research Grant, the Tier-1 Initiative, the University Excellence Fellowship, the Departmental Fellowship for Graduate Study, the Teaching Assistantship, the Dean's Fellowship, and the Public and Applied Sociology Award. Without this funding, my research would not have been possible.

I am grateful to the National Science Foundation's Law and Social Science Division for the Doctoral Dissertation Research Improvement Grant (NSF 15-514), which helped to cover many travel expenses and the transcription of dozens of interviews. Tufts University also provided generous support for my travels through various Faculty Research Awards, as well as funding from the Center for Humanities at Tufts to work on my book; the Tisch Faculty Fellowship helped fund additional research in Cidade de Deus. The American Association for University Women's American Short-Term Research Publication Grant provided invaluable financial assistance at a time when I most needed it.

Thank you to Kryssia Ettel, who transcribed hundreds of pages of interviews with great accuracy and efficiency. I also want to thank the Urban Affairs Association for selecting me for the 2017 Alma J. Young Emerging Scholar award. I am grateful to the Latin American Studies Association's Defense and Public Security Section and the Society for the Study of Social Problems' Conflict, Social Action and Change Division for selecting drafts of my research for best paper awards. I am extremely grateful to the American Sociological Association (ASA) for selecting my dissertation, on which this book is based, for the 2019 Best Dissertation Award, and the ASA's Section on Collective Behavior and Social Movement for the 2019 Distinguished Contribution to Scholarship Dissertation Award. Thank you also to the ASA's Section on

Peace, War and Social Conflict for awarding an Honorable Mention for the Best Article Award to my article, "Rethinking Favela Governance: Nonviolent Politics in Rio de Janeiro's Gang Territories," published in *Politics in Society*.

I was incredibly fortunate to be welcomed into the Sociology Department at Tufts University as I started working on this manuscript. Every faculty and staff member in our department has been supportive and offered helpful guidance on various stages of the process. Thank you to Helen Marrow and Freeden Blume Ouer, who have been as generous with their time as with their mentorship on transitioning into an academic role. Jill Weinberg generously read and offered suggestions on my introductory chapter. Rosemary Taylor, Natasha Warikoo, Adrian Cruz, Jon Dzitko, Sarah Sobieraj, Paul Joseph, Victoria Dorward, Katherine Blake, and Amy Pendleton have offered invaluable suggestions and enthusiasm for my scholarship. Caleb Scoville, Felipe Dias, and Daanika Gordon have helped me process questions and ideas and make decisions on how to handle difficult situations. Finally, I don't know how I would have finished my research without John LiBassi, who has spent dozens of hours helping me figure out how to send grant money to an informal neighborhood. Finally, a huge thank you to Carolyn Talmadge at the Tufts Data Lab for making such beautiful maps.

The Latin American Studies Program at Tufts has also been a welcoming and intellectually enriching space. Thank you to Nina Gerassi-Navarro and Christiane Soares, who were early supporters of my research in Brazil, along with Eulogio Guzman, Katrina Burgess, and Consuelo Cruz. Thank you to Katrina for continuing to mentor me throughout these years. My deans—Jim Glaser, Bárbara Brizuela, and Heather Nathans—have supported my scholarship and academic success in innumerable ways. Thank you also to Peter Levine, whose enthusiasm for my research and work in Participatory Action Research not only inspired more confidence in me about my work but also opened many doors for new research and teaching opportunities. Cedric De Leon, now at the University of Massachusetts, Amherst, gave me incredible encouragement as I transitioned from student to professor. I am similarly indebted to many of my students who are as brilliant as they are kind and fiercely committed to social justice: Sophia Costa, Maya Velasquez, Harper Wise, Tori Simon, Athena Nair, Rachel Totz, Mark Beckwith, Gabe Reyes, Selomi Dayaprema, Gabriella Cantor, Olivia Roskill, and many, many more.

Many people across academia in the United States and Brazil have been instrumental in getting this book written and published. Pablo Lapegna, at the University of Georgia, and Javier Auyero, at the University of Texas, Austin, were early supporters of my research in Cidade de Deus and helped open doors that led to a contract with Oxford University Press. They have also become wonderful colleagues and offered me guidance throughout my career. I am very grateful to my brilliant and supportive reviewers, who read and helped me revise an early draft of my book: Sonia Alvarez, Marie Berry, Eduardo Moncada, Sonia Fleury, and Keisha Khan-Perry. Their comments were incredibly insightful and helpful. Marie, in particular, has become a friend and mentor, offering me advice and encouragement at many turns. The anonymous reviewers of my book and related journal articles have also played an important role in helping me think through my arguments and revise the text. Jenny Pearce, Brinton Lykes, Michelle Fine, Julian Go, Raewyn Connell, Enrique Desmond Arias, Thiago Rodrigues, Alba Zaluar, Daniel Esser, and many others have given me their time and feedback as I developed my ideas and this manuscript. A huge thank you goes out to Shannon Oltmann, who helped me get this book over the finish line, providing excellent comments, edits and reassurance as I finalized each chapter.

It is an honor to have this book included in the Global and Comparative Ethnography Series at Oxford University Press. Thank you to James Cook, my acquisitions editor at Oxford, for helping me get through the long review and contract process. I am grateful to Alexcee Bechthold, my productions editors at Oxford and Kavitha Yuvaraj and her team at Newgen Knowledge Works for bearing with me as I asked endless questions about the production process and made last-minute revisions to my manuscript.

Finally, none of this would have been possible without my wonderful, loving, and supportive family back home. My son, Jordan, now 11 years old, put up with my constant trips to and from Brazil. While back home, he gave me endless snuggles and laughter that helped me get through the secondary trauma that came with working in a neighborhood with so much loss and violence. I am grateful to his father and stepmother for caring for him whenever I was away. My mother instilled in me both a commitment to social justice and the belief that I could succeed at anything I put my mind to. Thank you, mom, for reading drafts of my book and spending hours talking me through the stress and anxiety that comes with this process. My father, sister, brother, and stepmother have been encouraging and engaged in this long journey, cheering me on as I got closer to the finish line. Thank you to my partner, Henrique, and my stepson, Heitor, who have been bright lights on this journey, showering me with love and affection and helping relieve the angst that has come along the way. I am also indebted to many friends who have become like family to me, in particular Elicia Cousins and JoAnn Rojas, whose constant love and support have become essential to my well-being.

And thank you to anyone who takes time to read this book. I have written it for you.

Survivors

"Survivors"
By Valéria Barbosa (translation by author)

Living in chaos, in crossfire
is to live threatened, at all times threatened.
Not having a voice to be heard is to deepen the wound of the lack of
    public policies.
Government enters, power leaves
and the scourge of social differences
floods the being of the favelas.

What to do?
How to live?
Threats on all sides.
Gunshots, hunger, disease, unemployment and silence . . .
Changing this imposed destiny of colonial servitude is the duty of
    liberation science. Education!
Schools closed, mouth shut, body shot, eyes in tears

It remains to survive and scream to change this rotten power.

"Sobreviventes"

Viver no caos, em fogo cruzado
é viver ameaçado, em todos os momentos calado.
Não ter voz pra ser ouvido é aprofundar a ferida da falta de políticas
    públicas.
Entra governo, sai o poder
e a mazela das diferenças sociais
inunda o ser das favelas.

O que fazer?
Como viver?

Ameaças por todos os lados.

Tiros, fome, doença, desemprego e o silêncio . . .

Modificar este imposto destino de servidão colonial é dever da
ciência da libertação. A educação!

Escolas fechadas, boca calada, corpo alvejado, olhos em pranto

Resta sobreviver e gritar pra mudar este podre poder.

Introduction

Conflict Activism in Rio de Janeiro's Gang Territories

Politics in the Park

Latin America's gang territories, spaces governed in part or in full by organized drug gangs, are some of the last places one might expect to find non-violent activism. The rapid expansion of drug trafficking organizations in the 1970s and 1980s into poor urban neighborhoods across the region, coupled with routine invasions of increasingly militarized police forces, transformed these spaces into potent sites for the expanding drug trade and ensuing turf wars between rival gangs. Residents in these neighborhoods face the constant threat of being struck by a stray bullet while walking their children to school or making dinner in their kitchens. They must also contend with the risk of being intentionally killed by a gang member or police officer for disobeying their orders, snitching, speaking out against them, becoming embroiled in corrupt political schemes, or otherwise posing a threat to their power. Armed conflict and political repression have made collective organizing for social and political rights so challenging in gang territories that it might seem impossible. This is compounded by decades of racialized segregation, poverty, and urban exclusion, which further challenge residents' capacity to mobilize. Despite these seemingly insurmountable obstacles, non-violent activism plays a prominent role in the socio-political landscape of Cidade de Deus—or CDD as most locals call it—one of Rio de Janeiro's most notorious gang territories.

* * *

"Come closer, everyone!" Natalia gestured enthusiastically, inviting passersby to join the circle. She leaned into the microphone in her hand: "Testing, one two three . . . one two three." A few feet from our circle, homeless folks settling down on cardboard cots for the night raised their heads in interest. Cars zoomed by on their way from the city's downtown to wealthy neighborhoods nearby. CDD residents descending the bus from a long day of work looked

Activism under Fire. Anjuli Fahlberg, Oxford University Press. © Oxford University Press 2023.
DOI: 10.1093/oso/9780197519325.003.0001

over with curiosity. A sole police officer sat in the park's bullet-ridden police booth behind us, a presence both disconcerting and calming. At any moment, he could summon other officers to disrupt our group. Yet his relaxed demeanor also suggested that tonight the police were not preparing to invade the neighborhood and set off yet another gun fight with drug traffickers selling drugs just a few blocks away.

"Folks," Natalia said in her low voice, pushing her glasses up with her index finger, "we are here to share our opinions about the recent impeachment vote. If you have an opinion about it, come share it. The favela is never heard, but our voice matters. Mic, anyone? Who wants to go first?" She smiled at the other members of Art Talk, a collective of poets, hip hop singers, painters, sculptors, actors from Cidade de Deus. While their regular event was a monthly poetry open mic, today was a special occasion. Brazil's House of Representatives had voted two days earlier to impeach progressive president Dilma Rousseff, a move widely seen by left-leaning groups as a coup against the Worker's Party. It had triggered rage and fear among many CDD residents, who feared the loss of vital welfare programs under a new regime.

Art Talk members shifted uncomfortably, equivocating about who would take the mic next. A group of older men playing cards on a table farther back turned in our direction as more passersby joined in. In an effort to be helpful, I grabbed the poster I had made a few minutes earlier that read "What is democracy? Come share your opinion!" With Natalia's blessing, I began wandering the park inviting people to join our circle.

Natalia handed the microphone to Osmar, a man in his 40s who offered to read a poem off his phone. His voice echoed through a small speaker, which he had connected via a long extension cord to the police booth. I marveled at Osmar's sleight of hand, having convinced the officer to let us use his outlet to feed energy to the group's protest. Osmar paused awkwardly as he scrolled through his phone looking for his poem. He found it and began to read it passionately, decrying the injustice of a corrupt political system, pausing occasionally to allow his phone screen to reload. He finished and smiled, embarrassed, as the people standing around clapped and nodded in solidarity. Gradually, other Art Talk members gained confidence and stepped up to share their views about the latest political scandal, the corruption of their political system, their distrust of national leaders, and the effects this had on Rio's favelas, or poor informal settlements, which had been taken over by drug traffickers many decades earlier.[1] As crowd members gained confidence, their voices raised and they pumped their hands in fists as they raged against the system. Favela residents remained poor, they claimed, even as rich politicians stole public money. They decried the racism and brutality of the police, the destructiveness of the unequal distribution of urban resources, the state's investments in tourists and the rich at the expense of its own citizens, and the hypocrisy of the war on drugs, which criminalized poor Black people,[2] even as politicians engaged in their own criminal activities.

I looked anxiously behind us at the officer, searching for clues about whether he was planning to expel or arrest us. He barely glanced at us, seemingly uninterested in the anti-state, anti-policing discourses of the group. Why is he letting us get away with this? I wondered. And why isn't Natalia worried about the drug gangs, stationed only a few blocks away? Drug sale points, located on most street corners in CDD, allowed drug lords to keep their eyes on the street and oversee the comings, goings, and doings of the community. Surely they would hear about our protest on their turf. Yet Natalia appeared unconcerned.

Feeling emboldened by the speeches of other residents, Maria Rita stepped up to the microphone to add to the collective diatribe against the state. Though she usually preferred to be an observer in these overtly political events, Maria Rita had been infuriated by the impeachment vote. Her family and I had watched the grueling spectacle on television from her living room couch as the mostly white male House of Representatives had cast their vote one at a time in favor or against the impeachment. It had felt like an extremely long soccer game, with the running vote tally displayed on a scoreboard behind Chamber of Deputies president Eduardo Cunha. As the six-hour vote went on, anti-Dilma sentiment became increasingly enthusiastic. In exaggerated displays of masculine solidarity, the reps applauded and screamed so loudly their faces contorted and turned red. They high-fived and body-slammed each other with each anti-Dilma vote, finally hoisting the representative who cast the deciding impeachment vote aloft, crowd surfing him across the assembly floor. Maria Rita and her family had found the proceedings as entertaining as they did disturbing. But animated laughter at the absurdity of the scene gradually gave way to solemn silence as Dilma's—and the country's—fate was sealed. It was not a soccer match, after all.

The morning after the vote, I awoke to a message from Natalia on the Art Talk WhatsApp text message group suggesting that they organize a public Open Mic night to discuss the impeachment. Natalia had founded Art Talk five years earlier to bring together CDD artists. For her and many other local artists, Art Talk had become a space of not just culture but also politics. Or better, politics through culture. They were not able to engage in the types of mass protests we often see on the news, but in Cidade de Deus, these local artists were among the most vocal advocates for economic equality, democracy, civil rights, and racial justice. They called the event "Open Microphone is Politics: Respect the Popular Vote" and scheduled it for Tuesday night.

The Open Mic proceeded as planned. In total, around 10 people from Art Talk had been able to attend, and they were joined by a handful of passersby. For two hours the attendees took turns railing against the state and social injustice into the microphone as others clapped, nodded, or hooted in solidarity. While the event was smaller than Natalia had hoped, it seemed to fulfill two of her goals: to give CDD residents the opportunity to have a voice in the political process and to occupy public space with political claims-making. Holding the Open Mic next to the police booth, which had so frequently been at the center of gunfire, was a statement that the park did not belong only to its armed actors, but also to its unarmed residents.

As the Open Mic wrapped up, Osmar asked the police officer in the cabin to take a picture of our group. He agreed, dragging himself slowly from the cabin and taking the phone from Osmar. We huddled together as Natalia made a peace sign with her fingers, and we smiled into the phone—and at the military police officer behind it. Standing in the crosshairs between the police and the drug trade, Art Talk had transformed the park into a political space, a site for contesting corruption, racism, and violence. It was neither the first nor the last time residents organized around these issues. The open mic was one of hundreds of events organized by residents within and beyond the borders of their neighborhood to demand better conditions for the favela. But it left me with questions that the rest of this book tries to answer: What made this activism possible? How did activists manage to organize so publicly without incurring the wrath of the police or drug traffickers? And what, if anything, did this activism accomplish?

Repression, Violence, and the Spaces of Activism

In its effort to explain how Art Talk and dozens of other groups in Cidade de Deus have managed to protest violence and social injustice without getting killed, this book contributes to a much broader conversation about how social mobilization operates in contexts of extreme violence and political repression. Activism, which I define here as non-violent collective action aimed at social and political change,[3] is never an easy undertaking. Organizing for social change is a struggle even in countries with strong constitutional protections for citizens' rights to free speech, assembly, and protest, as well as more formal channels for changing laws. Activists face challenges to assemble resources, create a unified front, persuade people to act, stand up to power-holding elites, and achieve long-lasting political and social change. Furthermore, activists are never free from the threat of violence by state forces, as regular news images of police brutality against protestors in democratic countries have demonstrated.

Most of the world's population, however, does not live in countries with relatively functional democracies that provide political protections and civil liberties. The 2022 Freedom House report found that 80% of the world's population lives in a country categorized as "Not Free" or "Partly Free" (Freedom House 2022). These regimes are often characterized by one-party systems, limited (or non-existent) systems of checks and balances, severe corruption, restrictions on free speech and protest, and persecution against minoritized ethnic, racial, or social groups.

Political repression does not operate only at the national level. As the world rapidly urbanizes, political conflicts and restrictions are rescaled to cities. Urban centers have increasingly become the sites of ethnic, racial, and economic diversity, mass migration, national and international economies, and cultural and ethnic diversity. Consequently, cities are also core areas for conflict, militarization, and violent repression (Graham 2011; King 2021; Konaev 2019). Even in "free" countries, like Brazil and Mexico, violence and corruption at the urban or neighborhood levels limit citizens' ability to speak out against oppressive actors and policies. The rescaling of politics to the urban level also means that many of the images of repression of protest and activism are taking place in major cities, where both national and municipal leaders—and their security forces—are based.

Restrictions on political rights are sometimes formalized, declared by government officials, or written into state laws and enforced by state-sanctioned policing. Just as frequently, however, repression is enforced in more ambiguous or informal practices, such as when activists are imprisoned for crimes they did not commit or when states "hire out" repression to paramilitary or vigilante groups (Hunt 2009; Sheridan and Zuñiga 2019). Non-state actors, such as organized criminal groups, guerrilla fighters, and vigilantes also play a heavy role in restricting political and social organizing, such as when they assassinate journalists, human rights' defenders, members of oppositional political parties, and anyone else who poses a threat to their power (Dueñas 2019). It is not uncommon for officials in the state to engage in corrupt ties with violent non-state actors, making it difficult—and perhaps even irrelevant—to distinguish between "state" and "non-state" repression. This constellation of repressive tactics and actors can create an especially constrained and dangerous landscape in which to mobilize for rights (Córdova 2019; Krause 2018; Krook and Sanín 2016; Zulver 2022).

Paradoxically, while violent repression constrains activism, it also creates an even greater urgency for it: the fewer rights people have, the more they need them. The consequence of punishing activism, therefore, is not the disappearance of organized political and social action, but its reconfiguration (Almeida 2003; McAdam et al. 2001; Moss 2014). It transforms into what I think of as *conflict activism*, or collective action aimed at securing the rights and needs of a group of people in a context of political repression and the threat of physical violence. These threats may come from state or non-state actors, or, more frequently, from both. While groups may use a variety of tactics to achieve their goals, including deploying their own forms of violence, this book is interested in non-violent collective action, which rejects the use of violence, the threat of violence, or the direct engagement with armed actors to achieve the group's goals.

There are many documented strategies employed by conflict activism. One tactic we often hear about in the news is when dissenting groups engage in high-risk oppositional politics, which entails direct confrontation with the state or other governing actors in order to change policies or practices, or even demand regime change (Loveman 1998; Staudt 2009; Zulver 2022). Confrontational tactics can include public speeches against those in power, the circulation of petitions, sit-ins, and street protests, as well as more radical measures like hunger strikes among imprisoned activists and self-immolation in public spaces. However, direct activism in contexts of violent repression is often severely punished through imprisonment and death, leading movements to lose leaders quickly and forcing remaining members to change strategies in order to keep themselves, their families, and the movement alive (Ayoub 2010; McAdam 1982).

An alternative approach is to "hide" from the oppressive regime and instead mobilize underground until the political climate is more open to change (Lawrence 2017). In some cases, activists may go into exile and organize the movement from abroad (Gideon 2018; Henry and Plantan 2022; Moss 2022; Ong 2006), or ask transnational allies for help (Keck and

Sikkink 1998; Moss 2014; Roth and Dubois 2020). It is also common for activists to utilize symbolic and more "disguised" forms of protest. For instance, An Xiao Mina (2019) argues that in China, images of ordinary things, such as the sunflower and the Gobi desert's grass mud horse have become associated with protest against the regime. In other cases, songs, paintings, books, and other forms of cultural production may convey a group's protests. Due to their hidden or double meanings, these images or works can be difficult for a regime to interpret or to censor (Dunn 2016; Groves 2012; Johnston 2011). However, symbolic protest can be limited in its ability to achieve tangible political change if disconnected from more direct actions, and may also incur the wrath of a repressive regime if it becomes too blatant or visible. Many movements engage in what Oleg Yanitsky (2010) refers to as "differentiation," or a fragmentation between those engaged in more defiant activities and those focused on more normative (and safer) efforts.

While these are some of the strategies we have come to associate with conflict activism, the activism I observed in Cidade de Deus did not fit neatly into these configurations. CDD activists did not speak out against drug traffickers and rarely confronted the police. Nor did they organize underground or through hidden symbols. Their activities were public, and known to violent actors. As I describe in greater detail later in the chapter, CDD's activism hinged on occupying the political, social, and cultural spaces available for direct claims-making, while avoiding more dangerous people and demands. This included taking advantage of resources on multiple levels, capitalizing on gendered political spaces, and politicizing normative cultural and racial frames, while taking their demands to a variety of state and non-state actors outside their neighborhood. In many respects, they practiced what Lynette Chua (2012:714) terms "pragmatic resistance," or the maneuvering within openings to the formal legal structures and cultural norms while refraining from more oppositional mobilization tactics.

In order to do this successfully, CDD's activism did not conform to the typical forms and tactics we have come to associate with social movements. Instead, it employed *patchwork politics*, collective actions fragmented into many small-scale groups or clusters, rather than one cohesive movement. Each cluster provided a distinct set of resources, organizing strategies, and political voice to the neighborhood and connected to a diversity of urban and transnational social movements. Within CDD, this fragmentation afforded activists a kind of "political invisibility" (Gallo-Cruz 2020), whereby they were known to violent actors but not viewed as politically threatening to them.

Selina Gallo-Cruz (2020), in her study of women's mobilizations in Argentina, Yugoslavia, and Liberia, found that female activists were often perceived by regimes as non-threatening, which in turn afforded them "free spaces" in which to organize against violence. Similarly, the feminization of conflict activism in Cidade de Deus, which includes placing women in leadership positions and engaging in "women's work" of caretaking and social development, enables CDD's activists—whether female or male—to operate without being perceived as a direct threat to the masculinized network of drug gangs, police, and corrupt politicians.

Conflict activism is also racialized. Most activists I got to know identified as Black and centered demands for racial justice and against racist policing in their efforts to fight for their neighborhood and broader citizenship rights. By highlighting favela residents' shared experiences of racial discrimination and segregation, activists articulated a public discourse that positioned them in solidarity with, rather than in opposition to, drug traffickers, who have also been victims of racist violence. Outside of the neighborhood, their connections to myriad political actors helped them bring essential resources and rights to the neighborhood while connecting them to multiple allies and ideas. The outcome was a segmented but interconnected, feminized, and racialized sphere of non-violence that was grounded in Cidade de Deus, but extended into social movements across the city and the world.

The Activist Underbelly of Latin America's Gang Territories

In the last 40 years, Latin America has witnessed significant political openings and closures. Throughout the 1980s and 1990s, the fall of repressive dictatorships across Central and South America gave way to multi-party elections, progressive constitutions, expanded rights to free speech, assembly and protest, and institutionalized systems of checks and balances. Within these newly established political democracies, populations who had experienced decades, if not centuries, of state repression and social exclusion began to mobilize publicly, claiming membership and rights within a burgeoning new civil society (Gohn 2014; Inclán 2018; Paschel 2016; Staudt and Méndez 2015; Stephen 2010; Tarlau 2021). Traditional social movements focused on labor and land rights grew alongside new social movements concerned with the rights of women, queer communities, people of African descent, and indigenous groups. Over the last four decades, Latin America witnessed an era of expanded democratic engagement as members of historically disenfranchised groups pushed the boundaries of traditional democracy to broaden modern conceptions of citizenship and political participation.

At the same time that social mobilization was spreading like wildfire across the region, another phenomenon took hold in Latin America's poor urban neighborhoods, which challenged the very foundations of democratic engagement: the rise of "social violence" between drug gangs and the police (Duran-Martinez 2018; Rodgers 2009). In Brazil and many other countries, drug traffickers took advantage of growing urban inequality by installing their drug processing operations in the poorest neighborhoods where a lack of state institutions, coupled with easy access to unemployed young men, provided the ideal setting for clandestine operations. Drug lords have gone to great lengths to maintain control over these neighborhoods, killing those who speak out against them and co-opting neighborhood associations, elected officials, and community leaders who might pose a threat to their sovereignty (Arias 2017; Auyero and Berti 2015; Córdova 2019; Gay 2012; Molenaar 2017). At the same time, state police forces—with pressure and financing from the War on Drugs spearheaded by the United States—began launching brutal raids into these same neighborhoods, sending bullets flying and homicide rates soaring (Amnesty International 2015; Auyero and Berti 2015; Diamint 2015; Ramos 2015; Savell 2016). In many of these neighborhoods, darker-skinned men have been the most common targets of police violence, further racializing inequality and the denial of civil rights (Alves 2019; Vargas 2010).

As urban violence exploded across Latin America, so has the study of urban violence. In what Eduardo Moncada (2013) terms the "politics of urban violence," a vast body of scholarship examines the violent and corrupt relationships between non-state armed actors and the state's security forces and politicians (Barnes 2017; Davis 2010; Duran-Martinez 2018; Lessing 2017; Willis 2015). This literature documents the many barriers that impede residents of gang-controlled neighborhoods from accessing their political, civil, and social rights. In these areas, drug lords impose their own rules, prohibiting residents from speaking out against the drug trade or sharing any information about illicit activities to state authorities (Córdova 2019; Molenaar 2017; Perlman 2010; Silva 2008; Zaluar 1994). In turn, drug lords provide "security" against petty crime and interpersonal violence—which has often meant torturing or executing those accused of such crimes—as well as social assistance to needy residents in an attempt to gain legitimacy and support (Albarracín and Barnes 2020; Arias 2017; Barnes 2017; Penglase 2014). Community leaders and others suspected of subverting gang power are assaulted, expelled, or murdered, often in horrific, public displays of "performative violence" intended to reaffirm gang leaders' control over the neighborhood (Larkins 2015:13).

In many neighborhoods, drug lords placed their own men in charge of neighborhood associations and co-opted locally elected and administrative government officials through a combination of bribes and threats (Arias 2006a, 2017). Even today, local civic leaders remain afraid to speak out against drug traffickers (Savell 2015; Sonoda 2012). Constant invasions by the police, along with executions by drug gangs and militias, have transformed favelas and other poor urban neighborhoods into sites of "chronic violence," where high rates of homicides and other forms of physical violence sustained over many years provoke great social and psychological harm to residents (Pearce 2006).

The state's inability—or unwillingness—to assert its full control over these spaces has resulted in a kind of "fragmented sovereignty," wherein non-state actors constantly compete with state security forces to assert physical, legal, and social control over the neighborhood (Davis 2010). The result is "intermittent, selective, and contradictory" violence that is difficult to predict and challenging to navigate (Auyero, Burbano de Lara, and Berti 2014:94). Furthermore, although clientelism, or the exchange of favors for votes, has been common practice in poor neighborhoods for decades (Auyero 2001; Murillo, Oliveros, and Zarazaga 2021; Nichter 2018), the nature of clientelism has changed as politicians became increasingly dependent on the support of drug traffickers to win votes. A perverse kind of symbiosis between the favela and the state, based on both violence and illicit ties, sustains a cycle of brutality that benefits a few while destroying the lives of many more (Larkins 2015). A "new urban duality" has emerged between gang territories and the cities in which they are embedded (Koonings and Kruijt 2007:4).

Organizing against drug lords and corrupt state actors has created a minefield for community activists. The co-optation of neighborhood associations has rendered these political spaces, once central to favela organizing, either obsolete or outright dangerous for making demands (Gay 2012). While the nuances of these obstacles vary across Latin American cities, the rise of gangs has decreased electoral participation (Ley 2018), limited community engagement (Molenaar 2017), and stymied relationships with political elites (Córdova 2019). These barriers are compounded by segregated poverty and social exclusion, which further limits access to political, civil, and social rights in gang territories.

Not surprisingly, scholars of gang neighborhoods have been quite pessimistic about social mobilization under these constraints. According to Luiz Antonio Machado da Silva (2008:15), distrust between residents has made it challenging to "collectively articulate an organic and proactive understanding of shared living conditions," thereby limiting participation in grassroots movements and the influence of favela residents in public arenas. Favela historians have decried the "unraveling of civil society" (McCann 2014) and the corrosion of "law and possibility" (Fischer 2008:314) with the rise of the drug trade. Favela scholar Janice Perlman (2010), reflecting on the radical changes in Rio's favelas between the 1960s and early 2000s, found that the arrival of the drug trade severely eroded social capital, trust, and activist networks. Writing about the political shift in Rio's favelas with the rise of the drug trade in the 1980s, anthropologist Robert Gay (2012:81) notes:

> In Rio de Janeiro, the transformation of the situation from one of political solidarity, engagement, and hope to one of retrenchment, isolation, and fear has been as sudden as it has been dramatic, and has resulted not only in the virtual collapse of civil society, but also the reemergence of hierarchical forms of domination associated with the pre-democratic era. Poor neighborhoods and *favelas* in which clientelism and democracy intermingled to create a paradoxical kind of accountability . . . are now locations in which clientelism not only erodes democracy, but where the constant presence of violence makes change seem unlikely, if not impossible.

There is little doubt that life in favelas and other gang territories has become significantly more challenging since their takeover by gangs in comparison to previous eras. This shift has required residents in gang territories to respond to these challenges in creative ways. The most common is by engaging in what I have come to think of as the *politics of survival*, whereby people engage in social and economic strategies of adaptation to localized violence (Deckard and Auyero 2022; Jovchelovitch and Priego-Hernandez 2013; Silva 2008; Zubillaga, Llorens, and Souto 2019). The politics of survival may at times be collective, but, as I understand it, is not explicitly organized around political and social demands for change. These collectives might be better conceived as what Asef Bayat (2013) has termed "social non-movements," or lifestyle practices that assert one's everyday needs in urban space without making direct claims on political actors.

People in gang territories also deploy what James Scott (1987) defines as "infrapolitics," invisible tactics that resist direct confrontation, such as by using humor (Goldstein 2003) or re-appropriating discourses of mother-hood (Veillette and Avoine 2019) to reject physical, social, and symbolic violence. While there can be great power in re-writing social norms and scripts, some of these changes may be at the individual level and may not necessarily result in collective political action. Finally, some have argued that participation in gangs is itself a form of resistance to oppression and state violence, as gang members' resistance to the police, performances of oppositional cultural practices, and even perpetration of violence can serve as strategies to reject the roles and scripts imposed on them by an unequal and racist society (Bourgois 2003; Rios 2011). In Brazil, James Holston (2008) found that the drug trade used a discourse of rights to demand better prison conditions and treatment by the legal system, further demonstrating the resistance strategies employed by armed actors.

Survival, infrapolitics, and organized violence are all important ways of understanding resistance in gang territories. This book, however, is concerned with another form of resistance: collective action that aims explicitly to produce social and political change without the use or threat of violence. Given how many obstacles have arisen to democratic engagement in these spaces, it is not surprising that those looking back on how things used to be have emphasized the many closures to activism in gang territories. My objective, in contrast, is to examine the opportunities that remain, or have emerged, for non-violent collective action with the rise of gang-police violence, and how activists in these spaces are reconfiguring their efforts to keep social mobilization alive in a context of violence and repression. What I hope to contribute are some foundational concepts and ideas that enable us to theorize what I think of as *the politics of urban non-violence* in Latin America's gang territories. I do this by focusing on Cidade de Deus, one of Latin America's most dangerous gang territories, where activism remains a vital, if underreported, part of the neighborhood's life, vitality, and ability to both persist and remain connected to the city and broader social movements.

Re-writing Narratives of Urban Violence

Cidade de Deus is one of Rio de Janeiro's more than 700 favelas, or "sub-normal agglomerations," the formal classification by the Brazilian Institute of Geography and Statistics (IBGE).[4] Located in Rio de Janeiro's West Zone (see Maps I.1 and I.2), it is a medium-sized favela, with approximately 3 kilometers of distance between its two farthest points that someone in good physical health could cross on foot in about 40 minutes. At the time of the study, one-third of households subsisted on less than the minimum monthly wage and another third subsisted on less than two minimum wages (Fahlberg, Potiguara, and Fernandes 2020). Although, as Figure I.1 shows, CDD is an urbanized community, over 10% of residents live in auto-constructed shacks. It is primarily, though not exclusively, a Black and brown neighborhood, with only 19% of residents identifying as white (Fahlberg, Potiguara, and Fernandes 2020). With a population of between 37,000 and 60,000 residents, depending on which study you read, it accounts for less than 1% of the city's population (Portela 2017). And yet, thanks to the internationally acclaimed movie *City of God* released in 2002 and nominated for four Academy Awards, Cidade de Deus has become globally known. The movie vividly depicts the brutal tactics employed by local men involved in the drug trade against each other and against non-armed residents to gain

Figure I.1 Cidade de Deus
Photo by the author.

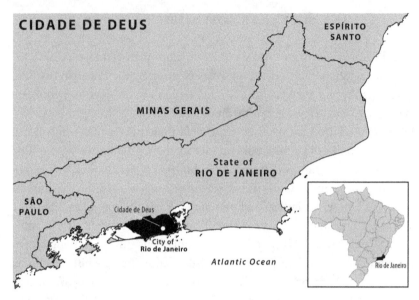

Map I.1 Map showing the location of Cidade de Deus in the State of Rio de Janeiro
Source: Tufts Data Lab

control over the local distribution and sale of drugs in the neighborhood. Corrupt police officers are also prominently featured, as they invade the neighborhood either to shoot (often arbitrarily) at young Black men they assume are drug dealers or collect bribes from actual drug dealers in exchange for allowing them to sell drugs. Although the movie is set in the 1970s and 1980s, much of the violence by drug gangs continues today. The movie, however, has transformed Cidade de Deus from a physical place into an international symbol.

For many, Cidade de Deus has become a symbol of criminality and violence, a place where poor people, lacking a work ethic and moral standards, resort to laziness, promiscuity, and crime to game the system. I heard some version of this narrative reiterated frequently by lighter-skinned Brazilian middle-class friends and acquaintances, often during heated political debates at barbecues, birthday parties, or gatherings to watch soccer games. Cidade de Deus, like other favelas, represents the feared and despised "Other," the space to which those who challenge the social order of the city must be removed, relegated, and contained (Amaral 2019; Burgos 2005; Penglase 2014). This view helps to justify the common belief in Brazil that

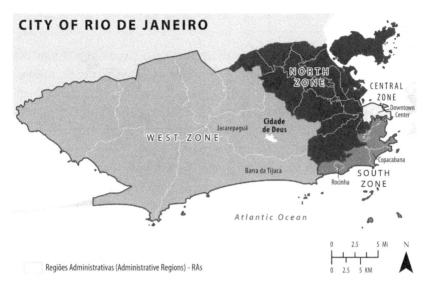

Map I.2 Map of the City of Rio de Janeiro
Source: Tufts Data Lab

·"a good criminal is a dead criminal," and has been reflected in the speeches of policymakers. For instance, Rio's former governor Sérgio Cabral once defended abortion rights by claiming that abortion would decrease the "factory of production of delinquents" in favelas (Paiva 2007), and Rio's more recent governor Wilson Witzel threatened to send a missile into Cidade de Deus to solve the problem of its "lazy criminals."

An alternative narrative posits that Cidade de Deus and Rio's other favelas represent intersecting experiences of victimization: the historical legacy of slavery, political and social exclusion, mass displacement, labor exploitation, racism, government neglect, and police violence (Alves and Evanson 2011; Carril 2006; Larkins 2015; Perlman 2010; de Sousa 2003; Valladares 2005). This perspective is found in scholarly books and journals, documentaries, the speeches of activists, some investigative journalism, and (occasionally) the speeches of progressive politicians. The two narratives compete for hearts and minds, not only in Rio de Janeiro, but across the globe, as spectators with a fascination often reserved for the most horrific of stories wait to see what the fate of this little neighborhood will tell us about the state of Latin American cities more generally. While these narratives are diametrically opposed in terms of their sympathy for the plight of favela residents, they both tend to center violence and poverty as the central themes in the favela experience.

In this battle for narratives about CDD, however, a voice—or rather, 60,000 voices—have been missing: those of the residents. How do they think about their own neighborhood? What does this community represent to them? And most importantly, what narrative(s) do they wish to contribute to the global conversation that has unfolded about them without their consent or participation? What are the stories they wish to tell?

I found the answer to this last question quite simply: I asked them. More specifically, I asked my first set of interview participants what stories they would like to see told about CDD. Consistently, my participants told me they wished someone would write about the "good things" in Cidade de Deus: "98% percent of residents are good!" several exclaimed, referencing a popular (unconfirmed, though plausible) statistic that only 2% of favela residents were involved in the drug trade. They were frustrated at how often journalists and scholars focused on violence and believed that this narrative, however well-intentioned, led to stigma associated with living in favelas simply by emphasizing some stories at the expense of others. To combat this view, participants showered me with evidence that there was much more to Cidade de Deus: the neighbor who ran a soccer league for children, the group that did art with children in the park, the organization that helped elderly people with physical therapy. These were the stories they wanted told, in the hopes of combatting the favelas-as-violence perspective that has become so popular. These were the stories residents felt proud to tell, the ones that made so many declare with conviction, "I am CDD!"

Cidade de Deus, like many other areas of conflict and poverty, has suffered from what I call *epistemic disequilibrium*, or a drastic imbalance in the types of narratives produced about a community or population which, in their to-tality, create an inaccurate or incomplete image of a place or a people. By focusing our stories and studies about conflict zones on violence, whether by gangs or the police, or even the violence of systemic inequality, not only do we overlook stories of non-violence, but we inadvertently reinforce the belief that these spaces are uniquely characterized by violence. This reproduces a "pornography of violence" (Bourgois 2001) and can also result in a denial of the heterogeneity, personal agency, and transformative capacity of these communities. This imbalance is particularly strong in literature on gang ter-ritories, where the wealth of studies on urban violence in Latin America have left readers with a sense that in gang-governed neighborhoods, violence is all there is. It is important to take stock of our field and ask ourselves, or better yet, our participants, what perspectives seem to be missing.

It is also crucial to acknowledge that many favela residents are themselves scholars. Renata Souza, Celso Athayde, Marielle Franco, Fernanda Amaral, among many others are (or, regrettably, were, in Marielle's case) well-established Brazilian researchers who combine their first-hand experiences of favela living with scholarly analysis. There are many people from CDD who have published books, articles, and poems. Their positionality affords them an insider view of not only the violences levied against favela residents, but also the survival strategies and forms of resistance borne in response to violence. Their writings have helped to balance the epistemic disequilibrium by emphasizing the creative responses of favela residents to injustice.

Once it became clear that CDD residents wanted outsiders to know more about the good things in their community, I set off to honor their wishes. In many respects, however, I was not qualified to do so. For one, I was not raised in a favela and possessed many privileges my participants did not. I was a white, American academic conducting research in a Black neighborhood where most residents live near or below the poverty line and have not had the opportunity to go to college. These differences alone created a significant imbalance of power between me and my participants. Furthermore, having received my training in a US institution of higher education, my views were grounded in epistemologies of the Global North, and I was operating under the pressures and expectations of the US academic system. The "white gaze" I carry with me was not only an inescapable aspect of my personal identity but also a professional hazard (Pailey 2020). I was, and still am, part of an academic system that perpetuates intellectual imperialism, whereby the theories produced in the Global North are viewed as superior to the epistemologies of the "subaltern" from the Global South (Alatas 2000; Connell 2007; Go 2016). I thus arrived in CDD with a great deal of social, racial, and epistemic privileges that limited my ability to fully understand the local context and radically increased the chances I would misunderstand and misrepresent residents' lived realities. As an outsider, I also wondered (and still wonder) whether I even had the right to tell residents' stories.

At the same time, my background and positionality did contribute some useful resources to this endeavor. I am fluent in Portuguese and have adopted much of the Brazilian culture after spending nearly a decade of my childhood years in Rio de Janeiro and many more years embedded in the Brazilian diaspora in Massachusetts. This has allowed me to traverse between Rio de

Janeiro and the US academic system with some ease. My fluency in English allows me to bring stories from the favela to an international audience, and my training as a sociologist has afforded me skills in research methods and data analysis, as well as knowledge of social theories that have helped me see the workings of activism in Cidade de Deus from a sociological vantage point. As one of my participants reflected after reading the first draft of this book, I became a "conduit of stories," using my lived experience as an American academic to render legible what I saw in Cidade de Deus to an international community. In order to address my limitations and take advantage of my contributions, I have engaged in a long and fruitful dialogue with myriad CDD residents who supported, advised, and critiqued me throughout the years-long journey of collecting data and writing this book. In this process, I have learned as much *from* and *with* them as I have *about* them. In the following sections, I describe the data I collected and how I drew on the principles of Participatory Action Research to address inequities and promote participation and mutual learning throughout my research and writing process.

Collecting Data in a Gang Territory

Cidade de Deus is not a neighborhood one can just visit on a whim. Heavily armed drug traffickers are stationed at many street corners and roam the streets regularly, surveilling residents and paying close attention to those they do not recognize. Outsiders must enter with a local resident or risk being questioned—or killed—by a gang member. I first visited Cidade de Deus nearly two decades before my fieldwork began, when I was a young girl living with my family in a small housing complex that abutted the favela. My parents had moved from the United States to Rio de Janeiro when I was three years old, and my mother, a psychologist, had started a program for children and women confronting sexual and domestic violence in Cidade de Deus. I grew up hearing about her work and experiences there and visiting family friends who lived in various favelas. My mother had only brought me to visit Cidade de Deus once, the day after a severe flood had destroyed much of the neighborhood and temporarily subdued violence between drug traffickers and the police. Although we moved back to the United States when I turned twelve, those early experiences instilled in me an appreciation for the complexities of poverty and violence. This led me to work as an advocate for domestic and sexual assault survivors, primarily with Latina and Brazilian women living in the United States and, later, into a more academic exploration of the lived experiences of violence.

When I started fieldwork many years later, I gained entry to Cidade de Deus thanks to Rosangela, a family friend who was raised there and maintained an active participation in several community-based organizations even after moving to a working-class area nearby. In 2013, the year before I began fieldwork, I contacted Rosangela and we began speaking regularly on the phone. She offered many insights into what was happening in CDD and what issues residents were discussing. She then put me in contact with Solange, the director of an afterschool organization I refer to here as Youth Promise. Solange and I corresponded for several months by phone and email, and I started volunteering remotely by creating an evaluation for a domestic violence group she was offering.

When I arrived in 2014, Rosangela and I hopped on the bus from her house to CDD and she walked with me through the neighborhood to Youth Promise. At the time, the neighborhood was under a brief period of control by the military police, who had forced drug traffickers to either flee or hide their weapons and drugs. This allowed me to walk the streets without risk of being shot, though many warned me that drug lords still maintained a close watch on those coming and going. My visible affiliation with Rosangela and Youth Promise offered me an acceptable reason to be there—to volunteer with a youth organization. I continued to volunteer at Youth Promise off and on for two years, helping with a variety of projects as needed. It was there that I met Maria Rita, one of the teachers, and we quickly hit it off. During my first two trips, I lived near Cidade de Deus with childhood friends, but after my second visit in 2015, Maria Rita invited me to stay with her family in Cidade de Deus. The following trip, I stayed with her, her older sister Esther, and Esther's two sons. We became extremely close, and I continued to live with them for every visit thereafter. Not only did Maria Rita and Esther teach me how to safely navigate an increasingly dangerous space and help connect me with new participants, they also offered invaluable opinions and suggestions on my project that have played an important role in my own analysis and writing. They have become like a second family to me, and we remain in regular contact even as I finish writing this book.

The research for this book is based on many types of data I collected over the seven years I spent deeply immersed in studying Cidade de Deus and informed by several studies I conducted after fieldwork was completed.

Between 2014 and 2020, I conducted fieldwork over the course of nine trips to CDD. While there, I spent my time volunteering with or visiting local organizations and collectives, meeting people in their homes and places of worship, chatting with people on the streets and in local businesses, attending meetings, presentations, parties, and other events, and traveling to other favelas and around the city. This segmented approach allowed me to document changes and continuities in CDD over time and helped me cultivate long-term relationships with dozens of CDD residents with whom I remain in close contact still today. During my time in CDD, I also conducted over 120 in-depth, semi-structured interviews with CDD activists and other residents, activists from other favelas, staff in urban-based non-governmental organizations (NGOs), elected officials, public servants, funders, researchers, and other relevant actors. I also conducted virtual ethnography over Facebook and WhatsApp throughout those years, remaining attuned to events and discussions, and interviewing my participants informally about these over social media. As urban ethnographer Forest Stuart (2020) has noted, social media platforms have become important sites of socialization, news sharing, and political action, and are just as important to our understanding of a community as physical observations.

I stopped collecting field notes on specific examples of activism in 2018 when Brazil's far-right president Jair Bolsonaro was elected to office. Following his election, activism across the country witnessed a new wave of threats from its national government and an emboldened conservative base. However, I continued to conduct interviews on questions related to race and knowledge in an effort to fill in some pieces I felt were missing from my original fieldwork. In any event, my core research had reached saturation by then, as new observations confirmed the findings and theories I had already developed. I also had the opportunity to present my findings and arguments to dozens of CDD residents, whose input and ideas lent credibility to my theoretical conclusions. I further triangulated my data by hosting two book workshops with the key participants of the book to ensure that my findings were both safe to share and reflected how activists themselves have experienced their fight for rights and resources.

In addition to this qualitative data, I reference statistics about Cidade de Deus throughout the book, data that comes from a project I co-led in 2017 with CDD resident Ricardo Fernandes. This was a neighborhood-wide survey of social development, insecurity, and social resilience with 83 questions on health, education, employment, infrastructure, mobility, social networks, and resilience, and the effects of insecurity on these. Ricardo and I designed the questions based on the input shared in five focus groups we led with one hundred CDD residents, in which we asked participants to discuss what issues were most urgent to them and how they handled them. For instance, the survey not only asked how many children were enrolled in school but how many days of school they had missed the previous year due to shootouts, maintenance issues, and teacher absences. We also documented how many years a participant had been awaiting a vital medical procedure, as well as whether they had "made a ruckus" (*fazer um barraco*) to get seen at the local health clinic. We hired and trained a team of residents from across CDD to administer the survey by randomly selecting 1–3 households or storefronts on each street of the neighborhood. Our team interviewed 989 respondents in total, a sample representative of the racial, gender, and age breakdown of CDD. The results were published in a full report in 2020 (see Fahlberg, Potiguara, and Fernandes 2020). Since the last census was conducted in 2010, our survey provides the most up-to-date information on social conditions in Cidade de Deus.

Participatory Action Research

The research for this book was collected using a Participatory Action Research, or PAR, approach. The roots of PAR trace back to 1970s Latin America, when mobilization against authoritarianism and economic inequality bolstered demands for progressive politics and participatory forms of decision-making among leftist groups in academia and in poor communities. PAR advocates for a leveling of the playing field between researchers and participants (Fals-Borda and Rahman 1991). It recognizes that each individual has a unique "standpoint," or way of perceiving the world based on their multiple identities (Fraser 1990). In particular, those most "distant" from centers of power are often best able to see what those at its center cannot (Collins 1986; Narayan 1998), thereby contributing questions and analyses to which someone like me may be less attuned. PAR thus argues for the inclusion of the research community in drafting questions, determining the most appropriate methods, analyzing the data, and disseminating findings (Fine et al. 2021). PAR also advocates for the acquisition of "serious and reliable knowledge upon which to construct power, or countervailing power, for the poor, oppressed and exploited groups and social classes—the grassroots—and for their authentic organizations and movements" (Fals Borda 1991:3). Research, rather than being conducted simply for the sake of enriching academic knowledge, should serve a political purpose: to improve the lives of historically marginalized populations.

I have sought to apply these principles in several ways, which I describe at length in the Appendix of the book and briefly here. For one, I sought to make my presence in the neighborhood beneficial in some way, however small. Throughout my time in the field, I volunteered with both Youth Promise and *SpeakCDD!*, a community-based newspaper that Rosangela co-founded with Sonia, another Cidade de Deus resident and long-time activist. I continued to lend a hand to other organizations and individual residents whenever possible.

I have also involved my participants in decision-making about the research questions, methods, and analysis throughout the project. In addition to asking participants what they wanted me to study, I involved them in my analytical process, regularly presenting my findings and theoretical arguments and asking for their opinions and suggestions. Sometimes these conversations happened formally, with groups of 20 or more people, and many other times they took place informally as we lounged in someone's living room or as I sat with a participant on a long bus ride. Each participant I spoke with offered a unique and valuable perspective. After I wrote the first draft, I invited 10 of the main protagonists featured in this book to read a translated draft of the manuscript and discuss it with each other and with me. We held two workshops where they shared their comments and critiques, and I have incorporated many of their suggestions into the final draft.[5] I signal some of these revisions throughout in an effort to acknowledge my participants' intellectual contributions.

In 2019, several CDD residents and I co-founded the *Coletivo de Pesquisa Construindo Juntos*, or the Building Together Research Collective, in an effort to create the institutional capacity for more collaborative research projects. The objective of our collective is to "give voice to the periphery" by collecting data with, by, and for favela residents. We have since led two additional projects. Through participation and action, our team has created data that not only reflects the interests and concerns of residents but contributes to social action. As one of my participants noted in our book workshop: "Our actions only make sense when done [in collaboration] with other people's hands, if it is done with other perspectives, if it is done with other experiences . . . it only makes sense when it is complemented by the doing of other people, by the experiences of other people." I would add that these "other people" must include those who represent the communities we seek to examine.

While a PAR approach is critical to addressing socio-political inequalities, it also contributes to the more academic goal of advancing social theory about society because, simply put, dozens of minds are better than one. Through "dialogical reflexivity," my participants and I, each with different social locations and lived experiences, come together to explore ideas, debate perspectives, and learn together (Yuval-Davis 2012). Through these conversations, we have all arrived at a fuller understanding of what life is like in a conflict zone and how activism operates in these areas. While no amount of participation and action will override the multiple historically entrenched and globally reproduced inequities between me and many of the residents in Cidade de Deus, I believe PAR moves us a small step in the right direction. Ultimately, I, like many of my participants, hope this book offers a new narrative about favelas and other areas experiencing armed conflict and repression so we might begin to think more systematically about the "good things" happening in the places we often associate only with violence.

Conflict Activism

Conflict activism in Cidade de Deus both does and does not operate in the ways we typically associate with social movements. According to Sydney Tarrow (1996:874), social movements are "sustained challenges to powerholders in the name of a disadvantaged population living under the jurisdiction or influence of those powerholders." Donatella della Porta and Mario Diani (2009:20) add that social movements are "linked by dense informal networks and share a distinct collective identity." Most of CDD's activists have been involved in challenges to power-holders—specifically government actors—by making explicit demands for resources, progressive public policies, racial and gender justice, and citizenship rights. CDD's activists are closely connected to each other as well as to activists in other favelas and urban and transnational social movements. They publicly espouse a common identity as favela residents working to combat violence and make demands for their neighborhoods. In both actions and identities, they are a social movement.

Social movements often coalesce around a set of core demands and strategies. They also tend to have leaders or spokespeople who are recognized as the voice of the movement and who may play a central role in decision-making. CDD's conflict activism, on the other hand, has no leader, no slogan, and no single issue. In fact, most of the people I profile in this book do not even call themselves activists, going instead by titles like "community educator" or "teacher." Rather, conflict activism in Cidade de Deus is a *field of action*, composed of diverse actors, collectives, and organizations with differing approaches to social change but united by their commitment to improving the neighborhood and advocating for the rights of favela residents through the use of non-violent strategies. They operate differently from drug traffickers, the police, and local corrupt state officials, refusing to use physical violence, the threat of physical violence, or any affiliation with "violent specialists" (Tilly 2003) to make their voices heard or their demands met. Although clientelist networks have been and continue to be one of the primary mechanisms by which poor residents obtain basic resources, activists do their best to circumvent local clientelist networks given how frequently these intersect with drug traffickers and corrupt security forces.

Instead, they have constructed a *sphere of non-violent politics* which operates politically parallel to and symbolically in opposition to the sphere of violent politics in the neighborhood. This sphere relies almost exclusively on licit forms of financial support, such as government grants, funding from private organizations, and donations from crowdsourcing and thoroughly vetted individuals. While, like drug traffickers, they also have ties to the state, these partnerships are based on official collaborations (funded by, say, a grant from the Ministry of Culture), rather than back-door deals with individual politicians. Activists adopt many of the tools of non-violent resistance. Based on my observations, Cidade de Deus activists engaged in at least 40 of Sharp's list of "198 Methods of Nonviolent Action" (Sharp 2013). These included writing letters to demand resources from municipal, state, or federal elected officials, creating alternative media, such as community-based newspapers and a radio station, using art and cultural productions to protest favela mistreatment, holding vigils, performing plays and music, holding assemblies, writing books and pamphlets demanding rights, refusing assistance from government aides or appointed officials, and creating alternative social patterns, vocabulary, and norms.

While hundreds of residents are involved in local forms of activism, they are not organized into one solid neighborhood-based organization or movement. Nor are local agencies affiliated with an overarching favela-focused social movement.[6] Instead, favela activists provide an array of direct services, grassroots organizing, cultural protest, and more explicit political work that are not held together by shared visions or tactics, but by their shared geographic space and informal ties across collectives. Across Cidade de Deus, I documented not one but three clusters of collective action, each with a core set of members, activities, networks, and visions about how to promote social change. I describe each of these in-depth in Chapter 2. The collectives in these clusters align themselves with, and participate in, external urban and transnational social movements and progressive political parties focused on a range of issues. Importantly, just as they must navigate local closures, they have also become adept at taking advantage of resources and political openings at the municipal, national, and international levels.

Despite several differences in how each cluster works to achieve social change, they also share important similarities, which are the focus of Chapters 3, 4, and 5. For one, all favela activists mobilize against violence, though they do not protest directly against drug gangs or corrupt state officials in the neighborhood, which would result in immediate threats, expulsion, or death (Perlman 2010; Silva 2008). While most of us think of violence as physical aggression, measured by homicide rates and armed conflict, activists are more concerned with the root causes of these issues. As I describe in Chapter 1, the physical violence perpetrated by gangs is a symptom of structural violence, such as economic inequality, residential segregation, punitive drug policies, neocolonial exploitation by the United States and other western countries, and the state's overall neglect of favelas and their residents (Briceño-León 2005; Galtung 1969; Winton 2004). Conflict activism in Cidade de Deus has focused primarily on addressing these broader forms of structural inequality, rather than the more immediate physical violence perpetrated by gangs, which would be too dangerous. They also mobilize against symbolic forms of violence, such as racism, gender inequality, and discrimination against favela residents. Finally, activists sometimes fight against more explicit forms of state violence, in particular police brutality (Alves and Evanson 2011; Dantas, Dantas, and Cabral 2020).

Taken together, favela activists have a multitude of demands relating to this broader view of violence, not only in Cidade de Deus but across Rio de Janeiro. According to Rachel Coutinho and Thaisa Comeli (2018:10), "In Rio's favelas . . . it is increasingly common for collectives and organizations to seek to rescue the history of residents and neighborhoods, to report abusive acts by the State, to fight evictions and white expulsion, to debate internal minorities within minorities, among other urban collective actions." They also fight to be treated with dignity and equality, and to have their citizenship rights respected. Ultimately, favela activists aspire to a "right to the city" (Harvey 2015; Lefebvre and Enders 1976) and to be fully integrated members of urban society: to get good jobs, receive a good education, access and be welcomed into mainstream urban spaces, be treated by police as citizens and not criminals, and to have a voice in the public policies that affect their lives.

Conflict activism has been allowed to operate under gang dominion thanks to its ability to maneuver into the emergent spaces for social action. In Chapter 3, I explain how the fragmentation and constant fighting between drug traffickers and the police have created social, moral, and gendered voids that activists have successfully learned to occupy. While the corrupt and violent ties between drug traffickers, police, and political cronies govern the physical territory and local systems of law and order, activists oversee the capturing and distribution of resources, the social infrastructure of the neighborhood, and the cultural and artistic development of the community. Activist organizations, which are run primarily by women and engage in what is largely considered "women's work," have taken ownership of the caretaking, social development, and cultural needs of the community. This distribution of local services reflects a *gendered division of governing labor*, whereby the security and formal political spheres of the neighborhood are governed through masculinized violence while the social and cultural spheres are run by feminized non-violence.

Although we have come to think of favela politics as a man's world, especially since the rise of the drug trade, women play critical roles in areas of armed conflict as caretakers of the community and mobilizers for peace, as well as in more formal political roles (Berry 2018; Cockburn 2004). Furthermore, women have been central in Latin American politics (Alvarez 1990; Stephen 2010; Zulver 2022), both through gender-based social movements and engagement in political parties or other institutionalized politics. In Brazil's poor urban neighborhoods, where gender is interwoven with race and class exclusion, many poor Black women have developed a political identity due to their multiple experiences of marginalization, exclusion, and violence. According to Keisha-Kahn Perry (2013:151), "blacks, women, mothers, and workers . . . constitute the *superexploited*, producing a kind of political militancy necessary to lead social movements." The Black women in Rio's favelas routinely suffer a disproportionate amount of violence, not only from gangs and the police but also from abusive partners, employers, business partners, and other predatory men. In many poor urban neighborhoods like Cidade de Deus, these overlapping forms of suffering have helped to produce a kind of collective identity built upon the shared experience of exclusion from political power (Baldez 2002; Zulver 2022).

Conflict activism also fills a psychological void. Neighborhoods depend not only on material resources but also on emotional ones: people need hope to function. There must be "good things" to balance out the "bad things." Activists occupy some of this symbolic space,[7] "doing good" when so many armed residents, police, and corrupt politicians are "doing bad." In fact, while drug lords and police maintain their power through coercion, activists govern through the consent and support of local residents. This creates a tense and fragile equilibrium. Violent actors remove residents' rights to peacefully reside in and move around their neighborhoods while activists provide spaces for safety, access to resources, and collaborative decision-making. They do what they can to make the neighborhood function as well as possible, while providing hope that someday things might be better. To be clear, my argument is not that activists are necessarily more moral than members of the drug gangs or the police—there are complex and deeply human reasons people join these violent institutions. Instead, I argue that non-violent politics gains legitimacy in the eyes of local residents because it has been symbolically constructed in opposition to its "immoral" opponents. Activists do the best they can to live by these standards, but even more important to the survival of their collective efforts is maintaining the appearance of morality. Non-violence, then, is as much a necessary social construction as it is an internalized ideal and pragmatic response to armed conflict.

These social, gendered, and moral spaces for action reflect the emergent opportunities for collective action in gang territories. However, favela activists must be strategic in how they take advantage of these possibilities. While drug traffickers have been willing to share control over social, cultural, and moral activities, they have less tolerance for sharing political power. Thus, activists must constantly toe a fine line between not obtaining too much power or money to be a threat to gang leaders but having enough power to achieve some success in fulfilling their objectives. It is not sufficient to simply avoid direct challenges to drug traffickers: activists must never become their competitors. In practice, this has meant having such a small budget that drug traffickers would not covet their resources, keeping organizations small, having many organizers but no single representative, and keeping as much distance as possible from corrupt political networks.

While activists have few economic resources, they have something just as critical: expert knowledge about how to navigate local codes of conduct. Like other residents, most local activists were born and raised in Cidade de Deus. They have learned and internalized the social norms of their community and know how to avoid confrontations with gang members. The depth of residents' local knowledge became clear to me as soon as I arrived and realized how little I had. Maria Rita and I often joked that we would write a handbook on how to comport oneself in the favela—and the book would be long! In Chapter 4, I argue that conflict activism succeeds in part by embedding itself within the dominant cultural practices and discourses of the neighborhood, thereby conforming to expectations of appropriate behavior while also making more explicitly political claims for citizenship rights. I refer to this practice as *political upcycling*. One particularly important form of political upcycling has been emphasizing their commitment to fighting against racism, which discursively positions Black activists in solidarity with Black drug traffickers, all of whom have suffered from racialized state violence and structural racism. Rather than challenge local norms, activists embrace the many connective threads that bind them to the favela and deploy them strategically to mobilize against violence and for the needs of their community.

Making Gains through Patchwork Politics

How big of a splash can one really make by proceeding so cautiously? For decades, scholars have been trying to figure out how to measure social movement "success," a concept that is as foundational to collective action as it is elusive to those who study it. Success could be defined as meeting a movement's desired outcomes (i.e. its demands), being recognized as legitimate spokespeople for the movement by its antagonists (Gamson 2015), or "winning major concessions from the holders of power" (Fishman and Everson 2016:2). Others may define success by a movement's capacity to effect long-term significant social improvements on a given issue, such as by achieving not only legal rights but also substantive funding for resources and a shift in how society views the issue.

While these definitions may be helpful for measuring the efficacy of large-scale social movements with established leaders, a specific list of demands, and a large following, it does not carry neatly into Rio's gang territories, where activism does not have a central leader, a consolidated list of demands, or a large constituency. Instead, CDD has a few hundred activists and a general vision: to make life better for their neighborhood by making the world a safer, more equitable place. Their successes can be measured in small but meaningful ways. Every time they help another favela resident gain a new skill, access food or medical care, get into college, or get a decent job, they have moved closer in their vision. Every time they contribute to bringing more housing, more medical services, more jobs, and more schools to the neighborhood, they have moved closer in their vision. Every time they have convinced someone that Black is beautiful, that police violence is wrong, that poverty is a result of inequality and not laziness, they have moved closer in their vision. With each small step, they have had another small success.

The larger point here is that conflict activists "do" politics differently than other movements. As Frances Fox Piven and Richard Cloward (2012:xi) have argued, "popular insurgency does not proceed by someone else's hopes; it has its own logic and direction." In a context of fragmented sovereignty, spatialized forms of social and economic exclusion, and limited resources, activism in Cidade de Deus has created a patchwork politics wherein different collectives focus on a range of issues, bring in diverse types of resources, target a wide array of allies, and deploy differing discourses that in their totality help to produce meaningful changes and improvements to the neighborhood and beyond. Thanks to the diversity of activities on the ground, local residents can in the same day enroll their child in a literacy class run by one collective, register for public housing secured by a second collective, and then meet a visiting Black American activist at an Open Mic hosted by a third. These disparate efforts, when seen from a birds-eye view, do ultimately enable myriad possibilities for favela residents and for transformational politics. Each activist group contributes a few pieces to a larger landscape that, when woven together, help to increase resources, curb inequality, address some of the root causes of violence, and ultimately promote a broad movement toward non-violence. Armed conflict and repression may prevent mobilization through traditional mobilization forms, but through patchwork politics, similar goals can be accomplished, or at least pushed in a similar direction.

Favela activists have also achieved a challenging feat: they have constructed democracy in the trenches. They do this by creating spaces of participatory democracy. In Chapter 5, I examine how activists in CDD have not only constructed spaces for open and peaceful dialogue but have also created partnerships with representatives from the state, private industries, large urban NGOs, university researchers, and a host of other actors. Lacking in resources and openings within their neighborhood, activists have reached outward. Through this process, they have constructed spaces for collaboration, as well as contentious politics, with the state and other actors that push forward the interests and needs of their neighborhood. In the absence of a large, "vertical" social movement, activism in Cidade de Deus has developed horizontally, enabling a plurality of political imaginaries and social practices.

At the same time, there are limits to what conflict activism has been able to accomplish, thanks largely to the constraints that are embedded within their organizational configurations. Horizontality may promote plurality and diversity, but it limits representation. In previous decades, when neighborhood associations had elected presidents and community assemblies, these representatives could speak *for* the community and could make demands on their behalf. They organized large groups of people across favelas to protest, resist evictions, and take landowners to court. Conflict activism in CDD does not mobilize large groups that can combat or expel the drug trade. Furthermore, too much success in mobilizing resources for the favela would disrupt drug operations by increasing state presence (and control) in these regions, which would surely incur violent repression. Thus, life in favelas can get better, but not too much better: an entire branch of the global economy relies on the exclusion of CDD and other gang territories to keep the drug trade alive.

Conflict activism has not changed the world or radically reconfigured conditions of living in Cidade de Deus. But it has made life better for thousands of favela residents, who would be in much worse shape if activists did not organize to provide these services. Activists also play meaningful roles in urban social movements, progressive politics, and humanitarian NGOs. And they construct an alternative form of political action in the shadows of the drug trade, enabling residents to engage in democratic dialogue and decision-making, cultivate non-violent and often productive ties to state officials, and fight for citizenship rights even when so many avenues for activism have been rendered impassable.

A Note on Racial Terminology

I think it's important for you to put this question in the book . . . it is important for us to announce to the world the complexity that is

racial understanding in Brazil and how much that sometimes stunts
some growth processes that the country can do.
                                    Leonardo's feedback during our book workshop

While anti-Black racism is a widespread problem in Brazil, it manifests differently than in the United States (Graham 2019). The United States has a
legacy of exclusionary and often legally institutionalized racial politics which
aimed to separate, isolate and subjugate Black communities (Massey and
Denton 1993; Gordon 2022). Brazil, in contrast, is characterized by a mass
process of miscegenation and *limpeza de sangue*, or "cleaning of the blood
line" through inter-marriage. Portuguese settlers forcibly impregnated slave
women in an effort to "purify" the African "race" and encouraged inter-racial
relationships (Wade 2009). Most Brazilians carry some mix of European and
African, as well as indigenous, ancestry, with varying combinations of phenotypical features, hair types, and skin colors. Consequently, racism in Brazil
operates along a continuum often referred to as "colorism," whereby those
with darker skin tones suffer greater amounts and forms of discrimination
than those with lighter skin (Filho and da Silva 2020). This continuum also
makes it challenging for many Brazilians to clearly identify with a specific racial category. Many people I met in CDD found the question of "What is your
race?" a complicated one.

Given these complexities, I have chosen to deploy racial terminology in
different ways throughout the book. I frequently refer to *racism*, an "ideology of racial domination" (Wilson 1999:4) in which "the presumed biological or cultural superiority of one or more racial groups is used to justify or
prescribe the inferior treatment or social position(s) of other racial groups
(Clair and Dennis 2015:857). Racism can operate against individuals but
also against neighborhoods, such as when the police invade favelas because
of the widespread perception of these areas as Black—and therefore "criminal"—communities (Nascimento 2019). Racism is also structural because it
is a constitutive element of the political and economic organization of society
(Almeida 2019). It is therefore embedded within institutions and widespread
practices that result in unequal opportunities for darker-skinned people and
favela residents.

Whenever I label particular activists or other actors as Black, white, or
pardo (mixed-race), it is because they have told me this is the racial category
with which they most identify. In the absence of this first-hand knowledge,
I describe the skin tones and features of relevant actors in order to document

the racial heterogeneity of, and power imbalances between, the people I am writing about, but without imposing my own categories onto them. For instance, I frequently observed tensions between private or state actors—who were mostly lighter-skinned and had more features often associated with whiteness—and favela activists, who generally (but not always) had darker skin and more African features. Finally, I explore in several chapters, and in Chapter 4 in greater depth, how racial categories have been politicized, how activists have attempted to combat the erasure of indigenous and African cultural practices by reclaiming Blackness and teaching other favela residents about Black history. In a country where racial identity is both subjective but also highly consequential in terms of (mis)treatment by police, employers, and society at large, racial terms and presentations of self become a political tool yielded not only by the state but by racial justice activists as well (Paschel 2016).

1

Cidade de Deus

A Contested Territory

Cidade de Deus is a great school with Masters who have made a university of survival of the floods, of the fire that burned down shacks,
their own and of their friends, of the sacrifice of being relocated a
great distance between their jobs and their homes . . . If it had not
been for the Guardians of this place, "the friends and neighbors"
who took care of our children while parents were working in the
Zona Sul,[1] today we would not have a history to tell.
—Valéria Barbosa, *The Great Guardian Masters of Cidade de Deus:*
Makers of Destinies.

Survival and Resistance in the Favela

I looked through the window of my taxi as it pulled onto the street corner,
down Jeremiah Road, and into the heart of CDD. I searched for Esther past
the frenzy of pedestrians, cars, bicycles, produce stands, and storefront
awnings with dangling toys and sandals. I knew Esther's calm gait, dark skin,
thin legs, and short black hair so well I would have easily spotted her in the
crowd. Instead, my eyes descended upon an obtrusive group of five or six
drug traffickers stationed at the *boca de fumo*, or drug sale point, just a block
down. This was the first of three *bocas* I would have to pass by on the walk to
Esther's house. Having just arrived from the airport with two large conspic-
uous suitcases that I would need to wheel past the *bocas*, I wished I could
have waited in the cab until Esther arrived. I could tell from my driver's anxious glances and exaggerated swiping of my credit card that he was eager to
leave the area. I exited the car, grabbed my suitcases as the driver lifted them
out of the trunk, and began to make my way down the road and into the
neighborhood. It was a path I knew well, as I had been living with Esther

Activism under Fire. Anjuli Fahlberg, Oxford University Press. © Oxford University Press 2023.
DOI: 10.1093/oso/9780197519325.003.0002

and her family off and on for the last 18 months. Yet the feeling of fear was always bubbling below, fed by the knowledge that at any moment I could be questioned by a suspecting drug trafficker or get caught in a shootout. I maneuvered down a side street hoping to avoid at least one *boca*, sighing with relief when I finally spotted André, Esther's youngest son, heading my way. He smiled broadly and made his way to me, greeting me with a bear hug and grabbing the handle of the larger suitcase. Though he had not yet turned 13, he towered over me. He informed me that Esther had gone to a different corner to wait for me. "She's terrible at reading her phone messages," André reminded me, rolling his eyes in jest. We chuckled and went looking for Esther, whom we found a few blocks away. As we walked to their home together, I tried to shake off the feeling of fear that Cidade de Deus engendered and focus on the people I was so eager to see again.

Once back at the house, Esther made us coffee with steamed milk and began filling me in on recent events. Things had been bad lately. Near-daily shootouts between the police and drug traffickers had provoked multiple challenges. Esther had had to close her storefront pizza business, which put a strain on her finances. Her neighbor's 82-year-old grandmother had been struck by a stray bullet and was still in the hospital. Because it was so dangerous to move about the streets, André had missed several days of school, and Maria Rita was forced to stay at work for lunch rather than walk home to eat with her family.

As if the constant threat of arme conflict wasn't enough of a problem, another of Esther's neighbors had been recently diagnosed with terminal cancer, and Esther's injury to her foot was not healing properly. Ismael, a lanky 18-year-old boy whom Esther had taken under her wing, had dropped out of his high school equivalency course. On top of it all, a pipe had burst directly into Esther and André's bedroom a few weeks earlier, flooding it with several inches of water that took them days to get rid of, created a terrible stench, and destroyed most of the furniture. CEDAE, the public water company, refused to intervene, claiming they only fixed maintenance issues in "public areas." This infuriated Esther since it was the poor maintenance of the neighborhood's pipes that had caused the rupture. "I was crying all the time," Esther lamented. I squeezed her arm and gave her a sympathetic smile, commenting on the injustice of it all. I knew, however, that somehow she would make it through this, as she always did.

The lament in Esther's voice belied the tenacity with which she led life. Like most Cidade de Deus residents, Esther had faced what could easily be considered an insurmountable number of tragedies to herself, her family members, and the many people in her neighborhood she cared about. Esther, like millions of other poor urban residents across the globe, was a victim of multiple, intersecting forms of violence and social exclusion. However, Esther was also constantly fighting back in her own creative and stealthy ways, starting several businesses, becoming adept at a wide range of skills, forming relationships with resourceful actors across the neighborhood, and helping her friends and neighbors find jobs, housing, and food. She was a devout evangelical Christian and often viewed the assistance she provided as living out her religious beliefs.

While Esther's response to the "chronic shocks" in her and her kin's everyday lives reflected her individual efforts to provide care and action (Fahlberg et al. 2020), two of her other family members responded to the injustices imposed on CDD through a variety of collective forms of action. Her younger sister, Maria Rita, was a computer teacher and the coordinator of an afterschool program for local children and adolescents, as well as an active participant in several other local social and political initiatives. Meanwhile, Esther's 27-year-old son Leonardo had co-founded an arts-focused community-based organization (CBO) and led several racial justice initiatives in Cidade de Deus and across the city. Several of Esther's other family members, including another sister, several nieces, nephews, and brothers-in-law were also active in local CBOs and their workplace unions. The time I spent in Esther's household and in dozens of other spaces across the neighborhood revealed both the challenges that Cidade de Deus faces due to multiple forms of violence and the range of responses that residents deploy to face these problems. This dynamic relationship between externally imposed injustices and internal responses by its residents has made CDD into a space that is constantly being made, unmade, and remade.

This chapter provides a description of Cidade de Deus, including the lived experiences and obstacles its residents must deal with, as well as the historical processes of exclusion and survival strategies that have transformed this neighborhood into a *contested territory*. I understand a contested territory to be a geo-political space whose meanings, boundaries, and hierarchies are under constant negotiation by a host of state and non-state, armed and unarmed actors. The most obvious contestation is between the local drug traffickers and invading police troops perpetually competing for territorial control. However, ordinary people also resist the violence imposed on them through a number of individual and collective strategies. Some of these tactics are focused on survival and economic mobility, others at airing grievances, and still others at achieving immediate and long-lasting social change. When we understand CDD as a contested territory, it becomes unsurpring that activism has emerged here. This collective, non-violent action is nested within and supported by the spirit of resistance which has become an inherent component of the favela identity and experience (Souza 2020).

Competing Borders

While the neighborhood of Cidade de Deus is well known across Rio de Janeiro, there are competing understandings of exactly where its borders begin and end. In Map 1.1, we can see that the Regional Administration—the sub-municipal branch of the government that oversees the maintenance and building of infrastructure—has delineated one boundary for Cidade de Deus. Meanwhile, the area designated as Cidade de Deus by the military police under the Unidade de Policia Pacificadora (UPP or Pacifying Policing

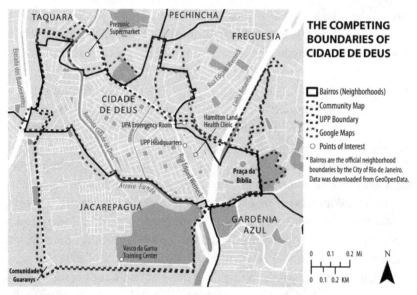

Map 1.1 The competing boundaries of CDD
Source: Tufts Data Lab

Units) encompasses a broader region. Google Maps, which is consulted by ordinary outsiders—taxi drivers, international visitors, investors, and families looking to buy real estate in nearby areas—has yet a third set of boundaries. To make matters more complicated, residents have their own ideas about where Cidade de Deus begins and ends. Map 1.1 illustrates each of these perimeters, showcasing not only divergences in the various boundaries but also the chaotic experience of trying to follow them all.[2]

At least some of this confusion can be attributed to the fact that CDD is constantly exapnding. As families outgrew their homes and new people arrived, many built new homes in peripheral areas, particularly along the southern and northern perimeters (see Map 1.2). Some of these areas, particularly those in the southern area known as Karatê, have grown into robust informal settlements and are widely considered to be part of Cidade de Deus. The drug trade—both their sales and their own homes—has also expanded into these areas. Given that these areas are extremely poor and have become hubs of gang activity, they have attracted the attention of the police. They have also been deemed worthy of demolition. Beginning in 2019, for instance, dozens of shacks were torn down along the southern corridor to make room for a new soccer stadium.

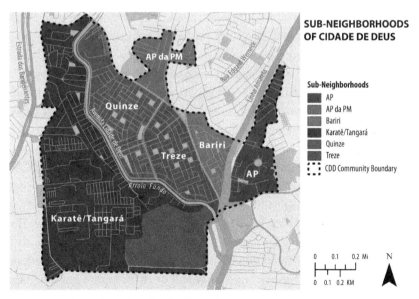

Map 1.2 Sub-neighborhoods of Cidade de Deus
Source: Tufts Data Lab.

Some of CDD's more financially stable residents have moved into the northern area, known popularly as AP2 or AP da PM. This area is relatively wealthier and Whiter than the rest of Cidade de Deus and is composed primarily of brick-and-mortar homes. In the community-wide survey I co-led with a team of CDD residents, our team debated about whether this region should be included in the survey, as many of the people who live there do not consider themselves CDD residents, and it is considered by the postal office to be another neighborhood. To make a more informed decision, we asked hundreds of residents on Facebook whether they considered this area to be Cidade de Deus. Approximately half of those who responded said it was CDD and half said it was not. Some of the reasons given for why it *was* Cidade de Deus included the fact that residents had migrated there from the central areas of CDD, that residents in AP da PM needed social services, and that the drug trade was selling drugs there. Other residents, eager to distance themselves from the stigma of living in a favela, opted instead to label their neck of the woods by its postal service address—Pechincha—a neighborhood widely viewed as more middle-class.[3]

The different meanings that travel with outward residential growth suggest that the "favela," like the "slum" or the "ghetto," is a social construct based on a set of shared understandings about what constitutes such spaces. When the favela, and the social meanings attached to it, expand into new areas, these areas become stigmatized and face similar treatments. When these meanings—including the income and skin colors attached to these stigmas—do not carry into new spaces, such as the case of AP da PM, residents could opt for a non-favela identity. Choosing between one's community and one's upward mobility was not easy for some of the people we spoke with, but it reflected a space for maneuver, agency, and escape. Liza Weinstein has argued that "the slum" is now "more a matter of politics than of science" (Weinstein 2014:9). It is a term given to the places we *think of* as underdeveloped, uncivilized, illegal, and therefore deserving of being neglected, bulldozed, or shot up (Arabindoo 2011). The same can be said for Cidade de Deus. There are is no agreed-upon set of coordinates that demarcate the borders of CDD. The state and private companies are not the only arbiters of CDD's boundaries, however: its residents, including both unarmed residents moving into new spaces or helping to construct meanings and drug traffickers traveling into these zones of expansion, shift and stretch the physical and symbolic limits of the neighborhood.

A Neighborhood and a Community

The term favela often evokes certain images: shirtless, dirty children living with their emaciated mothers in dilapidated shacks built upon steep hillsides. This is not what most of Cidade de Deus looks like. For one, Cidade de Deus is flat, having been built several kilometers outside the downtown area on former plantation land. CDD is also incredibly diverse. Half of residents identify as Black, another 30% as *pardo* or mixed race, and 19% as White. A handful identify as indigenous. CDD's residents are male, female, and a handful identify as transgender, and they are of many ages, sexual orientations, and educational levels.[4] Residents practice a variety of religions. Most are Evangelical and Catholic, but some are Jehovah's Witnesses. Additionally, in private homes, away from the condemning eye of local Christians, many residents practice religions with African roots, such as Umbanda and Candomblé.

Residents also distinguish themselves based on which "part" of the neighborhood they are from. Residents often think about CDD as broadly divided into six different sub-neighborhoods, each with its own history, parks, businesses, and different blends of public housing, including apartment complexes and houses, as well as privately built brick-and-mortar homes and handmade shacks.

Most areas of Cidade de Deus look more urbanized than is often expected of a favela or slum (see Figure 1.1). Slum upgrading projects in the 1980s and 1990s helped to pave many streets and install electrical lines and water pipes throughout much of the neighborhood. According to the 2010 census, three-quarters of CDD residents live in a home or apartment they own, and only 13% are renters (see Figure 1.2). Many of the people I met had lived in the same house their entire lives, next to neighbors who had also been there for decades.[5] However, approximately one-tenth of households in Cidade de Deus occupy informal, self-made shacks (see Figure 1.3). These shacks rarely have running water or electricity. The wood and cardboard of which they are made cannot protect them from bullets. They tend to be clustered near the least hospitable areas of CDD, such as near open sewage canals and the swamp.

The southern part of CDD, Karatê, is one of the poorest parts of the neighborhood, and the families living in shacks near the swamp were among the most vulnerable. When my team and I were assembly the survey, we spent a day talking to families in the area to capture their experiences. Many families

Figure 1.1 A street in CDD on a calm morning
Photo by the author.

Figure 1.2 "Os AP" or "The Apartments"
Photo by the author.

Figure 1.3 Auto-constructed shacks (left) across from a public primary school (right); the school sign is pockmarked with bullets
Photo by the author.

reported that they regularly dealt with rats, snakes, and other dangerous animals, and one woman told me that only one week earlier she had rescued her toddler from an encroaching alligator. However, residents also took great pride in what they had achieved despite so many obstacles. One woman gave me a tour of her shack, which she had built herself with plywood and other materials from a nearby demolition site. She was pleased with what she had accomplished. She had secured a bed for her and her 10-year-old son, had managed to connect some electrical wires to a light bulb and a television, and had decorated her home with colorful rugs and family photographs. Many of CDD's other shacks were adorned with small gardens and flags of soccer teams, and one particularly memorable shack was covered by a house-sized sheet with a printed image of what appeared to be the couple's engagement photo. While building and living in a shack comes with many challenges and dangers, the process of auto-construction also allows for creativity, self-expression, and at times, the construction of new practices and subjectivities (Holston 2008).

Figure 1.4 A side street
Photo by the author.

CDD has been largely left out of the formal economy, with only 16% of residents reporting participation in formal employment in our survey in 2017. Nearly a quarter worked informally, and over 30% had no paid work. Given the challenges of accessing Cidade de Deus, the neighborhood has been overlooked by large companies. Instead, over 20% of residents have started their own small businesses or worked for themselves. This has resulted in a vibrant local economy, particularly in the central commercial areas, which have shops that sell groceries, clothes, shoes, toys, and small appliances. There is an abundance of small nail salons, pizza fronts, ice creams stores, bars, barbershops, and gyms. While money and goods circulate, the informal economy does not provide enough: one-third of households lived below the federal poverty line, and another 34% lived barely above it in 2017.[6] In practice, this meant that while few people were dying of hunger, many could not afford even basic items, like new clothes, wifi, meat, or a cell phone bill.

There are also many public agencies in CDD, including seven preschools, nine primary schools that go up through age 14, a technical school for adults, a local welfare office, a health clinic, an emergency room, and some publicly funded social service organizations. As I briefly describe later in this chapter and in greater detail in Chapter 2, CDD's local activists have played a significant role in getting these agencies established and staffed. However, it was also common for agencies to shut down when the government stopped paying employees or maintaining the buildings. Even when they did operate, residents complained about over-filled classrooms, absent staff, bureaucratic red tape, and insufficient materials, all of which made it extremely challenging to actually receive the services presumably being offered.

CDD residents maintain close ties with neighbors, small business owners, and extended social networks. They congregate in local parks, restaurants, places of worship, and the streets. Longevity, communal ties, and shared experiences of marginalization have helped to lay the foundation for social resilience, or "the capacity for a group of people bound together . . . to sustain and advance their well-being in the face of challenges to it" (Hall and Lamont 2013:6). Residents are often quick to lend a hand when others need food, shelter, transportation, or childcare: it is hard to say no to hungry neighbors knocking on your front door. In our 2017 study, over 60% of respondents had helped a neighbor or a friend in the previous two years. The most common

Figure 1.5 Restaurante Cidadão, a soup kitchen in CDD that closed after two years
Photo by the author.

forms of help were giving donations of clothing, food, etc., cleaning a public area, helping people get jobs, and taking care of friends' children or elderly relatives or people who were sick. I knew many families who had taken in extended kin or informally adopted children whose parents were unable to fully care for them. It was also common for people to help neighbors and friends find work and for people with cars to provide their elderly neighbors with rides to appointments. Residents also fixed public equipment, including playgrounds, benches, and downed electrical wires, when public agencies did not arrive.

Favelas are often presumed to be on the losing end of "splintering urbanism," wherein the city's poor are cut off from other urban areas due to unevenly distributed transportation and communication technology (Addie 2022; Graham and Marvin 2001). In some respects, this is the case for Cidade de Deus. It can take over two hours to get to Rio's downtown area, often in hot, standing-room-only public buses. It also suffers from precarious infrastructure, including electricity that cuts out several times a week, flooding, and poor wifi access. However, Cidade de Deus is well connected to surrounding towns, thanks to the development of Rio's West Zone in the last 40 years. This enables residents to access a host of commercial and entertainment needs, while also exposing them to racial discrimination and mistreatment in mainstream urban spaces, like shopping malls and beaches. Discrimination is exacerbated by the fact that Cidade de Deus is one of the largest and most notorious favelas in the West Zone. Residents of surrounding towns tend to assume that any crime committed nearby—a mugging on a bus, a home invasion, a picked pocket—was committed by "bandits" from Cidade de Deus. However, residents resist these social barriers by inserting themselves into the broader urban society and economy. Most residents either own a phone with internet capabilities or have a family member whose phone they can borrow (Souza 2010). This enables them to be connected to family and friends across the city, as well as obtain news, music, videos, and ideas from national and transnational media platforms.

People are physically connected to the city as well. They are constantly coming and going from Cidade de Deus to nearby commercial and residential areas for work, school, shopping, leisure, and everyday tasks like mailing a package or buying supplies for a party. CDD residents provide critical labor to surrounding areas in the form of service work in storefronts and nail salons, construction, domestic work, garbage collection, and bus driving. Others attend university, and some have jobs in the knowledge economy as teachers and nurses and in other professional fields. They are also consumers patronising stores and restaurants in nearby commercial areas. Favela residents are both pushed out of mainstream urban spaces and also integral to the urban economy (Alves and Evanson 2011).

Cidade de Deus's boundaries are permeable to its residents. Given that most residents have lived in CDD most of their lives and are well known to the drug traffickers stationed in their part of the neighborhood, residents are usually able to move about the streets near their home without being questioned. However, if residents travel into parts of the neighborhood they don't visit regularly, they run the risk of being questioned by gang members. Furthermore, police forces enter on a regular basis and at unpredictable times. They frequently question residents—particularly dark-skinned men— and are well known to physically assault residents, imprison them unjustly, or shoot them. They also initiate gun battles with drug traffickers, sometimes on a daily basis, putting residents at constant risk of being caught by a stray bullet (see Figure 1.6). Finally, the ubiquity of guns in public spaces makes these areas dangerous even on an uneventful day. I recall one occasion in which I walked just a few feet in front of a young man distractedly swinging the trigger guard of his gun around on his index finger. It could have gone off at any minute, and in any direction. On another occasion, one of Esther's adopted sons came home and reported that he had witnessed a man shot in

Figure 1.6 A local bakery after a shootout
Photo by anonymous.

the street after presumably trying to steal drugs. He had said it so casually I asked him to repeat the story to make sure I had not misunderstood. When gun-holding young men get in fights, catch someone they believe is stealing, or are otherwise suspicious or angry, there is always the possibility that guns will be used to address the issue and that bystanders will be caught in the crossfire.

CDD is much less accessible to outsiders. While there are no official checkpoints that people pass through when they enter, drug traffickers stationed at main entryways keep a close watch on passersby and sometimes question people they do not recognize or those who appear out of place, such as someone who looks lost, stares at drug traffickers, or tries to take pictures or video of the area on their phones. Taxis and Ubers rarely attempt to enter the area, and when seeking an Uber one must walk to the main avenue for the application to work. Favelas have become inscribed into urban technologies as no-go zones. Residents who own cars must turn on their emergency lights and lower all windows when they enter so drug traffickers can see who is inside. The primary reason for this surveillance is to keep out undercover police officers, people who might share information with the police, or anyone working for rival drug factions or the militia. In practice, this means that if you do not have a good reason to be there, drug traffickers will likely force you to leave.

One legitimate reason to enter CDD is to "do good." Teachers, social workers, and religious leaders affiliated with an established organization in Cidade de Deus are perceived as helpful to the neighborhood and are usually allowed to enter without interrogation. This was my ticket in: as a volunteer for Youth Promise, I entered and exited their building multiple times a week so drug traffickers would see me as a social worker and leave me be. Outsiders may also enter if they are accompanied by a local resident. Finally, outsiders may also enter to buy drugs or to attend rave parties on the weekends, thereby sustaining the illicit drug economy without incurring its problems.

This boundary policing helps to retrench the experience of CDD as a community by reaffirming notions of who "belongs" in such a space. In this case, belonging is based on neighborhood residency, fluency in obeying local social norms, and ironically, on exclusion from mainstream urban society. However, within the dynamic borders of Cidade de Deus, residents have built social networks, systems of mutual support, and kinship ties that help people deal with many of the obstacles they face. In the following section, I describe some of the structural challenges that have made favela life so much more challenging than other urban spaces.

The Daily Struggles Created by Structural Violence

One of the greatest challenges to residents in Cidade de Deus and other favelas is the inaccessibility of the many rights and resources promised to them. As Brodwyn Fischer (2008) argues, the "poverty of rights" among Rio's poor is not due to a lack of progressive legislation, but to a lack of resources. Brazil has universal healthcare, through which the federal government funded the installation of hundreds of emergency rooms (known as the UPAs, Unidades de Pronto Atendimento). One was inaugurated in Cidade de Deus in 2010 (Figure 1.7). However, residents are routinely denied service because the UPA often lacks basic medical supplies, nursing staff, or doctors with the necessary specialty. Camilla, one of the coordinators at Youth Promise, had raised three children in Cidade de Deus. One afternoon at

Figure 1.7 The public health clinic in Cidade de Deus, Centro Municipal de Saúde Hamilton Land
Photo by the author.

Youth Promise, Camilla told us about her experience the previous day. After a visit to the UPA with her 12-year-old son Marcos who had broken his arm, she discovered that "the orthopedist only works on Thursday." Unfortunately, it was Tuesday. "I told Marcos, next time, you have to break your arm on a Thursday!" Camilla chortled, pleased with her joke. But the experience had not been so funny: she had lost an entire day of work shuffling him from the UPA to the public hospital in Barra, a 20-minute bus ride away, where he was finally seen several hours later. Additionally, as the conflict between the police and the drug trade escalated, the director of the UPA reported in a meeting organized by local activists that they had started operating as a "war hospital," given how many gun victims they were treating. This diverted resources from ordinary residents to the victims of police violence.

The public services outside CDD also posed challenges to poor residents. One afternoon, I was sitting on the couch when Esther arrived from the emergency room of a public hospital in another neighborhood. She had gone there after feeling her blood pressure drop. She sat on the couch and told me about the hours of waiting she had endured. "Three died there today," she mentioned, almost as an afterthought. "Three died? In the emergency room?!" I'd exclaimed, shocked by her nonchalant tone. One had collapsed and died in front of her, having been forced to stand in line at the pharmacy for hours after having had a heart attack earlier that morning. She had also seen a family huddled outside crying and hugging, which she assumed was from a second death, and rumors had been circulating around the waiting room of a third death. While many wealthier Brazilian residents pay for costly private health insurance to supplement public healthcare, few favela residents can afford this luxury. The consequences were severe: Esther had lost many close friends and family members to cancer, diabetes, and other illnesses that would likely have been treated successfully if they'd had access to better medical care. Fearing what might happen if she became complacent, Esther was quick to jump to action when she felt sick. I lost count of the number of times Esther would travel from the UPA to the hospital to the health clinic to a specialist, back and forth, in search of proper care. It was costly, time consuming, exhausting, and confusing, since she frequently received incorrect or contradictory diagnoses. The process often aggravated the very conditions for which she sought care (Figure 1.8).

Constant shootouts and fear of drug gangs and the police significantly exacerbated the already poor social infrastructure and residents' overall

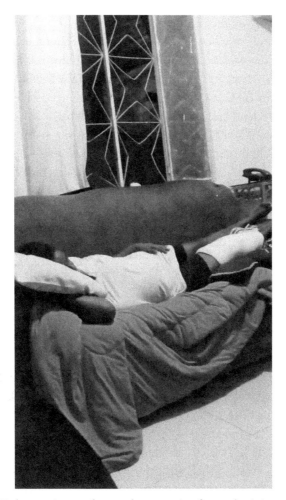

Figure 1.8 Esther resting on the couch recovering from a leg injury
Photo by the author.

quality of life. Our community survey found that over three-quarters of
households had mental or physical problems related to the stress caused
from constantly facing insecurity, including fear, anxiety, difficulty sleeping,
sadness, or high blood pressure. I personally knew of four women who died
of heart attacks after they or a loved one was caught in a shootout. Insecurity
created other problems: 88% of children had missed school the previous year
because of shootouts, and 45% missed more than ten days. Three-quarters
of children had also missed school because of teacher absences and maintenance issues, due in part to shootouts that made it difficult for teachers

and maintenance workers to enter the neighborhood. At least once a week, I woke up to find André stuck at home because of shootouts. I knew these unanticipated absences would severely affect his ability to learn, and later to compete with students from safe neighborhoods in college entrance exams. It was little surprise that Cidade de Deus's college-age residents were only half as likely to attend university as other Rio residents.

The repercussions of the frequency of school closings, which has been an endemic problem through most of CDD's history, has also affected its adult population: one-third of our participants reported not completing primary school,[7] and only 34% had completed secondary (high) school. This has major implications for poverty rates. Within our sample, 14% struggled to secure employment due to lack of educational qualifications, while an additional 8% had been denied employment because they lived in a favela.[8] The favela also suffered from poorly maintained and irregular public services. A third of residents did not receive their mail regularly. For some, this meant that work checks or other important documents arrived months late or not at all. Roads and sidewalks were covered in potholes, parks and playgrounds were in disrepair, leading to many injuries among children. Although electricity was costly, power went out regularly, sometimes multiple times a day, making it very difficult to operate businesses or do any work that required technology. Almost three-quarters of residents also had issues with overflowing sewers, clogged water pipes, and roads that flooded or had major potholes (Figure 1.9).

Although Cidade de Deus is often perceived as a site of physical violence, just as pervasive are its struggles with *structural violence*. According to Johan Galtung (1969), people often die or are injured without a specific aggressor. Instead, "the violence is built into the structure and shows up as unequal power and consequently as unequal life chances." In other words, economic, political, and social systems operate in ways that prevent some (or many) people from living a long, healthy life by denying them access to existing goods, services, and care. Structural inequities are exacerbated by *symbolic violence*, or taken-for-granted beliefs that legitimize a relation of dominance and submission, often by affirming negative beliefs about the oppressed group (Bourdieu and Wacquant 2004). In Rio, discriminatory and racist beliefs about favela residents justifies the challenges they face to survival and mobility (Vargas 2006). This is often manifest in a refusal by employers to hire CDD residents perceived as irresponsible or lazy, the mistreatment of darker-skinned customers who are suspected of being thieves,

Figure 1.9 A side street that routinely filled with sewage water after rain
Photo by the author.

and support for harsh policing practices in favelas deemed to be pockes of criminality. In these, and many other ways, the broader urban community creates additional barriers to economic and social mobility for favela residents while reinforcing the idea that they are unworthy of the full rights of urban citizenship.

CDD residents have developed a range of tactics to confront the everyday manifestations of structural and symbolic violence. For instance, when our team asked residents how they deal with poor service at health clinics and other government offices, they reported they had learned to *fazer um barraco*, a colloquial term for "making a ruckus," to get assistance. It was among the few non-violent "weapons" that they had at their disposal (Scott 1987), an individual tool of resistance that helped them obtain immediate service, even if it did little to change embedded structures of inequality (Fahlberg et al. 2020). If that didn't work, many residents turned to informal resources, such as self-medicating, starting their own small businesses, or fixing public utilities themselves. Camilla and her neighbors, for instance, had paved their own road several times because of flooding issues.

These examples showcase some of the many barriers that keep Cidade de Deus residents from enjoying a "right to the city," or full participation in the privileges and benefits of urban living (Harvey 2012). They represent not only physical but also structural and symbolic forms of violence, and they are frequently the issues that favela activists point to when making demands for more resources and rights. However, these challenges are not simply contemporary issues; they are manifestations of historical processes of segregated discrimination, racism, and neglect that characterize the relationship between Rio de Janeiro and its many favelas.

Cidade de Deus and other urban slums are frequently believed to be defined by scarcity and neglect: they emerge because the state and society refuse to provide the poor with sufficient resources and opportunities. This is a partial explanation. Modern urban societies are also built on the backs of slums like CDD and depend on them for both practical and symbolic purposes. For one, capitalism relies on poverty to function: favela residents provide "surplus labor," filling in the gaps of the formal economy as informal and cheap labor (Perlman 1979). Favelas also serve as the symbolic "other" against whom ideas about who "deserves" the benefits of citizenship are formed. By looking down on favela residents, wealthier groups reaffirm their status as "good" citizens who have earned their success through hard work and modern cultural values. As Engin Isin (2002) has argued, citizenship is founded on differentiation, on distinguishing between who deserves the benefits of full inclusion in the state and who should be left out. Some groups *must* be excluded to make included groups feel worthy. In Rio, favelas have become those sites. Its residents are viewed as morally and culturally depraved, mired in cultures of violence and poverty and therefore needing to be excluded and policed. It is upon this tension between exclusion and inclusion—being allowed in just enough to uphold urban hierarchies and their subordinate places within it—that Rio's many favelas, and eventually Cidade de Deus in particular, were constructed.

Colonial Legacies and the Making of Brazilian Sovereignty

To understand the creation of Cidade de Deus and its economic and sym-bolic meanings within Rio de Janeiro, one must return to colonial history, and in particular to the treatment of Black and poor citizens. Between 1501 and 1866, Brazil imported nearly 5 million slaves from Africa. Rio de Janeiro became a "nerve center" of the Atlantic slave trade, receiving an approx-imate 2 million slaves during the colonial era (Romero 2014). Portuguese colonizers relied heavily on Africans, as well as some indigenous slaves, to grow sugarcane, coffee, and a host of other lucrative crops. Runaway slaves created autonomous communities, known as quilombos, in which they set up their own internal economic and social systems, practiced African religions, and created new cultural forms rooted in those of their ancestors. In quilombos, writes Lélia Gonzalez (2018:264), there existed "a life parallel to the life of dominant society, to the dominant culture, to the dominant class." For Gonzalez and many other scholars, favelas have become modern-day forms of quilombos: racially segregated communities where excluded citizens resist their marginalization through autonomous counter-cultural movements (Leite 2000).

After Brazil gained independence from the Portuguese monarchy in 1822 and transitioned to a republic, the new Brazilian state relied on the policing of poor Black communities to affirm its sovereignty. Brazil's first national po-lice force was formed for the explicit purpose of quashing "internal enemies," including poor peasants, nomadic indigenous communities, and runaway or freed slaves. The Brazilian government frequently labeled these as "pacifi-cation" interventions aimed at "civilizing" insurgent rebels, though targeted communities were often slaughtered or taken as sexual slaves (Rodrigues et al. 2018). National security and state-building in Brazil thus relied largely on the killing of its own subjects (Husain 2009). Peter Wade (2009) further contends that participation in Brazil's nascent military gave young, mostly poor men opportunities to perform aggressive masculinity, gaining status and respect through patriotic violence. Many decades later, the over-policing of favelas reflects this legacy of building the state—and modern notions of masculinity and citizenship—through internal warfare against poor and ra-cially marginalized populations.

While these raids, particularly against Black and indigenous groups, were often justified by racial hierarchies, which posited non-White groups as mor-ally and culturally inferior to those of European descent (Quijano 2000), the construction of racial differences was not always convenient to political elites. As Brazil transitioned from an imperial monarchy to the new Brazilian Republic in 1889, the appearance of unity and solidarity became critical to forging a new national identity. In order to build the new nation, Brazilian statesmen began to deploy a rhetoric of a "racial democracy," suggesting that all racial groups had equal access to democratic rights (Goldstein 2003). While this was intended to strengthen patriotism and willingness to serve the interests of the country, it was not accompanied by full rights to voting or citizenship. Citizens were not denied the right to vote based on race. Instead, exclusions based on literacy, income, and gender prevented the majority of the population from electoral participation, including women and most Black and poor men. In practice, Black and brown Brazilians continued to suffer from state violence and neglect, even as policymakers clung to the myth of racial equality (Ana 2019; Vargas 2010).

In 1888, Brazil earned the unenviable title of being the last country in the western hemisphere to abolish slavery. Freed slaves were provided with few opportunities for upward mobility. Rural peasants were also thrown into poverty when oligarchs in northeastern Brazil took over rural lands or sold them off to foreign investors. Rural migrants flocked to Rio de Janeiro in search of employment and a place to live. Meanwhile (lighter-skinned) European migrants, who descended in droves on Rio de Janeiro and other Latin American cities during WWI and WWII, received a number of social supports to get back on their feet and integrate into Brazilian society.

Rural migrants arriving in Rio de Janeiro found themselves in a similar situation to recently freed slaves, having nowhere to live and little access to well-paid jobs. With few alternatives, they built shacks on Rio's hillsides near their jobs in wealthy residential and commercial areas. The first organized informal settlement in Rio de Janeiro was built in the late 1800s by soldiers released from the army after the destruction of one of the largest settlements of poor people in northeastern Brazil, famously misnamed the Canudos War (rather than the Canudos "genocide").[9] After the "war," soldiers—themselves from poor families—were discharged without employment. Many moved to the growing Rio metropolis looking for work and better life prospects. With nowhere to live, they built their homes on the Morro da Providência (Providence Hill), alongside recently freed slaves from the area (Valladares 2005:29). By the turn of the century, many other informal settlements, known then as cortiços, sprouted up along the hills lining Rio's downtown area and wealthy residential districts.

Rio's population doubled, from 500,000 in 1890 to 1 million in 1920. Governance over the growing Rio de Janeiro metropolis, the capital of Brazil until 1960, set the tone for the nation's urban planning agenda. Brodwyn Fischer notes that the European influence over racial and social ideologies and growing urban inequality "helped to convince many elite Cariocas (Rio residents) that new forms of social regulation—of criminality, of public health, of entertainment, even of architecture and urban design—were necessary to make Rio a fully 'civilized' city" (Fischer 2008:23). Rio's politicians and bureaucrats took on the role of refereeing social differences, mostly by ignoring the needs of its poorest residents. Their decisions, Fischer argues, "laid the foundations for a strikingly bifurcated form of urban growth, both deepening and broadening colonial inequities" (Fischer 2008:23). Urban development focused on wealthy, whiter districts, while poor housing areas were left to their own devices.

For the early part of the 20th century, cortiços remained on the geographic and symbolic fringes of the city. They were mostly small and fragmented, lacking infrastructure or a strong collective identity. Around this time, advances in medicine and public health in the United States and Europe spread to Brazil and provided urban professional elites the opportunity demonstrate their modernity by applying these "scientific" practices in poor areas, particularly through sanitation campaigns. However, their commitment to "sanitizing" cortiços soon turned into a mandate to destroy them altogether. As fear of disease-infested settlements spread, anti-cortiço campaigns took full force between 1902 and 1906 under Rio de Janeiro Mayor Francisco Pereira Passos, who razed shacks to make room for "wide avenues and sumptuous belle époque architecture" (Fischer 2008:35). Eradication of informal settlements would, in theory, rid the city of its "primitive" and "uncivilized" populations and create opportunities for industrialization and urban growth modeled after European cities.

The city's population doubled again between 1920 and 1940. Informal settlements continued to grow as well. They became more organized, building their own infrastructure, including wells, roads, and internal systems of governance. They were relabeled favelas, after the weeds that grew on Rio's hills. By 1950, approximately 7% of the city's population lived in favelas or, as the city formally termed them, "subnormal agglomerations." It is around this time that academic research in favelas began to take off as social scientists became fascinated by these "marginal" spaces (Perlman 1979). As Licia Valladares (2005) argues, social scientists have played a critical role in both reproducing and debunking popular beliefs about the "backward-ness," "laziness," and cultural "marginality" of favela residents.

Rio also experienced major political transitions during this time. In 1930, Getúlio Vargas led an armed revolution against the newly elected president and took over the presidency. Seven years into a turbulent reign, Vargas outlawed all political parties and established a dictatorial civil re-gime called the "New State." Elections were allowed only at municipal and state levels. Backed by the armed forces, the first Vargas regime outlawed po-litical manifestations, censured the press, and imprisoned "enemies of the state" (Carvalho 2001:113). Despite this, Vargas had widespread support from the people, particularly those in urban areas, thanks to his promises of electoral and social reforms and a fierce nationalist agenda that rejected the traditional oligarchical structure and the control of agrarian elites. Vargas ex-panded the franchise to women and lowered the voting age to 18. Civil rights were expanded as well. New labor rights included an eight-hour workday, restrictions on child labor, the implementation of work authorization cards, and a national minimum wage. Retirement and pensions also became legal rights.

While these social rights were widely beneficial to the working class, they were much less effective in strengthening citizenship among favela residents. Access to workers' rights required employment in the formal economy, though most favela residents worked in informal employment. Pensions and other entitlements required a birth certificate and other forms and the ability to navigate complex bureaucratic structures. Low literacy rates coupled with a lack of documentation among the poor meant that the obstacles were too great for many favela residents to obtain the rights provided by the state. Consequently, demands for infrastructure and social services—rather than race-based civil rights—became the core struggle among favela activists.

By the 1940s, the lack of political rights began to weigh on Vargas's power. In 1945, Vargas was deposed by his Minister of War, only to ascend to power again after a democratic election in 1950. Vargas's second regime spearheaded a wave of political openings, including regular elections for the president of the republic and national and regional legislative posts, freedom of the press, and freedom of political organization. Political opportunities grew in Rio's favelas as well. By the mid-20th century, rising literacy rates in favelas enabled more poor people to vote, thus forcing politicians to give at least the appearance of advocating for the causes of favela residents. Their support was inconsistent, however, and usually relied on a clientelist system of exchanging favors for votes (McCann 2014). Politicians operated in an old-fashioned populist fashion called "water-spigot politics," wherein local bosses "registered voters and brought out supporters and politicians, usually through intermediaries, by granting small concessions" (Fischer 2008:60–61), though these social services were usually inadequate and distributed based on political loyalty rather than need or right.

Many favelas became sites of active social and political organizing, thanks to both the internal needs of residents and the influence of external actors. Residents demanded more consistent urban services. They sent letters to politicians, organized street protests, and spoke out in the press. Among the most urgent issues were housing rights, particularly in areas where favelas were threatened with demolition or evictions, and access to urban infrastructure, including electricity, water, sewage, and education (McMann 2014). Increased attention to the "favela problem" among progressive urban elites had given birth to a new narrative of favelas as spaces of hard-working people with few resources and, for some more radical advocates, as a creative solution to the drought of urban housing and infrastructure. The growing Communist Party had come to see favelas as sites for popular mobilization. Progressive members of the Catholic Church opposed to authoritarianism and the violation of human rights had also begun to support activist efforts in favelas. In the 1940s a joint venture between the Catholic Church and the federal and municipal governments resulted in the creation of Fundação Leão XIII, which provided widespread social services, including healthcare and educational services to favelas in an effort to prevent the spread of communism in some of the largest favelas. Many of these groups also believed that urbanized infrastructure was a minimum requirement for human existence and set out to help favela residents obtain greater access to electricity, water, and public telephones. They also helped created neighborhood associations and organize collective mobilization against evictions.

In contrast to the urban "ghettos" of the United States, Rio's favelas had greater racial diversity thanks to the heavy presence of lighter-skinned rural migrants. Nonetheless, favelas were racialized spaces, viewed, policed, and neglected as if they were entirely Black neighborhoods (Ana 2019; Vargas 2006). Favelas were subject to regular police interventions to arrest "criminals" or to provide security for eviction campaigns, while also receiving far fewer urban resources than Whiter urban neighborhoods. Racial discrimination was not written into law but became a reality through the practices of the police, the municipal government, and urban elites.

While favela residents' access to infrastructure and other social resources progressed in a scattered and fragmented fashion, the national landscape of rights witnessed a decisive fall beginning in the 1960s. For one, the federal capital was moved from Rio de Janeiro to Brasilia in 1960 in an effort by then-President Juscelino Kubitschek to escape, in space and symbol, the old politics of authoritarianism and corruption by ruling from a newly built "city of hope," a utopia for democracy (O Globo 2013). The relocation of the capital resulted in a decline in both political and economic power in Rio de Janeiro. Additionally, a great deal of turbulence in national politics had led Vargas to commit suicide in 1954 in the middle of an economic scandal. By the 1960s, the country had been led by two leftist presidents. Party politics was becoming increasingly polarized between progressive populist leaders and conservative elites. The national economy was also in sharp decline. With support from Brazil's National Congress and the United States, which had come to associate all leftist politics in Latin America with communism (Gobat 2013), the Brazilian Armed Forces overthrew leftist president João Goulart in response to his plan to socialize the profits of large companies. Political rights were suspended, and the Congress elected army general Humberto Castelo Branco as president. Castelo Branco promised to return power to national industries, to expand foreign trade, and to promote the political stability deemed necessary for effective economic growth. Neighboring Latin American countries witnessed a similar fate as the anticommunist, pro-capitalist forces overthrew progressive leaders and imposed authoritarian regimes. For the next 21 years, Brazil remained under dictatorial rule. It was in this context—of dramatic national change and a complex and contradictory urban landscape—that Cidade de Deus was borne.

The "Favelization" of Cidade de Deus

Cidade de Deus was not intended to be a favela. Instead, the first houses in CDD were built by the state of Rio de Janeiro through its State Company for Housing (COHAB). COHAB was financed by the National Housing Bank (BNH), founded in 1964 under Castelo Branco, to "promote construction and acquisition of self-owned homes, especially among the classes of lower income, to increase opportunities for employment and to invigorate the civil construction sector" (Fundação Getúlio Vargas 2009). It is rumored that Cidade de Deus (or City of God) was so named in order to convince residents to take pride in their new community and commit themselves to building a formal, respectable neighborhood rather than a favela (Marcelino 2013).

Labeled a *conjunto habitacional*, or housing complex, Cidade de Deus was designed to accommodate families "relocated" (i.e., evicted) from informal settlements on land areas slated for redevelopment. It was part of a much larger political project in the city. Then-governor Carlos Lacerda had been elected in 1960 on promises to grow Rio's industrial potential and to reverse urban decay by removing unwanted shantytowns. He also believed that if the city's poor residents were placed in a formal neighborhood, they would adopt the "values" and behaviors of the wealthy, which would in turn "transform" them into "respectable urban citizens" (Valladares 2005). During Lacerda's tenure, 140,000 people were relocated, mostly from the areas near Rio's beaches, the business district, and wealthy neighborhoods, and displaced to more distant—and still undeveloped—areas. Lacerda received significant funding from the United States under John F. Kennedy's Alliance for Progress program,[10] in an attempt to combat the perceived risk of communism in Latin America's shantytowns through urban "renewal" projects. Kennedy's program was so influential that another housing complex constructed at the same time as Cidade de Deus was named Vila Kennedy.

Cidade de Deus was strategically installed in the Jacarepaguá region in the West Zone, which had been identified as a new site for the expansion of urban industrialization. While the Jacarepaguá region had some commercial areas before the 1960s, most of the land was vacant and undeveloped, having once been used by large plantations. "You know this land is built over a graveyard," Esther had lamented to me once, "We live on the bodies of dead slaves." Esther's comment reflected the continuities in racialized urban development. The legacies of slavery and state-sanctioned violence against Black bodies remains inscribed today in both physical spaces and the individual and collective experiences of urban segregation. Since then, many CDD residents have provided the manual labor for the construction of middle-class and wealthy neighborhoods in the surrounding area. Urban redevelopment became, in many respects, a new colonial project that continued to reaffirm the dominance of the city's white elite, constructed on the backs of poor Black laborers.

Many residents in Cidade de Deus arrived when it was first being built and have remained until now, raising families and building a community. The plan for Cidade de Deus held some promise, at least in theory, for offering former favela residents a decent life. In addition to individual houses, to which residents would presumably be allowed to earn the legal titles after paying them off at a substantially reduced price, Cidade de Deus had electricity, water and sewage systems, and some paved roads. However, the city provided the bare minimum to residents and left them to their own devices to make their homes and the area suitable for living. "We had no door, no bathroom," recalled Esther, who arrived in Cidade de Deus at age five in the first years of its construction. As many residents who had been lucky enough to receive a new public housing unit told me, the homes lacked internal infrastructure, such as a toilet in the bathroom or stairs to the second floor. From its very beginnings, residents were required to build their own infrastructure in order to have habitable homes. Those with less luck were put into smaller and less developed provisional homes, while others were forced to build shacks or extensions onto family members' homes. Fifty years later, many residents maintained a great interest in their neighborhood's history. Longtime resident Rosalina Brito created a website to document its early years, post photos, and share an interview she conducted with Cidade de Deus's architect Giuseppe Badolato:

Rosalina: Cidade de Deus was not built for the homeless. Who was it for, then?

Giuseppe: It was a BNH (National Housing Bank) town planning project for low-income people, who would have their own house paying 10% of their salary and who would provide labor, service for Barra da Tijuca that was in development.

Rosalina: Were you disappointed in what happened to your project?

Giuseppe: I was shocked when I saw Cidade de Deus abandoned by the public power, which should continue to invest in infrastructure—CDD was not designed to receive so many people.

In contrast to other favelas, which were dealing with forced evictions, slum demolition, and displacement from natural disasters, CDD was the receiving site of these urban refugees. While this spared CDD from the threat of demolitions, it encountered another set of struggles: to provide for the needs of a rapidly growing and extremely diverse population. In Cidade de Deus's first five years, thousands of newcomers arrived from 63 different favelas. Former Cidade de Deus resident Edir Figueiredo de Mello (2010:40) writes in his doctoral dissertation that "in the first years of the formation of the Housing Complex, the dominant representation of it, among a large part of the residents, was that of a multifaceted space, composed of a heterogeneous population differentiated according to origin criteria [i.e., the favela they came from] and types of home." This heterogeneity also created conflicts and distrust between residents.

Cidade de Deus continued to expand at a rapid pace into the 1970s. As the population swelled, the water and electricity supplies could not keep up. Roads paved with cheap materials began to break. Sewers clogged and canals filled with trash. There was never enough housing, medical supplies, or schools. Already accustomed to making do with few resources, Cidade de Deus's residents sprung to action. Some added extensions and second and third stories to their houses to accommodate their growing families and others built their own shacks. They paved their own roads, connected new electrical wires, extended water and sewage pipes, and started local cooperatives for tutoring and childcare. What once began as a formal housing complex quickly became informal. Cidade de Deus had been "favelized" (Neto and Nunes 2012).

"Favelization" elicits a negative sentiment of decay and marginality, of state neglect and urban exclusion. However, it can also be seen as evidence of social resilience. Gerardo Silva (2013:43) argues that although the term favela has many definitions, a central component is resistance and struggle. For him, "favela is a subjective determination, meaning a desire among the poor to remain in the city, to build quotidian strategies for a better life even in situations of precarity, violence and risk." In fact, the absence of government leadership in Cidade de Deus's social development engendered a number of early efforts to improve living conditions in CDD. Residents began mobilizing to provide the social services the government either would not provide, or for which it provided too little to keep up with residents' needs.

According to former Cidade de Deus resident and author Valéria Barbosa, many residents played an important role in organizing local development needs and filling some of the voids left by a neglectful state. Their goal was to improve urban infrastructure and provide cultural and athletic opportunities for residents. At this time, a progressive branch of the Catholic Church, which had been inserted in CDD and many other favelas, partnered with residents to organize community action projects (Netto 2016). One of the earliest initiatives was organized by Julio Grotten, a priest sent by the Catholic Church from the Netherlands, and a local resident, Senhor Nelson. Together they founded the first social service organization of Cidade de Deus. "This assistance center," writes Barbosa, "relied on the volunteer work of doctors, provided help to families in difficult situations, and worked in the Church space itself" (Barbosa 2012:46). Dozens of informal community-based organizations were also established, mostly run on a volunteer basis through donations with no stable sources of funding. Many cultural groups emerged as well. According to Cidade de Deus ethnographer Alba Zaluar, by the early 1980s Cidade de Deus had a large samba school, four carnival "blocks," or street bands, and several soccer teams. These groups helped bring residents together and many played a role in the political and social organizing of the neighborhood (Zaluar 1985:175). These were not without conflicts, however. These divisions had a spatial logic, representing different blocks of the neighborhood. Samba schools and soccer teams followed a clientelist logic, cultivating relations to individual politicians in order to obtain donations for the team or school and basic goods for participants while helping the politicians obtain votes from block residents. Nonetheless, cultural groups and social service initiatives served an important role in addressing the needs of the neighborhood while also building social ties and solidarity. Gradually, CDD transitioned from a site of chaos and distrust to a community with collective objectives and actions. At the same time, rising gang conflicts created new challenges to favela living and organizing.

Early Turf Wars

Unlike older favelas on Rio's hillsides, which were built in the first half of the 20th century and witnessed decades of peace before the rise of the global drug trade, Cidade de Deus faced high levels of violence almost as soon as it was created. As residents arrived from dozens of distinct communities, so too did local armed gang members. By the 1970s, distrust between residents sparked local turf wars. Socially constructed differences and hierarchies, based partly on arriving residents' various places of origin, came to define and constrain social networks. Armed young men appointed themselves the enforcers of security in a context of social distrust. Gangs sold drugs, primarily marijuana, and imposed strict punishments on residents who trespassed onto a rival gang's territory. People from one "block" could be assaulted, raped, or killed for crossing into a rival block.

Violence between gang members wreaked havoc on residents' lives and made it challenging for outsiders to navigate the territoriy. However, their actions should also be understood as a form of resilience in the face of economic exclusion. Alba Zaluar argues that the actions of drug gangs "can be interpreted as an individual revolt against adverse conditions, as a refusal of the types of employment destined to the poor population, as well as a participation in one of the most lucrative economies that we know of in the capitalist world" (Zaluar 1985:166). Writing about the drug trade in Harlem, Philippe Bourgois (2003) argued that state violence and the exclusion of the poor from decent and well-paid formal jobs catapult young men in search of resources and respect into an illicit economy that relies heavily on violence—often against their own kin and neighbors— as a form of resistance. Having been excluded from the formal economy and wealthy, White urban spaces, many young men in favelas join gangs to obtain not only much-needed money but also social status and respect, thereby producing a new form of citizenship that takes rights by force (Holston 2008).

Gangs also provided many practical services that the state did not. For one, they became the local enforcers of the law, policing a range of criminal activities, including petty theft, home invasions, domestic violence, and child abuse, often through the deployment of extremely brutal and public forms of violence intended to affirm their power (Larkins 2015). Gangs also provided residents with small favors, such as food donations, gifts for children on holidays, and block parties, in an effort to gain popular support.

Despite the gangs' presence in policing crime, women suffered extensively from violence during this time. Luz, an artist and activist in her early 50s, shared some examples with me of how physical and sexual violence led to other forms of aggression and social exclusion in her life. "At that time, the bandits of that period did not have pity for women, no, they would kill women, raped women, it was horrible," she recalled. These threats led to another problem for Luz: at age 12, her father ordered her to quit school. He claimed it was for her safety, though he had long advocated against women's education. Public violence offered him a legitimate excuse to promote patriarchal values. Three years later, Luz met and quickly married a boy who worked at the local butcher shop and moved out of Cidade de Deus. It was both an escape and an act of defiance against her father. Llthough leaving Cidade de Deus gave her a reprieve from gang violence, her husband soon became physically abusive. Several years and three daughters later, she returned to her parents' home to escape him. Her path back to her controlling father reflects the limits of resistance in a context of constrained housing and economic precarity.

Luz was not the only woman to have been caught between spaces of gendered violence. Esther had tried to flee the violence of Cidade de Deus by going to work as a nanny in a nearby middle-class neighborhood at age 15. This lasted for only a year before she had to run away from work one day when her employer's father tried to rape her. In Esther's case, both race and class inequalities further exacerbated the situation: a Black woman from a favela, the chances that the police would take an attempted rape report from her seriously were slim. She left the job, losing both her regular income and the safety it had provided before the assault.

Violence against women is often overlooked in conflict zones, in part because men make up the overwhelming majority of homicide victims and in part because the gendered component of violence is erased in discussions of political violence (MacKinnon 1994). When it is examined, there is often a focus on how intersecting forms of inequality—including those of race, class, and gender—produce multiple barriers to safety. While this cannot be ignored, we must also examine how women consciously navigate these terrains of insecurity. In her work on intimate violence along the journey across the Mexico-US border, Wendy Vogt argues that a focus on "intimate labors" allows us to recognize the resilience and agency women deploy to survive and minimize violence (Vogt 2018:137). In Cidade de Deus, the intimate labors of Luz, Esther, and many other female residents reflect not only intersecting forms of victimization but also agentic maneuvering between sites of violence. They reveal how women strategically moved between spaces, jobs, and kinship networks in order to maximize their safety and try to create a better life for themselves.

While gang rivalries created significant obstacles for moving about the neighborhood, they did not deter residents from working collectively to address mounting problems with housing, food insecurity, education, and healthcare. Throughout the 1970s and early 1980s, residents founded three neighborhood associations in which they gathered in assemblies to discuss the neighborhood's most urgent matters and create plans for how to address these problems. Residents' associations held elections for leadership posts, partnered with allies in NGOs and government agencies across the city, and prioritized structural changes based on rights rather than *assistencialismo*, or charity. Among the most well-established of these associations was the Council of Residents of Cidade de Deus (or COMOCID), founded in 1968. "The dictatorship permitted it, the registration of a statute for a community-based organization" explained Jefferson, an activist in Cidade de Deus for many decades, "but our statute had to meet two conditions: It had to be not-for-profit, and it had to be apolitical." By this he meant that they could not align themselves with any of the national political parties then emerging to challenge the legitimacy and political power of the dictatorship, such as the Worker's Party and Brazil's Communist Party. Rather than declare allegiance to a political party, COMOCID set out to organize around local needs. Their projects included registering residents' land titles and helping them obtain other legal documents, as well as advocating for better trash collection and sewage systems and resources to meet educational and healthcare needs. They spearheaded a petition asking the state to build a public health clinic, which was ultimately successful: the Hamilton Land Municipal Health Center, inaugurated in 1979 on Cidade de Deus's main avenue, continues to serve hundreds of residents a day.

The efforts of residents' associations was aided by the establishment of several state agencies to connect favela residents to the state. The Fundação Leão XIII, for instance, was founded in 1947 by national decree with the goal of integrating favela residents into the urban fabric by promoting "the moral and cultural elevation" of favelas (Valla 1981). In 1974, it was linked to the state's Urban Social Center (Centros Sociais Urbanos). National and municipal investments in these programs aimed to decrease communist, anti-state sentiment among the urban poor. Both institutions encouraged residents to organize into (apolitical) associations, providing trainings for favela youth, organizing local vaccination campaigns, and financing cultural events. CDD activists also found allies in local agencies. "We had a strong relationship with the doctors [at the health center], many of whom were [politically] on the left," a former COMOCID leader explained to me. They also partnered with professors and students at publicly funded universities to design a new housing plan for residents living in shacks and held several forums with teachers and other allies working for the state to discuss how to extend and improve public education.

Power Consolidated under the Comando Vermelho

The internal structure of drug gangs changed in the 1980s. The newly established drug trafficking organization known as Comando Vermelho, or the "Red Command," took over Cidade de Deus and forced a truce between rival block gangs. Ben Penglase argues that the Comando Vermelho, or CV for short, was the "bastard child" of the dictatorship (Penglase 2008:125). It was formed in Rio's prisons, where the dictatorship had incarcerated both petty criminals and political "subversives." The two groups conspired together to insert Rio de Janeiro into the growing global drug economy. When Brazil's dictatorship fell in 1985, hundreds of prisoners were released, and the leaders of the new CV went to Cidade de Deus and other favelas to enlist local gangs into their new economic project. Two other drug factions emerged as well, taking over other favelas. Favelas became the ideal locations in which to process cocaine and marijuana and prepare them for sale or export. According to de Souza, most of Rio's favelas, located in twisty hillsides, could not be easily accessed by police patrol vehicles, allowing drug traffickers to hide drugs, guns, and people from invading police (de Sosuza 2005). Furthermore, informal criminal gangs already operating in CDD and other favelas provided the new drug factions with easy access to an existing, albeit fractured, drug infrastructure and many unemployed young men. CV leaders—with connections to violent criminals across the city—subdued or bribed block gangs and appointed "managers" to run the drug operations for each block. In a perverse capitalist logic, a focus on growing their entrepreneurial strength through cooperation significantly decreased daily shootouts between neighboring rivals while also increasing their economic and political control over the neighborhood.

The growing power of the CV in Cidade de Deus and many other favelas gave the state's security apparatus an ideal new target. No longer charged with apprehending "political dissidents" under the dictatorship, militarized police forces in Brazil's new democracy set out to take down the CV, which was quickly establishing a "parallel state" within favelas (Leeds 1996). The rise of the CV also took on a symbolic dimension, representing the connection between the "threats" of political uprising during the Cold War and the "new threat" of narco-trafficking (Rodrigues 2016). According to Thiago Rodrigues, Ronald Reagan further promoted the "mechanism of the incessant production of enemies," thereby solidifying the ties between the United States and Latin America on the basis of fighting the "global threat" of leftist narco dissidents (Rodrigues 2016:68–69). The fight against drug gangs in Latin America had not only political but also economic objectives. As Dawn Paley (2014:4) argues, the War on Drugs is in fact part of a "war strategy that ensures transnational corporations' access to resources through dispossession and terror."

The consequences of this "drug war capitalism" were devastating to Cidade de Deus, as well as other favelas. Just as the consolodiation of the CV helped quell inter-gang fighting, a new violence spread between invading militarized police forces and a heavily armored CV. Rates of homicides and "death by acts of resistance" (i.e., murders by on-duty police officers committed supposedly in self-defense) skyrocketed. Ten thousand people were killed by police officers in acts of resistance between 2000 and 2010 across Rio de Janeiro (Misse, Grillo, and Neri 2015). Many residents described their memory of this time to me. "I saw people dying, you know," reported Luz. "Here, a lot of people dying. Many of my friends who came here . . . died." Nearly all of my participants had lost a family member to drug-police violence, many killed in gruesome ways.

Meanwhile, the CV set about institutionalizing its power by co-opting neighborhood associations and local politicians. Those working or speaking out against the CV, whether residents, outsiders (such as teachers or social workers), or government officials working in the neighborhood, were quickly and brutally expelled, bribed, or assassinated. What had been a chaotic and decentralized cluster of street gangs transformed into a highly structured and powerful illicit economic and political system that maintained its power by instilling fear in residents, controlling everyday behavior, and policing subversion. Even as democratic openings expanded across Brazil in the 1990s and early 2000s, a topic I explore in-depth in Chapter 2, an authoritarian governance flourished under the CV within the borders of the neighborhood. Their control was limited to favelas, however. Most of its leaders could not leave the perimeter of the neighborhood, lest they be caught by the police and imprisoned or killed. The CV also did not have broader political ambitions, such as taking over the government; it was motivated primarily by economic gain. Political control of favelas was necessary insofar as it allowed their daily operations to function smoothly.

Organized Violence and the De-Politicization of Activism

Transformations in the politics of violence in CDD had a chilling effect on community organizing. While at first the cease-fire between block gangs allowed neighborhood associations to recruit members from surrounding blocks, this was soon stymied as the drug trade closely surveilled the social actions of the neighborhood and began to threaten community organizers who opposed their power. COMOCID was dismantled. Geovana, one of COMOCID's leaders, resigned in the 1990s after she was brutally beaten and raped, likely by a man hired by local political rivals. The residents' associations that did remain were co-opted by drug lords, sending activists fleeing. Another local organizer was murdered by drug traffickers after he began to secretly mobilize residents in opposition to the drug trade. Rumors of the brutality with which he was killed circulated—and still circulate— among activists, spreading fear and preventing any organizing that interfered with the CV. The drug trade proved a greater obstacle to local organizing than 20 years under the dictatorship.

As residents' associations disappeared or became depoliticized, activists turned their attention to less explicitly political tactics, moving away from party politics and political organizing and toward addressing social and cultural issues, as well as more symbolic practices. Among the most memorable was the First of May Rendezvous (*Encontro*), a day in which activists invited all cultural groups—samba schools, soccer leagues, artist collectives, theater groups—as well as local food vendors and musicians to hold a large fair in the middle of CDD's main avenue. The event shut down the street and brought great public attention. "It was an affront," explained one of its leaders to me, "both to the existing powers in Cidade de Deus and to . . . all the rich neighborhoods that didn't want us to close down the street." Residents placed barricades in the streets and celebrated local culture and community. The event was a great success for many years. The activists I interviewed recalled the event with nostalgia as an example of how residents from many different social and political circles banded together to assert their right to occupy vital urban space. It ended abruptly in 1997 when the inauguration of the Yellow Line, a major highway that cut straight through the heart of Cidade de Deus, displaced hundreds of residents and made the main avenue a core artery for travel from wealthy neighborhoods and the urban center. The state forced residents to move the event to a distant, small area until it eventually fizzled out. Activism, however, did not stop. Activists adapted to a changing physical and political landscape to create new strategies to demand urban rights and improvements to the neighborhood. Cidade de Deus was, and remains, a site of contestation, even as some avenues for change are rendered impassable. However, with each transition, activists bring with them their history of resistance, social networks, external allies, and repertoires of collective action that can be reconfigured and redeployed as new closures and challenges arise.

Destruction and Development

The history of Cidade de Deus, like that of other favelas, is not only about destruction but also about development. Although the state has done little to help and much to harm Rio's favelas, it also relies on the cheap labor, tax dollars, and votes of favela residents. It aspires to see not the total but only a partial destruction of favelas: enough to keep residents alive and working, submissive and subservient. At the same time, Brazil—like many other countries in the Global South—aspires to gain and maintain legitimacy on the international stage. High rates of urban violence and inequality can become an embarrassment to political leaders who are made to look incompetent. Rio de Janeiro, like many other cities, promotes just enough development to maintain an image of economic progress and a commitment to democracy.

In CDD, state investments in development have come in fits and starts, often sparked by a combination of internal changes and external pressures. Between 1980 and 1990, the favela population of Rio de Janeiro increased by 41%, and many favelas became so large they could not easily be destroyed and relocated. The increasing strength of the CV and other drug factions over these neighborhoods further challenged the ability of the police to enforce evictions. After decades of "urban renewal" projects that promoted mass evictions and displacement of favela residents, city officials finally began to accept that favelas were there to stay. Support for investing in urban development in favelas replaced the previous policy of displacement.

At the national level, Brazil's dictatorship was crumbling in response to growing international pressure and a national debt crisis. In 1982, direct elections were held for state governors for the first time since 1965. Leftist governor Leonel Brizola was elected on a platform of investing in the social needs of the city's poor and working classes. He appointed socialist anthropologist Darcy Ribeiro as Secretary of Special Projects, and together they opened 500 Centros Integrados de Educação Pública (CIEPS, Integrated Centers of Public Education), most of which were installed in or adjacent to favelas. "The goal was not merely to educate," writes favela historian Bryan McCann (2014:93), "but to make the CIEPs the engines of deeper social reforms" and to transform the harsh realities of the city's favelas. One CIEP was built on the outskirts of Cidade de Deus and still operates today, providing technical courses and a secondary education night school. In 1989, Brazil inaugurated a universal healthcare system, known popularly as the SUS, which provided critical health care services to millions of favela residents.

In 1996, Cidade de Deus experienced a disastrous flood that is still etched into the neighborhood's collective memory 20 years later. Cidade de Deus's untended canals, clogged with trash and tree trunks, overflowed after several hours of heavy downpours, sending over a meter of water and mud into most homes, and completely destroying many shacks. Over twenty years later, I still vividly recall walking through CDD's muddied streets with my mother and sister. Images of the devastation—wrecked shacks, piles of rubble, the bodies of those killed in the flood covered by tarps, a doll, children's flip flops— remain etched in my mind. I can only imagine the impact it has had on those who lived through it. Accounts varied about the number of deaths: some estimated 50, others 100. Esther believed it was many more: "There are a lot of bodies that were left, they gave some estimates but not all the bodies were found . . . There was a lake that [people] had covered up [to build shacks over] . . . but that used to have a whole other community. People couldn't leave because of the lake . . . they were stuck and died . . . They were buried." For Esther, the tragedy was not only that they died, but that their lives were never counted: "They went away with their houses, documents, everything." When the bodies and the documents were washed away, they had ceased to count. They never died because, according to state records, they never lived. This was the most egregious example of citizenship denied (Glenn 2011).

While the flood of 1996 continues to be remembered as one of the most traumatic events in CDD's history, it also paved the way for greater government investments in Cidade de Deus's physical and social infrastructure. Media coverage about the flood awakened both the government and private companies to the need for greater attention to and investments in the neighborhood. Esther recalled how many donations of clothes, appliances, furniture, and mattresses were sent to the area. Residents took advantage of these external resources, quickly rebuilding the neighborhood.

In 2002, another event brought renewed attention and resources to CDD. Fernando Meirelles produced a movie based on the book *Cidade de Deus*, authored by former resident Paulo Lins. It showcased the extreme violence of Cidade de Deus's drug traffickers in the 1970s and 1980s, with a backdrop of poverty and informality. It was not intended to be an ambitious project and was made on a tight budget, casting several local residents who were on screen for the first time. However, the extreme violence and "exotic" setting captivated international audiences. By 2003, it had been nominated for four academy awards and had won several international prizes. It made its way onto movie screens and television sets across the world. Suddenly, Cidade de Deus's reputation as a violent neighborhood went global. With the spotlight now cast on Rio's severe issues with urban inequality and violence, the mayor of Rio de Janeiro, Cesar Maia, turned his attention to the area. The city's reputation with the international community became an impetus for development.

In 2003, the mayor and his Secretary of Security Luiz Eduardo Soares, created the Entrepreneurial Forum of Rio, which brought industrialists, private investors, the World Bank, and other weighty actors to the table together to invest in Rio's favelas. With much advocacy from local activists, Rio's municipal government helped to fund the construction of 618 new public housing units and a public preschool in one of the poorest areas of the neighborhood, and it began construction of a secondary school. These investments have been mired with challenges, however, which I describe in detail in Chapter 2. In a published narrative about Cidade de Deus's history, residents offer the following reflection on the role of the state in their neighborhood: "We (Cidade de Deus) are the consequence of years of short-term and discontinued projects—schizophrenic projects permeated by clientelist-electorate interests, tempered with corruption . . . We are children of mediocrity and a lack of seriousness by an exclusionary and centripetal state, with a few rare and honorable exceptions worthy of our respect" (Comitê Comunitário de Cidade de Deus 2014). Development in CDD comes in waves, as growing violence and poverty eventually generate sufficient tragedy or public humiliation to garner the attention of the state and private investors. Under pressure from outsiders, they promise to invest more resources into the area but ultimately do so begrudgingly and unevenly (Fahlberg 2019). As the rest of the book demonstrates, activists stand ready to capitalize on these ebbs and flows of public attention, ensuring that external opportunities are directed into material changes in CDD.

A Temporary Peace

By the time I began fieldwork in Cidade de Deus in 2014, the neighborhood's appearance had changed completely from that depicted in the movie. In addition to being much more urbanized, there were no men selling drugs on the streets. On a handful of occasions, armed police officers from the military police's Pacifying Policing Unit, or UPP, drove past me as I walked down the road. I had arrived five years into a controversial "pacification" project spearheaded by then-Governor Sérgio Cabral and his newly appointed Secretary of Security Mariano Beltrame. The UPP program aimed to expel armed drug traffickers from the city's many favelas and impose a "policing of proximity," characterized by 24-hour surveillance by specially trained military police officers and more dialogue between the police and community leaders. As in previous instances of development under pressure, the UPP had sprung from Rio de Janeiro's newly appointed role as the host of the 2014 World Cup and the 2016 Summer Olympics. As the international spotlight again descended upon Rio, new resources were invested to contain violence and promote favela development.

The UPP in CDD began its work in late 2008 when the military police launched a series of planned invasions in armored vehicles known as *caveirão*, or big skull. Invasions were sometimes announced ahead of time on the television or shared through clandestine channels in order to give drug traffickers the opportunity to leave, rather than stay and fight. Most chose to flee. Several were caught and executed or apprehended, and the remaining put away their guns and moved around CDD as civilians. In February 2009, Cidade de Deus was declared "pacified." Four UPP precincts were then installed throughout Cidade de Deus. A similar process (with varying degrees of "success") took place in many other favelas. A total of 38 favelas or favela complexes were appointed a UPP precinct, accounting for almost half of Rio's 1.6 million favela residents according to the state government (Governo do Rio de Janeiro 2014). Rates of homicide reportedly dropped by as much as 75% in some favelas. Early polls suggested that residents in occupied territories were overwhelmingly supportive of the intervention, noting that shootouts had decreased, people felt a greater sense of safety and stability, and everyday life could finally run as it did in other urban neighborhoods (Cano, Borges, and Ribeiro 2012). Investments were brought in through the "UPP Social," a social service initiative administered by the state government in areas with a UPP presence. Cidade de Deus received a number of "public-private partnerships" as well. The UPP Social also provided courses to residents, such as karatê and ballet classes. Many were taught by officers in the UPP force.

Residents had a mixed reaction to the UPP. As I have noted elsewhere, most residents I talked to believed that the UPP brought peace and safety, which allowed them to travel throughout the neighborhood without the constant fear of being shot (Fahlberg 2018). This peace was also symbolic: it transformed the favela into an ordinary urban neighborhood, defined in part by the constitutional right to come and go. Finally, residents who participated in the social programs offered by the UPP, or whose children participated, and even those who just heard about them, were excited to see investments by the government in their neighborhood. However, most Black men I interviewed were opposed to the UPP, as they were frequently the victims of unprovoked and physically violent police searches. Furthermore, few residents believed the UPP would stick around very long; most beneficial government interventions did not last. Many scholars and racial justice activists had a more critical perspective, contending that the UPP program represented strategies of "humanitarian militarism" (Savell 2016), neoliberal accumulation (Freeman 2012), and the amplification of the "penal state" (Franco 2014) which further entrenched racial segregation and militarization (Alves & Evanson 2011).

By 2017, the peaceful era of CDD under the UPP had become a distant memory. In 2014, Comando Vermlho drug traffickers began to reclaim parts of the neighborhood, selling drugs openly on street corners and parading through the southern part of the neighborhood with exposed weapons. This was exacerbated by an economic recession in the State of Rio de Janeiro beginning in 2015. One-third of the budget for public security was cut in 2016, freezing the salaries of police and other public employees for several months. Rumors began circulating that UPP officers were accepting bribes from drug traffickers to allow them to sell drugs in some areas of the neighborhood. In response, the more aggressive arm of the military police, known as the BOPE (Battalion for Special Policing Operations) began to invade in their armored vehicles, often sparking armed confrontations with drug traffickers. As one resident explained to me, "The UPP comes for money, the BOPE comes for blood." In 2015 drug traffickers became more audacious, gradually setting up *bocas de fumo* closer to the commercial areas of the neighborhood and waging occasional drive-by shootings of UPP precincts. By 2016, drug traffickers were selling drugs on every major street corner and shooting back at the police, who now invaded almost daily. Homicides returned to pre-UPP rates, and people again were forced to hunker behind furniture or throw themselves onto the ground as bullets flew around them.

The UPP, like most state interventions, was temporary. It provided yet another example of uneven development, reflecting only a partial and tenuous interest in affording favelas resources that were just enough to stay afloat but never sufficient to experience more permanent security and urbanization. By 2017, not only were gangs, drugs, and shootouts back, but structural violence, including poverty and high unemployment rates remained high. The UPP also did little to change local organizing practices. Activists, like other residents, assumed that the CV had continued to surveill the neighborhood even at the height of the UPP's power and would eventually return in full force. To prevent gang retaliation once the UPP left, residents and activists continued to operate as if they were still under the control of drug traffickers. I describe these practices in greater detail in Chapter 3.

The UPP has nonetheless become a meaningful event in the history Cidade de Deus. Economic investments into local infrastructure and new social programming may have been insufficient, but many believed they were better than nothing. Some of the projects started or funded by the UPP Social helped to provide residents with supplemental education, gave children opportunities to learn new skills, and provided some infrastructure improvements to parks, fields, and other public areas. As I describe in Chapter 2, the UPP also provided an opening for collective action, helping to fund some cultural collectives and decreasing the distance between favelas and the state. While this distance grew again after Dilma's impeachment, some of the seeds sown under the UPP are now bearing fruit, which I discuss in greater detail in Chapter 2. The UPP also had an important symbolic value: it provided residents a glimpse into what life *could* be like if it were free of violence. For many, it was the first time they felt like urban citizens instead of urban outcasts. While most of the activists I profile in this book were fighting for their rights to the city long before the UPP cleared the streets of drug gangs, other residents were now able to envision what a safer and more developed CDD might look like. Many young people coming of age under the UPP joined local organizations and movements in hopes of finding peace again, but without militarized policing.

Conclusion

Cidade de Deus is not only a neighborhood, it is a space that is constantly being re-created by both external and internal forces as the state and myriad armed and non-armed actors struggle for control and survival. As the government intervenes through bursts of investments coupled with waves of security and development initiatives, residents employ a range of creative strategies to survive, adapt, help their neighbors, and resist state violence and urban exclusion. Not all responses are defined by non-violent collective action. Many strategies of resistance are individualized and not explicitly political, and some are violent. But in their totality, these many practices reflect a broad terrain of contestation. It is within this terrain that activism has taken hold, building off the efforts of local residents constantly searching for new ways to fight against the broader forces that push them out of urban society.

Even residents not directly involved in local social movements have played vital roles in creating a neighborhood that enables activism. Rafael, a volunteer teacher at a local afterschool program, shared with me all of the different ways he had supported social movements. These included teaching, hosting children's parties, writing grants, sweeping floors, and many other activities. For Rafael, each person contributed something of value, even if this value was not always acknowledged or rewarded:

> I think that there is no such thing, for me there is no differentiated work, each one has its importance, everyone has their importance. Intelligence is not unique. An astronaut is not more cultured than a guy who sweeps the street. These are functions that depend on each other in the world, in a universal context, we depend on each person to do something. You depend on the guy who made the notebook for you to write, understand? So, these are practical things where we have this perception, it is a way of looking [at things], it is a perspective that many people do not have.

While most Cidade de Deus residents were never directly engaged in conflict activism as I have conceptualized it in this book, they make up the community around which activists rally. Their problems are the problems that activists work to address, and their contributions, whether directly through local collectives or indirectly—as family members, friends, the local barber, teacher, or garbage collector—are essential to the scaffolding upon which political and social action is laid bare. By engaging in their own, unique forms of action, adaptation, and resilience, they help create an environment in which the politicization of everyday problems is not an aberration but a central component in the meaning of favela living (Souza 2020).

2

Milking the Resource Matrix

Democracy, Development, and Digital Devices

Mobilizing Political Opportunities

Many of the activists I got to know in Cidade de Deus had been involved in collective action for decades. Sonia was among the most well-known and respected activists I interviewed there. When I asked her about what life had been like growing up Cidade de Deus, she immediately began recounting her engagement with social action. According to Sonia, her spirit of activism was inspired by her mother, who was among the early pioneers of CDD's social movements. Her mother participated in a women's group in one of the local residents' associations in the early 1970s, before it was co-opted by drug lords. She was also a poet and songwriter and served as a *zeladora de santos*, or "caretaker of saints," in the spiritist Afro religions of Candomblé and Umbanda.

Her mother's engagement with political, cultural, and social issues rubbed off on Sonia. In the early 1980s, when Sonia was 16, she and her friends decided to start a theater group. "We were watching the violence in Cidade de Deus, all this stuff happening, sitting in the samba school, listening to the drums beating and we started talking, like 'Let's start a theater group?'" she remembered. "We wanted to protest, to show our community, through art, the things that were worrying us about Cidade de Deus." They began to produce plays addressing social themes like domestic violence, sexuality, prostitution, and LGBTQ rights, and they held workshops to promote members' political consciousness. The group surged to 60 members and found financial support from the state-run Instituto Leão XIII and other public and private agencies. Sonia explained how she and her colleagues persisted: "Even though Cidade de Deus had problems, which happened a lot, the drug war will never end, right? From the moment that money rolls, then things get complicated. But even then, in this period, we were doing it, always participating in social movements here inside Cidade de Deus."

Activism under Fire. Anjuli Fahlberg, Oxford University Press. © Oxford University Press 2023.
DOI: 10.1093/oso/9780197519325.003.0003

Sonia remained active in the local cultural scene, but also went on to serve as a school monitor at a public school and became an active member of the teachers' union. In 1997, a group of CDD residents with university degrees started a college entrance course in the neighborhood. Sonia enrolled in the class and with great effort got into college and received a degree in social work, enabling her to get a job as a public servant. As opportunities for participation in collective action shifted, Sonia adapted to the changing political landscape. However, the continuities between these efforts remained salient for Sonia:

> The social movements here inside Cidade de Deus are always making demands and something here that is very precarious, not only in Cidade de Deus, but also in communities[1] in general: the lack of public policies, right? . . . we feel the absence of this government investment, you know, public policies, but even so, we are always making demands, joining forces, for us to achieve our goal. That's our goal here in Cidade de Deus.

When I met Sonia in 2014, she was 48 years old and still very involved in local social movements. She had become a poet, like her mother, and regularly attended Art Talk Open Mic events. She, along with her close friend Rosangela and several others, started a community-based newspaper that shared stories about "the good things" in Cidade de Deus while also critiquing government neglect and abuse in the neighborhood. The newspaper was founded thanks to a collaboration between a journalism program at a prominent university in Rio de Janeiro and local residents. The journalism faculty provided CDD residents with trainings and student interns to help keep the newspaper running, though Sonia and her colleagues did most of the heavy lifting chasing after stories, interviewing locals, collecting data, and writing the articles. Sonia also remained engaged with several community-based organizations (or CBOs) in the neighborhood, collaborating on a range of social and cultural projects.

In Chapter 1, I argued that activism in Cidade de Deus is situated within a contested territory, produced by both external forces and a variety of internal forms of resistance. As Sonia's story suggests, among these legacies of resistance was a variety of organized non-violent forms of action, which many older activists still alive today had participated in throughout their lives. While not all of the activists I met in Cidade de Deus were old enough to boast such a lengthy history of social action, the legacy of organizing in

Cidade de Deus provided contemporary activists with repertoires of collective action, or "arrays of known possible interactions that characterize a particular set of actors" (McAdam, Tarrow, and Tilly 2001:49). Over the years, activists have learned from their own and each other's experiences, taking advantage of educational and financial opportunities and creating strategies they could draw upon to adapt to changing contexts.

Throughout her life, Sonia's activism was also shaped by external opportunities. These included the growing popularity of unions, funding from both state and private agencies, federal affirmative action policies for Black and low-income Brazilians to enter university, and a host of programs that provided education and facilitated networks between activists in Cidade de Deus and external institutions. These resources reflect openings in the political opportunity structures or "exogenous factors [that] enhance or inhibit prospects for mobilization, for particular sorts of claims to be advanced rather than others, for particular strategies of influence to be exercised, and for movements to affect mainstream institutional politics and policy" (Meyer and Minkoff 2004:1457–58). While Sonia's activism was engendered by her personal drive—inspired by her mother's activism—it was also shaped by the repertoires of action she developed over the years in concert with other activists and by resources, allies, and openings outside of her social network. Sonia's activities and forms of mobilization shifted over time, accommodating to external possibilities as they came and went.

In this chapter, I examine how these external political opportunities have shaped the repertoires of collective action in Cidade de Deus. I describe three different "clusters" of non-violent collective action that compose the terrain of favela activism in contemporary Cidade de Deus: transformative assistance, community militancy, and cultural politics. I identify some of the political and economic openings that have enabled their rise. These openings can be traced to several global, national, and municipal shifts, which include (1) new rights and resources that emerged with the transition from dictatorship to democracy in the 1980s; (2) increasing funds for favela development with the rise of progressive populist leaders, including the election of Rio de Janeiro's leftist Governor Leonel Brizola in 1982 and the rule of the Worker's Party over Brazil from 2002 to 2016; and (3) globalization and the democratization of information communication technologies (ICTs), which enabled favela activists to gain entry into—and resources from—the global public sphere.

These political opportunity structures have created what I term a *resource matrix*: an array of economic, social, political, and cultural openings that offer a scattered landscape of supports to social mobilization. It is particularly important to consider this resource matrix in areas of conflict, where leadership and politics are fragmented. While much has been written about the importance of political opportunity structures in promoting social change, these opportunities do not simply arrive at the door of marginalized groups. CDD's activists have played a vital role chasing after external resources and configuring their collectives to gain access and membership to emergent political institutions and openings. In a neighborhood characterized by a dearth of private or public resources, conflict activism survives by "milking" the resource matrix, capitalizing on every opportunity that becomes available, while still working toward their larger goals of improving the neighborhood and promoting broader social change. A key role of activists in conflict zones, then, is to identify, access, and bring external resources into their community and to utilize them creatively to resist violence and address inequality. In CDD, activists succeed at milking the matrix by "clustering" around particular sources of funding, political practices, and external allies. Activists become proficient in how to access them, developing ties with the actors who can connect them to those resources and learning the discourses and practices used in each space to signal worthiness of particular types of support. In other words, the fragmentation between these clusters reflects a divide-and-conquer approach, whereby residents disperse in order to capitalize on the variety of political opportunities opening at different times and via distinct avenues.

Democratization and the Expansion of Rights

Like much of Latin America, Brazil was under dictatorial rule for more than 20 years—from 1964 to 1985—which restricted many of the political rights allowed under more democratic regimes. The dictatorship criminalized many forms of contentious politics and imprisoned and killed dissidents, including politicians, activists, and intellectuals. It abolished direct voting and in 1968, suspended habeas corpus for those arrested for threatening "national security." The death penalty was legalized and newspapers and other media outlets were severely censored. Nonetheless, groups continued to mobilize against the regime. Workers' unions organized massive strikes to demand better wages. Among the most vocal and charismatic leaders of union organizing was Luiz "Lula" Inácio da Silva, a founding member of the Worker's Party who would, 30 years later, go on to be elected president of the country. While the conservative branch of the Catholic Church supported the dictatorship, progressive priests who subscribed to liberation theology played an important role in speaking out against the regime. The Worker's Party and progressive leaders in the Catholic Church became influential in favelas, working with residents and neighborhood associations to spearhead grassroots organizing around housing rights and "popular education" aimed at increasing literacy and critical thinking among the poor.

For many years, the dictatorship maintained power in part by inflicting terror and in part thanks to significant improvements in the national economy during the late 1960s and 1970s, which were widely hailed as Brazil's "economic miracle." By the late 1970s, however, skyrocketing inflation, unemployment, and poverty sparked widespread discontent towards the state. Across Latin America, other authoritarian regimes were also facing internal pressures from mass street protests of unhappy citizens. International human rights organizations worked with activists across the region to spread accounts of political violence by dictatorships to US and European audiences and called for accountability of repressive regimes and open elections. With pressure from the United States and Europe, authoritarian regimes began to weaken, ultimately conceding to democratic elections. As the dominoes began to fall around Brazil, a transition to democracy seemed imminent. Massive street protests emerged across major Brazilian cities as Brazilians demanded *"Diretas Já!,"* referring to direct representative presidential elections.

In 1982, democratic elections were held for state governors for the first time since 1965. The military regime hoped they would win elections, thereby reinforcing their power through "legitimate" means. While many allies of the military's political party did win elections, opposition parties, including the growing Worker's Party, also won seats and grew their political power and legitimacy. In 1985, the first presidential election in 20 years was held through an indirect electoral vote. President-elect Tancredo Neves died before he could take office, however. José Sarney, the representative of the opposing party who had been listed on the ballot as vice-president to appease the opposition, took office instead. His reign was disastrous, as were those of his successors. The currency changed four times over the following eight years in the middle of six different experiments with economic stabilization. Mary Kinzo (2001:8) argues that this "succession of failures not only aggravated the economic and social crisis, but also compromised the capacity of the state to govern, making the problem of governance a permanent reality."

However, democratic openings continued to emerge. The literacy conditions for voting were lifted and rights to free expression, press, and public assembly were reinstated. Activist leaders and left-leaning political parties collaborated to design Brazil's 1988 Constitution, which was lauded as one of the most comprehensive and progressive constitutions in the world. It guaranteed a broad array of political, civil, and social rights, expanding entitlements related to retirement, the rights of people with disabilities, and maternity and paternity leave (Fleury and Pinho 2018). Penalties for racism and torture were increased. The new constitution also guaranteed universal rights to healthcare, which laid the foundation for the inauguration of a universal healthcare system two years later. In 1989, the first direct presidential election was held. Three years later, President Fernando Collor would be impeached for embezzling public funds during a period of high inflation and economic instability. Brazil's economy finally stabilized in the late 1990s under President Henrique Fernando Cardoso and continued to improve after the election of President Luiz Inácio "Lula" da Silva in 2002.

Despite, or perhaps because of, the poor governance of its leaders, Brazilian citizens have taken advantage of the democratic *abertura* (or opening) to organize thousands of social movements around a wide variety of issues. From labor and housing rights to identity-based movements around indigeneity, Black rights, and gender rights, among many others, social organizing has proliferated in Brazil. Brazilian cities have become important hubs of protest, and it is now common for people to launch strikes and street protests. In 2013 and 2014, for instance, millions of Brazilians took to the streets in reaction to a hike in bus fares. As protests grew, participants also demanded better healthcare and education, more accountability for corruption and police violence, and more employment, among other things (Ricci 2014; Vicino and Fahlberg 2017). The favela activism I witnessed after 2014 emerged in this wider context of mobilization across the country for an array of issues and demands.

Brazilians have faced several highs and lows in their journey to redemocratization. On the one hand, the shift to democratic elections enabled citizens, including favela residents, to vote in largely fair multi-party elections. This has resulted in the election of many progressive politicians at the national, state, and municipal levels who have supported significant social and cultural initiatives, described in the following section. Protections guaranteed by the new constitution also provide favela activists and other social movements the right to organize and make public demands for their rights, to speak out against government officials, and also to work collaboratively with the state—luxuries that people in many other conflict zones do not have. At the same time, many of these rights are limited by police violence against protestors, as well as the war on drugs described in Chapter 1, which overwhelmingly targets poor Black people in favelas. The biases in the legal and criminal justice systems result in a "disjunctive democracy" that violates the civil rights of Black Brazilians, who are unable to benefit in practice from many of the rights they have on paper (Caldeira and Holston 1999). Finally, as the impeachment of Collor and the imprisonment of Lula in 2017 for fraud demonstrate, corruption has remained endemic in Brazilian politics. Democratic elections are not, on their own, enough to curtail centuries of clientelism and political manipulation, or to ensure that elected officials will govern effectively.

Despite these challenges, there is a meaningful difference between organizing collective actions in a country with expansive political and civil rights and mobilizing in one without these protections. While Cidade de Deus is replete with political closures, it is also embedded in a democratic country, however imperfect. The conflict activism in Rio's favelas benefits from a progressive constitution and the right—at least in law—to organize and engage in both contentious and collaborative politics with the state. The activism I witnessed also benefited from stability at the urban and national levels, as elections were generally viewed as legitimate, and there were no significant threats to the national government from international or civil armed groups. While the impeachment of President Dilma Rousseff in 2016 was viewed by many left-leaning Brazilians as an illegitimate "coup," the transition to her replacement, Michel Temer, was peaceful. My point is not that Brazil's democracy is working well. But when we consider the instability and violence faced by activists in sites of domestic and international warfare, it becomes clear that national stability allows for activists to operate in a more predictable and less volatile political arena than many others. As I demonstrate in this chapter, favela activists have benefited from these openings, deploying a host of strategies to engage with the state and make demands for resources.

Development and New Fountains of Funding

Another important opening that began to emerge with the fall of the dictatorship was a growing concern for social development, both nationally and in favelas. In 1982, a "reformist wave" swept Rio de Janeiro with the election of Governor Leonel Brizola, who had run on a vision of "brown socialism" (McCann 2014). Brizola spearheaded many improvements to infrastructure, housing, and social services in Rio's favelas. He also put a stop to favela removals and appointed five key favela leaders to positions in state and city government. While these reforms were limited by a number of factors, including a long period of high inflation and the hemorrhaging of government funds to corrupt political leaders, many favela activists cultivated political ties and a shared identity and vocabulary with the rising progressive leadership, which would be activated repeatedly over the following 40 years.

The economy finally stabilized after President Henrique Cardoso created the Brazilian real in 1994. However, economic stability came at a cost. Like many other national leaders across Latin America (and the globe), Cardoso jumped on the neoliberal bandwagon, restricting the power of labor unions and decreasing regulations for foreign investors. Unemployment rates rose, especially in large cities (Filgueiras 2006).

By the 1990s, a tenuous commitment to improving favelas in Rio de Janeiro had begun to emerge. Several new social development projects were created to urbanize many favela neighborhoods. Rio's 1992 Master Plan explicitly declared the city's objectives of "integrating the favelas into the formal city" and "preserving their local character." With funding from the Inter-American Development Bank and the municipal government, the Program Favela-Bairro invested USD$300 million in upgrading 38 favelas, with a focus on infrastructure and social services, mostly directed toward mid-sized favelas (Urani 2008). The city's stated commitment to improving favelas was an important detour from its historic approach of evictions and provided a symbolic reframing of its poor areas as spaces that needed investment rather than exclusion from the urban fabric (Atuesta and Soares 2016; Pereira 2008). Many of these improvements were made hastily and with cheap materials, however, and after only a few years of wear and tear, they began to quickly disintegrate (Perlman 2010).

New social programs for the poor emerged after 2002 when Lula was elected president of Brazil on a leftist platform. Under Lula's governance, several national programs were funded that improved the social landscape in favelas. One of these was the extremely popular *Bolsa Familia*, or Family Purse, a welfare program that provided conditional cash transfers to families living below the poverty line. Participating families were required to keep their children enrolled in school and take them to regular medical checkups, among other obligations. Widely hailed as a model for conditional cash transfers in other countries, Bolsa Familia reduced poverty from 13% to 3% between 2003 and 2015. Rio's municipal and state governments also began providing a number of benefits to low-income families, including free or reduced-fare bus passes and low-cost electricity and internet access.

These national wealth redistribution programs benefited millions of favela residents across the country. In the survey my team and I administered in 2017, 19% of CDD's households received income from Bolsa Familia, and a total of 48% of households received some kind of public assistance, such as transportation passes or reduced electricity costs. Lula also spearheaded the PAC, or Growth Acceleration Program, which sent federal funds to municipal governments to invest in social and urban infrastructure improvements. PAC money has supported several urbanization efforts in Cidade de Deus in recent years, including the construction of new housing and the installation of a local emergency room, or UPA (Unidade de Pronto Atendimento). Cidade de Deus was also the recipient of the programs Território da Paz (Territory of Peace) and Espaço Urbano Seguro (Safe Urban Spaces). Both of these funded various infrastructure improvements, such as the construction of parks, soccer fields, and paved roads and the expansion of sewer systems, as well as social services and cultural activities.

In an effort to improve the national security landscape, Lula launched PRONASCI, which has been described as the "PAC of Security." Its objective was to improve public security through prison reform, the retraining of police officers in non-violent forms of conflict resolution, and the provision of education and jobs to vulnerable youth. It funded many social projects, including rehabilitative services for youth and prisons for women and young adults (Urani 2008). While PRONASCI funding was terminated in 2011, it benefited many favela residents through investments in social development (Ruediger 2013).

Another important shift under Lula and Dilma was an expansion of rights related to housing and urban inclusion (Stefani 2021). Lula's first term included the inauguration of the Ministério das Cidades (Ministry of Cities), which redistributed funds and responsibility for urban rights to three levels of government and included opportunities for citizen participation in local planning. In 2009, during Lula's second term, the public housing program Minha Casa Minha Vida (My Home My Life) was established to offer housing subsidized by the federal bank to low-income residents for a small monthly fee. After 10 years of regular payments, residents gained the title to the home. For many years, the program was a major success, with three million homes being delivered by 2016, primarily to female heads of household.

The expansion of social investments began to wane after Dilma Rousseff's impeachment and the ascendance of Michel Temer to power. Temer, a member of the more conservative Brazilian Democratic Movement Party (PMDB), spearheaded multiple austerity measures, including a 20-year cap on federal spending and slashes to Bolsa Familia and many other public programs. At the same time, Rio de Janeiro fell into an economic recession; programs that provided subsidized meals were closed down and state-run welfare programs eliminated. Maria Rita, Esther, and I spent many nights watching the news and worrying about yet another federal program under attack by the new president. While these austerity measures continued over the following years, many seeds had been sown in CDD's activist circles under the Worker's Party and were already bearing fruit. While financial opportunities declined after 2016, the organizational infrastructure developed in the previous decades remained sturdy.

The Global Civil Sphere

Political and economic openings have also been accompanied by Brazil's participation in the global civil sphere. The internet was first "inaugurated" in Brazil in 1992. During much of the 1990s, it was utilized primarily by researchers and activists in NGOs, who used email and newsletters to communicate and share information with other researchers and social movements. Use of the internet exploded across the globe in the 1990s, and Brazil was quick to join the fray. By 1998, one million Brazilian citizens were connected to the internet, primarily from wealthy and middle-class groups. The widespread installation of "LAN Houses," or internet cafés, in poor neighborhoods in the early 2000s helped expand and democratize internet access (Aguiar 2021). The transition to wifi also afforded people the option to access the internet via personal phones or computers, further facilitating internet access. In 2009, the state of Rio de Janeiro launched the program Rio Estado Digital (Rio Digital State) which provided free, though often spotty, wifi hotspots in many favelas. A combination of technological advances and state programs have thus helped connect Rio's favelas to each other, the city, and the global online community. Favelas still remain underrepresented in internet use, however, reflecting an ongoing digital divide that entrenches their subordinate location in the city (Nemer 2022).

Despite these challenges, favela residents are nonetheless active on social media platforms, particularly WhatsApp and Facebook, as well as Twitter, Instagram, and other popular sites. As I describe later, it has given activists entry into what Manuel Castell's calls the "global civil society," where a variety of actors and institutions at local and international levels mobilize to discuss and address problems provoked by globalization (Castells 2008). Participation in the global civil sphere via information communication technologies, or ICTs, allows social movement organizations and individuals to share information, discourses, and tactics (Young, Selander, and Vaast 2019); expand their social and political networks (Anderson 2021); cultivate new relationships; and connect movements with elite allies across the world (Hunt 2019). Many movements, including those focused on gender, racial, and class injustice, have gained momentum through online networks of solidarity that articulate shared challenges as products of global institutions— patriarchy, colonialism, and capitalism—and connect disparate groups to transnational social movements (Arbatli 2017; Mohanty 2013; Smith 2016). ICTs have been especially beneficial to activists in conflict zones across the globe, allowing them to organize below the watchful eye of repressive regimes, while also reaching out beyond their border to seek support from transnational allies (Moss 2022). Participation on social media and connectivity to international institutions and movements has given activists access to allies, resources, ideas, and communities they can turn to in the face of a closed national political landscape.

Against this backdrop of political, economic, and technological openings, several new political formations emerged in Cidade de Deus. Each of these political forms clustered around a different configuration of resources, networks, and political discourses, all of which are embedded in history, national politics, and international openings and pressures. Some are riding the wave of the rise of NGOs, thanks to funding provided under multiple Worker's Party initiatives, and utilizing funds to provide social assistance to needy residents. Others, particularly those who were once active in anti-dictatorship movements, adopt more of a militant approach to demand rights for the neighborhood. A third cluster, led primarily by a younger generation raised under the Worker's Party and networked into the global public sphere through social media, is taking advantage of political openings to demand broader forms of social change. I describe these in greater detail next.

Transformative Assistance

Cidade de Deus is home to dozens of CBOs and informal collectives, known locally as *projetos*, that provide services to the neighborhoods. CBOs and *projetos* are an important part of the civic life of Cidade de Deus and offer many residents a semi-formal space for giving and receiving support to and from fellow residents facing similar challenges. Among those who responded to the survey my team and I organized, 2% claimed to have founded their own NGO or *projeto* and 8% of our participants reported being a volunteer for one of these in the previous two years. In a population of 60,000, this would equate to nearly 5,000 volunteers. The social service landscape in Cidade de Deus offers a vast array of supports to favela residents. Youth Promise, the organization for which Maria Rita worked, offered morning and afternoon classes five days a week, every week of the year except during summer and winter holidays. The Center Dona Otávia offered elderly women a place to learn sewing and other skills they could use to earn an income, while also providing them an informal support system. The Center for Racial Justice, when it had the funds, provided percussion lessons to youth coupled with classes on African culture; it also led trainings for women on how to create African hairstyles, a skill that could generate an income.

There were many others. The Senior Center provided physical therapy, aerobics, percussion classes, free lunches, and other basic care needs to the neighborhood's elderly population. Esther's son Leonardo and two colleagues founded and ran a theater group inspired by the one Sonia had led many years earlier. It offered adolescents acting classes and helped connect them to theaters and television producers across the city. Many groups provided professional dance classes to young adults, several of whom performed in competitions and cultural centers across the state. Another offered the popular *forró* dance classes to adults. *Projetos* were constantly popping up to provide soccer, jiu-jitsu, and dance lessons, help people obtain employment or a high school diploma, provide computer literacy courses, and much more.

The social service landscape in CDD also included publicly funded and administered organizations, staffed primarily by residents who often worked collaboratively with private CBOs to service the population. The Teen Connection, a project run by the municipal government, offered a host of technical and professional courses and certificates, as well as college preparatory courses and computer classes. The local health clinic employed nurses from CDD, as well as "health agents" who provided case management to needy families with small children in some areas of Cidade de Deus. For several years during the height of the UPP, SESI Cidadania offered a children's library, physical education, and classes on "citizenship" for children. There were also a few medium-sized NGOs on the outskirts of the neighborhood that tended to hire CDD residents. These included two large early childcare and elementary school facilities, which provided basic health and educational services to the families of enrolled children. While I return to the relationship between private and public social services in Cidade de Deus in Chapter 5, the important point here is that private CBOs operate within a larger field of social services financed and administered by a range of private and public actors. Local residents insert themselves into this landscape as employees and volunteers, and also frequently start their own groups.

There were so many different activities, classes, and other types of assistance in Cidade de Deus that one resident, Isabella, founded a Facebook page in 2011 called CDD Connects to facilitate the connection between those in need and those providing for those needs. The page shared dozens of announcements every week, ranging from flu vaccine clinics to a new karatê class to a high school equivalency course. By 2017, CDD Connects had nearly 100,000 followers, demonstrating how citizen engagement in digital technologies could promote information sharing and the strengthening of local ties (Amaral 2021; Custódio 2017). Dozens of other Facebook pages have also been created to connect residents with similar interests, including pages for particular religious groups, cultural practices, and interest in the history and news of the community. CDD Connects and other similar sites that have emerged since 2011 reflect the importance of these digital technologies for promoting social cohesion and collective efficacy in a context of fragmented and often violent political relations.

CBOs operate like other NGOs in that they are private, not-for-profit institutions dedicated to social actions to improve society. NGOs became increasingly popular in the years following re-democratization, as Brazilian activists institutionalized the demands of their social movements through formal associations. However, the transition from a movement to an institution eroded some of the more radical politics of these groups as they moved toward collaboration with the state. By the 1990s, civic organizations were no longer "derived from processes of mass mobilization but more punctual (specific) mobilizations," driven toward "servicing the needs of some pluralistic entity, rooted in humanitarian objectives" (Gohn 2013:239–40). These were less geared at contentious claims-making and more toward what Gloria Gohn (2013) calls "citizen participation:" small-scale and institutionalized forms of assistance. The shift was formalized with the passing of the Nonprofit Law in 1999, which established the legal concept of Public Interest Civil Organizations (OSCIPS) (Alves and Koga 2006). Furthermore, the creation of various councils, committees, and conferences with both state and civic actors across multiple levels of government also inspired more collaborative efforts to address social issues. The rise of CBOs in Cidade de Deus, therefore, was not especially unique to favelas but rather an outcome of a national shift in the configuration of collective action with the emergence of an organized civil society supported by—rather than opposed to—the formal state.

Across the globe, another major transition was underway, as western countries shifted away from the welfare state and toward neoliberalism, pressuring developing countries to do the same. According to David Harvey (2005:2), neoliberalism—also called advanced capitalism—is "a theory of political economic practices that proposes that human well-being can best be advanced by liberating individual entrepreneurial freedoms and skills within an institutional framework characterized by strong private property rights, free markets and free trade." Neoliberal economics calls for the deregulation of the market, a greater emphasis on individual freedoms and individual responsibility, the expansion of the state's control over the social order through policing, criminal courts, and incarceration, and the privatization of its social sphere, among other things. Although Brazil witnessed a "softer" shift to neoliberalism than many other Latin American countries, President Henrique Cardoso, who governed from 1995 to 2002, restricted the power of labor unions and decreased regulations for foreign investors, which contributed to high rates of unemployment, especially in large cities (Filgueiras 2006).

This shift also impacted favelas. By the early 2000s, violence in favelas was so great that the municipal government feared sending public servants from outside the neighborhood in to service the community. Rio de Janeiro's mayor Cesar Maia advocated for the outsourcing of public services directly to favela residents, in many cases placing residents' associations in charge of overseeing community garbage collection, public childcare programs, and healthcare programming for families. The state also appointed "community agents" who helped connect favela residents with public benefits. This shift created both new opportunities and new challenges. Journalist Fernanda da Escóssia (2003) sums up the consequences of this approach:

> Among the advantages [are] the ease of the hiring process, the genera-
> tion of local employment and the easy access to dangerous places, since
> the labor(ers), recruited in the community, have free transit. The risks are
> the transfer of responsibilities from public authorities to civil society, po-
> litical patronage and, in the case of Rio, the appropriation of [residents'
> associations] by criminal groups, such as drug traffickers.

In 2003, the Inter-American Development Bank and the World Bank pro-vided R$115 million to Rio's municipal government to promote favela devel-opment. The city transferred the funds to private NGOs to carry out the work. Some of these NGOs directly serviced favelas and others commissioned lo-cally based CBOs to do the work. While this put thousands of favela residents to work, they were usually paid far less than public servants in the same occupations working outside the favela.

Many scholars have been critical of the privatization of social services in the neoliberal era, arguing that this shift has exacerbated income inequality (Harvey 2005; Wacquant 2009). In Brazil's informal settlements, however, the state was not doing a great job of promoting equality even before the ne-oliberal era. In favelas, where the state has a long history of inefficient and underfunded public goods, the shift to relying on NGOs and CBOs offered an alternative with some possibility for improved services. Unfortunately, public grants and private donations to NGOs and favela CBOs have been wholly insufficient to address the many needs of these communities. Government incompetence only made matters worse. In 2017, for instance, the municipal government failed to invest R$230 million they had received in loans from the Bank of Brazil and the Brazilian Development Bank slated for construc-tion projects mostly intended for favelas. The city councilman appointed to investigate the stalling of these projects claimed the issue was due to a lack of attention and oversight (Magalhães 2018). While there are many concerns regarding the privatization of the social sphere, including an overreliance on private companies whose primary concern is profit, it does offer an alterna-tive development path in a context of a fragmented, corrupted, and ineffi-cient public sector.

The turn toward privatization has enabled CDD residents to take on an important role in providing for the social, economic, and psychological needs of the neighborhood's most vulnerable residents. At the same time, the dearth of public or private support for favela-based CBOs has left most of these small groups with insufficient resources to pay their staff and provide for the needs of the neighborhood's residents. Youth Promise, one of the neighborhood's most formal and well-funded CBOs, only had the capacity for 150 to 200 full-time participants and served an additional 50 to 100 families through workshops, fieldtrips, and holiday parties. In a neighborhood as large as Cidade de Deus, these services barely scratched the surface of the population's needs.

The barrier to accessing resources is also exacerbated by the informal infrastructure of most favela CBOs, which makes them ineligible for large government or foundation grants. These grants tend to go to formal NGOs located in more central urban areas, a topic I explore in detail in Chapter 5. While large NGOs do offer a number of services in many favelas, particularly in the favelas closer to Rio's downtown area, in Cidade de Deus, small resident-run CBOs do most of the heavy lifting. Often, they receive small grants from larger NGOs to provide the services for which the grant-giving NGO was contracted. Consequently, most of the "employees" in Cidade de Deus's CBOs are either volunteers or receive irregular stipends when small streams of funding become available.

Many CBOs have attempted to become formal NGOs. According to Wellington França (2019), the process for this formalization involves several steps and occurs when:

> two or more people invite friends and neighbors with the idea of creating an entity, hold a meeting, draw up a statute, elect among themselves leaderships for the exercise of positions of Executive Board, Fiscal Council, and Coordinators of technical or thematic commissions. They seek the assistance of a lawyer and register the constituent acts in the registries specializing in civil registries of legal entities.

It is an exhausting process that requires administrative knowledge, endless patience with bureaucratic loopholes, and constant upkeep. Rosangela, for instance, was the retired director of a childcare center who volunteered for the Center Dona Otavia. She spent several years attempting to formally register the CBO so they could become eligible for federal grants. Often when

I visited her, she complained about the inumerous hours she had spent traveling on long bus rides across the city and in long tires lines attempting to obtain the proper signatures, letters, and documentation. Even with her expertise and time, she faced multiple bureaucratic hurdles.

Not surprisingly, many private social service initiatives are never formally registered and remain in the realm of informality. While we often think of informality in relation to housing or employment, it also extends into Cidade de Deus's civic sector where the systems of mutual support hold an ambiguous identity of organized social actions that lack the documentation to prove their legitimacy. This ambiguity creates many challenges for CBOs and small NGOs. According to Colin McFarlane (2012:89), "the informal–formal relation is both a seemingly modest descriptor and a powerful distinction that has an active effect on urban imagination and practice." A bulletin published in 2008 by the Audit Offices of the Municipality of Rio de Janeiro, claimed that "Despite the evident social importance of NGOs, it is evident that not all of them have the financial, administrative, technical and operational suitability to contract with the Public Power" (TCMRJ 2008:3). Political exclusion of favelas is facilitated, in part, by pushing favela civic life outside the formal bounds of the state. This has a spiraling effect, enabling the government to deny them the funding they need to become formalized and procure larger funding sources; civic belonging itself is denied to favela CBOs, and the view of the favela as "marginal" to the state becomes entrenched by bureaucratic exclusions.

The outsourcing of social services from the public sector to NGOs and CBOs has also been met with another challenge. Brazilian scholars frequently charge NGOs with subscribing to *assistencialismo*, translated roughly as "welfare" or "charity." I first heard the term from Leonardo, Esther's older son, who argued that the *assistencialista* approach to social change was *atrasado*, or behind the times. Leonardo believed that NGOs (among which he counted Youth Promise and Cidade de Deus's other CBOs) were great at addressing the immediate needs of desperate people but did little to challenge inequality or violence in a more systemic way. In a similar vein, researchers Natália Lourenço and João Paulo dos Santos (2011) argue that the *assistencialismo* model prevents the poor from becoming conscious of their constitutional rights, thereby entrenching their dependence on the state and their subordinate class status. By making poor people reliant on donations and funding from the state or the private, for-profit sector, NGOs become victims of a "social interventionist model of the neoliberal policies in force" wherein marginalized populations are given just enough resources to survive but not enough to overcome their oppression (da Silva Porto 2005:1). At the same time, *assistencialismo* helps to destroy democratic processes by entrenching clientelistic practices, such as when specific politicians use the provision of social services to get votes (Instituto Millenium 2012).

In line with some of these criticisms, Cidade de Deus's individual CBOs rarely engage in contentious politics aimed at either the state or private corporations. Because CBOs are focused on offering services to extremely needy people (of which Cidade de Deus has many), they rely on friendly ties to potential allies across the city (and the world), leveraging these ties to obtain donations, volunteers, small government grants, or funding from private institutions. For instance, Solange, the director of Youth Promise, welcomed nearly all offers of support, provided there were no known ties to the drug trade (a strategy I take up in Chapter 3). Just before I first arrived, she had hosted two foreign student volunteers from the Netherlands, including one who lived in Solange's house for a short, but very stressful time. She received visitors traveling from other countries as well and was constantly receiving messages of support and donations from people in Europe and the United States, as well as from wealthy donors in Rio de Janeiro. She worked hard to maintain good relations with government agencies and private foundations who supported Youth Promise with small or medium-sized grants.

While CBOs do not directly protest or otherwise confront the state or private companies, I argue that their potential for transformative change exceeds the critiques of Leonardo and many NGO scholars. Beneath their emphasis on social assistance is a subtler but nonetheless critical component of the logic of social action that undergirds the political imaginaries of Cidade de Deus's CBOs: they believe that by transforming individuals, they can transform society. This is neither a top-down approach to change nor even a bottom-up, grassroots approach, because it does not involve community organizing. Their focus is heavily on the individual and, at most, the family. Yet they provide much more than just charity: they offer the social and psychological building blocks necessary to cultivate successful, politicized individuals who, at the very least, will practice the types of active citizenship characteristic of a just, non-violent society and, at best, might actually become leaders of these transformations.

They do this in several ways. Solange told me that what most drew her to social work were "the transformations that we see happening in people's lives." As she explained to me:

SOLANGE: What moves me to continue this work is the transformation we see in people, small as it is, but most of the time it is crucial for people to lift themselves up, you understand? This is what makes me love my job.

ME: Have you seen a lot of these transformations?

SOLANGE: Oh boy! Many, many . . . I get really happy when I hear people say, "Oh, that email you sent about the job opening I sent to a friend and she got the job." Or I run into a mom in the street: "Do you remember me? I am the mother of so-and-so, he is working at x place." Or the very student, we run into them, you know? And all happy he says: "Oh, I'm attending university because of that job I got." So, you see, there are a lot of people, a lot of people who, from the work that I do, who are grateful to me for what they were able to accomplish because of our activities, they were able to lift themselves up, know you? This makes me very happy.

Jefferson, a karatê teacher and director of a local cultural center, told me that their goal "really is to work with culture, with a new vision, not simply seeing people as human beings, but also as protagonists of the process of cultural construction of Cidade de Deus." Jefferson used karatê as a means to teach his students about learning discipline, respect for others, and the importance of working hard to accomplish personal goals. He proudly noted that many of his students had decided to go to college or seek professional employment rather than settle for low-paying, low-skill jobs or join the drug trade. By helping favela youth obtain professional skills and jobs and gain entry to competitive public universities, Solange and Jefferson hoped to reverse some of the barriers created by segregated inequality and the exclusion of the favela from mainstream institutions. CBO leaders also hoped that they could prevent young people from entering the drug trade. Maria Rita explained this logic to me:

> This generation, we have to start opening their horizons, open their eyes to something else, right? For when they choose, to make a different choice. Sometimes you come from a family that the father is a drug trafficker, the uncle is a drug trafficker, the mother is addicted, there are people who are like that . . . So the negative points add up . . . Here we can get him in touch with other things, [so] that he can amplify his vision: "No, I can be a computer programmer; I can be an athlete; I can be a teacher," so that he has these opportunities, [he can] see that it is not at all impossible, that he can have it too.

Maria Rita, Solange, Jefferson, and other CBO leaders focused on what they believed they had some control over: the cultivation of a strong self-esteem, viable economic alternatives to selling drugs or living poverty, and a commitment to non-violence, which could help to interrupt the cycle of violence and place youth on a new path toward inclusion in the economic and political urban centers of power. In the meantime, they hoped to decrease the number of potential "soldiers" in the drug trade, thereby subverting gang violence indirectly.

CBO leaders themselves are quite adamant that they do *not* subscribe to *assistencialismo*, which has become a pejorative term within the social service sphere. When I presented a first draft of my book manuscript, in which I termed their model of change "transformative *assistencialismo*," CBO leaders were quite unhappy with the term. In an effort to respect my participants' own narratives of their work, I revised the name to "transformative assistance," a label that reflects a similar idea but moves away from such a loaded term. However, my participants also emphasized that *assistencialismo* does remain alive and well in CDD and other favelas and that several NGOs and *projetos* do little to help lift families out of poverty in an effort to maintain dependence, class inequality, and even political control over desperate residents.

As I show in the remaining chapters, CBOs also contribute to political mobilization in another important way: they provide a safe, politically neutral space in which more explicitly political ideas and projects could be fostered and organized. Many CBOs hired teachers with a broad range of political perspectives, and some of these taught their students about systemic injustice, racism, police brutality, class struggle, and the harms of authoritarianism. Youth Promise and other well-established CBOs also "rented" out space (usually for free or at low cost) to local collectives who touted more radical perspectives. Cultural activists, who I describe later in this chapter, were frequently reliant on CBOs to gather and organize. Thus, while providing social assistance may emphasize charity over structural change, CDD's CBOs seek to also create transformation by providing people with pathways away from poverty and violence and creating possibilities for more radical politics.

Community Militancy

In contrast to Youth Promise and other CBOs, which have taken advantage of more collaborative avenues for state support, the Residents' Board emerged as a direct resistance to exclusionary urban politics. In the wake of the release of the movie "Cidade de Deus," Rio's mayor Cesar Maia was under pressure to do something—or at least *act* like he was doing something—to address the violence and under-development of the city's many favelas. Maia and National Secretary for Public Security Luiz Eduardo Soares invited members of the newly founded Business Forum of Rio, composed of local business leaders and investors, to develop a plan to address urban poverty. Cidade de Deus was at the top of their fix-it list. State officials and representatives of the Business Forum scheduled a planning meeting in a meeting room of one of Cidade de Deus's residents' associations and invited several important actors: representatives from the United Nations; O Globo, Brazil's media giant; several federations of business conglomerates; Viva Rio, a mega NGO in Rio de Janeiro; and a large and well-known NGO that was founded in Cidade de Deus but ran most of its activities in other favelas (Pfeiffer 2014). Conveniently, they had not invited other local CBO leaders who had been leading neighborhood development efforts in CDD for decades.

"We found out [about the meeting], and that we weren't participating" Carmen recounted to me. A tall, imposing woman with long wavy black hair and tan skin, Carmen was born and raised in Cidade de Deus and had founded a CBO called the Environment League in 1998. Originally founded to provide literacy classes to mothers and other low-income residents, the league has, in more recent years, created curricula to teach students about the environment, trained residents in recycling collection, and established 14 recycling "points" across the neighborhood. "Hold on!" Carmen exclaimed, recounting the mayor's development initiative, "How can it be that the institutions of Cidade de Deus are not being invited to discuss a social intervention in Cidade de Deus?" Carmen and many other CBO leaders were appalled.

They fought to gain entry to the meeting. They sent letters to all possible allies on city council and went to City Hall and knocked on office doors demanding that they be included in the development plan for their neighborhood. According to Carmen, they were finally allowed into the meeting after calling a friend at a major newspaper, who in turn called the leader of the meeting and threatened to leak the story. Clara, who had founded a small CBO to offer childcare and sewing classes to CDD residents, chuckled as she recollected the scene: "Imagine me, a favela resident, with pitch-black skin, a woman, arguing with these important people to let me in. I wasn't going to sit around and let them make decisions about our community without us!

And you know what? We got in!" As Clara's narrative suggests, entry into the meeting was as much about symbolic representation—of having Black, female favela activists at the table—as it was about the material implications of social development.

Once inside, they were told to listen quietly to the mayor's presentation. However, the plans proposed by the government had not taken into account the concerns of local residents, and Carmen had interrupted loudly, accusing the group of ignoring the voices of those whom their plans would most affect. Feeling embarrassed, the directors of the meeting ended the meeting and gave the CBO leaders that weekend to put together a better plan. "The meeting was on a Friday," Carmen remembered, "and we worked all weekend on the plan." Carmen and her colleagues divided up into teams, surveyed local residents about their needs, and wrote them up. "We spent hours putting together the plan and trying to get it typed up." As Carmen recalled, they could only find one working computer among all the CBOs, and they took turns drafting the document and making edits.

The final product was a 50-page document with detailed demands for neighborhood improvement, including better trash collection, community gardens, a community bank, a high school, additional public housing, better infrastructure, and more resources for the local health clinic. On Monday morning, they pulled together just enough funds to cover their bus fares and headed to the scheduled meeting with municipal officials and forum representatives at City Hall, 30 kilometers outside Cidade de Deus. According to Carmen, "We were exhausted by Monday morning. But we did it. And they were shocked! They didn't think that we could do it . . . We dressed up in our best business attire, you know, looking professional, and there was that whole thing of, poor people don't dress this way, which really threw them off." Their hard work paid off. State officials agreed to adopt their proposal. To date, the Development Plan of Cidade de Deus, developed by its CBO leaders, remains the official plan for identifying where and how to invest in the social development of the neighborhood when funds—and political will—become available.

Over the following years, the group established itself as the Residents' Board and founded an institute registered as an NGO that could apply for grants. The board would identify the most urgent needs and the institute would gather funds to realize some of these goals. The board partnered with the Business Forum of Rio, UNESCO, researchers in some of Rio's public universities, SESI (the social branch of Brazil's industrial complex), LAMSA[2] (a private highway construction company), and a host of other private and public partners in order to make their demands a reality. Between 2005 and 2009, they helped to create several new literacy classes and establish a community-based newspaper and radio station (Pfeiffer 2014). The board also worked with municipal officials to increase the number of trash collection days, to clean up debris sites, and to add "community cleaners" to sweep the main streets. It successfully mobilized the municipal government to construct hundreds of new housing units for families who had lost their homes in the 1996 flood. In 2011, the Residents' Board secured a grant from the Municipal Secretariat for the Development of Economic Solidarity to open the first Community Bank in Brazil. The bank produced a neighborhood-based currency to promote local investments, and the project was hailed as a model for community-based economic development across Latin America. The currency remained in operation until 2014, when the bank—one block from the UPP Station—was robbed and all the money was taken.[3] Even in 2017, board members remained hopeful that someday they could re-open it.

Board members also organized a coalition to demand the building of a secondary school in Cidade de Deus. This multi-year effort entailed multiple steps, including several meetings with local residents and potential partners as well as with state deputies and secretaries,[4] submitting multiple letters, petitions, and other written requests, collecting evidence of the "demand" for a secondary school in Cidade de Deus through surveys, and filing multiple documents. And, when this all proved insufficient, they accosted the governor in the middle of a live televised interview and demanded that he sign the mandate for a secondary school in Cidade de Deus. Embarrassed and caught off guard, the governor signed the mandate, and the state finally invested a supposed R$6 million into the construction of a the school. The project was halted after two years when, according to the governor's office, the funds ran out. In 2017, Carmen re-initiated the coalition in an effort to reignite the fight for secondary education in the neighborhood. I attended several meetings, which included partners from Farmanguinhos (the federal association for health research[5]), researchers from Pontífica Universidade Católica (a prestigious private university in Rio), and staff from SESC, a social service organization funded by Brazil's commerce sector. My research team and I contributed by adding questions in our survey to measure demand for secondary education in Cidade de Deus. Even as I write this book, the battle for the school continues, with progress being made slowly and with great effort.

According to the updated Social Development Plan of Cidade de Deus published in 2010, the board aims to "establish a dialogue with the Public Power (the state) with the goal of the construction of urgent and necessary public policies in collaboration with residents of the neighborhood, in a context in which government initiatives are directed towards this" (Pfeiffer 2010). In other words, their objective is to direct state resources to Cidade de Deus and to ensure that these are implemented with input from local residents. In many respects, the board operates as an urban social movement. According to Manuel Castells (1983:xviii), urban social movements include three elements: "1) demands focused on collective consumption . . . 2) defense of cultural identity associated with and organized around a specific territory, and 3) political mobilization in relationship to the state, particularly emphasizing the role of local government." Unlike individual community-based organizations that focus on serving the needs of individuals, the board was concerned with social development projects utilized by all of Cidade de Deus's residents. Importantly, these demands were targeted explicitly at the "Public Power," which they viewed as responsible for providing the services that favela residents needed to become full urban citizens.

Thirty years after Castells's original work, more recent literature on urban social movements has focused attention on how activists work to address the "contradictions of the neoliberalization of the urban" (Mayer 2013:70). While neoliberalism has certainly affected Rio's favelas, the Residents' Board works to address issues that have plagued their neighborhood for decades thanks to historic legacies of spatially concentrated exclusions. It is the community, and not neoliberalism, that lies at the core of their efforts. Consequently, the activist model employed by the Residents' Board is better described as *community militancy*, based on an unrelenting fight for their neighborhood through both collaborative and contentious, though always non-violent, politics. The term is theirs, not mine: board members regularly referred to themselves as "militants" to define their shared struggles and collective action. According to Carmen:

We are not volunteers, we are militants. Volunteers come from time to time and do an activity. We are militants. Militants commit themselves to making a change, commit themselves to studying about that. Every day [we] are there.[6] Every day there, having money or not we'll be there. So we militate. We fight for the community no matter what, even when there is no money, no time, we fight for the community.

Board members have re-appropriated the term "militancy" from the collective resistance against the military dictatorship in which many board members had once participated. Though anti-dictatorship mobilization was led primarily by members of the working class with support from student, labor, and farmworker movements (Santana and Pimenta 2009), favelas had also been activated in the struggle in response to housing insecurity and under-development (Souza 2006). Several board members and other community militants had been key leaders of CDD's early movements for housing rights during the dictatorship. Several had also been active members of the Worker's Party and viewed the fight for favela rights as a contribution to the larger guerrilla movements against the regime.

When I arrived in Cidade de Deus in 2014, its community militants were still employing the multi-pronged strategy they had used under the dictatorship, which combined popular education, contentious claims-making, coalition building, and a focus on expanding resources in favelas. At the time, the upcoming World Cup and Summer Olympics, which would shine a bright light on Rio de Janeiro's violence and inequality, pressured then-Governor Sérgio Cabral to invest more heavily in favela upgrading. The Residents' Board took the opportunity to update Cidade de Deus's Social Development Plan and to work with various private and public funders to demand these improvements. They had succeeded in pressuring the government to build a new set of public apartment complexes to house families who had been living in temporary homes since the 1996 flood. These were inaugurated in 2014 and had enough units to house nearly 1,000 families. But the board was also furious with the UPP Social, the social branch of the UPP policing program, for building some of its own "new" projects—including a Youth Recreation Center, with shiny linoleum floors and air conditioners that local residents flocked to—rather than direct funds to community-based organizations that had spent years doing much of this development work without government support. At one board meeting I attended, Geovana, a long-time community militant and active board member, had railed against the UPP Social, which had just won the UN-Habitat award for promoting development in favelas: "We're the ones promoting development in favelas! And here comes the government and gets all the credit!" she'd exclaimed. Board members nodded in a shared sense of anger and invisibility. In our book workshop years later, Carmen added to this critique:

I would like it to be documented that when the UPP enters, we were very well organized, and when we presented this process to the UPP, they simply said they were not going to execute it. There were two UPP coordinators [at the time], . . . and I remember what they said: What we did until then didn't matter. What mattered was what they were going to do going forward.

For Carmen and many others, the success of the Residents' Board—an autonomous civil society organization—threatened the control and influence of the state in Cidade de Deus. Wishing to take the credit for social improvements, and fearful of the organizing capacity of the board, the UPP Social disrupted what had been, for many years, a cohesive contentious movement.

Ultimately, the Residents' Board succeeded in fits and starts, with an eye for the ebb and flow of political opportunities in the municipal and national political arena. Obtaining government support had never been easy; in most cases, board members had to employ a range of collaborative and contentious strategies to succeed. The most common strategy was to organize councils, committees, and meetings with private organizations and public administrators—who often were referred to as "partners" or "collaborators"—with an interest in investing resources in Cidade de Deus. I attended several of these, and in nearly every one of them, board members asked pointed, direct questions of their "partners" in government or private organizations, quizzed them on their level of commitment to the neighborhood, pointed out power differences between them and these "collaborators," and often turned down offers for projects that were unlikely to bring meaningful improvements to the community.

As I describe in Chapter 5, board meetings were often long, contentious, and stressful. But board members were steadfast in their approach. In addition to meetings with potential allies, they also engaged in letter-writing campaigns, in-person lobbying of representatives and public administrators, and the strategic placement of news stories about Cidade de Deus's development needs in newspapers. Community militants thus filled the vacuum left by the city's half-baked slum-upgrading efforts, identifying shortcomings and drawing on historic repertoires of contentious politics to demand long-term improvements to social infrastructure. They also strategically targeted political openings, particularly moments in which the government's failures in CDD have been most visible to the international public. The Residents'

Board was not the only model of political activism, however. Next, I describe how cultural politics provided a third cluster of social change.

Cultural Politics

I stepped into the bar shyly, searching unsuccessfully for a familiar face. To my left, a man sat shirtless, nursing a glass of beer, his large belly protruding out from the wall against which he leaned. I stepped toward the back, where the bartender wiped down the counter and chatted amiably with a small group of men, glancing intermittently at the soccer game on the television behind them. Wandering over to the bartender, I asked if this was the place where Art Talk was gathering. I was at the address they'd sent out on WhatsApp, though the place wasn't what I had imagined for a poetry reading. The bartender pointed at a bouquet of plastic flowers on a table behind me, and I turned just as Cibele walked in, her hands full of bags. Relieved, I greeted Cibele, and she handed me a stack of flowers to weave through the iron bars that separated the bar from the street. Cibele turned to organize the remaining decorations—Christmas tree lights and large sheets of red fabric—and I went to task, threading wire stems through the thick iron bars.

Cibele was a light-skinned woman of around 25 I had briefly met at an Art Talk meeting the week before. Her dark curly hair accentuated her thick black eye liner and large gauge earrings. I didn't know anyone else who looked like her in Cidade de Deus, and I wondered if she was even from there. Before I could ask, a van pulled up. Two dark-skinned men got out. A man with Cybele long dread locks and dozens of tattoos down his arms opened the back of the van and began removing large, brightly colored paintings. Having finished with the flowers, I was tasked with hanging the paintings on the bars. Suddenly, Cibele realized she could not find the Art Talk banner, which she normally hung behind the microphone. She searched agonizingly for it, until she came across a painting of Frida Khalo that had been in the van. She placed it on a shelf behind the mic. "Here! This will do!" she exclaimed, satisfied with the substitution. We pushed tables off to the side and arranged the chairs to face the microphone and Frida. The men brought in a large sound speaker. I stepped back for a moment. Aside from the shirtless man, still staring aimlessly past us, the bar had transformed into a stage—a sparkling, flowery, feminized theater.

Soon, other Art Talk members began arriving, greeting each other warmly, looking for ways to help set things up, and purchasing beer. Within an hour, around 25 people of various ages, skin tones, tattoos, piercings, and gendered presentations of self were congregated. Some sat on chairs, others on the floor, and many others stood outside the bar chatting and smoking. As I later discovered, though Art Talk was run by Cidade de Deus residents and most events took place within the neighborhood, a number of those in attendance that night were from neighboring, middle-class areas or from favelas in other parts of the city.

Natalia, a very thin 25-year-old woman with an androgynous appearance walked up to the mic and called the evening to order. In later conversations I had with Natalia, she had identified at times as Indigenous, at times as Black, and at times as Black-Indigenous. As it turned out, discussions of racism and racial identity were an important component of discourse in Art Talk. While most Art Talk Open Mics did not have a theme, they had made an exception for this one, calling it "Women against the Coup" in reference to the recent vote by the House of Representatives to impeach Workers' Party President Dilma the week before. Natalia had invited the most prominent female poets from Cidade de Deus, including Dona Mia, a spunky woman in her 70s who had become one of the cultural icons of the neighborhood, as well as several other Black female poets. Over the course of the next four hours, dozens of people got up to the microphone. This is an excerpt from my field notes after the event:

> The microphone was open to anyone, and several people read poems that weren't necessarily political, and some that were written by other poets. A couple of people read poems written by their friends. Some people sang their poems. Seu Zé, an older man, was especially entertaining as he had brought outfits for each of the characters that he performed. He performed a couple of poems about the police that were especially provocative and interesting, and I wish I could have filmed them. There were poets from all walks of life, some seasoned, some great, some timid, some novices . . . . Although I don't recall all the moments, there were some that were especially memorable. Carina was a 30-something-old tall Black woman with long braids wearing a long dress, and she was a formidable poet. She cried passionately several times as she recited her poems, and it was hard not to feel the pain of the poem with her. One was about the pain of giving birth to a stillborn child . . . . Natalia had also invited a young woman whose

nickname was LilyQ. At the beginning of the Open Mic she had hung several pages with provocative quotes about women's sexuality and equality in sex. Some read: "You want a shaved vagina but you give me a hairy asshole" and "If you don't like kissing after oral sex, then you are repulsed by your own body." LilyQ had a very sexually empowering speech that included the importance of being open about sex so that women's rights could be respected. Natalia asked her several provocative questions about her own sexuality, and Natalia herself even made a few comments about preferring large penises and having bought a few sex toys from her shop.

While some poems focused on personal issues, the majority had political undertones as poets criticized the corruption in Brazil's government, renounced police brutality and the violation of the rights of favela residents, especially of its Black population, and decried violence against women. Others celebrated women's sexuality and called for the protection of lesbian, gay, and transgender people. Many had opened their poems by exclaiming: "Long live democracy!" as they lifted their fists to the air. These were greeted with cheers of solidarity from the crowd. Through songs, poems, and rap, Art Talk transformed the bar into a site for making demands for democracy, safety, a more equitable distribution of resources, and an end to racial discrimination. This was true in the paintings as well. One painting featured a small white house with two windows and a triangular red roof sitting alone on a bucolic green pasture. It did not resemble any house in Cidade de Deus or Rio de Janeiro. I asked Luz, the artist whose experiences with gendered violence I described in Chapter 1, about her paintings. The house, she told me, represented a place of quiet because her own house was so noisy from the blasting music of the *baile funk* parties hosted by drug traffickers, as well as the loud sermons coming from nearby evangelical churches and the screams of children playing in her street. How wonderful it would be to escape it all, she reflected aloud. Another painting was of Batman, his face half in the light, half in the dark, which Luz explained was meant to reflect the good and the bad sides of humanity. A passerby looking at these paintings would be unlikely to see the symbolism in them, but, lining the iron walls of the bar that night, they contributed to the collective airing of grievances in the favela.

When all the poets had concluded their readings, Natalia ushered us out onto the street. A few minutes later, the 550 bus rounded the corner onto our road, and two dark-skinned men from our group stopped the bus to talk to the driver, who appeared confused and petrified. A few seconds later they gestured us over, and we crowded in front of the bus to pose for a group photo. It was intended as a symbolic gesture: the 550 route began in Cidade de Deus, passed through another favela, then down Rio's wealthy commercial district, past several beaches, and ended in Leblon, one of Rio's most expensive neighborhoods. As Natalia later explained to me, stopping the bus on its journey signaled their efforts to interrupt the systems of inequality that exacerbated the social and economic distance between the poor and the rich.

On my way out of the Open Mic, I ran into Maria Rita's neighbor Jordana, a Black 20-year old sporting long, colorful braids and bright green lipstick. She had been at the open mic after returning from university two hours away with two of her white middle-class friends. "You don't find this kind of thing in Zona Sul," Jordana noted, referencing a wealthy district of the city. "Only here in Cidade de Deus are you going to see a poetry Open Mic in the middle of the sidewalk, at a bar." Jordana was referring at once to the informality with which artistic events took place in Cidade de Deus and to the unique logic and form of politics in the *favela*. Poetry, rap, paintings, and a host of other artistic practices allowed favela residents to develop political subjectivities that were both public and hidden and to demand change in a manner that was both public and indirect. At the same time, they transformed everyday public/private spaces, like parks, open bars, and streets into sites of protest and claims-making for the rights of citizenship.

While Art Talk is the largest and most well-organized artist collective, Cidade de Deus is filled with *produtores culturais*, or cultural producers, people engaged in the creative economy through both traditional forms of art, such as poetry, painting, song writing, and theater, and more contemporary digital art forms, such as graphic design and film production. There are also many community journalists, novelists, hip hop artists, classical ballet dancers, martial arts fighters, and soccer players. Many of them are autodidacts: they learned their trade through informal apprenticeships and lots of independent study and practice. Yet, much of what they produce is so good you would not know its makers did not have a professional degree, which is a valuable reminder that informality should not be confused with mediocrity. In fact, Cidade de Deus residents have produced movies and documentaries, performed in international dance troupes, made internationally acclaimed music, won national and world championships, and played for international sports teams. Many, if not most, of Cidade de Deus's artists have sold their art or been employed by businesses outside the favela.

Art transports the favela into the urban and global knowledge economy, offering poor citizens economic opportunities, new social networks, and, for
some, a platform through which to make broader critiques of inequality and
state violence.

While Cidade de Deus is often imagined as a site of violence, it is also a
site of great cultural vitality. Art provides an avenue for personal expression, contributes to personal well-being, and can promote the construction of shared images and values within a subculture. Furthermore, artistic
creations are "among the first manifestations of collective resistance, and art
becomes a crucial and fundamental way of conveying demands, struggles,
and the collective identities constructed by the act of resisting oppression"
(Déa 2012:5). From the freedom songs of the civil rights movement and
the anti-war posters of the Vietnam War to critical theater performance in
anti-Apartheid South Africa and photography during the Arab Spring, art
"play[s] a key role in social movements and wider currents of social change"
(Reed 2019:13). Cultural activists in Cidade de Deus do exactly this: they utilize artistic expression to critique the political, economic, and symbolic systems of oppression that entrench concentrated inequalities, thereby offering
local residents a narrative that holds the state, capitalism, the patriarchy, and
racism responsible for their struggles.

However, cultural activists contribute more than just symbolic forms of
protest. Many are directly engaged in politics either as employees in municipal government, candidates or campaign staff for political candidates,
or members of formal social movement coalitions, and some have held several of these roles. In many cases, local artists engaged in these institutionalized political spaces in the hope that they could make some kind of positive
changes from within the formal state. The desire to make institutional change
inspired Leonardo, an actor and co-founder of a performing arts organization for adolescents, to campaign for a city councilman from another favela
and to participate in the founding of a national movement that addressing
the impact of Brazil's drug policies on poor Black citizens. Jordana had
started her own YouTube channel dedicated to telling positive stories of the
favela. Natalia, meanwhile, would go on to run for city councilwoman, and
many Art Talk participants would become loyal volunteers on her campaign.
They protested the state while working for it and in opposition to it, all in an
effort to change it.

Just as the Residents' Board and Cidade de Deus's CBOs emerged in a
particular social, political, and economic context, so have Cidade de Deus's

politicized artists. For one, national investment in the arts has grown steadily since the National Foundation for the Arts (Funarte) was created in 1975, followed 10 years later by the establishment of the Ministry of Culture. In the 1990s, President Fernando Henrique Cardoso promoted the slogan "Culture is a good investment" in an effort to push the neoliberal agenda of private investments in the arts (Calabre 2014). The shift in perspective that took place with Lula's election in 2002 marked a new era, as the government invested in "public policies for culture," arguing that culture itself was a basic right. Funding for the arts increased substantially. The Secretariat for Identity and Cultural Diversity (SID), established in 2003, was charged with channeling government funds to artistic groups and initiatives for "popular cultures" (a euphemism for poor people), indigenous, LGBT, and the elderly, among others. These programs largely continued to expand throughout Lula's two terms and Dilma Rousseff's first term.

Brazil's shift to democracy also decentralized power, placing states and municipalities in charge of the distribution of federal investments and capturing their own, private investments. This urbanization of the nation-state has made Brazil's cities the sites for social conflict and contentious politics (Davis and Duren 2011) while also offering urban citizens great proximity to—and power over—political and economic decision-making. In Rio de Janeiro, the nationalized oil company Petrobras was among the largest "patrons" of the city's cultural landscape. In 2011, they established a partnership with the State Secretary of Culture and the Observatório das Favelas, one of the largest and most highly regarded favela-based NGOs. According to Petrobras, "we seek to sow seeds to develop actions in the field of culture that would increase the recognition of the role of favelas in the construction of the city's identity. The idea of the project is to make known and recognize their richness and cultural plurality" (Barbosa and Dias 2013).

Funds for culture in favelas increased even further during the height of the UPP, as Rio de Janeiro's governor and mayor attempted to prove to the world that they cared about favelas. By 2014, these funds were paying dividends. In 2011, Art Talk won a R$25,000 award[7] from the state's Secretary of Culture, which allowed them to purchase a van for their equipment and to hold streetside open mics throughout the city . They went on to win several other small grants that financed supplies and transportation. Rosangela, a poet and the co-founder of a community newspaper, was selected for a national book prize by the federal Ministry of Culture. The award paid for her to publish her book and a CD of original songs. Leonardo's theater group received funding from Funare and was invited to present a play at one of their annual events. Meanwhile, Luz showcased her paintings at various cultural centers and fairs across the city, many of which had been sponsored by the Ministry of Culture or large private foundations.

Affirmative action policies have also played a critical role in promoting education and political action in favelas. In 2004, the State University of Rio de Janeiro began to require that 20% of newly admitted students be Black. Six years later, the Federal University of Rio de Janeiro implemented quotas for public high school graduates and low-income students. Then, in 2012, the federal government passed the Law of Social Quotas, which required that half of new openings at Brazil's federally funded universities (considered the most prestigious in the country) be earmarked for graduates of public high schools and a quarter for students from households earning 1.5 times the minimum wage or less. These quotas have been part of a larger movement across Brazil to value the inclusion of the poor and people of color in higher education. Dozens of preparatory courses for college entrance exams were offered—some by volunteer favela residents, others sponsored by private companies—in Cidade de Deus and other favelas. I met many CDD residents who had taken advantage of these openings to enroll in university, where they not only gained formal degrees that could be leveraged for jobs and status outside the favela, but also received training in history, sociology, and critical economics. With both knowledge and formal degrees, young favela activists have brought these resources into local networks of cultural resistance.

Beginning in 2016, however, funding for social programs began to wane. For one, the Worker's Party, which had been responsible for a spike in cultural investments and a general shift in perception about the rights of the poor, witnessed a dramatic fall with President Rousseff's impeachment and the imprisonment of dozens of Worker's Party leaders embroiled in the Lava Jato corruption investigation. As the investigation unfolded, leaders of the Workers' Party, including Lula himself, were charged with accepting large kickbacks in exchange for construction deals and operating permits granted to Petrobras, the nationalized oil giant. The scandal also hastened the decline of Petrobras, already underway after years of poor management, and exacerbated an ensuing economic recession. Cultural programs that had been funded directly by Petrobras were suddenly abandoned. The new, fiscally conservative President Michel Temer immediately initiated widespread cuts to investments in culture and education, along with many other social programs. Then, two months before the 2016 Summer Olympics, the State of Rio de Janeiro faced an economic crisis thanks to revenue losses from Petrobras, mismanagement, and the overwhelming costs of the mega-events. While the economic decline continued well into 2017, cultural producers remained firm in their endeavors, searching for other streams of funding and taking advantage of the skills and networks they had developed at the height of Brazil's cultural investments.

Fortunately, cultural producers were not reliant solely on the municipal or federal government. In fact, cultural resistance has risen alongside and in connection with the global public sphere (Castells 2008). Their access to information communication technologies, such as the WhatsApp text messaging service, Facebook, Twitter, and email facilitated connections to activists, donors, and media across the globe, specifically activists in trans-national social movements focused on racial justice and gender-based issues. Leonardo and 20 of the youth from his theater group received funding from a German theater group and flown to Germany to perform there. Natalia spent six months in North Carolina as an exchange student, where she learned English and had the opportunity to study philosophy and sociology, learning ideas that later informed her poetry and critical writing. Rosangela worked as a journalist for an international feminist community newspaper and attended a number of international feminist conferences across Latin America. There were many other examples of activists' connections to countries across the world, demonstrating that favela activists were not restricted by either neighborhood politics or the ebb and flow of government resources. While conflict activism does expand, contract, and become reconfigured in response to political openings, the international community has become an important source of solidarity and support, a theme I discuss at length in Chapter 5.

Conclusion: A Patchwork Politics

This chapter has demonstrated how activists tend to cluster around particular resources and networks in an effort to channel as many national and international opportunities as possible into the favela. As they become proficient in grant applications, grassroots organizing, and cultural connection across favelas and countries, activists bring in a wide variety of resources that benefit local residents, improve the overall well-being of the neighborhood, and insert CDD into broader social change movements.

The result is a patchwork of opportunities, services, and political views that make Cidade de Deus a better and more inclusive place to live. In lieu of one consolidated social movement, activists have dispersed into several organizational forms that each bring in a particular set of resources but that, in totality, help to produce a great variety of opportunities and political visions. The dispersion of organizations, projects, initiatives, and events across the neighborhood is a product of a dynamic, disjointed, and multi-dimensional field of opportunities outside of the neighborhood. It is an imperfect solution to intersecting and deep-rooted problems. But when taken together, these collectives provide local residents with access to many of the elements that contribute to political participation and social change: the basic public goods needed for survival, organized mobilizations around collective consumption, creative expressions of shared identity, and avenues into the formal and transnational spheres of political power.

Although this chapter has laid out three distinct clusters of collective action, activists and other residents navigate in and out of these groups as new funding sources become available, personal relationships grow or fall apart, or even as the security landscape shifts. Maria Rita, for instance, was a long-time employee at Youth Promise and tended to focus her energy on applying for grants from the government and private foundations that could be used to keep the organization afloat. However, she was also engaged in cultural production, teaching her students how to design websites or new apps and attending many of the events hosted by local artists. A 2013 study by the Observatório das Favelas found that of the 62 entities engaged in cultural production in Cidade de Deus, 27.4% were CBOs and another 27.4% were informal organizations (i.e., projetos) (Barbosa and Dias 2013). Carmen, one of the core leaders of the Residents' Board, also ran her own CBO, where youth learned, among other things, how to transform recycling materials into artistic products. Jefferson, the karatê teacher, published several books and was among the organizers of Art Talk. Leonardo's organization used the arts to promote the social and political development of youth, and could be viewed as both a CBO and a site of cultural resistance.

For local activists, the distinctions between these three clusters of change were not always apparent or even perceived as relevant. The first time many local activists came to see these as distinct approaches to collective action was when I presented some of my findings to them and invited their feedback.

I received no rejections to my analysis; instead, we spent the following two hours discussing the many shared challenges activists faced in a context of endemic corruption, extreme insecurity, and a racist and exclusionary government. It was what they had in common, more than what differed, that our diverse group rallied around.

Nonetheless, making these distinctions is helpful for two reasons. The first is that, even while residents move between these clusters, each has a unique logic and set of practices that demarcates it as distinct from the others. How one operates and funds a CBO requires a different set of skills, resources, and networks than how one organizes an Open Mic event, and it may very well attract a different audience and offer different benefits. CBO leaders learned to master the language of grant applications, community militants became fluent in contentious political activism, and cultural actors had to navigate a broader cultural and social scene within and beyond CDD. Each cluster followed a particular set of norms and practices, and each was based on a distinct view of how to address violence.

Second, there were often conflicts between the leaders of these groups, who did see their ways of making change as fundamentally different from—and better than—the others. Older activists who had organized under the dictatorship and were now involved in community militancy often felt snubbed by the younger generation of cultural activists who spent less time in CDD and more time traveling around the city. Young artists, in turn, viewed the Residents' Board and other formal institutions as outdated and too focused on place-based bureaucratic practices. Additionally, more radical activists were sometimes critical of CBOs who focused on social services, sometimes at the expense of organizing for more structural change. There was no shortage of disagreements, and these sometimes erupted and led to cleavages between collectives.

Conflict zones are often examined from the lens of political and physical closures, as researchers identify the many overlapping obstacles that hinder organized activism. However, even areas suffering extreme violence and poverty exist within a broader national and global landscape that is teeming with new economic, political, and social flows that can, with struggle and strategy, be channeled into even the most hostile terrains. As I discuss in Chapter 5, the ties that local collectives foster with external allies are not only productive of new opportunities but also reproductive of global, racialized, and classed inequities. It is important that these ties are not overly romanticized. But it is just as important that they are not overlooked. For activists in areas of extreme violence, in dire need of whatever crumbs they can gather to feed and sustain their community, their ability to disperse and cluster around existing political opportunities is an important repertoire of action that keeps people and political ambitions alive in a context of violence and scarce resources.

3

Violent Clientelism and
Gendered Governance

Introduction

"We aren't going to serve as a stepladder for politicians. We definitely aren't! (*Não vai mesmo!*)," Isabella exclaimed, justifying her refusal to praise the work of the candidates for city council on her Facebook page. Isabella had become a lightning rod for local politics since her page, CDD Connects, had gained tens of thousands of followers within only a few years. Founded in 2011, CDD Connects was a digital platform for sharing all types of useful information, including the many free or low-cost services being offered by community-based organizations, promotions at local businesses, news about government construction projects, and bus routes shut down due to shootouts, among other things. In a neighborhood characterized by informal economies, irregular public services, and few reliable news sources interested in publishing anything but stories of police invasians and homicides, CDD Connects filled an essential need for information about everything else that was happening across the neighborhood. Her first posts had been about local services being offered: a new computer course, a vaccine clinic, distribution of school supplies, and other public programs, some organized by the government, others by local CBOs (community-based organizations). Isabella also wrote stories about community issues, such as broken pipes, unpaved roads, and under-staffed schools. She frequently tagged municipal policymakers in her posts, demanding that they address these problems. As the page gained in popularity, however, so did her own status and power. Not surprisingly, when the 2016 municipal elections for mayor and city council rolled around, political candidates were eager to get their ads marketed on her site, which could quickly reach nearly every resident in Cidade de Deus and many others living nearby.

Isabella decidedly turned down every request to post campaign flyers on CDD Connects, regardless of the sum they offered to pay her. She had

Activism under Fire. Anjuli Fahlberg, Oxford University Press. © Oxford University Press 2023.
DOI: 10.1093/oso/9780197519325.003.0004

recently been avoiding some of her own friends who were running for office. "Politics is a topic that I hate, that I don't understand, and I don't believe in it," she'd told me as we splayed across Maria Rita's couch a few weeks before the election. "Instead of speaking gibberish (*falando besteira*), isn't it better to stay silent?" I nodded in agreement, but I knew from many previous conversations that Isabella's refusal ran much deeper than a supposed lack of understanding about politics, which she actually had in abundance. Instead, Isabella feared being caught up in a game that everyone in CDD knew to be corrupt and dangerous. She hated what she called *politicagem*, or the tendency for politicians to engage in clientelism and take the credit for the hard work of favela residents and public servants without providing them proper compensation. And she, like most of my other participants, feared becoming involved in relationships with elected officials who might have some connection to drug traffickers or other violent actors, such as the *milicia* or the police.

However, Isabella was among dozens of residents whom I came to see as extremely politically active. While we frequently view participation in politics as running for office, joining a campaign, or working for the government, we might also define politics as contestations over who gets what, when, and how (Lasswell 2018). In this broader view, politics involves intentional and strategic engagement with power structures in order to obtain resources and make demands for rights. Defined this way, politics can be the purview of any member of civil society who is engaged in claims-making, whether within or outside the formal political system. This allows us to recognize the work of people like Isabella and other favela residents as political. Few activists in CDD run for office or become closely affiliated with elected officials, and most refuse to ask for favors from state officials, particularly those with suspected ties to local drug lords. Yet local activists were constantly organizing to address the needs of their neighborhood and make demands for resources and citizenship rights.

It is widely argued that gang territories are governed by the politics of violence, composed of the webs of illicit ties between drug gangs and state officials, mediated through bribes and threats that ultimately determine who gets what and how (Arias 2017; Barcellos and Zaluar 2014; Gay 1993; Larkins 2015; McCann 2014). This view is partially correct. In Rio's favelas, gangs and *milicia* cultivate alliances with politicians in order to co-opt local governing bodies—including some civic associations and state-run agencies—and obtain the resources they need to keep their operations lucrative while quashing any direct threat to their authority. However, although such violent networks operate with great force and resilience in Cidade de Deus, they are not the only mechanism through which politics is enacted. Favela activists like Isabella and the participants of many collectives I described in Chapter 2 also play an essential role in local governance by bringing in and distributing resources and creating possibilities for social and cultural development. In order to remain effective and safe, activists have developed a host of strategies to resist co-optation by gangs or use the threat of violence to push forward their objectives. In other words, alongside the politics of violence operates a politics of non-violence. Together, they govern the neighborhood.

This chapter examines how these two political spheres manage to co-exist somewhat peacefully and to share power in a context of segregated violence and poverty. The central argument is that in Cidade de Deus, and I suspect in many other conflict zones, the politics of violence and non-violence are relational political forms which operate through a *gendered division of governing labor*. While the masculinized politics of violence controls formal political institutions and the management of law and order, the feminized sphere of non-violence maintains the social and cultural development of the neighborhood. To be clear, there are many women involved, directly or tangentially, in the drug trade, and there are hundreds of men involved in non-violent activism. However, each sphere performs a set of tasks that are generally attributed to masculinity or femininity. Furthermore, while the most powerful actors in violent governance are almost entirely men, the leaders of CDD's non-violent politics are primarily women. As I will demonstrate, the gendering of political spheres is critical to the survival of non-violence in areas of conflict and repression.

Just as in a traditional patriarchal family, these gendered spheres are not evenly balanced. Drug traffickers maintain ultimate control over what activities are allowed and how to enforce those boundaries. Meanwhile, non-violent activists must squeeze into the social and cultural spaces that drug traffickers do not fill, creating a semi-autonomous sphere of social action that is constantly at risk of being co-opted or harmed. The preservation of this balance requires that activists draw on internalized, often subconscious practices developed over years of living under violent politics, as well as more consciously determined strategies of action and avoidance to remain both effective and alive.

Politics through Violence

The power of the drug trade over Cidade de Deus is hard to miss, being a pervasive presence in both the physical spaces of the neighborhood and everyday economic and political issues. I had an opportunity to learn about some of its many facets on a warm night in April 2016, when Esther and I headed to a poorer section of the neighborhood to sell pizzas at her friend's luncheonette. Armed drug traffickers roamed many back streets openly, displaying their dominance by showing off weapons tucked into the back of their pants, yelling loudly at each other from down the street, and zooming past residents on noisy, high-end motorcycles. Many also wore thick gold chains and boasted the latest model of cell phone. These "spectacles of consumption" demonstrated their dominance over the territory by embodying a masculinity based on both physical power and styles of leisure (Larkins 2015; Zaluar 2010). It set them apart from—and above—other residents.

Visible symbols of gang membership[1] are especially critical in a context of urban warfare in an informal neighborhood where there was no official uniform to distinguish narcotraffickers from unarmed residents. As I described in Chapter 1, a five-year ceasefire between the police and the drug trade had begun to unravel in 2014. It had started, I was told by many residents, when UPP police began accepting bribes to allow gang members to sell drugs on particular street corners. However, more aggressive branches of the military police were soon sent in to crack down on these open displays of power by the drug trade through armed police troops ready to wage direct combat. Drug traffickers, noticing fissures within the police, become bolder, shooting back instead of paying bribes. Their forces and their determination had grown, and they were ready to battle the police for complete control of the neighborhood. They began by growing their visible presence in Karatê, one of the poorest areas of CDD, which abutted a large swamp and could not be as easily accessed by police vehicles as other areas. At night, armed men wandered the streets freely, participating in street parties and mingling with other residents.

This was the kind of scene most activists would avoid. Though street parties are a permanent fixture in favelas, activists usually avoided socializing where drug traffickers were likely to hang out. They did not want to risk being caught in shootout crossfire, and they certainly did not want to be seen talking to gang members. Esther, a long-time CDD resident who was not directly active in collective organizing, was less concerned about the appearance of "mixing" with drug traffickers than her sister Maria Rita, who worked for a well-known CBO and had a reputation of honesty and legality to uphold. Esther knew many gang members since birth and had no problem asking the "managers" of drug sale points for favors on behalf of needy families: a food basket, protection against an abusive partner, or permission to occupy a government-run apartment unit. Esther's ability and willingness to navigate between CDD's violent and non-violent political spheres positioned her as what one activist termed a "nebulous person," someone who could— and would—traverse between the gang, ordinary residents, and the activist sphere, thereby preserving a sense of connection between distinct socioeconomic forces.

Esther's friend Claudia had gone on a long trip to visit family members in the northeastern state of Bahia and left Esther in charge of her pizza shop. Esther had prepared dozens of treats, individual-sized pizzas, *empadão*, and açaí. It was a festive night. The pizza shop sat across from a bar blasting funk music. Adults gathered in small groups drinking beer, while children jumped excitedly on a large trampoline that took up much of the main road. The yellow streetlamp cast shadows down the side street behind us, and I could make out the bodies of two scrawny girls chatting as a small child ran between their legs. In contrast to the part of CDD where I lived with Esther and Maria Rita, composed primarily of finished brick and mortar homes, the homes here were only semi-finished. Exposed brick had been layered to make second and third stories. Bedsheets hung in empty windowsills, blowing in the wind. Residents I spoke to in this area often referred to their homes as "under construction," though few had been able to invest in improvements in recent years. The roads were made of dirt, and I imagined the challenge of keeping these homes clean of the dust.

Esther and I squeezed into Claudia's luncheonette, a tiny space with a giant freezer, some shelves, and a dusty old microwave. There was barely room for the two of us, although once we lifted the metal gate we could stand outside in front of the luncheonette and watch the festivities. While Esther sorted the food and chatted with friends coming over to greet us, I stood around nervously trying to look at ease and non-curious. I knew I stood out. I worried I might be perceived as an undercover police officer, spying on an area that drug gangs had designated their own but which they still had to "defend" from invading police. Seu Tony, Claudia's husband, had not gone on the trip with his wife and was hanging around outside. He came over to chat with me. After a tense conversation in which I tried to convince him that I did not work for the government, he eased up and began telling me about his life. He shared many stories with me about his formative years, his marital issues, and the soccer players he used to manage in hopes of getting them signed to major teams.

He explained that soccer is the only way to leave CDD and make big money (for young men, I believe he meant). It is an escape from favela life, if you can be so lucky. But making it in soccer was a dangerous game in favelas. Assuming you had skills, the opportunity to play on a team, and get a coach from a professional league (in Brazil or abroad) to notice you, you then had to finance your trip to the recruiting city or country, as well as the field and the equipment to practice ahead of time. According to Seu Tony, who hoped he might make it big someday by being the agent of a successful player, the state did little to help poor aspiring players be competitive in the market. Once a local politician had offered to cover the transportation and field costs for one of Seu Tony's players and to give the player a R$300 stipend, in exchange for Seu Tony's helping him get votes. This patron "relationship" only lasted four weeks, after which time the politician stopped giving him money, and Seu Tony had to pay the rest of the field fees out of pocket. In response, Seu Tony stopped helping him earn votes. "Here, every politician is dirty," he told me.

Seu Tony's experience reflects one of many entanglements favela residents have with corrupt politicians, which can end badly when one side does not live up to their end of the deal. In a well-functioning democracy, financial and material resources are distributed through public policies to those who qualify, regardless of the candidates for whom they voted. In favelas, how-ever, people received state resources through clientelism, whereby resources are distributed by individual politicians directly to their friends and allies who help them get elected (Chasteen 2016). In Rio and across Latin America, clientelism has been so pervasive, particularly in poor neighborhoods with little control over the urban or national political process, that it has become embedded in everyday life (Auyero and Benzecry 2017).

In Rio's favelas, drug traffickers often mediate these relationships, serving as brokers between politicians, who need the support of local drug lords to garner votes from the favela, and local residents, who need money or other types of resources to make ends meet or to grow a business venture (Arias 2006b). The result is a violent configuration of clientelism, wherein involve-ment in political networks is interwoven with armed illicit actors and always tinged with the threat of exile, torture, and death for residents who fail to meet the demands of the politician or gang lord. Enrique Desmond Arias, drawing on over a decade of research on politics in Rio's favelas, argues that these neighborhoods are governed by "micro-level armed regimes . . . that alter political practices within the same urban and national-level institutions [and] also generate particular localized political orders" (Arias 2017:2). In Cidade de Deus, where drug gangs have governed the streets since the 1970s, the gang-led micro-regime is sustained through illicit ties to political actors, making any involvement with politicians a potentially deadly affair.

Those who rise to power in this system are those who are willing to play the game and incur the risks. This includes of course drug traffickers and corrupt politicians, but also local "big men," or favela residents—usually men—who are not directly involved in either the drug trade or politics but who accept resources in exchange for political favors (Penglase 2014). Seu Tony offers a prime example. Seu Tony was among the lucky ones, however, as he survived the unraveling of his agreement with his benefactor. In other cases, the exchange of favors in CDD can end much more badly. According to Seu Tony, many aspiring soccer players end up being "sponsored" by the drug trade. Few are recruited to major teams, however; the rest return to CDD having spent the gang's money with little to show for it and no way to pay it back. Seu Tony told me about one player who was murdered after he returned to CDD without fame or money and was unable to pay back his sponsor in the drug trade. I left that night with a clearer understanding of both the physical and economic mechanisms the gang utilized to affirm their control of the neighborhood.

We returned the following night to sell pizzas again, but this time I sat talking to Rafael, Seu Tony's son, who was in his late twenties. Rafael opened up about his experiences in CDD immediately. "I have already lost more than one hundred friends, more than one hundred. I've seen a lot of stuff here," Rafael reported matter-of-factly. We sat in folding chairs staring at the intersection. He pointed to different spots nearby, reporting the executions he had witnessed. Some were killed by drug traffickers who suspected them of being undercover spies for the police. Others had been shot by the military police during an operation or for refusing to pay the bribes they charged. The very state actors charged with citizen protection were among the greatest perpetrators of violence in Rio's favelas.

Suddenly, we heard fireworks in the distance and the street went quiet. The fireworks had been a warning that the *caveirão*, or armored vehicle of the BOPE (the Battallion for Special Operations), similar to a SWAT team, was riding through the neighborhood. The children and armed men scurried out of sight so quickly it seemed more like a reflex than a negotiated plan of action. The rest of us looked down the road in apprehensive silence. Sure enough, barely a minute passed before the *caveirão* appeared. I held my breath as it drove past us, only a few feet away, as slowly as a person walks. The rifle tips of the officers inside stuck out of small holes pointed directly at us. I could see the whites of some of the officers' eyes. Reaching the end of the road, the *caveirão* turned around and drove past us again. I said a silent prayer that they would not shoot at us and that the drug traffickers would not shoot at them. A few minutes later, we heard fireworks from another area of the neighborhood, alerting us that the *caveirão* had moved on to another place. They left in peace that night, though on many other nights these incursions ended in shootouts and death.

Violent governance in Cidade de Deus operates through a combination of cooperation and competition between drug traffickers, the police, and corrupt politicians who rely on extortion, bribes, threats of violence, and actual violence to perform dominance over the neighborhood and each other. This political arrangement has a distinctively masculine characterization. For one, although both men and women commonly asked drug traffickers for favors and resources, most of those with the power to distribute such favors are men. Furthermore, displays of physical and consumptive power allow men to signal their dominance in the masculine hierarchy. In his research on gangs in Medellín, for instance, Adam Baird found that "Like soldiering, the capacity for violence is a rite of passage into the gang and a definitive assertion of male adulthood" (2018:203). While more affluent or lighter-skinned men may perform hegemonic masculinity through high-skilled jobs or electoral politics, gangs and the police become some of the few institutions in which poor, darker-skinned men can exercise masculine power and status (Baird 2018; Bourgois 2003). While in less violent contexts it may be common for women to be key political brokers in clientelist networks (Auyero 2001), in gang territories, violent clientelist networks have been constructed as hypermasculine spaces that enable individual men to showcase their dominance over the territory.

This model of governance empowers individual drug lords and politicians while draining actual government institutions of political power. As noted in Chapter 1, drug traffickers under the Comando Vermelho gradually took over favela neighborhood associations in the late 1980s and 1990s, killing or expelling their presidents and placing their own puppets in their place (Gay

1993; Perlman 2010). In CDD, the four "RAs," or Residents' Associations, now do little more than rent out rooms in their buildings for birthday parties or dance classes. According to one local activist, "We don't have a functional Association here in CDD. It doesn't work here." As several participants told me, residents have not been allowed to vote for new presidents in nearly twenty years. The role of the RAs, which had once been sites of enthusiastic debate and discussion about how to address the needs of the neighborhood, has been essentially de-politicized in order to ensure that residents did not have a space to organize against local gangs (Fischer 2008; McCann 2014; Perlman 2010).

CDD also has a Regional Administration office, a branch of the municipal government charged with overseeing local construction and development projects and distributing housing titles and other neighborhood-based resources to CDD residents. I tried four times to get an interview with the director, but she was never in her office and failed to show up to appointments I'd scheduled with her assistant. The building itself was falling apart, with large puddles of water spread throughout the concrete floor and giant patches of mold on the ceilings. Most residents had no idea what the Regional Administration did. Many participants believed it was co-opted by gangs. Some of the evidence for this, I was told, included how often individuals with connections to the drug gang were issued permits for large block parties, as well as rumors that some of the public goods administered by the Regional Administration often ended up in the hands of gang members, who then determined which residents could access them. When I asked one of my participants if they thought the director of the Regional Administration had been bribed, they replied, "If not bribed, then threatened." If the carrot did not work, the stick was sure to do the trick. In a space where so much of the "real" politics happened behind closed doors, residents used small pieces of evidence and rumors to make a best guess about who controlled what (and whom) and to determine which institutions had the potential to address residents' demands for improvements. While I have no personal knowledge about the veracity of these claims, the more important point here is that residents believed them. The perception of corruption among local government made the Regional Administration an ineffective space for claims-making.

Although I heard over and over from residents that "they (drug gangs) don't mess with me" (*eles não mexem comigo não*), it was clear that the drug trade had a more implicit power over the neighborhood. The network the gang cultivated through favors and threats had rendered formal political spaces inadequate, if not outright dangerous, for demanding a fair distribution of resources or meaningful representation with government officials. Drug traffickers also administered law and order, since the police only entered to search for drugs or make arrests and rarely (if ever) policed interpersonal crimes. Drug lords "assisted" residents with "protection" from petty crime, including theft, vandalism, and bar fights. They sometimes policed child abuse and domestic violence, and I knew several women who only found peace from an abusive partner after asking the local drug lord to intervene. I also heard of men being horrendously tortured and killed after accusations of child abuse, often with very little, if any, evidence of guilt. In theory, these interventions are meant to establish a reciprocal relationship between drug gangs and the community (Silva 2008; de Souza 2005). However, this relationship is far from even: drug traffickers can impose their demands at any time through the threat of violence while residents rely constantly on their good graces. Additionally, the safety and freedom that residents must give up far exceeds the benefits of gang-mediated law and order.

When I learned that Rafael's son was taking soccer classes with one of the local community-based organizations, I breathed a sigh of relief. From what I had observed, there was a decent chance that drug traffickers were not involved in funding this CBO, which more likely was receiving support from a government program or private philanthropist. It would be less likely that the boy or his family would have to "repay" a debt for soccer training or risk violent retaliation for non-payment. Taking classes through a CBO would put some distance between the child and the violent tentacles that reached into so many neighborhood spaces. I secretly hoped the child did not display too much talent, however, lest he also get trapped in the costly dream of making it big—which no local CBO could afford to fund on their own. But in CDD, the dream of making it big was also critical to keeping hope alive in a neighborhood with so few alternatives. Fortunately, violent clientelism was not the only avenue for obtaining resources or becoming politically engaged.

Non-Violence as Political Sphere

While local drug traffickers joust with the police and corrupt politicians for control over the physical territory and the enforcement of law and order, they are not the only favela residents who manage the neighborhood.

Community-based organizations, the Residents' Board, community journalists, and art collectives also play an essential role in overseeing the community through the provision of social and cultural resources. While we commonly view the government as responsible for governing its citizens, the concept of *governance* recognizes that a broad array of both state and non-state actors can partake in these tasks. As Mark Hufty (2011:405) explains:

> Governance does not presuppose vertical authority and regulatory power as the concept of "political system" and the traditional idea of "politics" do. It refers to formal and informal, vertical and horizontal processes, with no a priori preference . . . Using a governance perspective permits the inclusion of all political processes, including formal ones, those embedded in larger social systems, and unrecognized ones.

In informal neighborhoods and conflict zones, where the presence of the state is often weak and/or fragmented, it is essential to examine the role of non-state actors in local governance. In Cidade de Deus, activists have deployed a host of strategies to identify, access, and distribute resources to the neighborhood, help to improve living conditions, and advocate for residents' rights. This often involves working with state officials in the social service branches of the state and with private philanthropic organizations in order to direct resources to the most urgent issues. Community-based organizations were often the first stop for residents looking to address a variety of needs. Access to food, help finding a job, care for children or the elderly, the development of new skills, even basic health care were often administered by CBOs who carefully managed funds from government grants and private donors to spread resources as widely as possible. They also partnered frequently with staff from local public institutions, inviting them to talk about welfare and healthcare benefits or organizing joint events for the neighborhood, such as vaccine drives or courses on citizenship rights.

The Residents' Board has also played a critical role in advocating for the development needs of Cidade de Deus. In recent years, the board worked with municipal officials to increase the number of trash collection days, to clean up debris sites, and to add "community cleaners" who swept many of the main streets. The board successfully mobilized the municipal government to construct new housing units for families who had lost their homes in the 1996 flood and were living in temporary homes. Geovana, Carmen, and the other board members spoke fondly of this project. They worked with the architecture department at Rio's state university to meet with displaced residents and collectively design models for the houses in which they wished to live. At the same time, they refused to allow outside contractors to take on the project, insisting that Cidade de Deus residents be trained, organized into a cooperative, and hired to build the homes. Though their original request was for 4,000 units, they succeeded in securing the construction of 618 homes, which have now been inhabited for over a decade. The board also secured partners to fund the establishment of a community radio station that shared public interest stories and information about courses and upcoming events. Youth Promise—with a great deal of support from Solange and Maria Rita—had embraced the task of overseeing the radio station.

In 2011, the Residents' Board worked with a local social development organization to secure a grant from the Municipal Secretariat for the Development of Economic Solidarity, which allowed them to open the first Community Bank in Brazil. As I detailed in Chapter 2, the board has helped bring multiple forms of development to the neighborhood, including a local currency, several additional public schools, more resources for the local health clinic, and a host of other improvements. Often, board members succeeded by partnering with urban NGOs, private companies, universities, and allies in various branches of the municipal and state governments. The board also created an online portal in which government and private actors could learn about the board and local CBOs to promote new partnership and funding opportunities. Some of the partnerships were with various secretariats at the municipal and state levels, public research institutes, federal and state universities, the social service branch of private conglomerates, and international organizations, such as UNESCO and Action Aid, all of which provided funds or other resources to offer the types of trainings or services that addressed the demands in the development plan.

Isabella also took a leading role in addressing immediate issues through CDD Connects, which became so popular that not only residents but also politicians and state administrators followed the page. Isabella routinely posted stories about government mismanagement of buildings, public spaces, and public social services, tagging the Regional Administration and calling for them to intervene. In 2015, for instance, she made and posted a video of water pouring out of a pipe near a preschool that had been without water for weeks.

Do the basic math: This video is 36 seconds. How much water was wasted during this recording? Now multiply that by 1 month uninterrupted. A lot, no? This leak is on Travessa Lilas. Because of this waste, the Monica Preschool is without water. Residents claim they have called and filed complaints, asked for solutions at the "pretend" office of CEDAE [the city's water company] and still this clean water is going to waste. Maybe the Regional Administration of Cidade de Deus can ask the people of "Conservethemselves" to resolve this issue ☺.

In a reply to the post, that same day, the Regional Administration said they had already sent a team to fix the problem. The next day, another resident replied on the post that no team had actually come. Five days later Isabella replied that the water was still leaking. Finally, a full week later, another resident replied to the thread that CEDAE workers were on site and working on the leak, thanking CDD Connects for helping get this done. Isabella's Facebook page is replete with hundreds of such stories, in which a resident sounds the alarm about broken infrastructure, piles of garbage, downed wires, water shortages, and many other public issues. Isabella did not hesitate to tag the Regional Administration and call out various branches of the municipal government for their neglect and demand attention. By publicly "outing" their failures, Isabella managed to exert pressure on state institutions to address public maintenance issues in the neighborhood.

CDD Connects had also achieved incredible success locating missing children and adults. While finding missing people may be the police's job in other areas, in CDD, Isabella was residents' best hope. I was constantly amazed by how frequently CDD Connects shared pictures and information about someone who had gone missing—where they had last been seen, what they were wearing, etc.—only to post a picture with the words "Found" stamped across the post a day or two later. Over the years, the number of located people reached into the hundreds. Through the prolific reach of the Facebook page, CDD Connects successfully filled an essential role that neither the police nor the drug trade fulfilled.

CDD's art collectives were vital in distributing cultural rights and resources to the neighborhood. Local artists routinely organized events inviting children and adult members of the community to paint benches and posts in colorful designs, to create murals, and to perform dance, theater, and percussion shows, among many other events. "Art in the Park" was among the favorite and most long-running events. Organized by an older man with a long, white beard and Luz, the artist discussed in Chapters 1 and 2, Art in the Park provided a variety of art supplies, paper, and canvases for children to sit outside in the park and paint together. Through these and many other events, activists provided the community with access to materials and the opportunity to develop artistic skills that the severely under-resourced public schools often were unable to offer. In other cases, poets and writers from the community partnered with the public schools to provide poetry and writing classes in the schools. While private schools in Rio de Janeiro, and many public schools in the United States and Europe provide their children with these cultural rights, in Cidade de Deus, local activists have had to fill this space.

Drug traffickers and unarmed activists are central actors in neighborhood governance. While the drug trade enforces law and order, controls formal political associations, and imposes territorial control, the sphere of non-violent politics locates and distributes social and cultural resources, addresses residents' urgent issues, and promotes civic engagement. In contrast to violent clientelism, whose connections to the state are often through illicit ties with corrupt officials and the police, non-violent politics connects to social institutions within the government via licit channels, such as by administering a grant from the municipal government, co-organizing a community event with public servants, or calling elected officials to demand their rights be upheld. Both groups of favela residents (drug traffickers and activists) take leadership in managing the everday affairs of the neighborhood and cultivate relationships with state actors, and both have become central to local governance.

Given the many risks involved in sharing governing power with armed actors, activists were intentional about keeping their practices as separate from those of the drug trade as possible. While ordinary residents like Seu Tony and Esther were at times willing to ask drug lords for favors for needy families or aspiring athletes, activists were not. The leaders, staff, and volunteers of CBOs and *coletivos* were decidedly committed to avoiding any connections to violent clientelism. I did not know of any activist who owned a gun, and I never heard any story or even rumor of an activist utilizing their ties to a drug trafficker or other armed resident to gain an advantage in a relationship. While most activists did know one or several members of the gang they avoided close relationships with gang members at all costs. Additionally, as I detail later in this chapter, they refused resources connected to drug traffickers or anyone believed to be associated with the drug trade, thereby preventing the kind of repayment expectations that Seu Tony had faced.

This is not to say activists never broke the law. Rumors occasionally circulated that some CBO leaders pocketed money from government grants to pay their own bills, which fomented suspicion and distrust between activists. Residents pointed to evidence of corruption in CBOs when, for instance, a CBO won a government grant but did not offer the promised activities. Given how rarely the public was privy to detailed information about the funds any given CBO received or how they were spent, what people believed about a CBO or its leaders was often more powerful than the truth. The ease with which rumors of corruption could spread also reaffirmed the very slippery slope that activists faced in preserving their reputation and legitimacy in the eyes of the community.

Activists could also be accused of putting their desire for fame and status above the needs of their clients or colleagues if, for instance, they accepted an offer to give a talk about their organization's work, were interviewed by local newspapers without consulting others, or vied for a job in a large urban NGO, presumably leaving their colleagues—and their community—behind in pursuit of success. In a context where being poor and from a favela severely limited one's chances of rising in the ranks of urban society, activism had become one of the few avenues for urban respectability, and some activists used their work to climb the NGO ladder. Finally, as I describe in the Appendix, the only man I ever felt directly threatened by was a leader of an important favela-based cultural movement. As Lee Ann Fuji (2011) has noted in her research on political violence in Rwanda, fixed categories of "perpetrators" and "victims" severely oversimplify and misconstrue the dynamism and fluidity of violent acts on the ground. Activists, like drug traffickers and other favela residents, are people with layers of complexity. Just like other people, they could engage in theft, backstabbing, and interpersonal violence, even while participating in movements and espousing values that advocated for nonviolence, equality, and social justice. At the same time, they worked hard to preserve their reputation and avoid any rumors of illegality or immorality in order to distance themselves and their collectives from the sphere of violent governance.

Keeping this distance was further complicated by the fact that most activists had connections to individual drug traffickers through kinship ties or other social networks. Given how many young men joined (and sometimes left) the drug trade, most people were connected to someone in a gang, or someone who had once been in a gang. Esther and Maria Rita knew several young men whom they had helped to care for as children who eventually decided to join the drug trade. Additionally, most of the children and vulnerable adults who received services from local CBOs were related to people in the drug trade. As I describe later, the impossibility of avoiding all ties to violent clientelism made the *performance* of non-violence of utmost importance. Even as activists acknowledged and sometimes engaged in interpersonal relationships with people connected to the drug trade or corrupt politics, they worked hard to keep these actors in the realm of "weak ties," they avoided any formal or informal partnerships with corrupt or violent actors, and they regularly expressed their commitment to peace and social justice. Individuals could not always be kept apart, but the activist sphere positioned itself as economically, politically, and morally separate from violent clientelism.

Although non-violent politics stood, in many respects, as an oppositional force to the drug trade, drug traffickers generally allowed CBOs and informal collectives to continue their work without constant threats, extortion, or other disturbances. I did hear of a handful of cases in which activists had been warned by drug traffickers to stand down when their protests directly challenged drug traffickers, and I have no doubt that there were other such cases that were never shared with me. However, within the constraints imposed by gangs, activists were largely able to oversee the cultural and social development of the neighborhood without the interference of or threats from them. Why did local drug lords allow activists this freedom and this power? How have non-violent politics managed to survive within a context of violent clientelism?

When I asked activists these questions, they often cited the common saying: *If you stay away from them, they stay away from you.* My observations of how activist groups operated—keeping great distance from gangs—suggests that this was certainly an important component of the explanation. I had found this to be true in my own experiences of fieldwork in Cidade de Deus. I never intervened in the drug trade's affairs, and to my knowledge they never intervened in mine. However, given the long history of the execution of leaders of civic associations and the co-opting of political organizations, the relative autonomy of non-violent politics in Cidade de Deus hinged on more than just separation. Politics in CDD rested on a number of invisible social forces and more consciously intentional practices that had to be navigated with great caution. These include the gendered division of governing labor, the spaces created by the fragmentation of sovereignty, and a strategic avoidance of any participation that could be tied back to drug gangs.

The Gendered Division of Governing Labor

Rosangela and I stood in front of a bright yellow aluminum door surrounded by a sky-blue cement wall with yellow trim. On the door was a poster announcing an upcoming computer class. It was my first day in Cidade de Deus, and Rosangela had kindly offered to bring me to Youth Promise.

Rosangela rang the buzzer, and a voice came on: "Good afternoon?" "Hi, it's Rosangela and Anjuli," Rosangela responded. The door buzzed open, and we made our way through an open veranda with shiny white tiles and sky-blue walls to a narrow hallway and turned a sharp right up uneven cement stairs to the second floor. We came to a small landing packed with over a dozen children chatting animatedly. Some stood, others sat squished together onto the three chairs lining the hallway. Over their heads we could see into the main office, which was also packed with children gathered around two large office desks. Rosangela nodded her head toward Solange, a white, middle-aged woman with short curly blonde hair sitting behind a large desk in a swivel chair she had turned to face two girls of about ten years of age. It was impossible to hear her over the laughter and chatter of the other children, but from the girls' bowed heads and the stern look on Solange's face it seemed clear that they were being scolded. After a minute, she pointed at the two girls, and they turned to each other and uttered what appeared to be half-hearted apologies. "Come get your snacks!" a woman's voice resounded over the noise from the kitchen next door. Excused, the two girls ran off to join the other children lining up to receive their snacks—a juice box, saltine crackers, and a piece of chocolate packaged into small paper bags.

Solange made her way out of the office and over to us and gave me a warm hug, welcoming me to Youth Promise. The two girls, she told us with a sigh, had exchanged some unpleasant words and a few pushes before the teacher intervened and sent them down to the office. We watched as the sea of children dispersed down the steps with their snacks. "Good-bye, Tia Solange!" some of the children shouted,[2] glancing at me with curiosity. Within five minutes, the children were gone, and Youth Promise fell silent. Solange apologized for the craziness and proceeded to introduce me to the two women in the kitchen: Andressa, who had been handing out snacks, and

Vanda, who helped with cooking and cleaning. "Sure smells good in here," Solange noted as she lifted the lid of a pot of steaming chicken. A tall man with abnormally smooth ears, characteristic of martial arts competitors,[3] descended from the third floor. "This is our wonderful jiu-jitsu teacher," Solange smiled as she made the introduction. After I greeted each of the staff with the typical kiss on each cheek, Solange and I made our way back to the office where we spent the next hour talking about Youth Promise and how I might be of help.

Throughout my many trips to CDD and my time volunteering at Youth Promise, I was able to observe Solange's motherly approach to her flock of children, volunteers, and staff. It was not uncommon to find Solange behind a desk surrounded by children, hard at work applying for a grant, or bent over putting ointment on a child's skinned knee. Her other staff, nearly all women with the exception of a few male teachers, were similarly caring of each other, the children in the program, and the children's parents. This care came in the form of affection, education, and the provision of services, as well as disciplining practices intended to address problematic behaviors. Solange, Maria Rita, and Camila also worked tirelessly to help the caretakers of their youth—usually mothers or grandmothers—find food, housing, transportation to a job interview, or solutions to any other urgent need, though this type of social service work fell outside of their organization's formal programming. Youth Promise also had a strong social media presence, which they utilized to showcase the children's activities, send messages praising the projects the children accomplished, and affirm their commitment to racial justice and gender equality. The regular postings also provide evidence that the funds they received were being put toward the promised events and resources.

Solange and Youth Promise's motherly style in caring for the community represented a feminized approach to activism that I similarly observed among many other activist groups. The Residents' Board was run by several strong, fierce women, including Carmen, Clara, and Geovana, who tackled the social development needs of the neighborhood, in many respects acting as the caretakers of the community. Most of CDD's art collectives are also run by women and engaged in practices we might think of as feminine: hosting activities for children and youth, helping to beautify the physical landscape, and encouraging the social and educational development of its residents through courses and skill-building workshops. Across the spectrum of CDD's "clusters" of political organizing, women's leadership plays a central role in enabling local activists to organize politically without upsetting the local structures of masculine governance.

Feminized non-violent politics can be understood as occupying an oppositional space to masculinized violent governance. While there were many men involved in local activist efforts, male leaders were in the minority and were sometimes viewed with distrust and suspicion by other residents. The few male leaders I knew made frequent public remarks about the leadership roles of various women in their organizations. Leonardo, himself a local CBO leader, emphasized to me that this sphere was governed primarily by women. Meanwhile, Jefferson, the karatê teacher and president of a cultural CBO in CDD, was constantly praising the hard work and leadership of the women in his group, emphasizing that his role was mostly to carry out their orders. Additionally, activists, particularly those most well-known in the neighborhood, were expected to perform femininity by expressing their concern for vulnerable populations and their commitment to care work. For instance, several of the male activists I met worked as educators, teaching courses to children and adolescents on acting, photography, dancing, or writing that incorporated themes around human rights, while also engaging in other types of social organizing or political work. By taking on some of the many activities associated with care work, female and male activists enacted a feminized role in the neighborhood.

It has become common to associate politics with men and masculinity. In fact, in 2016, women held only 13% of elected municipal posts and 10% of national representative positions in Brazil (Cazarré 2016). Men are more likely to be asked to serve in high-level government posts, and men are often the spokespeople or appointed leaders of contentious, anti-institutional politics, including labor unions and many social movements. Furthermore, as previously noted, gang territories are often governed by informal networks of male "specialists of violence," corrupt politicians, and local "big men." However, for all that has been studied and written about masculinity in gang territories, we have paid much less attention to its symbolic opposite: femininity. When studies of politics in areas of violence and conflict focus on clientelism and the ties between armed actors, this brings attention to relations between men and the ways in which masculinity becomes connected to violence. While masculinity and violence are central to understandings of politics in conflict zones, they only represent half of the gendered field of power that characterizes this environment. Cynthia Cockburn reminds us of the importance of applying a more complete gendered analysis by asking, *where are the women?* (Cockburn 2004). By looking toward the women and forms of femininity in conflict zones, we can shift our lens away from clientelism and notice other forms of political action. For instance, in her exploration of housing activism in a poor neighborhood in the predominantly Black Brazilian state of Bahia, Kheisha-Kahn Perry found that Black women were "key political interlocutors between local communities and the Brazilian state for greater access to resources. They are the foot soldiers of the historical struggle for social and territorial belonging, participatory urbanizing policies and improved living conditions for black citizens in Brazil" (2013:15).

As Perry's finding suggests, when we move our focus away from electoral politics and clientelism and toward the fight for resources and rights, women—and in many cases, Black women in particular—emerge as meaningful political leaders. Across Latin America, women have played key roles in community organizing, service provision, and demanding resources from the state (Berry 2018; Zulver 2022). According to Perry, Black women play key economic and social roles in their neighborhood and often serve as "mediators of familial and social relationships within their communities, influencing political decisions and how important resources such as land are distributed" (Perry 2013:15). Women's political leadership in poor neighborhoods emerges from the gendered distribution of socio-political roles, which places female bodies in a position to understand and advocate for community needs (Fernandes 2007).

Solange's approach to leadership also demonstrates the centrality of motherhood in activist work. Motherhood is often viewed as one of the greatest social contributions with which women are tasked. In poor neighborhoods, where mutual assistance is crucial to survival, women are expected to care for their own biological children as well as other family members and vulnerable people. Esther herself was a mother figure to nearly a dozen adolescents whose mothers had died or were abusive, and she was often called upon to assist sick or hungry neighbors. While some men did also embrace parental roles beyond their families, the expectation and burden of this care remains strongly feminized.

Drawing on her research in the poor *barrios* of Venezuela under Hugo Chávez, Sujatha Fernandes argues that women's social role as mothers pushed them into community care work, which in turn transformed women into political actors. According to Fernandes, barrio women "utilized a maternal-centered notion of responsibility and nurturance as the basis of their political identity" (2007:122). In the context of male-dominated Chavista networks and institutions, women's involvement with the local needs of their neighborhoods provided them a unique space in which to become politically active. She writes:

> Despite male leadership and authority, the growing presence of women in local assemblies, committees, and communal kitchens has created forms of popular participation that challenge gender roles, collectivize private tasks, and create alternatives to male-centric politics. Women's experiences of shared struggle from previous decades, along with their use of democratic methods of popular control, such as local assemblies, help to prevent the state's appropriation of women's labor for its own ends. (Fernandes 2007:98)

As women occupy the spaces of social development not properly filled by the state or, in the case of CDD, by armed drug traffickers, the leadership over activities that began as an extension of motherhood transform women into political subjects. Ironically, the very act of performing traditional gender roles produces its opposite: the private sphere becomes public, and women's domestic work turns political.

In contexts of armed conflict, the gendered division of care work is further entrenched. Mothers (and grandmothers, aunties, or non-biological female guardians) are usually the primary caretakers of the men killed in armed conflict. When they become organized, women's groups also become powerful advocates for peace and mobilizers against armed conflict (Zubillaga, Llorens, and Souto 2019). The anti-dictatorship movement led by the Madres de la Plaza de Mayo in Argentina in the 1970s is perhaps the best-known example of politicized motherhood. However, stories abound of women protesting against state brutality targeted against their children (Diego Rivera Hernández 2017; Gallo-Cruz 2020; Hasić, Karabegović, and Turković 2020; Santiago et al. 2017). When maternal grief for the loss of a child due to racialized physical and structural violence becomes expressed through activism, it becomes what Erica Lawson terms "public motherhood," rather than a "private expression of pain" (Lawson 2018:713). Thus, while motherhood may not be commonly associated with activism, "gender and motherhood become the foundation for work that is implicitly and explicitly political and often transgresses social boundaries within local communities" (Vogt 2018:189).

In contexts of violence, motherhood can serve as a strong unifying force. Rosangela had once made the point that "there is no difference between mothers of PMs (military police) and mothers of criminals—both worry about whether their sons will return alive." As mothers and caretakers, women bear a heavy emotional toll from the constant worry that their children might be killed in conflict. This fear and pain can be generative of action. Women have become embroiled in anti-violence work in regions under armed conflict across the globe. In Sierra Leone, women mobilized against the war and promoted the reintegration of ex-combatants at higher rates than traditional leaders or international aid workers (Mazurana, Carlson, and Anderlini 2004). In Colombia, women's groups have helped to promote healing, peace-building, and collective memory projects in the aftermath of the decades-long civil war (Menés 2020), even when the risks of activism were high (Zulver 2022). In Mexico, feminist groups actively decry *feminicidios* and militarized violence (Staudt and Méndez 2015). And in the gang territories of Caracas, mothers help to resist violence by negotiating truces between gangs or using the power over their (armed) sons to pressure them to respect cease fires (Zubillaga et al. 2019). While women often become involved in anti-violence activism to protect their families, friends, and their neighborhoods, they are also uniquely positioned to advocate for peace and help rebuild war-torn communities.

The politicization of femininity in CDD was also reflected in the fervor with which Residents' Board leaders, such as Carmen, Clara, and Geovana, fought for social development in their neighborhood. By engaging in grassroots organizing, these powerful women extended the care discourse beyond the children and families in their organizations to the entire community by fighting for collective resources and services. By connecting their political efforts to communal caretaking, they could leverage this feminized role to legitimize more explicitly contentious claims-making. This extension of the domestic sphere outward to the neighborhood is not unique to Cidade de Deus. In a context of both poverty *and* warfare, women's community organizing has become even more accentuated and necessary. When clientelism becomes conflated not only with corruption but also with violence, non-violent activism becomes relationally tied to the feminine. According to Marie Berry:

> As is frequently the case in the developing or post-socialist world, non-governmental organizations (NGOs) can represent a dynamic space in between the public "male" government realm and the private "feminine" one. Such an in-between space—or "third sector"—must be

considered when looking at women's political power," particularly after war (2018:12).

While CDD was still very much "at war," Berry's point remains salient: the sphere of non-violence operates as a feminine space in contrast to the male sphere of violent clientelism. When non-violent politics becomes feminized, it comes to be perceived as subordinate and not directly threatening to the masculinized violent sphere. (Male) drug lords are less likely to be intimidated by female CBO leaders, particularly when these leaders are engaged in feminized labor. Thus, by placing women in leadership roles, the sphere of non-violence performs the "private" work of caretaking, but does so in collective and public spaces that enable it to serve a political role, yet one that does not directly confront violent clientelism.

There were both benefits and costs to the gendered relations of politics in Cidade de Deus, however. For instance, different people received different rewards for their participation in each sphere. Men participating in masculinized violent politics could bolster their claims to hyper-masculinity, which could be rewarded through promotions within the gang and access to material objects such as guns, motorcycles, money, and drugs, as well as women. Men engaged in violent clientelism were also much more likely to be killed. Meanwhile, women participating in the feminized sphere of non-violence were rewarded with praise for their commitment to community work and their moral contributions to the neighborhood, a theme I return to in Chapter 4. However, feminized social services came with few financial benefits. Most activists worked for very little money, if any at all. The work was exhausting on many fronts. Maria Rita, Solange, Carmen, and many others had often told me how emotionally draining the work was, having to expend many hours of labor for little pay while constantly worrying about the vulnerable children and families they served. Meanwhile, Geovana, one of the board leaders, who was in her 60s when I met her, had no retirement savings and was beginning to have serious health issues. She worried about how she would survive and get the care she needed.

While individual women gain moral capital from this work, what motivates men to participate in non-violent activism? For some men, CBOs provided an avenue to "get ahead," allowing men with more political ambitions to demonstrate their dedication to the neighborhood, to gain support when they ran for public office. Solange, Geovana, and many other activists I met were suspicious of male volunteers who aspired to a political life, approaching them with a high degree of caution, fearful of being taken advantage of or—worse—becoming inadvertently embroiled in illegal schemes. Most male activists I met, however, had no desire to run for office and did not appear to obtain any reward from this work beyond participation in activities they believed in and had been dedicated to for many years. I believe that CBOs and informal collectives provided a safe space in which to enact alternative forms of masculinity that did not cater to hegemonic values of violence, aggression, competition, and corruption.

In an analysis of how transgender men enact different constructs of masculinity, Miriam Abelson found that transgender men frequently enacted "transformative masculinity," which aimed to "fundamentally alter the gender system" by promoting gender equality whenever they were in safe spaces, such as in female dominated spaces or LGBTQ-friendly groups (Abelson 2014:562–63). These same men felt more constrained in expressing views of gender equality and defending women in more male-dominated spaces. Abelson's study ultimately points to the importance of spaces and their gendered meanings in creating the potential for alternative expressions of masculinity. In Cidade de Deus, Youth Promise and the many other organizations and collectives dedicated to non-violence provide physical and social spaces in which men who aspire to enact masculinity differently from the drug trade and Brazil's corrupt politics can safely perform transformative masculinity. Within this political sphere, the meanings of masculinity can be challenged and re-written, allowing men to "be men" by working against violence, rather than participating in it.

Fragmented Sovereignty and the Spaces for Civil Society

The autonomy afforded to CDD's sphere of non-violent politics has also been aided by fragmented sovereignty. Governance of conflict zones can take many different forms, which vary based on the approaches of criminal regimes to territorial control, relationships to state actors, and community relations (Magaloni, Franco-Vivanco, and Melo 2020). In his typologies of criminal-state relationships across Latin America, Nicholas Barnes identifies four forms of "arrangements" between the state and non-state armed actors. On one end of the spectrum, he argues that confrontation between criminal gangs and the police is the most competitive type of arrangement. On the other end of the spectrum, criminal groups can be "directly incorporated into the state apparatus, allowing criminals to engage in violent and illegal activities with impunity" (Barnes 2017:973). The politics of the *Comando Vermelho* gang that dominates Cidade de Deus lies on the "confrontational" end of the spectrum, though they also engage in some collaborative relations with local-level officials. This arrangement results in constant disequilibrium, whereby competition between state and non-state armed actors makes it difficult for any one entity to assert complete control over the territory. Since political alliances are fragile and may be disrupted at any time, drug lords may be so focused on maintaining the upper hand in their daily battles with the police that little impetus remains to exert coercive control over small-scale civic associations. The result is a complex landscape of multiple state and non-state actors who take on different roles and activities.

Such instability and diversity are not just features of Cidade de Deus. In an analysis of shifting patterns of citizenship and sovereignty in the modern era, Diane Davis (2010:402) argues that non-state armed actors are creating new imagined communities in contexts of poverty and political exclusion. Particularly in "brown zones," where state institutions are weak or absent, drug gangs are able to compete for territorial control and local sovereignty, thereby fragmenting power, governance and citizenship.

The fragmentation of sovereign rule is both destructive and productive. In Cidade de Deus, violent confrontations produce chaos and disorder, putting residents' lives at risk and making everyday living unpredictable and incredibly stressful. Local activists had to constantly contend with this chaos, often canceling meetings at the last minute due to shootouts nearby. However, the chaos also created spaces for civic engagement and governance. Given the limited power of the Comando Vermelho gang over the civic life of the neighborhood, activists were able to help fill the governance void. Enrique Desmond Arias found a similar phenomenon in Rocinha, Rio's largest favela. According to Arias, there was a greater density and independence of civic associations in gang-controlled Rocinha than in Rio das Pedras, where vigilante *milícia* groups are more tightly connected to the state and exert greater control over civic life. In Rocinha, much like in Cidade de Deus, the gang's "uneven relationship with the state prevented it from fully dominating local social life" (Arias 2017:161). The "divided governance" between gangs and the police thus created opportunities for non-armed actors in Rocinha to establish local organizations without constant oversight from gangs, provided they did not engage in street protests or mobilization activities that threated drug operations.

Marie Berry, in her research on gendered politics in post-war Bosnia and Rwanda, argues that war has transformative power, producing radical shifts in the social and political context, which can create opportunities for women's leadership. War, she claims, "can loosen the hold of traditional gendered power relations as it restructures the institutional and structural layout of society," leading to the increased participation of women in "informal political capacities" (Berry 2018:14). This argument can be usefully extended to gang territories. In Cidade de Deus, where armed conflict between gangs and the police have been raging for over fifty years with no end in sight, gendered possibilities emerge not from the end of war but from fragmented sovereignty, which engenders both political disorder as well as space for alternative forms of political leadership. Since state officials cannot impose complete control over the neighborhood and drug lords are too busy defending their territory to manage the paving of roads and the staffing of schools, non-armed residents take on a vital role in the management and maintenance of the neighborhood.

This division of governing labor appeared to work well for the Comando Vermelho. The economic viability of the drug trade relies on favela activist efforts, who help to promote social development and keep the neighborhood functioning. Paved roads allow middle-class customers to drive in to purchase drugs, and functioning hospitals enable injured gang members to receive care for bullet wounds. Individual drug traffickers, most of whom were CDD residents, also benefited from these services. Drug traffickers are, after all, people with physical and emotional needs. They need water, food, and clothes to survive. They have grandparents who need companionship and medical care, they have children who need to be cared for and educated, they have girlfriends and wives who need reproductive care and job training. In their efforts to improve the neighborhood, activists also maintain the basic conditions of development needed for the survival of drug traffickers and the successful operation of the drug trade.

Non-violent politics thus operates as a parallel force to criminal governance, filling the gaps in services that have emerged thanks to the fragmentation of state sovereignty. While drug traffickers mediate relations with armed state actors, activists cultivate ties with public administrators and policymakers in the social branches of the state. As the image in Chart 3.1 illustrates, the state engages with both armed and non-violent groups in CDD to administer governance. On one side, the state's security apparatus negotiates territorial control and law and order with drug gangs; on the other

Gendered Division of Governing Labor

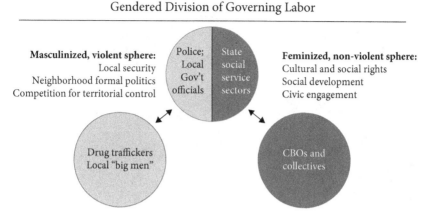

Masculinized, violent sphere:
Local security
Neighborhood formal politics
Competition for territorial control

Police;
Local
Gov't
officials

State
social
service
sectors

Feminized, non-violent sphere:
Cultural and social rights
Social development
Civic engagement

Drug traffickers
Local "big men"

CBOs and
collectives

Chart 3.1 Gendered division of governing labor

side, various state branches that deal with health, education, housing, and development work with activists to implement new projects, improve services, distribute resources, and promote participation in civic groups and activities. I look more closely at the relationship between activists and the state in Chapter 5. The important point here is that the fragmentation of sovereignty in Cidade de Deus has bifurcated local governance, such that activists also cultivate relationships with the state in order to improve neighborhood conditions and administer services to residents.

It is important to note that occasionally drug lords also helped to provide some basic services in the neighborhood. For one, drug lords issued "mandates" or rules, that were displayed in spray paint across the neighborhood or disseminated through word of mouth. One apartment complex, for instance, had been spray painted with the phrase: "Whoever is caught stealing will die. Signed CV." Another mandate had been painted on a cement wall: "Don't throw trash here. CV." These signs were often effective: I never saw any trash near no-trash warnings from the Comando Vermelho. The same could not be said for state signs. I once walked with Isabella past a giant heap of trash in front of a sign the municipal government had installed that read "No trash allowed here" (Figure 3.1) Chuckling, I pointed out the irony to Isabella, who simply responded, "If only the CV would put up a sign, the trash wouldn't be here."

The drug trade also offered charity to needy residents. According to Leonardo, one of the local managers for the drug trade spent

Figure 3.1 "Attention: Forbidden to throw trash"
Photo by the author.

R$60,000—approximately USD$15,000—a year on "cesta básica," or gift baskets with food and basic supplies to be distributed to needy families. He also recounted another time when he was helping to collect and hand out Christmas presents for poor children as part of a local *projeto* and he and his colleagues saw a man with a well-known affiliation with the drug trade taking photos of the event with his phone. They went over to ask him what he was doing, and the man asked what the event was all about and whether the UPP was paying for it. When they told him it was all funded by donations, he was shocked. "You got all this from donations? Without any help from anyone?" He went off and talked to someone on the phone, who said, "Man, we aren't doing anything to help? See what they need." Leonardo mentioned that all the soda was getting warm because they had no ice. Soon a whole truck full of ice showed up, paid for by the local drug manager. In small ways, drug gangs contribute to social needs, often in one-off situations like this one. These contributions were mostly symbolic, helping them show their support for the community without having to do much. They were not involved in the everyday management of civic life, however, leaving the organization of associational life to local activists instead.

Figure 3.2 A UPP police precinct in CDD, which remained under construction for several years
Photo by the author.

A Tenuous Co-Existence

While gendered governance and fragmented sovereignty provided opportunities for non-violent political action that CBOs and collectives could wiggle into, activists also had to engage in much more conscious decision-making to circumvent violent political networks. Drug lords were not eager to share power with community leaders, and activists knew this well. People with too much power—such as those with wealth, many religious or social "followers," or political connections—were more likely to have access to financial resources the gang leaders might want; or they could become a liability if they decided to speak out against the drug lords. Favela activists thus had to be extremely vigilant over their own financial success and social status in the neighborhood. Members of the Residents' Board were especially careful to minimize their positions of authority. Many times, Geovana, Clara, and other board members emphasized to me that they were *not* representatives of the community. To be a community representative

Figure 3.3 A "caveirão" or "big skull" armored vehicle driving through Cidade de Deus
Photo by anonymous.

would be to classify oneself as a political leader and become a target for co-optation or violence.

Solange and I had many conversations in which she shared with me her worry about securing enough funds to run Youth Promise, but she also was fearful of getting too much money. Her success, she explained to me, was a double-edged sword. On the one hand, providing many activities and resources for the kids in her program was exciting and helped them fulfill their mission. On the other hand, it made people suspicious of how she was managing to do so much in a community with so few (legal) channels for obtaining money. She worried people would spread rumors that she had received funds from the drug trade or corrupt politicians, which could destroy her reputation. Since the government and private institutions rarely invest heavily in favela-based organizations, CBOs that appear to be well-funded—that have nice equipment, expensive electronics, modern furniture, and new uniforms and backpacks for their participants, etc.—are often believed to be tied to violent clientelism. Solange was adamantly against accepting donations from any actor with ties to the drug trade. As she explained to me, no money was free in CDD. If she accepted a donation tied to the drug trade, that debt would eventually be called in, which could include being asked to store guns or drugs in her organization, or even repaying that donation with funds from a government grant. She also rarely accepted donations from individual politicians, regardless of known ties to the gang. Given the track record of many Brazilian politicians, who were often involved in corruption schemes and sometimes arrested and put in jail, Solange worried that her organization might inadvertently receive illegal funds and face legal consequences.

I had been in her office once when she turned down an offer for free t-shirts from a local state representative. "Imagine," she told me after she hung up the phone, "we all put on the t-shirts and then he's going to want to come and take a picture with us for the newspaper with the shirts. And then he goes and gets arrested for some dirty game, and there I am, smiling like an idiot next to him." In a neighborhood where corruption was so closely tied to violence, Youth Promise could not afford even the appearance of impropriety. Solange also turned down an offer from a local resident to use a building he owned to hold dance classes. Though Youth Promise desperately needed more space to host activities, Solange had heard rumors that the building owner was related to a local drug trafficker. Worried that he might eventually ask for "favors," she decided the space was not worth the risk.

However, there were times when Solange bent her own rules. I was surprised when I learned a few months later that she had accepted financial assistance from another state representative, who would be coming by to pay a visit to Youth Promise. João Carlos, a dance teacher at Youth Promise, explained her logic to me. According to João Carlos, young politicians are more likely than older ones to be corrupted. Although there are plenty of older corrupt politicians, he explained, if a politician is already seasoned and still hasn't shown any sign of corruption (a public scandal, consorting with a suspicious crowd, etc.) then there is a better chance that he is not corrupt. Thus, CBO leaders like Solange had created certain logics to guide their decisions and attempt to avoid dangerous clientelist networks as much as possible.

Other activists I talked to had similar concerns as Solange and, with few exceptions, espoused a refusal to accept illegal money. While it would be impossible for me to know for sure whether CBOs and collectives always turned down resources with known ties to gangs or corrupt actors, what I did witness was a host of groups subsisting on virtually no money at all. Activists' refusal to accept donations from individuals with potential ties to violent clientelism heightened the financial burden of CBOs and collectives and made it extremely challenging to pay workers a living wage or even a small stipend. They often lacked money to pay electricity bills, fix broken computers, or even buy printer paper. Most counted on small donations from private individuals or from stipends provided by larger NGOs outside the favela. Youth Promise succeeded in large part because Solange, with much help from Maria Rita, had become highly adept at obtaining funding through government grants, philanthropic organizations, and private donations. Maria Rita spent tireless nights on the couch writing grants and drafting reports. Most other groups that had managed to provide consistent services over several years had also benefited from the assistance of someone with research and writing skills who knew how to read and complete funding applications. However, many organizations did not have members with those skills and were thus unable to sustain large or regular operations. While the lack of money limited their effectiveness, it was also protective, as it prevented organizations from being suspected of gang involvement or becoming too powerful or threatening to gangs. CBOs and other local groups thus remained economically subordinate to local drug lords, retrenching the unequal divide between gendered political work.

In addition to maintaining a distinctly independent economic network, activists also had to be extremely cautious about avoiding becoming involved in social issues that impacted drug gangs. The Residents' Board was especially at risk of ruffling the wrong feathers in their efforts to fight for improvements to the neighborhood's development landscape. Geovana, one of the founders of the board, offered a useful lens into how she and her colleagues navigated these challenges. Her own strategies were informed by a well-known story of a 1980s activist, João de Mendes, an activist who had been killed after organizing against local drug traffickers.

Much like the Residents' Board in the 2000s, João had helped to organize residents to advocate for housing rights in the 1990s. Instead of mobilizing political action aimed at the municipal government, João organized a housing cooperative, in which he gathered money from residents and put it toward the construction of new homes. João had initially received tacit permission from the drug trade, who wanted to see improvements in the availability of housing but could not themselves be the public face of the movement. However, according to Geovana, João began to "*conscientizar os moradores*," to raise awareness about political issues among residents. He held secret meetings in his house at night, when he knew the drug traffickers would be out selling drugs, talking about how residents should have the power in the community and that they should not allow the drug trade in their neighborhood. His plan backfired. According to Geovana:

> They [the drug traffickers] went and got him at his house, put a hood over his head, took him out of his house and made him dig his own grave, put a gun in the hand of a young boy [and made him shoot him]. He died, was buried. The women came to my house [to tell me. He was shot] in front of the women. He was killed and buried.

During one of our informal after-dinner chats, Esther and Maria Rita began talking about João de Mendes without my bringing it up. Apparently, his murder had become a part of Cidade de Deus's collective memory. According to Esther, he had been brutally tortured before he was finally killed. While the details that Esther recalled of his death seemed to vary from Geovana's account, João's death served as an enduring reminder of what happened to those who attempted to challenge the drug trade.

I asked Geovana how she had managed to avoid the same fate as João. According to Geovana, "I always, always had the wisdom to never directly attack them head on (*bater de frente com eles*). I never challenged them directly." She explained her strategy to me by referencing a talk show she hosted on the local community radio station in the late 1990s with several colleagues:

> I'd get home and the drug traffickers [from my block] would cluster around me on my way home, and say, "Miss Geovana, we are listening to you." So it was a message (i.e. a threat). I did my work that didn't deal [with the drug trade]. But we also didn't announce the *baile funk*, or the deaths of [drug traffickers]. We didn't announce any deaths actually, so we wouldn't have to announce theirs either, you understand? So you had to have wisdom to not affront [them] . . . Our philosophy was the following: we are not police, we are not the justice department, we are not responsible for security. This issue was not our business.

I asked Geovana if they were conscious of this approach, if it required explicit discussion to navigate when and how to talk about security issues or anything related to the drug trade: "No, it was just common knowledge, it was understood . . . I just learned it . . . You notice that people are not talking about that. And sometimes people from Cidade de Deus would come and say 'Oh, we want to talk about this,' and [we'd say], 'No, we don't talk about that issue. Not that issue.' "

As Geovana's response suggests, CDD's activists survive by completely avoiding any discussion of security issues or the drug trade. Instead, they focus on social development issues and explicitly reject requests by residents to bring up matters of insecurity. Furthermore, like Solange, Geovana also avoided any collaborations with drug traffickers and did not allow them to participate in her mobilization efforts insofar as she could avoid it. Thus, activists make an explicit effort to keep their activities as distant from drug traffickers as possible by avoiding any close relationships with politicians or residents believed to have ties to drug traffickers and refusing to publicly discuss issues related to insecurity and criminal justice, which might come across as a challenge to gangs.

Overall, this strategy seemed to be effective, but had its limits. Carmen, affirming during our book workshop the importance of avoiding direct confrontation with drug gangs, explained: "If I had confronted them, I would no longer be alive. And some people say, oh, but you don't fight. We do! Political confrontations, confrontation of ideas, of education, of culture, of ideology, we do confront things." Through this logic of confronting political and social inequities but leaving the drug trade alone, the board had helped to secure a number of important improvements to housing, healthcare, and education in Cidade de Deus. However, once resources came into the neighborhood board members could not always control how they were distributed. Paved roads, for instance, were not only beneficial to residents who could drive their cars and bicycles with greater ease; they also allowed drug traffickers to fly down them on their motorcycles and the military police to roll in with their armored vehicles. The schools they helped get built were constantly shutting down due to shootouts, and most schools were littered with bullet holes. Community projects had at times been forced to close if their activities were located in an area that drug traffickers needed for their own activities. Not unlike gender relations within a patriarchal society, the masculine sphere of politics maintained its dominance over the feminized sphere of non-violence.

Conclusion: On the Edge of Electoral Politics

In 2016, Natalia, the founder of Art Talk, declared her candidacy for City Council. She had announced her bid at one of the monthly open mic meetings, and the audience had fallen silent. I wondered if they were trying to figure out if she was joking, or maybe they believed it was a terrible idea or were worried for her safety, but they were certainly not enthusiastic. Electoral politics was neither an effective nor a safe avenue for making social change in favelas. I feared her candidacy would destroy her reputation, or her life.

I was also curious about what would unfold and quickly volunteered for her campaign. Though over a dozen Cidade de Deus residents had opted to run for City Council that year, Natalia had been only one of two activists I knew who was running for office; most activists would have never even considered the idea. Natalia's party flyer labeled her a "Partner of the City," followed by this description:

> Natalia has a lengthy history of student struggles. She participated in the Municipal Association of Higher Education Students. As a resident of the Cidade de Deus, she founded Art Talk, making her a cultural reference in the city. She is leader of the movement #PeaceCDD against violence. This candidate for city council intends to create grants for poetry readings and cultural circles, to bolster sports projects in favelas, to territorialize the budget for Culture, and stimulate Economic solidarity. She wants to support public college preparatory courses and fight for wifi in the parks.

Natalia had gotten Dona Iracema to write her candidacy song. Dona Iracema was a cultural icon in Cidade de Deus and a beloved member of the artistic community. The refrain for the song, which played over and over on the loudspeaker in front of Natalia's campaign headquarters, teased residents: "I like womeeeeeen . . . (long pause) . . . in politics!" The pause had been intentionally provocative, at once advocating for LGBT rights while also emphasizing women's political empowerment. Natalia also publicized her campaign over a megaphone as she rode on the back of a motorcycle. "The favela needs women in politics!" She shouted into it. "The favela needs to be represented in politics!" As Natalia told me, she believed her leverage came from being "a young female cultural leader from the favela."

Natalia did not win. In fact, of the 51 city councilors elected in 2016, only one of them—Marielle Franco—was from a favela. Marielle was a Black lesbian sociologist who had advocated fiercely for racial justice and gender rights. She and Natalia had been active in the same circle of young favela activists. Once in office, Marielle continued to advocate for progressive politics. She spoke out against police violence and exposed extrajudicial killings in favelas. In March 2018, her car was attacked; both Marielle and her driver were shot and killed. Her murder has had a lasting impact on favela activism.

While many have since dubbed Marielle the "seed" of a larger movement, her execution demonstrates the extreme risks of engaging in formal politics, particularly around issues so closely tied to violent governance networks. The "women's work" of caring for the community can, and in many cases has, transitioned into a radical feminist politics that dares to demand total inclusion in the formal political system and accountability within the criminal justice system at the highest levels of the state. While a handful of brave activists continue to follow in the footsteps of Marielle and Natalia, most of CDD's activists refuse to engage in electoral politics. Many also have become so disillusioned with Brazil's government apparatus that they perceive running for office as not only risky but also ineffective for producing meaningful change. Avoidance of formal politics coupled with a somewhat peaceful co-existence with drug gangs remains the most common path for non-violent action in favelas. It offers an important reminder that, if we are to study non-violent politics in other areas of extreme violence, we must look beyond the formal political system and local clientelist networks. And we must look for the women.

4

Political Upcycling

Anti-Violence Protest through Education, Culture, and Racial Solidarity

Bentinho, you're going to grow	Bentinho, você vai crescer
And learn to listen . . . and to speak . . .	E vai aprender a ouvir . . . e a falar . . .
By questioning you also learn	Perguntar também se aprende . . .
The things of the world, and the world of symbols . . .	As coisas do mundo e mundo dos símbolos . . .
You're going to plant and sow knowledge . . .	Você vai plantar e colher conhecimentos . . .
You're going to do and learn what is culture . . .	Vai fazer e aprender o que é cultura . . .
You're going to recreate the world . . .	Você vai recriar o mundo . . .

Pablo das Oliveiras, 2019

Violence Talk

"This is *not* a war!" exclaimed Leonardo excitedly in reaction to my having just called the police-gang combat in favelas "urban warfare." He threw his hands in the air to emphasize the importance of his point. Heated debates had become among our favorite activities over the years. It was nearing midnight. I sat on the curb outside Esther's front door while Leonardo stood in the middle of the narrow street, a few feet in front of me. I scanned the street for drug traffickers. The intersection just around the bend was among the most popular *bocas de fumo* in the neighborhood. Armed men on motorcycles and on foot constantly passed us to get to and from the *boca*, especially at night when sales and use of drugs ramped up. Several armed

Activism under Fire. Anjuli Fahlberg, Oxford University Press. © Oxford University Press 2023.
DOI: 10.1093/oso/9780197519325.003.0005

men had passed us already. I always felt anxious discussing violence in public areas where drug traffickers might overhear us, but Leonardo seemed unconcerned. Leonardo's cousin, an economics student at a prestigious public university, leaned against an old car and watched our debate with interest. The rest of the family had already retired for the night, bored by our debate, which would likely go on for many more hours. "Well, if it's not a war, what *is* it?" I retorted.

"It is a genocide!" Leonardo exclaimed, throwing his hands in the air again. I should have anticipated his response. Leonardo was a fierce racial justice activist and was among the founding members of a national NGO advocating for the decriminalization of drugs as a long-term solution to aggressive policing in favelas. He echoed the views of many other activists and scholars who have long been referring to police-gang violence in Rio as a genocide, evidenced by the thousands of killings of young Black men by the police each year (Dantas, Dantas, and Cabral 2020; Marques Junior 2020).[1]

I looked around cautiously as I prepared my response. I didn't disagree with Leonardo, but we both enjoyed the debate too much to stop now. When no armed men were in sight, I pointed out that drug gangs also were responsible for thousands of homicides. Leonardo retorted by blaming colonialism and slavery for the strength of drug gangs. I replied that many other residents in CDD called it a war, to which he responded that Reagan's War on Drugs had popularized this term and now even favela residents had internalized that notion. Leonardo had some excellent points, as always, and I eventually conceded and transitioned to a new topic, making a mental note to incorporate his arguments more explicitly into my analysis. But what most struck me about that conversation was how openly he discussed gangs, police, and violence, even as armed men walked by and paid little attention to our noisy banter. No drug traffickers came by to monitor or stop our debate, and neither Leonardo nor his cousin—both well versed in the dos and don'ts of favela living—felt the need to censor our conversation. To the contrary: Leonardo's enthusiastic retorts could be easily heard by those around us.

What enabled him to speak so freely about drugs and violence near drug traffickers? One explanation could be that he was protected by his status as a long-time CDD resident who was well known and well liked by most of the neighborhood, including drug traffickers. Or perhaps no one overheard the details of our discussion. But I suspect Leonardo spoke with ease because he had become adept at navigating the unspoken codes of the favela. Leonardo, like the other activists in Cidade de Deus, had learned to construct

anti-violence narratives within political frames that fit into the larger symbolic fields of the neighborhood. Favela residents, and activists in particular, knew what was tolerated and what was not, and they instinctively
maneuvered the terrains of acceptable political discourse as they constructed
the narratives around which to mobilize non-violent action.

In Chapter 3, I examined the gendered spaces that have emerged in Cidade
de Deus for political action, enabling activists to take on a role in the social and cultural governance of the neighborhood while drug traffickers
remained occupied with security matters. However, favela activism is not
only about the everyday work of governance, but also about public, collective mobilizations against violence. What, then, enables activists to engage in
public forms of non-violent action in a context of armed conflict and political repression?

To answer this, I focus in this chapter on the symbolic spaces that activists
have constructed for their anti-violence work and the strategies—some
negotiated consciously but most enacted intuitively—that they deploy. If
Chapters 2 and 3 were about what activists *do*, this chapter is about what
they *say*, not only among themselves but on public platforms, such as the
streets and social media. I argue that activists engage in *embedded resistance*, framing their activities and organizations to conform to the ideologies,
values, beliefs, and meanings of the neighborhood. In other words, activists
do not speak out against the norms permitted by drug traffickers but rather
work within them. At the same time, they push the bounds of local narratives
by engaging in *political upcycling*, or a reappropriation of local discourses,
identities, and cultural tools to produce new forms of resistance and collective action. They build upon, rather than go against, the symbolic fields of
power in Cidade de Deus.

Social movement scholars use the term "collective action frames" to mean
"action-oriented sets of beliefs and meanings that inspire and legitimate the
activities and campaigns of a social movement organization" (Benford and
Snow 2000:614). Often, frames are deployed to gain momentum, legitimacy,
and mass mobilization among a large group of followers. In Cidade de Deus,
however, frames had a more primal function: to ensure the survival of local
activists. Activists were just as concerned with staying alive as with gaining
support from other residents. To do this, activists relied heavily on their
local, organic knowledge, or a deep understanding of the norms and values
of their neighborhood, in order to both fit in and speak out. As I demonstrate, activists connected local norms and narratives to campaigns for peace

and justice in several ways. First, I provide examples of three different ways in which activists fight against violence within the limits allowed by drug traffickers. I then examine how education and culture, which have strong moral and social power in the neighborhood, provide platforms for residents to engage in more political action. I then detail the importance of organizing against racism in helping to create solidarity across the neighborhood, and between activists and gang members in particular.

Protest within Limits

"This is Lucas Canuto, who was shot to death this afternoon in Karatê," began Isabella's Facebook post on CDD Connects in June 2014. Below the post was a picture of a boy with tan skin and dark, thick hair, standing on a dirt soccer field dressed in a dirty soccer jersey. "A boy of 12 years of age, according to sources, a studious boy, totally of the good (*hiper do bem*), who had a promising future. May God receive him in a good place . . . and comfort the heart of the family. This is a great sorrow for CDDforALL. #mourning." In news articles, witnesses were quoted reporting that the boy had been killed by a stray bullet while five men in Cidade de Deus were shooting at the police (Torres and Guimarães 2014). While the shooters were not identified, they were most likely involved with the drug trade, since few men not involved in gangs openly carry weapons in CDD.

Stories like these are all too common in Cidade de Deus and Rio's many other favelas. These incidents usually begin with a provocation by the police followed by an armed response from drug gangs, often ending with the deaths of gang members, and sometimes innocent civilians. They have become a feature of everyday living, and residents have constructed particular narratives through which to protest against them. Not surprisingly, families are outraged at these deaths. How they respond is instructive of the possibilities of and limits for protest in gang territories.

Family members of "innocent" people[2] killed during shootouts often organize peaceful marches to celebrate the person's life and speak out against violence. In the case of Lucas, where there was ample evidence of his lack of gang involvement, residents were quick to rally. Shortly after his death, his family and friends marched from Cidade de Deus to the local cemetery in Pechincha, the next neighborhood over. Many in the crowd were children. They held signs that read "I just want to be happy, living in the favela where I was born,"[3] and photos of Lucas. "We don't want problems, we don't want issues," his cousin told reporters. "We just don't want Lucas to be forgotten." The phrase "we don't want problems" has become a euphemism favela residents use to communicate indirectly to local gang leaders that they are not challenging the drug trade's actions. The march was small, not particularly well organized, and composed largely of women and children, further evading the appearance of threat to gangs. A news article reported that one of the protestors swore at the UPP police precinct as they walked past it. While protesting against the drug trade was not allowed, showing contempt for the police aligned with the interests of drug gangs and was therefore tolerated by gangs.

Within these constraints, peaceful marches after tragic loss have become a repertoire of collective mourning, even among residents with no affiliation to local CBOs or collectives. Activists took advantage of this opening to organize street protests against violence more generally and the police in particular. For instance, in March 2017, local activists organized a peaceful protest in Cidade de Deus's main park after a series of raids by the police, which had resulted in multiple shootouts and the deaths of four CDD residents.

"Today is a day for protest, to respect life, for dignity, for the right to come and go with safety through the streets of the favela," Natalia posted in a short video on Facebook, inviting people to attend the event. Another local activist posted a similar video calling on residents to participate: "I'm asking all of my friends to come in white, to show that we don't support this violence. This peaceful protest is an act against the violence that our community has suffered, and many innocent victims are losing their lives . . . We need answers from the government of the state and our city. We cannot stand this violence anymore." Approximately 50 residents attended wearing white, holding signs that read "We want the right to come and go" and "CDD Demands Peace." Between 2015 and 2017, a handful of other such protests were organized after the deaths of civilians during police invasions. Like marches organized by victims' families, these protests were also relatively small and composed of many women and children (Figure 4.1). They also avoided any direct mention of gangs. The difference, however, was their more explicit and united calls for action by the state. Rather than mutter discontent under their breath, activists held their banners high, decrying the harm provoked by routinized and aggressive police invasions and demanding that the government halt police raids (Figure 4.2). Activists had a clear target—the state—and a clear set of demands—a stop to policing operations. By

Figure 4.1 Rally for peace after weeks of intense police invasions and shootouts
Photo by anonymous.

conforming to the pre-existing forms of collective mourning tolerated by drug lords, activists were able to launch a more explicitly political event.

While these occasional protests were tolerated by drug traffickers, street marches and rallies created many risks. On several occasions when I was in Cidade de Deus, my activist participants had refused to attend these marches out of concern for what might unfold. For one, marches held after a death sometimes turned chaotic as angry protestors set fire to trash bins or blocked main avenues. Additionally, it was rumored that the drug trade often sent their men to surveil the event or to initiate riots, and activists, like many other residents, feared they might get hurt or caught in a confrontation between gangs and the police. Finally, the possibility remained that the police might retaliate or that drug gangs might return fire.

Natalia told me about an occasion in which she and a group of peaceful protesters were taking a minute of silence to remember the lives lost in a recent police operation when some police officers arrived on the scene. The protestors noticed this and began encroaching on the police chanting "Justice! Justice! Justice!" "They could have started a confrontation with the

Figure 4.2 "Stop Killing Us!" poster from the rally for peace
Photo by anonymous.

police," Natalia recounted. "It was this automatic thing, like a crowd mentality." Two of her fellow organizers went over to talk to the police and managed to draw the crowd back to the center. Around the same time, an armed drug trafficker drove by on his motorcycle. Fortunately, the police did not notice him, or if they did, they chose not to fire at him. Although the protest ended without violence, it left a mark on Natalia:

> We were in the park doing a peaceful protest, but later we realized that it could have gone to shit, like a serious brawl, and then [our collective] would get a bad name, you know, inside the favela, trying to get people to come out and protest.

Given the many risks to both physical safety and reputation that came with street organizing, some activists have found social media to be a safer space to protest against violence than the streets. They are not alone: many activists living in conditions of extreme violence and political repression have found digital spaces to offer new, safer avenues for protest (Mina 2019). However, given the many overlapping connections between activists and gangs and the possibility that even private posts could be shared outside of their immediate network, online activism had to follow many of the same rules as activism in the streets. Residents could focus on general demands for peace, or protest against the police, but never the drug trade. Natalia herself made the most of her anti-violence stance through her social media platforms. Figure 4.3 depicts a short but effective poem she wrote after getting stuck in a shootout on her way to buy bread. She recounted to me afterward how she had lain on the bakery floor with the workers and other customers waiting for the

Figure 4.3 "Breakfast: Two loaves of bread and eleven bullets"
Poem by Natalia.

shooting to stop. She collected some of the bullet casings on her way home. The poem reads "Breakfast: Two loaves of bread and eleven bullets" and quickly went viral across activist networks in CDD and several other favelas.

Leonardo also used poetry to decry violence. Consider this post on his Facebook page in 2017, after months of increasingly lethal police invasions:

> Armored vehicles/military police enter
> Lots of shots fired.
> Schools are closed.
> Workers don't work.
> Buses don't pass by.
> Bodies on the ground.
> Families in desperation.
> Mourning in the streets/Facebook
> This is the weekly, monthly routine in Cidade de Deus
>   for more than 40 years. Forty years.
> Nothing has changed.

The main culprit identified here is the police, although the "shots fired" were also from gangs. The major disruptions to schools, work, and transit were similarly provoked by shootouts between police and gangs, although only one of these parties is mentioned. While this is partly because, in Leonardo's worldview, the genocidal police are in fact the main perpetrators, his framing also enabled him to publicly condemn violence and the chaos it caused without risking his life. Isabella used a similar strategy to speak out against violence. Below is a post by Isabella on CDD Connects in July 2017, after a month of intense shootouts between the police and gangs:

#Shots = Something given by someone who holds a gun in their hands.
#Confrontation = When armed men with or without a uniform engage directly (*batem de frente*) and confront each other.
#Operation = Something "previously" agreed upon by BOPE, Choque, Core, dogs, helicopters, motorcycles, drones and armed vehicles.[4]
#Shootout = Any of the above. Anyone without a weapon in hand in hearing a gunshot says it's a shootout. In the dictionary, the word shootout can be added to synonyms of fear, dread, terror, risk, death, impotence, panic.

So it doesn't matter if it's one shot, a confrontation, or an operation. Shootouts are always defined by the bad feelings of those who aren't shooting.

Isabella's post clearly rejects the use of weapons in the resolution of conflict and, like Leonardo's, brings attention to the severe psychological damage caused by shootouts. She is also careful to only mention the state's security forces, including the BOPE, Choque, and Core. However, her reference to "armed men with or without a uniform" implies that she deems the drug trade at least partially responsible for the terror. She then references their relational opposite, "anyone without a weapon in hand," advocating for non-armed residents without directly challenging the perpetrators. Through these discursive twists, Isabella and Leonardo, like other local activists, are able to publicly condemn armed conflict.

This focus on a more generalized anti-violence discourse came about not only because protest against gangs was off limits. It was also motivated by the recognition among activists that everyone, including members of the drug trade, was harmed by unrelenting state violence. In early December 2016, shortly after the police had murdered several boys presumably connected to the drug trade, I had a conversation with Camilla, a worker at Youth Promise, over Facebook Messenger. She felt a deep pain out of empathy for the mothers, though she did not know any of them. According to Camilla, "The families continue to suffer, independent of who they are. Before God, we are all brothers [and sisters]." This was a collective trauma, a shared experience of victimization. Camilla, like many others, believed that even though the boys may have had some involvement with the drug trade, they did not deserve to be killed, much less in such an inhumane manner.

In fact, most of the residents I came to know well in Cidade de Deus disclosed to me that a close relative of theirs—brother, boyfriend, husband, uncle, cousin, son—had participated in the drug trade. Most had been killed, either by other drug traffickers or by the police. While neither activists nor other residents rooted for the *institution* of the drug trade—all of them wished it would end—their own experiences of loss provoked great sympathy among them for both the families and the *individual* young men who joined the gang. They hated the system but empathized with the foot soldiers of the gang. I knew one young man whom Esther had spent many years trying to help who, after being harassed and beaten by the police multiple times for being young, male, Black, and sitting on the wrong street corner, eventually joined the gang out of a deep sense of despair and hopelessness that any other opportunities would come his way. So while activists genuinely wished for a peaceful resolution to drug conflicts, they also recognized that individual drug traffickers were mostly young, desperate men with few alternatives. For them, the real issue was not the drug trade, but the state.

It is therefore not surprising, then, that favela residents have directed their anti-violence protests against the police and state violence more generally. This is common across Rio's favelas. Marcos Cardoso, for instance, found that in the favela Pavão-Pavãozinho and neighboring favela Contagálo, people routinely criticize the police. In particular, complaints centered around accusations of corruption, the use of excessive violence and extra-judicial killings, and violent policing interventions that threaten the safety of residents. Residents were also angry that, despite all of this show of force, the police allowed the drug trade to continue (Cardoso 2013). In fact, most favela-based protests published in the media focus on street protests against police invasions, which most closely mirrors the mobilization strategies we typically associate with social movements. During the time of my fieldwork, many of the favela-based protests against the police related to killing of "innocent" residents (i.e., those not involved in drug gangs) by UPP officers or by BOPE police during a "pacification" operation (FolhaPress 2015; Mattos 2017; Platonow 2015). Often, mothers or wives were centered in these protests (Vianna and Farias 2011). The Rede de Comunidades e Movimentos contra a Violência, or Network of Communities and Movements against Violence, was one such organization of mothers and other family members of people who had disappeared or been killed by the police. This suggests that conflict activism directly targets perpetrators of violence who they believe will not retaliate, while only indirectly protesting against those who are nearest and hold the greatest power over their lives.

The State is the Problem

"To talk about violence in the favelas is also to talk about a series of violations of fundamental rights—human, civil, political, social—and not only phys-ical violence, which results in an increasing number of deaths," write Rachel Coutinho da Silva and Thaisa Comeli (2018:9). In Cidade de Deus, as in other favelas, armed conflict is one manifestation of many broader and deeper forms of inequality and injustice, which I referred to in Chapter 1 as structural violence. While anti-policing protests were one target of activist mobilization, most favela activists were concerned with addressing structural violence, which they viewed as the primary cause of their suffering. By focusing on systemic violence perpetrated by the state and Brazilian society more generally, activists were able to avoid censorship (or worse) from gangs. Consider this Facebook post by Luis Henrique, a local activist who had worked for several CBOs:

> Structural and systemic violence kills bodies, but not only does it not end at the identified target. The blood spill is sometimes "only" the final stage of the process that persecutes, marginalizes, dehumanizes and, finally, murders certain groups of subjects. Today, one more mother passed away after learning about her son's murder.

In this post, Luis Henrique is not concerned with protesting against gangs, but rather in speaking out against the deeper forms of injustice that led both to the death of a grieving mother and to the murders of favela residents—including drug traffickers. Although no one killed the boy's mother, she died from violence nonetheless.

In Latin America, where poverty and aggressive policing are so endemic, the connections between them are many. In her work on urban violence, Caroline Moser (2004:4) argues that:

> The "livelihood security," of the poor and their ability to access resources to ensure survival are closely linked, in an interconnected vicious cycle, to violence. This relates not only to the spatial, economic and social constraints that the complex layering of endemic violence imposes on their daily lives, but also to the fact that, as citizens, their insecurity is closely linked to the failure of the state's public security systems to protect them.

For Moser, and for many other scholars of urban violence, the state's neglect in providing social services on the one hand and its tendency to over-police poor neighborhoods on the other hand creates a context of chronic violence wherein no single experience of harm can be understood in isolation from the others (Auyero, Bourgois, and Scheper-Hughes 2015; Briceño-León 2005; Gupta 2012; Pearce, McGee, and Wheeler 2011). For Luis Henrique, like the many other activists I interviewed, structural violence created the foundation in which armed conflict could flourish. The deaths caused by gangs were a symptom of a much larger problem: a lack of access to good employment, education, healthcare, and housing left young men with few viable alternatives (Zaluar 2004). The point was not to excuse the killings of innocent victims like Lucas, but to recognize that violence by drug gangs was rooted in systemic, historic, and pervasive forms of inequality. Urban violence for them was not measured by bodies or bullets but by the daily experiences of suffering and denial of the full rights of urban citizenship.

Thus, rather than mobilize against drug traffickers, activists have focused their energy on addressing the root causes of violence, which was both much safer within their context and also more likely to produce long-term changes. Bete, a CDD resident and psychologist who volunteered with several CBOs, expressed the fight succinctly and poetically on Facebook:

195 years after the proclamation of independence we continue to choose death.
Death in the favelas.
Death on the asphalt.
Death in the hospitals.
Death in education.
Death in dignity.
Death in citizenship.
Death of the poor.
Death to those who confront the system.
Death to those paid to maintain the system.
The only ones who don't die are those creating the system.

Below her post was a photograph of a cement wall with a Brazilian flag painted on it. Nearly a dozen large bullet holes had been torn into the wall. Her message was clear: the very foundations of national citizenship are under attack by the destructive powers of an unequal and oppressive system.

These kinds of direct protests against endemic corruption are not only a feature of favela activism but have become a common complaint across Brazil. In the massive street protests that took place in Brazil's largest cities in 2013, the greatest complaints among protestors included heavy-handed policing, poor public services, and endemic corruption (Ricci 2014). Sparked by a hike in the bus fare and over-spending in preparation for the 2014 World Cup games, the protests attracted one million participants and reflected a deep and widespread sense of anger across the country over endemic and

Figure 4.4 "Abandoned by Thieving Politicians." Graffiti on a wall in Cidade de Deus
Photo by the author.

systemic issues (Vicino and Fahlberg 2017). Though I met only a few people in Cidade de Deus who had attended the 2013 protests, the same complaints echoed in the daily discourses of favela residents. I continued to hear anti-state grievances over the years, often posted on Facebook and other public channels. One of Youth Promise's workers shared a meme on Facebook that read: "Dear criminals, please, rob our politicians . . . they have our money. Thank you." Around the same time, another resident who was extremely active in his labor union, uploaded several photos of areas of CDD that were flooded, where heaps of garbage had not been collected yet, and then a photo of a sign with the logo of the Municipal Government. "I already knew this was going to happen!!" his post reads. "Who is is the culprit??" (Figure 4.5).

Such public protests against the state reflect an important difference between political repression in favelas and many other conflict zones: Brazil's favelas exist within a national context of political democracy. While Brazil's democracy has been widely charged with being racist (Nascimento 2016; Perry 2013), disjunctive (Caldeira and Holston 1999), exclusionary

E u já sabia que isso iria acontecer!!!.
Quem foi o culpado??. See More

👍 Like   💬 Comment   ➤ Share

Figure 4.5   Facebook post of a flood in Cidade de Deus reads "I already knew this was going to happen!! Who is the culprit??"
Photo by the author.

(Carvalho 2001; Fischer 2008), and unequal (O'Donnell 1993), it does not impose the same limits on free speech and assembly as more authoritarian regimes which deny, in both law and practice, the rights to speak out against the government. In 2018, before the election of Jair Bolsonaro, Freedom House (2018) categorized Brazil as "free," explaining that "Brazil is a democracy with competitive elections and a vibrant civil society sector. However, economic and political crises have challenged the functioning of government. Corruption, crime, and economic exclusion of minorities are among the country's most serious difficulties" (Freedom House 2018). The country scored 31/40 in political rights and 47/60 in civil liberties. This is not to say that protesters and social movement leaders in Brazil do not face threats; they are sometimes killed under suspicious circumstances. The murder of progressive city councilwoman Marielle Franco in 2018 reflects the dangers that continue to exist for those who challenge the police or the dominant regime. However, favela activists and other local residents regularly made demands on state actors and aired their grievances in public forums without retaliation from the government. While these demands were often ignored, activists did not constantly fear imprisonment or retaliatory violence.

By focusing on structural violence as the object of their claims-making, rather than targeting the physical violence caused by drug traffickers, activists are able to fit into the normative discourses of the favela and the country. While activists still had to be careful not to accuse specific politicians or police commanders of corruption, who might retaliate in self-defense, these more generalized protests against the state, or even more focused—but public—demands made on specific branches of the municipal government, were much less likely to provoke retaliation. Rio's favela activists thus benefitted from the political rights guaranteed by the constitution and were protected (to a point) from state retribution. In this way, favela authoritarianism within a national political democracy operates differently than authoritarian regimes at the national or regional levels. While drug traffickers limit some forms of free speech and assembly, activists can still articulate demands on the state, provided they focus on structural or systemic grievances and do not expose corruption among politicians in cahoots with the local drug faction.[5]

Addressing Stigma by "Doing Good"

While many activists took advantage of discursive openings in Cidade de Deus to protest against the police and systemic inequality, the most common approach to anti-violence activism was to focus on "doing good," by helping others and refraining from engagement in interpersonal forms of violence. For most residents, "doing good" meant engaging in activities of mutual aid, like taking care of other people's children, donating food baskets to poor families, cleaning up garbage in public areas, or giving car rides to the elderly or disabled people. It was a widespread practice and one highly valued in a community with so few public services. "Doing good" was not only an individual act but also a means of social resilience or collective form of survival in a context of urban informality and state neglect (Fahlberg et al. 2020; Seeliger and Turok 2014; Theron and Theron 2013). As I argued in Chapter 3, even drug traffickers relied on local services and assistance to get care for their families.

In addition to helping others, residents widely embraced a spirit of non-violence. Non-violence in Cidade de Deus operates along a continuum. On one end of the spectrum is a commitment to not use physical (or sexual) violence against others, essentially requiring non-action. The other end involves more active (often organized) efforts to dismantle systems of violent oppression (Nojeim 2004). Most favela residents I met (activist or not) expressed commitment to the more passive kind, which Gene Sharp (1959) refers to as "generic nonviolence." In favelas, many men emphasize their commitment to non-violence by refusing to participate in the drug trade or perpetrate physical interpersonal violence (Borde, Page, and Moura 2020).[6] Activists built upon the moral commitment of favela residents to help others and to refrain from violence in order to broaden their participation in non-violence.

Isabella, for instance, founded CDD Connects in order to counteract the popular view of favelas as places of violence and criminality by sharing thousands of stories about the "good things" people were doing. The idea emerged when Isabella realized that people did not know about the services that were offered in Cidade de Deus and would often travel by bus to far-away business districts to get things resolved. According to Isabella, "It made me realize that the bad news circulates, but the good news doesn't, understand? That was missing. Then I said: 'I'm going to make a news channel, a news channel to talk about the good things that are here in Cidade de Deus.'"

Since 2011, Isabella has not only advertised local services, classes, and resources, she has also written stories about the positive things residents were doing for the community. One of these stories was about a young woman teaching children to rollerblade, another was about a famous ballet artist who performed on the international stage, others about martial artists competing in televised matches. Every time I visited CDD, Isabella would tell me with glistening eyes what new story she was working on, barely able to contain her excitement. For Isabella, the goal of CDD Connects was to resist and reverse the popular narrative that favelas are sites of violence and criminality (Amaral 2019; Zaluar and Alvito 1998). However, it was a choice that came at a high cost and required a great deal of boundary setting. Isabella had put much thought into what she would and would not publish. She was regularly contacted by major newspapers looking for details about shootings and policing operations and largely refused to provide these. She also refused to post most stories of shootings, the few exceptions being to honor victims like Lucas. She told me back in 2016:

> If I wanted to, the page could have more than 100,000 likes if I talked about shooting and death. People are just waiting for us to talk about violence, but I don't want to talk about it. I created the page to talk about what's good in the community. If I go to talk about each shooting, there will be no space left to talk about everything else.

In a place where violence is such a consuming narrative, both within the neighborhood and for people outside the favela looking in, the conscious act of reversing the narrative is a political act. Isabella was humble about this, though: "I do nothing more than exercise my citizenship, trying to improve my community," she told me. By 2018, CDD Connects had reached the 100,000-likes mark and was well on its way to even greater popularity. Perhaps Isabella had misjudged the desire across Cidade de Deus and the city for more stories about the good things in Rio's favelas.

Luis Henrique, like Carmen, Leonardo, and many others, espoused their commitment to organized political activities intended to radically transform their neighborhood and society more broadly, or what Johann Galtung (1969) refers to as "positive nonviolence." Consider Luis Henrique's post about a meeting he attended in 2017:

> Yesterday, I was at the office of Civics in Action. I was with other invited guests and participants reflecting about "non-violence" as an agenda and a practice in a world of violences . . . I am grateful for having learned about, and now be able to carry in my fight and actions, the history and fight of some men and women present, who represent an image and similarity to the true resistance in the margins, the militancy of the base and the possible revolution; how the lives that feed me every day in our Cidade de Deus. US FOR US.

For activists in Cidade de Deus, non-violence was not simply about doing good without doing harm. They participated in movements, both within and outside Cidade de Deus, that aimed to systematically address the neglect and over-policing of favelas, to resist racism and favela-based discrimination, and to promote political and economic reforms that would bring greater justice and rights to Brazil's urban poor. Their efforts could best be termed "nonviolent resistance," which Erica Chenoweth and Kathleen Gallagher Cunningham (2013:271) define as:

> the application of unarmed civilian power using nonviolent methods such as protests, strikes, boycotts, and demonstrations, without using or threatening physical harm against the opponent. Civilians challenging the state through nonviolent struggle employ irregular political tactics, working outside the defined and accepted channels for political participation defined by the state . . . Ordinary people use nonviolent resistance to pursue

a wide variety of goals, from challenging entrenched autocrats to seeking territorial self-determination to contesting widespread discriminatory practices.

This definition helps to situate activism in Cidade de Deus both in relation to other forms of non-violent action in favelas as well as the broader field of social movements. On the one hand, favela activists are more organized and intentional about social transformation than most favela residents. On the other hand, they rarely engage in "protests, strikes, boycotts and demonstrations," as the definition suggests. While academics and activists might understand non-violence as a strategic political process, its less subversive corollary, "doing good things" was not considered political or threatening to gangs. Doing good was not only permitted but widely condoned across the neighborhood. It provided activists with a moral space in which to organize political efforts. It also gave activists a discursive opening through which to advocate for public services and to speak out against domestic violence, sexual assault, and child and elder abuse. As I discuss in Chapter 5, a focus on issues that transcend favelas, such as structural violence, racism, and gender violence, has also allowed favela activists to situate themselves within broader urban and transnational social movements with similar political objectives and narratives.

The "Criminal," the "Worker," and the "Educator"

It has been widely noted that two oppositional social categories have emerged in Rio's urban imaginary to distinguish between "bad" and "good" favela residents: the *bandido* and the *trabalhador*, or in English, the "criminal" and the "worker" (Penglase 2014; Zaluar 1994). "Criminals" are viewed as those who engage in theft, assault, or work for the drug trade but usually excludes those committing white collar crimes, such as the sale of pirated goods, for instance (Cardoso 2013:173). Meanwhile, "workers" constitute those who receive their income legally, which can include formal employment (i.e., employment that is documented, taxed, and protected by labor rights laws) and informal employment, such as doing nails or fixing cars, with wages paid under the table. Given the difficulties favela residents experience in finding formal employment, the category of *trabalhador* has been broadened. According to Ben Penglase (2014:89), "to fall into this category one must be neither a drug dealer nor a *viciado* (drug addict)." In favelas, the *trabalhador* thus includes anyone with an ethic of hard work, regardless of current employment status (Oliveira and Nuñez 2014).

However, there is a third social category in favelas that has gone overlooked: the *educador*, or the "educator." The educator encompasses not only formally employed teachers but also volunteers and staff at social service organizations, community journalists who provide information (education) to the neighborhood, soccer coaches, ballet teachers, and anyone else providing guidance, knowledge, and nurturing. Most activists in fact call themselves educators and other similar names, such as "community educators" or "social educators." Some also go by "community communicators." While educators technically are also "workers," they have a unique role in the community that is not only accepted but widely embraced.

These three social categories exist in a moral hierarchy. The worker, for instance, stands morally above the criminal. The worker is considered to be blameless in the police-gang wars and to be an urban citizen deserving of state protection due to their participation as a laborer in the capitalist system. Criminals are "bad" due to their involvement in illicit activities and armed conflicts with the police. In the minds of many residents—both in the favela and beyond—drug traffickers deserve to be killed or jailed for breaking the law and do not deserve the full rights of urban citizenship. The educator, in turn, is situated at the top of the moral hierarchy of the favela, perceived as someone who has responsibility over the next generation, to ensure that children of the favela become workers rather than criminals. The educator keeps the children under their care safe during shootouts and builds up their self-esteem in the face of police brutality and discrimination from society. The educator helps children gain skills and knowledge needed to be successful in the broader urban society as professionals, athletes, or artists. The educator is also selfless, choosing a profession that is poorly remunerated (if remunerated at all) for the benefit of the broader community. Perhaps most importantly, in the eyes of many, the educator is the only hope that the favela might not be poor forever.

Being an educator is a much safer public persona in Cidade de Deus than activist, which could be perceived as a more political and trouble-making identity. Outsiders who came to Cidade de Deus to teach or care for children were among the few allowed entry into the neighborhood. One young light-skinned woman from outside Cidade de Deus who worked at Youth Promise told me that the drug traffickers always let her enter Cidade de Deus in her car because they knew she was a teacher. "Let the teacher pass!" they would yell at pedestrians every morning when they recognized her through her car window. I have no doubt I was also given access to the neighborhood thanks to my affiliation with Youth Promise and other CBO workers. Being viewed as an educator in a favela is much safer than being seen as a researcher.[7]

Notably, the role of educator is not considered political but social: educators exist solely to help children and other vulnerable populations stand on their own two feet, not to run for office or sabotage drug operations. Educator as a social category is therefore not viewed as threatening to gangs. In fact, because workers—who make up the vast majority of residents—highly respect and rely on educators to help them raise their children, gangs must respect the moral superiority of the educator if they are to maintain their own legitimacy in the community. The social importance of educators was true for gang members as well: many CBOs had the children of drug traffickers enrolled in their organizations. As Maria Rita and many others told me, even gang lords hoped that their children would receive better opportunities than they had and be spared the risks of gang involvement.

"To Educate is a Political Act!"

The activists I met in Cidade de Deus have built on this moral structuring to create a unique location that intersects with both the social and the political spheres. Their status as educators afforded them a wide berth on *how* they raised the next generation and *what* they taught them. Within the confines of CBOs or collectives, activist-educators not only taught their participants about how to be a good citizen and a hard worker; they also taught them about racism, structural violence, and the importance of collective action. Carmen offered a great example of how activists used their role as educators to produce a political consciousness. Carmen founded and ran a CBO called the Environment League, which offered literacy classes and various activities aimed at teaching children and adolescents about preserving and caring for their environment. Yet Carmen's approach was explicitly political. She told me once:

> The youth who come to the Environment League, they have to have some formal education. What does this mean? We say that it's a political education. The methodology and philosophy from Paulo Freire is political. Oh,

people say, "But is this party politics?" People who say this don't know what "politics" means . . . If they come here, they will study about housing, they will work, they will learn about health, they will learn about gender issues, they will study about social movements . . . They will understand the history of education, they will learn about the formation of the favelas, their own history in this place.

This type of political education bore fruit. I once attended a meeting in Cidade de Deus hosted by several local activists and public institutions to discuss the impact of a recent uptick in policing operations on the neighborhood. The police battalion commander had come to defend his operations to the participants. Carmen attended, along with several adolescents and young adults from the Environment League wearing matching t-shirts with their organization's logo. When the lieutenant finished speaking, a 19-year-old woman from Carmen's group took the mic and challenged the lieutenant by noting that the police abuse of power made dialogue between them and local residents extremely challenging. Carmen's hard work raising youth from the favela to make vocal claims for their rights was paying off. As Carmen noted, she, like several other activists, drew inspiration from the work of Paulo Freire, who published his seminal book "Pedagogy of the Oppressed" in 1968 while in exile from the Brazilian dictatorship. In it, he laid out a theory of praxis, where he advocated for literacy courses paired with critical education about oppression and resistance. According to Freire (2000:49–50), "If what characterizes the oppressed is their subordination to the consciousness of the master . . . , true solidarity with the oppressed means fighting at their side to transform the objective reality which has made them these 'beings for another.'" By educating young adults in Cidade de Deus about oppression and resistance, activists were not only teachers but also cultivators of a future generation of social change makers.

Not all CBO leaders were as political as Carmen, though even CBOs with less politicized leaders still offered important spaces for a political education. Solange, the director of Youth Promise, for instance, rarely discussed politics of any kind. She was not affiliated with a political party and did not actively adopt the Freirian pedagogical approach. However, many of the teachers at Youth Promise were more intentional about teaching the children how to think critically about injustice and inequality. Luis Henrique once invited me to participate in a course on communication and text production he ran twice a week for adolescents and young adults in the computer lab at Youth Promise. The students took this and three other courses as part of an educational series, including photography, digital citizenship (taught by Maria Rita), and social development and citizenship. Luis Henrique had begun the class talking about theories of communication, which took off after WWII. He used a variety of examples of popular videos, ads, magazines, and newspaper articles to reflect on these theories.

The students had been tasked the previous week with each taking a picture of something in their environment and developing a narrative about why they took the picture, what it was about, and why it mattered. All the projects had to be within the area of human rights or, as Luis Henrique explained, "our constitutional rights, of which we have many!" As I looked over the students' shoulders, I saw their themes: cruelty to animals, the environment, trash collection, the challenges faced by homeless people, leadership roles among black women, public insecurity. Roberto (one of Esther's "adopted" teenagers) was doing his project on refugees in Cidade de Deus with a focus on Haitians. As I scanned the students' projects, Luis Henrique commented to me: "We are not just here to spend down the time, we want to develop the subjectivity of the youth." He had a particular kind of education in mind, which taught youth about their potential as political actors capable of fighting for social change.

I was especially struck by a short essay written by one of the students at Youth Promise and a photograph he took of his younger brother standing in the street near one of the main roads that cuts through CDD. The essay offers a great example of how politics gets produced within Cidade de Deus:

Crooked Future

Every day, at the end of the day, I take this path, which is from my girlfriend's house to mine. That is, from the home of my future wife—the woman I intend to have a life with—to the home where my mother and my brother are—people with whom I maintain a strong affective bond. And, along the way, a street sign always gets my attention, which identifies the name of the street, *Avenida Cidade de Deus* [City of God Avenue]. My interest may seem strange, but the crooked aspect of it seems to give me cause to reflect on the reason for why it was that way. What happened to the sign for it to be that distorted? Perhaps the entrance of the police, in the *caveirão*, inside the favela? Maybe the . . . no. I can't stop thinking about this. The movement to "save" the community through the process of militarization of the favela, justified by the fight against the drug trade, which directly affects the routine of the residents (working mothers, parents, students, children).

How much is our future and our freedom worth? Is the war against drug trafficking worth all this daily violence against the dignity of our residents? The damage is not merely structural, it is human. They hold us accountable for our obligations (to the law), but they distort our rights. Neglect is not accidental, it is daily. But why did I tell you about my family in the beginning? Simply because this street sign makes me think about the future, above all, of my relatives; will the future of my brothers be crooked too? And my children? My mother worked—and works—hard to give me some autonomy and strength to keep fighting. But this sign pounds in my head all day long: How long until our story falls? Our neighborhood? This struggle to hold ourselves up is daily and comes from every resident, every working mother. Every teacher. And as long as we have strength, we will resist to the end.

In this text, the author connects the constant threat of violence faced by his family members with the brutality of the police, sponsored by the global war against drugs. The essay identifies the hypocrisies of state action, the disconnect between the state's harsh enforcement of laws and its failure to uphold favela residents' civil rights. It also emphasizes the author's commitment to join in the resistance against injustice. While CBO leaders like Solange did not always articulate these ideas in public forums, they provided the spaces in which a critical consciousness could be constructed by teachers and other staff/volunteers. Within the boundaries of the educator role, CBOs and collectives promote a multi-generational vision of social and political change.

"Only Art Saves"

Cidade de Deus is not only teeming with bullets, it also abounds with artists. If you ask most people in Cidade de Deus what they think is good about their neighborhood, they will tell you it's a place filled with culture. "Culture" includes everything from athletics and dance to music, poetry, painting, and sculpting. In fact, Cidade de Deus has gained a reputation as one of the hubs of cultural vitality among Rio's favelas. The sounds of singing echo from hole-in-the-wall churches on most nights and from most blocks, while residents gather for parties to play and sing their favorite *pagode* or samba songs. CDD was also the birthplace of funk, a type of heavy rap music in which rappers speak of marginality, violence, and pride in their resilience and unity. In 1994, Cidinho and Doca, two rapper-DJs from Cidade de Deus, wrote a funk song that became internationally famous and acclaimed as the "hymn of the favela." Cidade de Deus also boasts an impressive roster of world-renowned UFC, MMA, Tae Kwon Do, and Jiu Jitsu fighters, professional soccer players, ballet and contemporary dancers, and hip hop artists. In the 2016 Summer Olympics, Cidade de Deus native Rafaela Silva took home Brazil's first gold medal in Judo. In a neighborhood where inhabitants face so many challenges, it is little surprise that local residents have so much pride about the breadth and quantity of famous athletes and artists from Cidade de Deus. Culture is Cidade de Deus's second claim to fame, after extreme violence.

Cultural production is thus a popular and normative activity in Cidade de Deus. At least two-thirds of the 82 Facebook pages with the words "Cidade de Deus" or its abbreviation "CDD" in the title that I found were dedicated to various cultural forms or to publishing news about upcoming cultural events or stories about local artists.[8] Art is also everywhere in Cidade de Deus, as local artists paint telephone poles, park benches and murals. Some murals list the names of residents killed in recent years. Even drug traffickers produce or sponsor the production of art. One can often hear funk music blasting from the speakers at drug sale points. Particularly popular among drug traffickers is the *proibidão*, or the "big prohibition." The *proibidão* is a type of funk music that exalts the drug trade and substance abuse. It had been prohibited during the height of the UPP; playing it loudly was thus a form of resistance. In a setting in which many activities or discourses are strictly prohibited, cultural expression is widely embraced and encouraged.

Art and culture play an important role in social movements and have become especially vital to sustaining activism in areas of political repression and conflict. In China, for instance, An Xiao Mina (2019) notes how images of sunflower seeds and memes with the desert animal grass mud horse have become symbols of anti-government oppression. Given that it can be difficult for the government or internet censorship algorithms to distinguish between the literal meanings of these objects and the more subversive meanings attached to them by anti-regime activists, they are more difficult to control than explicitly political images and activities. In Argentina, El Salvador, and Mexico, the mothers of *desaparecidos*—missing men and women—carried photographs of their family members in marches as a way to protest against

state-sponsored violence. As Cynthia Bejarano (2002:140) notes, the innocence of the young people in the pictures, combined with the intimacy of the
photographs, had an "insuperable" impact. Hundreds of additional examples
of music, cartoons, photographs, posters, and many other art forms can be
found on the Human Rights Foundation (2022) website, showcasing how
art has been deployed by pro-democracy activists in countries under dictatorship to demand greater political and civil rights and mobilize for regime
change.

The production of art is also an important mechanism for representing
and preserving culture. In the context of political repression, art allows
marginalized groups to assert their shared identity and values, thereby
preserving a sense of community and solidarity even while a regime attempts
to silence or fracture it (Duncombe 2007; Park, Burgess, and McKenzie
1984). In other cases, art becomes a form of countercultural production that
aims to reject dominant capitalist and racist value systems (Burawoy 2012;
Elsner 2001; Williamson 2010). In contexts where a regime is determined to
eradicate an ethnic or racial group, cultural preservation itself becomes an
act of resistance.

Rio's favela residents use art and culture to protest inequality and violence, while also reaffirming their commitment to their community's local
experiences and values. In favelas, art has become an expression of subjectivity, or "cultural protagonism" (Meirelles and Athayde 2016:111), a form
of constructing and transforming both oneself and the world within and beyond the favela. According to Jorge Barbosa (2017:112),

> Despite the stigmas of poverty and violence that still mark favelas, the
> richness of their expressions is undeniable, as are their significant ways of
> representing and affirming their cultural difference. In this sense, culture
> is not lived exclusively through objects or artifacts, but rather as an action,
> expressively relational, corporeal and intersubjective, as it expresses paths,
> memories, values and life projects.

Cultural production allows favela residents to challenge the status
quo, construct alternate realities, and create community based on shared
vulnerabilities and world views (Barbosa 2017; Meirelles and Athayde 2016).
While favelas have become well known for their artistic creativity, this cultural production has also created a bridge between local values and political
resistance.

Activists in Cidade de Deus have taken advantage of the symbolic space they occupy to air political grievances. Whether in bars or public parks, Art Talk could protest against violence through prose, performances, and paintings without arousing suspicion. It blended into the cacophony of music and vibrancy in the background. Additionally, because participation in art and culture is so prolific in favelas, activist art created an avenue through which ordinary residents could become more involved in political action. One woman I got to know at local poetry events joined Art Talk because her adolescent daughter was a poet. In her efforts to support her daughter, she had not only begun writing poetry herself but had started to help Natalia organize more political activities, such as the open mic profiled in the book's Introduction and Natalia's campaign for city council. Cultural activism offered those residents with few artistic resources or formal training the opportunity to join a community united by a shared belief that art could change the world and their neighborhood.

I also met several painters who used this vehicle to speak out against state violence. Luz once showed me a painting of her and her family unloading trash bags of their belongings from a garbage truck. It was one of her earliest childhood memories. "I remember being so excited to ride in the garbage truck," she told me, and had felt inspired to make the painting. Reflecting on it after the painting was complete, she realized it carried another message: "When I painted this, I was remembering how much fun I thought it was back then to ride in a garbage truck. But then I looked at it afterwards, and thought, you know, I think this is a message, that even though they treated me like trash, I'm here surviving, thriving. Their plan to throw me away didn't work." Another of Luz's paintings depicts a young Black boy caught in front of an armored vehicle—reminiscent of the opening image of the main character in the movie *City of God*—caught between the drug trade and the police in the 1980s. The message of the painting is clear: the police car is more armored than before, but ordinary residents are still stuck between the guns of the police and the guns of the drug trade.

Cultural activists also used their skills in more collective and systematic ways. In 2012, Sonia, Rosangela, and a handful of other residents partnered with a group of graduate students and faculty at the Federal University of Rio de Janeiro to found a community-based newspaper called *SpeakCDD!*. While newspapers in themselves may not fit squarely into the category of art as we usually think of the term, this newspaper was filled with drawings, poems, pictures, and stories of the cultural endeavors of CDD residents. Most of the stories published in the paper were also about artistic events: literary festivals, field trips to museums, an organized event for children to paint in the park. It was a site for the making and sharing of cultural activism. There were also many stories documenting poor infrastructure and unreliable state services. The introductory message by the editorial board in its first issue offers a valuable summary:

"A lot of work and one more newspaper is on the street of Cidade de Deus"

One more time we come to the streets with the SpeakCDD! newspaper. This newspaper is the result of much hard work and dedication by each of its members, all of whom are residents of Cidade de Deus. [It is for] all residents interested in exchanging ideas with their neighbors and showing people outside our neighborhood what happens in our favela beyond the gaze of the large commercial media (the most common newspapers accessed in newsstands and on television).

In this edition, the reader will learn about the situation of abandonment of CIEP Luiz Carlos Prestes, one of the Spaces for Child Development of the Municipal Government, in the article by Solange. You will also see the real situation in which residents in areas with construction by the Bairro Maravilha project are living, based on the perspective of Sonia, reporter for the newspaper. You will also see how the Community Bank is running after it was inaugurated in 2011 in Cidade de Deus, by Joana.

Cidade de Deus participated in June in the event by the United Nations that united diverse countries to discuss issues related to the environment in Rio+20. Here, the reader can accompany the event in the pictures by Angelica. And you will also learn about the House of Culture of Cidade de Deus, Art Talk, and the participation of our community in FLUPP (The Literary Congress for Favelas) and FLIP (The International Literary Congress of Paraty). There are so many things happening in Cidade de Deus to tell you about!

Follow the newspaper *SpeakCDD!*. Read it. Distribute it. Collaborate as a reporter, get to know our group and our independent project. The newspaper is also on the internet. Just visit us and send us a message. Cidade de Deus always had a voice, now we have [a place] from which to shout.

I include this lengthy introduction as a way of demonstrating the explicit connections that residents made between culture and protest. The newspaper itself was arguably a work of political art: the first edition was 16 pages long, filled with colorful images and stories about the many events organized and/or attended by Cidade de Deus residents and reports of how government interventions were and were not fulfilling residents' needs. In 2014, Rosangela published a story about the inauguration of the House of Rights in Cidade de Deus, the first of its kind in Brazil, which offered a space in which residents could apply for birth certificates, employment cards, drivers' licenses, and a host of other documents. In the article, Rosangela bemoans the thoughtlessness behind the inauguration proceedings: only government officials were allowed to participate in the ceremony; there was no space for local residents. The local press (i.e., Rosangela and other Cidade de Deus journalists) were not allowed to take pictures, and there was too much policing. Worst of all was how the event let down a group of children from Cidade de Deus who had been invited to perform a song and had practiced several times for it. At the last minute, the event organizers decided there was not enough time for the children to perform. According to Rosangela:

> At the same time and at a park very close to the location of the inauguration, the plastic artist Carminho was conducting a workshop with children and their families. On one side of the park, children making art and expressing themselves, and on the other, children leaving an event without having performed. Since the stage was organized only for the governor, the authorities closed their eyes to a future president of the nation who was there playing his drum without being able to get their attention.

This is one example of how the paper offered residents a space to describe and reject the many ways they were neglected and excluded by the state, while also emphasizing the protagonism and skills of their community. Over the following five years, the paper published special interest stories about art and culture in Cidade de Deus, the many activities organized by local CBOs and the Residents' Board, and the neglect of the state. Articles included stories of famous athletes and artists from Cidade de Deus, information about how to adopt a child, the winners of a municipal grant for Local Actions (i.e., social projects in favelas), the Gay Rights Parade in Cidade de Deus, the founding of a community-based radio station, and the challenges of securing employment in the formal market. Many stories praised the virtues of literacy and the importance of encouraging education and reading among young children.

Every issue carried at least one, if not several, stories decrying urban violence and the consequences of this for local residents. For instance, a 2014 issue included a story by Sonia titled "Where is public security?" that prominently displayed a picture of Natalia and Jefferson speaking to a large audience at the International Literary Festival. The event was located just across the street from the Regional Tribunal for the State in the center of Bangú in a busy commercial area. "The presentations were wonderful," wrote Sonia, "we felt like the participants were ingesting culture, leisure, and citizenship." After describing some of the presentations, Sonia went on to describe the unfolding of a shootout between police and a group of men trying to rescue someone on trial, which resulted in the death of an eight-year-old boy walking down the busy street with his grandmother. The article concludes: "We spent part of a wonderful day with the beauty of poetry and concluded our programming with much pain and indignation about this tragedy. Governors, where is public security?" On the next page, a different story juxtaposed protests against violence. A large picture displayed four residents and three priests from Cidade de Deus's Anglican church smiling into the camera holding yellow brochures. "Cidade de Deus has entered into a fight against domestic violence against women" reads the headline. The comparison of these stories of violence and non-violence reflected the possibilities for mobilizing against violence through art. The final page of the issue offers another cartoon critiquing the government, this time about its failing public healthcare system (Figure 4.6). The doctor yells "Next," but his patient has already died and decayed, so only his skeleton remains. Importantly, no story or cartoon in any of the issues I read directly mentioned the drug trade. However, the newspaper was nonetheless almost entirely dedicated to speaking out against violence and affirming residents' continued struggles for peace, safety, and citizenship.

In addition to articles and paintings, Cidade de Deus's cultural activists were prolific performers of spoken word, hip hop, and rap. MC Claudinho was among Cidade de Deus's most popular musicians, who founded a slam hip hop competition in 2014. He explained to me that "It was based on the idea of a cultural circle, but our idea was a more political intent than for entertainment, because the idea was to make young people reflect on matters that have to do with their reality, with their daily lives." According to Claudinho, the early hip hop battles were initiated to give young men in gangs a place to battle without killing each other. It was a place in which they could earn respect and express aggression through words, rather than physical violence.

Figure 4.6 "What about health?" it reads. "Next!" calls the doctor. Cartoon by CDD artist depicting a patient who has died after having waited too long to receive services from SUS, the national public healthcare system
Picture taken by the author of a cartoon printed in a SpeakCDD! Newspaper article.

Hip hop battles helped to decrease homicides but, for MC Claudinho, had little cultural value. Instead, the hip hop battles he organized had a theme, and participants were required to rap about that specific topic:

> We presented themes about politics, like UPP, the Lava Jato,[9] fraud by [former Governor Sérgio] Cabral, discovery of the purchase of votes during the World Cup in Rio . . . These are issues that affect us directly but we do not read about it often. The young men competing in the battle already knew that they had to learn about the subject in order to win, so they would go and read, and get informed about the issue. And the audience that is going there is sitting there wondering what the fuck is the *mensalão*?

The *mensalão* was a political scandal that broke out in 2005 in which members of the Worker's Party were accused of buying votes for favored legislation with government funds. Claudinho's centering of this and other political issues in hip hop battles provided a political education to favela

Figure 4.7 A local artist giving me a narrated tour of some of CDD's many murals. This one documents important events in the neighborhood's collective memory
Photo by the author.

youth through music. In addition to the hip hop battles, he invited many guest speakers, mostly Black people from the favela who had become writers, poets, athletes, and other professionals. His goal was to give youth an alternative set of role models, "because the only role models they have are drug traffickers," he explained. He also hoped that by helping young people network with established artists outside the neighborhood, they could find a way to gain financial rewards for their work. Both *CDDSpeaks!* and MC Claudinho's politically oriented hip hop battles demonstrate how activists have utilized the normativity of cultural production in favelas to generate a critical consciousness that publicly condemned state violence, neglect, and corruption.

Figure 4.8 "Travel through the world is my home. Every place is my home." Art piece designed by a CDD artist, hung in the UPP police precinct
Photo by the author.

Race as a Mechanism of Solidarity

Race politics—including negotiations of racial identification and anti-racism organizing—was another form of embedded resistance that inserted local activists within normative values, images, and discourses. In particular, advocacy against racism positioned activists in solidarity with, rather than in opposition to, drug traffickers, who are almost entirely dark-skinned.

Figure 4.9 "The problems of the favelas we must irradicate." Mural in CDD
Photo by the author.

Activists deployed many discursive and political tactics in their fight against the historical legacies and contemporary injustices of racial discrimination.

According to sociologist Aníbal Quijano (2005:107–8), the concept of race, in its contemporary sense, did not exist before European colonialism began in the 1500s. It was during this time that social categories like "Indian," "Negro," "mestizo," and "white" emerged. The terms not only characterized phenotypical differences but, more importantly, legitimized unequal locations of power. Negative connotations were attached to ethno-racial groups at the "bottom" of colonial hierarchies in order to justify the subordination and exploitation of these groups by European settlers. Race, writes Quijano, "revealed itself to be the most effective and durable instrument of universal social domination . . . The conquered and dominated populations were placed in a situation of naturalization of their inferiority." For many favela activists, there was a close connection between slavery and modern-day racism in policing, poverty, and the rise of drug gangs: urban violence, in their perspective, was a racialized phenomenon. Thus, to fight against violence also required mobilizing against the symbolic forces of racism.

Among CDD's activists, race politics has been transformed from a tool for domination to one of resistance (Nascimento 2016; Paschel 2016; Vargas 2010). Most of the activists I met in Cidade de Deus proudly identified as Black. While many of these activists had dark skin tones and other phenotypical features often attributed to African ancestry, others who identified as Black had skin tones and hair structures that would have allowed them to pass as *pardo* (mixed race) or even white. When I explored racial identification in interviews with several activists in Cidade de Deus, they explained to me that the label was as much about skin color as it was about their understanding of race politics, racism, and racialized resistance. Activists not only publicly identified as Black, they also taught community members about colonialism and Black history and inserted anti-racism narratives into their fight against state violence and social injustice. By discursively connecting their fight against violence and oppression to racism, race was transformed from a social construction to a political construction, a symbolic device that emphasized solidarity across the favela around shared ancestry as well as shared vulnerabilities, urban exclusion, and state violence (Paschel 2016). Keisha-Kahn Perry similarly found a connection between race and resistance in activist collectives in Salvador, the capital of Bahia in northeastern Brazil. According to Perry (2013:xviii), "The complex racial politics of identification are linked to gender and class consciousness and identification as blacks, women, and poor people . . . Neighborhood activists are far from confused about the validity of blackness as a social category."

In Cidade de Deus, several activists deployed presentations of self that signaled membership in the African diaspora and participation in Black culture. These included wearing their hair in corn rows, braids, or dreads, listening to Black rappers, wearing clothes made by Black artists, and practicing religions with African roots, such as Candomblé and Umbanda. Even lighter-skinned activists found a way to leverage Blackness as a political tool. "I'm white," Solange told me once, pointing at the beige-colored tone of her arm. "But my soul is Black." I had raised my eyebrows in curiosity. She continued: "I don't know most of my ancestors, but Brazil is entirely descended from Blacks. I really respect this lineage." Solange's Caucasian features made it difficult for her to legitimately claim Blackness, but she had nonetheless found a way to align herself with African ancestry and culture, thereby demonstrating the salience of Blackness as a political construct in favelas' resistance movements. Many other lighter-skinned activists I met similarly pointed to whatever evidence they could find to identify with Blackness, including having dark thick hair, having children or parents who were Black, or living in a racialized community. However, this extended beyond an individual commitment to racial justice. Once, when Luis Henrique and I were discussing how many favela activists were Black and I mentioned Solange as the exception to the rule, he shrugged and defended her Blackness. He referenced Solange's curly hair, calling it a "white Afro," and reminded me that she was a migrant from Northeastern Brazil, a decidedly non-White part of the country. Both Solange and Luis Henrique thus felt compelled to define her as Black in an effort to legitimize her leadership within CDD's sphere of non-violence. Meanwhile, Maria Rita had been on a years-long mission to help her students and neighbors appreciate their African roots and take pride in thinking of themselves as Black. Favela activism, when understood as a political construct, is Black, regardless of the skin tones of the individuals within it.

Blackness as a political construct has not only helped to situate injustice and violence within a postcolonial lens, it also symbolically aligns the plight of activists with the well-being of drug traffickers, who are overwhelmingly darker skinned. Leonardo's labeling of police-gang conflicts as a genocide undergirded by racism—described in the introduction of the chapter—was a discursive device that helped to publicly position activists as allies of the drug trade, rather than opponents. In this narrative, drug traffickers were viewed as victims of racist police violence and racialized poverty. By connecting both oppression and resistance to race, activists constructed a symbolic sphere of action that identified a shared problem against which to fight (i.e., racism) and identified gang members as victims and potential allies rather than the targets of claims-making. This narrative has allowed many activists in Cidade de Deus to fight against violence without threats from drug gangs. In 2017, for instance, MC Claudinho launched an album about race and injustice in Rio de Janeiro, including the song "A Declaration on CDD." It illustrates how an anti-racist discourse was leveraged to produce internal unity among favela residents as victims of state violence, while also identifying a common enemy, the racist state:[10]

> Cidade de Deus only wants peace
> Police only kill poor
> society does not like Blacks
> for us always death penalty
> Swallow your cries, kid
> pistol in our face because of a joint
> Police take bribes, but don't accept checks
> We have no escape, the king of hard knocks
> knocks us down . . .
> Better days for CDD

Quilombo of war, rest and leisure

The dream persists only if happy

Police who arrest lawyer is a judge

As this song demonstrates, rap is used as a tool to discursively connect anti-Black violence by the police with corruption and neglect by the state. The constant use of the term "us" suggests a unity between drug traffickers and other Black favela residents. By emphasizing the ways in which racial discrimination is so harshly levied against Black favela men, MC Claudinho connects his fight for justice to the victimization experienced by drug traffickers. It is not difficult to see why drug traffickers would allow MC Claudinho and other artists with a similar message to perform their songs publicly. At the same time, his songs served as a vehicle for making broader demands for racial justice. MC Claudinho viewed his music as part of a global Black musical movement spearheaded by artists like James Brown and Nina Simone. For MC Claudinho, all expressions of Black identity were political, even if they were not directly confrontational:

Every Black person, he is already a militant from the moment that he is born . . . Sometimes we emphasize this thing of militancy in the speech, in the field of knowledge. But if you are born Black, you will have to militate to survive. If you are a single mother, exhausting yourself to put food on the table, man, you are militating! If you listen to the lyrics in Nina Simone's music, she will not tell you to pick up a gun or participate in a protest, but she will talk about the difficulties of being a Black woman. And this is already a militancy. The hair that Black people use is political; if I have sexual relations with a Black woman, this is political, everything, everything is political, because it is going against the Eurocentric flow.

When viewed through this lens, Black members of drug gangs are also part of this militant resistance. Through slam poetry, spoken word, rap, and hip hop, dark-skinned youth from favelas have created a platform to air their grievances, to connect their experiences of racism with state violence and poverty, and to join a global movement for racial equality (Lopes and Facina 2012; Sousa 2019). What MC Claudinho and other musicians had experienced in Cidade de Deus came to be understood as a symbol of violence and injustice more broadly; their art, in turn, was intended to address these at the symbolic level.

Learning Race

Many activists I spoke with were concerned with the death of education favela residents received about Black history or their own racial identity. Solange,
for instance, told me about her observations interviewing people for a survey
being organized by the United Nations to track and offer assistance to families
in extreme poverty. Solange noted that most people said they didn't know
what their race was. Even people with dark skin whom most would clearly
label Black didn't know their race. "Oh, is there yellow on there?" Solange
repeated what some had asked her; she peered into her outstretched hands,
imitating the participants looking over onto her checklist: "Put *pardo.*" "People
don't know what they are," Solange bemoaned. It was an interesting observa-
tion and one that I had heard many times from other activists concerned with
the fact that so few favela residents had learned about Black history or their
own connections to slavery and to Africa. Maria Rita, who had worked for the
national census a few years earlier, had come across the same situation: even
dark-skinned Brazilians often struggled to choose a racial category.

For activists, the lack of education about race and Black history in the
home and in schools has limited favela residents' awareness about structural
violence and their own identities. João Paulo's story is a case in point. I met
João Paulo at Youth Promise, where he taught courses on photography and
citizenship to children and young adults. He has tan skin, some African facial
features, and thick dark hair he wore in dread locks. When I asked João Paulo
what race he identified as, he responded unequivocally that he was Black.
Later he allowed me to interview him about it. He informed me that he hadn't
always self-identified as Black:

> [When I was growing up], there wasn't this thing, this discussion that you
> defined yourself, how do you define yourself, you know, at home, nobody
> ever talked about it. [No one ever said], "my son, come here, let's talk . . . so-
> ciety is like this, and, like this, due to your skin color, how you identify your-
> self," so this was a construction through my experiences. So I learned, you
> know, in the political militancy that I have already participated in, the
> Catholic Church, understand? [And] other NGOs. So this was a construc-
> tion, you know.

João Paulo's mother was white and his father was Black, he told me, so
he had been brought up to believe that he was a mixture, a product of the

miscegenation that presumably characterizes all of Brazil. He connected this to the lack of discussion about race in Cidade de Deus and the public education system:

> If we went to walk around Cidade de Deus and do research on [race], many people will not know what to say, because that still, it's a lot, you know. People know that prejudice exists, but they can't talk about it. Brazil is not prepared for that, we don't talk about slavery, we don't do any work around how much it created Brazil, and we have a population that has a very large educational deficit, you know . . . schools didn't discuss race, they didn't have history books, they didn't talk about Black culture.

For João Paulo, the schools did not fulfill an important social role in educating children about Black history and culture or encouraging pride in one's Black ancestors. Since his own parents had not done this either, it wasn't until adulthood that João Paulo was exposed to alternative views of race, when he began participating in CBOs in Cidade de Deus and other favelas. Especially critical to his early political formation was the *Pastoral das Favelas*, a progressive social service branch of the Catholic Church which espoused the more radical teachings of liberation theology and called for the engagement of the Church in resisting oppression and injustice. Civic and progressive religious organizations in favelas have thus played a central role in educating poor Brazilians about racial injustice and the power of racial politics to resist not only racism but all forms of oppression.

João Paulo's work at Youth Promise and many of the other activities he engaged in were aimed, in part, at promoting this alternative education, teaching young favela residents about racial injustice, Black history, and human rights. Many other local activists inserted racism and colonialism as a leading component of their educational work. Some organizations, like the Center for Racial Justice, used their professionalizing courses to cultivate pride in African hairstyles, dark skin, and the strengths of the Black community. At Youth Promise, Luis Henrique, Maria Rita, and other staff often explained to children the harms of more "invisible" forms of racism.

Leonardo took advantage of his acting classes to teach children about racial pride. He told me once with a mischievous grin how he had tricked his students into reflecting critically on the contradictory messages they received about race and beauty. He had begun the class by asking students if they believed that God, or whatever power they believed in, was just and fair. "Yes," they'd replied. He then went on to describe how God created one person with straight, blonde hair, light eyes, white skin, small pointy nose and sent that person off to be beautiful and happy. Then God created another person with a large nose, thick lips, curly hair, and dark skin, and ordained that person to be ugly and unhappy. "Is that fair?" Leonardo had challenged the children. "Chao! Chaos!" Leonardo yelled smiling as he recounted the children's reaction. "What do you mean, teacher??" they'd questioned him. Leonardo recounted his response to me:

> "Is God fair? He made two human beings, there is a human being who has everything perfect, he has straight hair, he is white. There is another who [people say], hey, potato nose, I don't know what else . . . If this same God created both of them, he is the most incompetent of all of us!" "How can you say that, teacher?" and another, "It is not that! No, everyone is the same, everyone is beautiful." Then I was like: "The same, we aren't. But we are all beautiful, I like that one." "But how can you say everyone is beautiful when people are like, 'Gee, so and so is ugly. Are you saying that potato nose is ugly? Because people are prejudiced." The kids were starting to get the point I was making. So I said: "Let me explain, what happens is that we, human beings, constructed ideas about what is perfect and what is not perfect. Only this is a construction and we are contaminated by it daily, we see it on TV, the presenter you like, does he have a nose like yours? And the hair. . . ?! [implies the answer is "no"]. So we are there all the time internalizing these ideas about what is beautiful, about what is perfect . . . And then [you walk] through the company you are going to work in. Until you get to the boss, you passed a thousand people, but you walk past like four Black people: one sweeping, one washing, one cleaning . . . You build the idea that their clothes are ugly. Because of that, everything influences you on a daily basis. So when you think she's beautiful and she's ugly, it's because it's built up in your head. Not because she is really beautiful or in fact she is ugly." Wow, man.

In the absence of Black history teachings in public schools, CBOs like Leonardo's have become the spaces for educating favela residents about racial discrimination and pride. In his analysis of racial justice activism in Los Angeles and Rio de Janeiro, João Costa Vargas (2010:xxii) argues that "The ongoing marginalization and premature, preventable death of disproportionate numbers of Black persons in the African Diaspora create the very conditions for the revolutionary transformation of our societies. . . . By revolutionary I mean a frontal, unapologetic challenge to the institutional-ized, cognitive, and cultural sources of oppression, which translates into var-ious forms of combat against the state, corporations, the elites, and all forms of bourgeois segments, even those within the left" (2010:xxii). The shared experiences of victimization because of one's skin color has the potential to create communities of collective action against state oppression and the legacies of colonial rule. In favelas, where racial discrimination is combined with extreme poverty and lethal police operations, the political construction of race holds an especially critical power in constructing shared identifies and political imaginaries about radical social change.

Cidade de Deus is not the only place where consciousness raising about racism is unfolding. The Black Movement (Moviment Negro) across Brazil has, for decades, pushed for a re-education about African ancestry, slavery, and modern forms of racism and racialized resistance (Gomes 2019). It is slowly paying off: between 2012 and 2019, there was a 36% increase in people who declared themselves Black, according to the Brazilian census: in 2019, 9.4% of Brazilians considered themselves Black, up from 7.4% in 2012. The number of people who view themselves as *pardo* also increased by 10% during that time, thereby increasing the proportion—and influence—of Brazil's darker-skinned majority.

Scholars have charged Brazil's Black Movement with being overly fo-cused on cultural politics without organizing around more concrete po-litical demands (Hanchard 2006). While there is some truth to this across Brazil and in Cidade de Deus, there is also an important political change that occurs when more people identify as Black or *pardo*. As many activists in CDD explained to me, this growth signals an expanding community of Black and brown people who have learned about the violence committed by co-lonialism against their ancestors. This shared history promotes an identity tied to shared experiences of racial discrimination, but also racial empower-ment. This helps to create unity within a severely politically fractured com-munity and a shared narrative around how violence unfolds and how it can be resisted.

Race, Gender, and Class: An Intersectional Perspective

Many residents found ways to incorporate racial justice work with demands for women's rights, recognizing that racial oppression impacts Black women differently than Black men. Jordana, Maria Rita's 20-year-old neighbor, used her degree in journalism to highlight cultural projects in favelas and to connect these to issues of race, gender, and violence. Jordana identified proudly as a Black woman. She wore colorful, stylish outfits, often wove strands of red or blue into her braided hair, and wore bright green lipstick that contrasted vividly with her dark skin. Jordana had moved to Cidade de Deus one year earlier to be closer to her university, the Federal University of Rio de Janeiro, one of the most prestigious public universities in the country. She was one of the busiest people I knew in Cidade de Deus (and in general), constantly shuffling between classes, internships, and volunteer work. I often saw Jordana at midnight as she arrived home, exhausted, after a two-hour bus ride from her university. Her constant engagements in Rio's downtown area and other favelas in the city meant that she was rarely in Cidade de Deus.

She had won a full scholarship to her university and had opted to major in Social Communication. In addition to her studies, Jordana was an intern in a research lab that studied culture in the city of Rio de Janeiro and had joined the section on "cultural manifestations from the periphery." Her training as an undergraduate student involved attending cultural events, interviewing artists in favelas, producing texts or videos on these, and offering critical analyses of how these shaped and were shaped by literature and other cultural movements. I asked Jordana how she understood the term "cultural manifestation." This was her response:

> Cultural manifestation is a protest, right, when you create . . . your reality, you know. It is a manifestation. A song, for example rap, is a manifestation, right, you put into words what you live daily and give rhythm to it and disseminate it. So it is a manifestation, a protest made here [in the favela], and it is seen [by people outside]. It is a production . . . it is a form of authorship, you know, of those who live that daily, so that is why it is a manifestation, a protest. It's cultural because it's art, right? It is not a mobilization of [political] protest. It's also mobilizing, but it's through another means, right? A more artistic means.

Though Jordana was commissioned to cover events in many Rio de Janeiro's favelas, she had recently done a story on a self-defense group organized by young women in Cidade de Deus. The group had termed itself Girl Power. Jordana explained why she viewed Girl Power as a form of political resistance:

Girl Power would not necessarily be considered a political act, right, but when you think about all the violence that women suffer, especially women from the periphery [i.e., the favela], and ultimately most of these women are Black, and, you know, when we recognize the violence they suffer daily, I think you need to make a form of defense, resistance. Because this is a form of resistance for women.

As Jordana noted, self-defense classes were not typically considered to be political. But for her, offering these for Black women in the favela was not only a way of arming women with tools to protect their physical and sexual rights, but also of raising awareness of their constant risk of being assaulted. In the two years following this first interview, Jordana covered dozens of stories about similar events.

In January 2018, Jordana started her own YouTube channel dedicated to telling stories about the favela. In her introductory video, Jordana smiles into the camera and exclaims "First of all . . . ," and points at her extremely large earrings that read: "Out with" on the right ear and "Temer" on the left. "Out with Temer" had become a popular slogan among leftist political activists across Brazil since Michel Temer's takeover of the presidency after Dilma's impeachment. Jordana continues: "Secondly, I am here to talk a little bit about what Favela is. Favela is love, it is art, it is freedom, it is theater, it is dance. Favela is life," she proclaims, standing in front of a colorful favela housing complex. "This project" (i.e., her channel), she explains, "proposes to debate themes that are not necessarily discussed in traditional big media. Here we are going to talk about you, your experiences, your lives, your values, what you do, what you like, what you do not like, for you to see yourself here on this little screen." True to her word, the videos on her channel showcase favela residents describing their everyday lives and explaining how they express resistance and identity through their artistic expression. In one video, Jordana reflects on a Samba School that put together a set for the 2018 Carnival parades on slavery in contemporary Brazil. She notes that the parade "shows the favelas as a current *quilombo* [i.e., former community of runaway slaves], as a place of resistance, and as a shelter, since our demands are not being met by the state." The parade had been produced by a Black choreographer from a Rio favela. In both the choreographer's rendition of modern-day racism and Jordana's journalistic reflections of it, art and cultural production have enabled Rio's poor to decry their continued racial, political, and gender subjugation.

Jordana's words and activities demonstrate the important relationship between race and gender in favela activism. While in the previous chapter I discussed the gendered dynamics of governance, and in this chapter I have talked about race as a unifying political construct, it is critical to examine how the experience of being both female and Black intersect in Rio's favelas. As many scholars have noted, Black women's double experience of marginalization—plus, as in the case of favela residents, the experience of poverty—places them not only in a unique position of being the "superexploited" but also of having the greatest urgency in making social change (Perry 2013; Theoharis and Woodard 2009). Writes Brazilian scholar Valdenice Raimundo (2016:136):

> With regard to the struggle for life, understood in the daily resistance it welcomes . . . it is the anonymous black woman, the economic, affective and moral support of her family, who plays the most important role. Exactly because with her strength and courageous capacity to fight for survival, she transmits to her most fortunate sisters the impetus of not refusing to fight for our people . . . Black women have always needed to be part of the struggle for better living conditions and this was done through different forms of organization, from the slavery period, in the post-abolition period and up to the present day, with organizations that have not always accommodated themselves in formal ways, but that have always been constant.

As this quote suggests, the experience of racial oppression also becomes the motivator for action. In fact, Jordana was one of many Black women in Cidade de Deus drawn to favela activism. Isabella, Maria Rita, Carmen, Clara, Natalia, and many other women I have profiled throughout the book identified as Black. It was not only their gender, but also their experiences of racism—including individual experiences of discrimination as well as the recognition that their entire neighborhood had been racialized—that provoked them to organize against violence and inequality. The sphere of non-violence thus enables Black women to gain political power by helping to mobilize their community, while also creating a symbolic connection to drug traffickers and other residents harmed by racial discrimination and the legacies of colonialism.

Researcher Nilza Rogéria Nunes (2021:103) refers to Black female leaders in Rio's favelas as "favela women" and argues that it is their location at the intersection of race, class, and gender that informs both their social identities and leadership in social mobilization in favelas. These "favela women," she finds, are active in a range of activities and spaces, including collectives and CBOs, social movements, religious institutions, and in some cases political parties in order to improve social conditions, healthcare, and education in favelas. Similarly, Anne-Marie Veillette (2021:90) finds that Black women from Rio's favelas have played an active role in organizing against police violence, driven by a resistance rooted in "Amefricanidade," a concept that highlights "the African diaspora's multiple and intensive traditions of resistance across the Americas." Notably, these scholars find that "favela women" were not necessarily motivated by traditional feminism that advocates specifically for women's rights, but rather by a kind of "popular feminism" that focused on improving conditions for their community and for people of all genders (Nunes and Veillette 2022). This finding reflects my own: CDD's Black women leaders organized to address the needs of those around them, not on the basis of gender, but on the basis of a broader quest for peace and equality.

While Chapter 3 noted how the feminization of non-violent politics has created space for activists to participate in the neighborhood's governance, an intersectional perspective allows us to recognize the significance of both gender *and* race in constructing this political sphere. Additionally, race and gender intersect in Cidade de Deus to inspire activism that is not only racialized and gendered but connects to anti-colonial and anti-patriarchal movements elsewhere and in previous eras. As I discuss in Chapter 5, connections to Black women in other favelas and across the city and the world have helped to inspire many of the favela activists in Cidade de Deus. Jordana once shared a graphic of a Black woman on Facebook. In her Afro-style hair is written, "We are the granddaughters of the Black women you couldn't kill" (Figure 4.10). Slavery and its legacies have made the survival of Black women in Brazil an act of resistance and have motivated a commitment to more organized political action within and beyond the favela.

Conclusion

When examined through the lens of cultural embeddedness, we can see how non-violent favela activism has been able to flourish, even in spaces typically characterized by violence and political repression. Favela activists are not only political actors; they are also residents raised in and by their community

Figure 4.10 "We are the granddaughters of the Black women you couldn't kill"
Photo by the author.

and socialized within shared identities, values, and meanings. While some of the discursive tactics described in this chapter were strategically and carefully negotiated, others were much more natural performances that required only that favela activists subscribe to the dominant frames they have become so accustomed to reinforcing in everyday interactions. However, activists "upcycle" these practices, stretching local meanings to a more political place than other residents, drawing connections between local narratives and social movement frames that speak out against state violence, racism, and structural inequality.

Culturally embedded resistance thus allows activists to connect local value systems to more radical and transformative social movement discourses, thereby opposing violence without explicitly resisting the status quo. In some respects, activists deploy "weapons of the weak" by relying on the tools and discourses that have been made available to them in an extremely constrained environment. When examined more closely, however, we see that these discourses have been reappropriated to resist violence through organized and non-violent practices. Through a strategy of political upcycling, they draw on established discourses to oppose structural violence and armed conflict. They maneuver into existing social categories to create new ones. They cater to shared pride around cultural creation to construct new political imaginaries. And they deploy shared racial identities to justify organized action against the legacies of colonialism and its more localized and dangerous consequences.

5

Ties that Strengthen, Ties that Bind

Favela Activists in Urban Politics and Transnational Movements

A favela cresce, de cima para baixo, de baixo para cima, elástica,
como serpente viva, social, ondulante. Se uma palavra a define é
"movimento"

The favela grows, from bottom to top, top to bottom, elastic, like a
live serpent, social, undulating. If there is a word that describes it, it
is "movement."

Renato Meirelles and Celso Athayde, 2016

Introduction

In 2014, Solange founded the Community Coalition, a network of local
community-based organizations (CBOs), public employees, and administrators
working on social service provision in CDD along with researchers from several of Rio's universities and private citizens who volunteered in Cidade de
Deus. They communicated via a WhatsApp text messaging group in which
they shared information about new courses and programs, grant applications,
job openings, and other local initiatives. They also met in person monthly. In
the meetings I attended, participants introduced themselves and described
their programs so colleagues could help connect their clients—primarily CDD
residents—to relevant services. Each meeting, a handful of participants whom
Solange had identified ahead of time provided a more detailed presentation
or live demonstration to the group about their organization and what it could
offer CDD residents. Participants also asked questions about these projects,
gave each other advice on where they might get financial support, donations,
or volunteers, and brainstormed potential collaborations between their re-
spective organizations.

Activism under Fire. Anjuli Fahlberg, Oxford University Press. © Oxford University Press 2023.
DOI: 10.1093/oso/9780197519325.003.0006

The meetings were held in the Youth Center, a building owned and run by the municipal government in Cidade de Deus, which had one of the few air-conditioned meeting spaces in the neighborhood. It was a coveted space, but Solange's good relationship with Youth Center staff had enabled her to secure it for the meetings. Most meetings I attended had between 15 and 25 participants. Those who worked for the government were often mid-level administrators, such as the directors of the local welfare clinic or primary school. Few public servants in attendance had significant control over the policies governing the distribution of state funds, but they offered valuable information about which grants had recently been announced and how to apply for them, and often shared other types of resources, such as lending space for a CBO in the school gym or providing a social worker to teach a course on healthy relationships. In a neighborhood where public policies were implemented in a limited, uneven, and unpredictable capacity, these street-level bureaucrats enacted critical gatekeeping roles, becoming conduits of information, making the state itself more legible and accessible to favela-based CBOs, and creating productive interpersonal ties with those typically marginalized by the state. The Community Coalition created a space where favela activists could meet with people from the state and from private institutions outside the favela to work together to solve local problems. Though Solange kept the meetings on task, she welcomed input from all participants about how frequently to meet, which topics to discuss, who should be invited to present, and more. After the meetings, participants mingled casually while nibbling on cookies and sipping coffee, bonding over their shared struggles of trying to help the neighborhood with so few resources.

The Community Coalition was one of several networks that connected favela activists with the world beyond their neighborhood. In fact, although poverty, violence, and racial exclusion have contributed to making Rio de Janeiro "divided" and "fragmented" (Fahlberg and Vicino 2015; Rocha 2005; Ventura 1994), favela activists struggled fiercely against this social isolation. They frequently received visitors from the "outside," including public servants from the state's social service branches (the health clinic, welfare office, schools, etc.), as well as residents from other favelas, employees from private NGOs across the city, and middle-class residents who volunteered in local CBOs. Favela activists were also constantly on the go. Solange and Maria Rita regularly attended meetings in large NGOs based in downtown areas, Carmen founded a sister organization in another favela, Leonardo worked on various urban social and political campaigns, and Natalia was constantly headed to meetings and cultural events across the city. Many Cidade de Deus activists were also invited to discuss their work at conferences and roundtables in universities and with NGOs located in other states. Several activists had been offered scholarships to study abroad or to perform on stages across the world.

Favelas and other poor urban areas are typically characterized by their social, economic, and political isolation from the rest of the city (Beall, Crankshaw, and Parnell 2014; Ribeiro and Telles 2011; Rocha 2005). However, activists exert critical resistance to this inertia. The cultivation of ties outside the favela has been essential to promoting social change. At a basic level, these ties resist the marginalization of the favela by strengthening its connectivity to the broader urban and global society. Activists' integration into social and political spaces helps to bridge the favela with other urban spaces and movements across the city—and beyond—thereby positioning the favela within broader networks of social change. Through these networks, activists have managed to make demands for social services, development needs, civil rights, and social inclusion in the urban fabric. This movement across spaces has been especially critical in a context of local violent governance: because political demands cannot be made to neighborhood-level corrupt and dangerous leaders, they take their claims to municipal, national, and global actors who have more resources and fewer dangerous ties to favela-based drug traffickers. Their demands are more safely and effectively articulated outside the favela.

This chapter is concerned with examining the different types of networks that favela activists cultivate, how they are leveraged to make demands for resources and rights, and how they help to foster new spaces and channels for democratic claims-making. How, it asks, do these networks produce immediate and potential opportunities for social change? At the same time, these ties present challenges for favela activists, who often occupy subordinate roles in external networks, even within urban and transnational social justice movements. Favela activists are highly reliant on large and comparably wealthy urban NGOs, their white allies in universities and progressive political parties, and Black middle-class intellectuals in Rio de Janeiro and across the world. This has limited their ability to advocate for favela-specific issues in movements that may have political or identity-based concerns but do not struggle with segregated poverty. Ironically, the very spaces of urban and transnational solidarity that help them expand democracy and fight for justice also retrench the subordination of favela activists. With few financial resources and even less political leverage, however, favela activists have little choice but to align themselves with external allies who may take more than they give in return. Despite these inequities, the willingness and capacity of favela activists to cultivate ties with external allies have helped to deepen democracy and expand resources and rights in a context of armed conflict and political repression.

Participatory Democracy in the Favela

Democracy in Brazil has gotten a bad rap. Writing in 1993, shortly after Brazil and other Latin American countries transitioned from dictatorship to democracy, Guillermo O'Donnell charged Latin America's nascent democracies with unevenly distributing citizenship rights and responsibilities across their territories. According to O'Donnell, in certain "brown zones," or areas with high rates of poverty, informality, and "brown" skin, the state did not assert its full authority, leaving residents with "weak" forms of citizenship, where they relied on clientelist ties without meaningful political representation to obtain even the most meager of resources (O'Donnell 1993). Only a few years later, Theresa Caldeira and James Holston (1999) aptly noted that Brazil had become a "disjunctive democracy," whereby the enforcement of civil rights was reserved for white, and usually wealthier citizens, relegating Brazil's Black and poor people to contend with police brutality, routine violations of civil rights, high incarceration rates, and few protections from the legal system. While the increase in social and political rights under the Worker's Party helped to address some forms of inequality, Brazil's democracy continues to be extremely violent, racist, and exclusionary even 20 years later (Amaral 2019). From the perspective of many Cidade de Deus residents, Brazil hardly feels like a democracy at all.

Similar charges have also been levied against other national democracies with significant subnational forms of violence. In many regions across Africa and Asia, for instance, violence has become a pervasive tactic to ensure victory in local elections (Kongkirati 2016; Wahman and Goldring 2020). In South African cities, the rise of vigilantism not only reflects a violent and ineffective state control apparatus, but creates extra-judicial pathways to crime prevention (Smith 2019). In many cities, the rise of asymmetric urban warfare by populations excluded from the political and social benefits of national democracy further erodes citizenship rights in targeted populations. Urban conflict threatens the very stability and strength of the national state in fragile democracies (Beall, Goodfellow, and Rodgers 2013). While political violence poses many challenges for free and fair elections and large-scale social movements, does urban conflict serve only to erode democracy?

The answer depends on how one defines democracy. While democracy is often conceived as a national form of government based on fair elections, institutionalized accountability, and freedom of speech and assembly, among other elements, the concept of "participatory" democracy emphasizes civic engagement at the local level. Participatory democracy can be understood as both a practice and a set of values. In the first case, participatory democracy creates spaces in which citizens can debate, deliberate, discuss, and provide input on and influence over local state politicians and bureaucrats (Baiocchi et al. 2011; Bherer, Dufour, and Montambeault 2016). These dialogues may be collaborative or conflictual, provided they create opportunities for open discussion and collective decision-making (Cornwall and Coelho 2007). In the second case, participatory democracy is defined by a set of principles that promote inclusion, meaningful debate, representation of diverse voices, and collective decision-making (Young 2000). In theory, spaces of participatory democracy help strengthen (national) democracies by empowering citizens to be politically engaged and to hold their leaders accountable (Fung 2009). Furthermore, radical imaginings of participatory democracy have hoped that participation "could transform the inegalitarian relationships between the state and society and that it could help to emancipate and empower citizens in every sphere of their daily lives" (Bherer et al. 2016:226). In these "intermediary" spaces between the state and society, collaboration and contention unfold to allow debate between heterogeneous actors and views, thus becoming "crucibles for a new politics of public policy" (Cornwall and Coelho 2007:2).

Participatory democracy projects—including those spearheaded by local governments as well as those led by civic organizations—became popular across the United States in the 1960s and 1970s, and in Latin America in the 1980s and 1990s after the fall of dictatorships. Thanks to social movements that advocated for more horizontality and inclusion in decision-making, there has been great concern about how to increase participation of ordinary citizens in the making of public policies (Montambeault 2015). Some particularly well-known examples include participatory budgeting in Porto Alegre (Baiocchi 2005), landless peasant movements in rural Brazil (Wolford 2010),

Citizen Power Councils in Nicaragua (Bay-Meyer 2013), and the communal councils in the barrios of Venezuela under Hugo Chavez (Wilde 2017). Studies of these arrangements share a common concern for the extent to which participatory democracy is able to overcome the clientelist practices of Latin American regimes and promote meaningful inclusion of citizens in decision-making. When we shift our focus away from national elections and the enforcement of rights toward spaces of collective dialogue and decision-making, it becomes apparent that Cidade de Deus activists are building and strengthening democracy by creating spaces for meaningful conversations (and arguments) between representatives of various state and non-state institutions, who work together to address the needs of favela residents. They do this in large party by creating ties with allies within the state.

Allies in the State

There are plenty of reasons to argue that the state is unresponsive, or even antithetical, to the needs and concerns of favela residents. However, the "state" is a complex concept, and one that must be more closely examined if we are to fully comprehend its relationship to favelas and, in this case, favela activism. While we often think of the state as the institutions of government, it is also useful to consider the many groups, actors, and individuals who are part of the bureaucratic apparatus of the state. In Brazil, in addition to officials elected by popular vote to legislative branches, there are also appointed officials who oversee various *secretarias*, or agencies charged with executing laws and overseeing the implementation of governance. Within these offices are administrators at various levels, as well as public servants, such as teachers, doctors and nurses, and garbage collectors, who engage in the most direct forms of service provision. Favela activists have spearheaded contentious tactics to pressure state officials, particularly those in positions of power, to fund new projects in CDD, implement public service programs, and uphold their citizenship rights. They also cultivate collaborative ties with many mid-level administrators and lower-level public servants. These mid-level actors did not often have control over major decisions at the municipal or state level, but they became invaluable allies as activists sought resources and worked to implement changes in the local implementation of services. By strengthening their connections to a range of state actors, they promoted participatory democracy in Cidade de Deus.

I got to know several of the state administrators that had become allies to favela activists. Carlos, for instance, was a tall, smiley, light-skinned man in his late 20s who was well liked by local activists. Carlos was hired as the field coordinator for the UPP Social and was tasked with mapping all the public institutions and services already existing in the neighborhood. He was also charged with facilitating dialogue between the municipal government, the private sector, and civil society (i.e., favela residents and CBO leaders). He described his work this way:

> You have a demand, someone else has an offer, and we make this connection, that's what happened here in this "network" [The Community Coalition] meeting, this is one of the aspects of the Program: creating networks in the territories so that the tripod will work. What [composes] this tripod? It is public services, private initiatives and civil society organizations. For something to work this tripod has to happen. So we make a dialogue between these three potentialities, in these three Representations, of the civil society organization, of the private initiative and also of the public services.

Carlos had fostered positive relationships with many CBO leaders, and several of them commented to me about their fondness for him. He was born and raised in another favela, which afforded him a certain legitimacy among favela activists that more affluent state administrators did not have. According to Carlos, this upbringing also afforded him a useful and more holistic perspective on state-favela relations than other state actors had. In his role at the center of this "tripod," Carlos had set out to promote partnerships that were in the interest of favela residents. He describes a potential collaboration with the Children's Institute, a powerful national organization funded by a public-private partnership that reigned in millions of reals each year to support a range of social, educational, and artistic programs for Brazilian children:

> Let me give you an example: The Children's Institute had a project to train young people, and then they got in touch with [the UPP Social] saying the following: "Look, send me the contacts of the partners of institutions, you know, associations, local leaders there in CDD so that we can make a partnership there, so that they send the young people for training to the Program that will happen in Barra." And we were like, "Wait a minute. Give you their contact info? I'm not going to give their contacts. We have their

contact info, but what is your goal, what is the objective, who is behind this?" "Oh no, you can't say who the funder is?" I said: "Then we cannot give their contact, if this is not clear. What we can do is mobilize the whole community, the leaders, we put them in a room for you to present the project, then you say what you can give them, that you cannot say who the funder is, so if they want to do the partnership with you, all right" . . . So you go there and be clear, because I know how Cidade de Deus is, I know how people here think, . . . what their ideologies are. You understand? So we have an understanding of how to proceed . . . Pre-determined projects will not come here, they will not work in Cidade de Deus.

As the moderator of these relationships, Carlos saw himself as a kind of gatekeeper, attempting to protect favela organizations from corrupt private organizations that might prey on them, while also ensuring that local CBOs had the opportunity to decide for themselves which organizations they were willing to work with. Isabella was especially fond of Carlos, who had played a central role in helping her and other community members work with COMLURB, the municipal garbage collection company. Through their collaboration, Isabella and Carlos had succeeded in increasing trash collection days and locations. Unfortunately, Carlos lost his job shortly after our interview, when funding for his program was drastically cut. However, he offered an example of a positive and productive relationship between the state and favela activists, driven in part by Carlos's own background as a favela resident and personal commitment to protecting the interests of CDD's activist organizations.

Patricia offered another example. She was the director of the local welfare office, which provided assistance to families in extreme poverty and crisis in Cidade de Deus. Patricia and her team of three social workers were responsible for enrolling poor residents in CadÚnico, the government's platform for distribution of public benefits, such as the Bolsa Familia cash transfer program, public housing, and aid for utilities. However, as Patricia explained to me, she had little control over which families received aid: all she could do was enroll them in the database and wait for them to make it through the system. The welfare office was also severely understaffed, with 4 social workers to attend 500 families. Despite this, Patricia had found ways to make herself useful to local CBOs. I first met Patricia at Youth Promise, where two of her staff taught a weekly class about citizenship rights and obligations. Solange and Maria Rita had both spoken fondly of their partnership. They met regularly with Patricia to coordinate the distribution of resources to Youth Promise's families and the provision of various training programs for its youth and caretakers. I ran into Patricia on several occasions at various meetings in and with local CBOs, and both she and Carlos were regular participants at The Community Coalition meetings. While Carlos and Patricia are only two examples, they showcase the ties between local-level state administrators and CBOs, who often worked collaboratively to push state resources as far as they could go and to provide whatever personal assistance and protections they could within the limits of their roles.

As Françoise Montambeault (2015) notes, participatory democracy often has different degrees of success. In the case of Cidade de Deus, networks of local and state service providers helped activists and local government actors expand resources and improve the practices of state agencies, reflecting the agency of mid-level administrators (Baiocchi et al. 2011). However, they could not single-handedly reverse national trends, such as the austerity measures spearheaded by President Temer or endemic corruption in the political system, nor could they rid Cidade de Deus of armed conflict. While The Community Coalition has provided favela activists, state administrators, and other public and private actors across the city spaces in which to dialogue and work together to solve local problems, not all meetings between the favela and the state have been collaborative. As the next section illustrates, meetings between activists and more powerful urban actors have also been characterized by contentious forms of claims-making.

Contentious Collaborations

The Residents' Board meeting was scheduled for 2 p.m. I had been eager to attend this particular meeting, as the board was in the process of revising their charter and restructuring the organization in order to make it more compliant with federal laws and, thus, more competitive for obtaining federal funding through the National Bank. I stepped into the building run by the Residents' Board where the meeting would be held, greeted some of the staff on the first floor, and headed upstairs to the "conference room"—a small classroom filled with old wooden student chairs, likely donated from a school. Though the space would be tight for such an important meeting, it was the only room with an air conditioner.

Beatriz, a thin woman with brown skin and a small Afro, walked up, introduced herself to me with a friendly smile, and offered me a thin plastic cup for coffee. I declined, choosing water instead. It was too hot to drink the Brazilian *cafezinho*, a dark, syrupy coffee filled with sugar. We chatted amiably as the other participants slowly arrived. Beatriz had recently been hired as one of two paid administrative staff at the Institute for a Better Neighborhood, a CBO founded by the Residents' Board a few years earlier to serve as what they called their "executive branch." While the Residents' Board identified the needs and priorities for improving Cidade de Deus, the institute had been founded to apply for grants that could be used to fulfill the board's vision. The institute had recently received a grant from a large, well-funded urban NGO called the Association for a Better Tomorrow (ABT), which received large state and private grants and distributed these to small CBOs in favelas to provide direct services to residents. ABT also provided some of their own direct services to favela residents through their main office closer to Rio's downtown, including job trainings and assistance with navigating the job market. Among their recent projects had been helping the Residents' Board streamline and formalize their legal status so they could apply for federal and private grants themselves and be less reliant on ABT and other urban NGOs to fund their work. ABT had hired two legal experts to lead the restructuring of the board's charter and organizational practices.

I recognized many of the people arriving to the meeting, several of whom I had already interviewed: Clara, Carmen, and Geovana, profiled in Chapter 3; Rafael, a white middle-aged man with a scruffy white beard and oversized clothes who founded a CBO dedicated to helping artists and clothing designers become financially independent by selling their goods and training them in commercial sales; Carlina, a frail Black woman who walked with a slight hunchback and who was at the institute every time I came over, though I was never clear exactly what she did. Several people I didn't recognize also arrived and took their seats. Most of the participants in the meeting were darker skinned. At the front of the room, two 30-something, light-skinned women dressed in business attire had arrived and got to work setting up a projector and computer. Simone, one of the directors of ABT who had been charged with overseeing the restructuring of the Residents' Board, sat off to the side. She was a middle-aged, light-skinned woman with short, light-brown hair.

Finally, the meeting began. The nicely dressed women in the front introduced themselves. They were lawyers with expertise in executing land policy, particularly around urban and rural settlements on public and private land. They had been commissioned by the ABT to revise and help "improve" the board's legal statute to make it compliant with the National Bank so they could qualify for large federal grants. The board founders had drafted the statute themselves nearly a decade earlier and had re-written it several times over the years. After finally getting the projector to work, the lawyers projected the document with their mark-ups and edits onto the screen. The document glistened with red underlines. Comments, cross-outs, deletes, and edits filled the right column. Few words had been left unmarked. I felt my entire body tense in reaction to the image and could only imagine the stress this must have provoked in the documents' authors sitting next to me.

Alessandra, the lawyer who appeared to be in charge, began reading the top of the document, proceeding line by line and commenting on the areas she and her colleague found problematic. I did my best to follow their critiques, which were mired in obscure legal jargon. For instance, the lawyers were concerned about conflicts of interest in the statute. In particular, they worried that members of the Residents' Board—the institute's governing body—were also among the possible recipients of institute funds. They also challenged the board's requirement that all members be "juridical" people—representatives of registered CBOs—rather than "physical" people—i.e., individuals. They claimed that this prevented people with no leadership role in a CBO from having a say in board decisions. They also noted that many CBOs struggled to keep their paperwork up to date. What would happen if a CBO's registration papers expired? Would they be excluded from the board? Could they continue to participate at meetings until they could renewed their registration? The lawyers made their way through the document highlighting issues and attempting to explain inconsistencies and requirements. "We are going to suggest we change this to this," stated Alessandra, pointing at new text she had written in to replace the institute's text. "Sound ok?" Participants squinted at the screen attempting to make sense of her recommendations, but before they could respond, Alessandra took their silence as approval. "Ok, onto the next line," she continued. I looked around the room, which had fallen silent as people attempted to keep up with the fast-paced, technical presentation and Alessandra's complex logic for changing so much of their original document.

The silence did not last long, however. Rafael jumped in to explain their logic behind what the lawyers saw as a legal inconsistency: "We are an association of institutions," he explained, describing the lengthy history of how the

Residents' Board had been founded entirely by CBO leaders and why they had decided to keep that structure. The lawyer interrupted him before he could finish to explain why this was legally problematic. Jair, a middle-aged man who had been active in Cidade de Deus's social movements for decades and was hired alongside Beatriz to assist with the restructuring process, jumped in to propose a possible compromise between Rafael's point and the lawyer's concerns. Before he could finish, Alessandra interrupted him to explain why his solution would not work. Another participant interrupted her loudly: "We are a forum of discussion around political decisions!" Another participant jumped in to explain to the lawyers, with frustration, that the goal of the institute was to implement the decisions made by the board. "I understand, but my job here is just to clarify" the lawyer remarked condescendingly, despite her obvious preference for keeping her proposed changes.

All over the room hands were shooting up as people shifted uneasily in their chairs, eager to lay claim to their history and their own narrative of it. Somehow Clara managed to get her turn in the rowdy crowd, suggesting that ultimately "juridical" people were the only ones who had the capacity to execute whatever decisions the board made and that it would not be fair for residents with no commitment to social development to make decisions about the neighborhood if they were not in a position to actually carry them out. Simone, ABT's director who had been silent until now, jumped in animatedly: "Outsiders can still help by being part of the Institute!" she exclaimed as she pointed vigorously at herself, eager to ensure that her own role in the improvement of Cidade de Deus was not discounted. After multiple attempts to be heard, Geovana raised her voice authoritatively and proclaimed that democracy was not always about expanding decision-making power, but about deepening and affording more substance to the process. The board, she explained, contributed to democratic engagement by increasing social development and demanding public policies for Cidade de Deus rather than by simply including a growing number of voices in the decision-making processes. I looked back at Simone, the ABT director, who by now had retreated from the confrontational debate and was on her phone scrolling through her Facebook newsfeed.

The lawyer, tired of listening to the increasingly angry dissent among participants, shifted from the "open floor" model to a hurried explanation of the remaining comments and edits in the document. To my right, Carlina, who had been sitting with her hand raised for the last thirty minutes, rubbed her forehead in anguish and whispered in my direction, "I don't work for them." Giving up on getting a word in, Carlina got up and began serving us water, for which we were extremely grateful. Another participant behind me added loudly, "This is so rude." By now, the other lawyer was engaged in a heated debate off to the side of the room with another participant. Finally, the room erupted into total chaos as Alessandra exclaimed, "You will need to explain this to me because I'm *very* confused!" and Rafael began to shout, "The politics for the fight for Cidade de Deus *is* the Board and the Institute!"

Finally, Carmen, sitting off to the side, lunged forward with her hand in the air in a display of control. The room quieted as Carmen took command. She recounted the history of some of their struggles, what motivated the decisions outlined in the statute, and why some of Alessandra's suggestions had not worked in the past. "They have worked for me," Alessandra remarked. "Well then you must be much prettier than me," Carmen retorted facetiously. I chuckled to myself as Alessandra shifted uncomfortably. Tensions finally began to ease as Carmen offered suggestions for how they might recon- cile some of their differing perspectives and why some parts of the statute could not be changed. In what appeared like an effort to wrap up the conten- tious meeting, Carmen extended a peace offering by noting that they were all benefitting from the knowledge they had gained from the lawyers during this process. The lawyers agreed to take another look at their edits and in- corporate more of the board's demands into the statute. After four hours, the meeting finally ended, though more because of everyone's exhaustion than because much progress had been achieved.

Fighting to be Heard

There are two stories in this anecdote. Perhaps the more obvious one is the denigration and condescension with which the lawyers criticized the hard work of the favela activists. The race and class dynamics were difficult to ignore, as the professionally-dressed, lighter-skinned lawyers "educated" poor, dark-skinned favela residents about what they saw as the (many) inadequacies of their plan. While the meeting may have been labeled a col- laboration, it also revealed some of the negative sentiments held by middle- class urban society about the favela—that they are uneducated, informal, irrational, culturally "other," and "inferior" (Perlman 1979). Spaces of par- ticipatory democracy, like this meeting, embody the power differentials be- tween state and private actors and favela activists. They create a space for the enactment of white saviorism, where more powerful urban actors "assist" and "educate" favela actors about how to do things "the right way." This reinforces a classed and racialized hierarchy between the city and the favela upheld by rigid and hard-to-follow bureaucratic practices meant to exclude those without formal training. It also belittles the local forms of knowledge and practice developed by favela residents to address challenges and needs specific to their neighborhood. Participatory democracy may place a diversity of urban actors in the same space to dialogue about an issue of communal importance, but these actors bring with them their prejudices and stratified access to resources and bureaucratic knowledge and power.

There is another story here, however: favela activists fought back. They refused the dominant narrative, and they resisted the lawyers' forceful suggestions and demeaning attitude. While the fight had been difficult to watch, it had been a fight! And it was a collective fight, as board members banded together to refuse the bureaucratic logic of social change and class inequality that the lawyers attempted to impose on them. By fighting back, activists demonstrated the logic behind their actions and the thoughtful ways in which they deployed local capital. It was based on the belief that "no one knows more about how to survive poverty than the poor themselves" (Appadurai 2001:29). Had the lawyers in fact listened to board members, rather than seeking to correct them, they might have been able to appreciate the complex and challenging political landscape within which the fight for social development unfolds in favelas. While the lawyers may have been correct that the board's charter would not meet the standards of the National Bank, the favela activists' locally embedded approach to their organizational policies and practices was equally valid and rational within the local context.

The more I got to know board members, the more I was able to fully understand the logic of the practices they had developed and why they did not match the demands of the National Bank (or the lawyers). In particular, I came to appreciate the challenge of maintaining democratic spaces for decision-making in a neighborhood governed by drug traffickers and corrupt politicians. Although the role of violent politics had not been fully articulated during that one meeting just described—in part, I suspect, because these issues could not be safely discussed in such a large forum—it became increasingly visible through my conversations and interactions with local activists. As it turns out, democracy must be closely guarded—and therefore, exclusionary—in a context of violent clientelism.

Democratic Exclusions in Spaces of Violence

Both the Community Coalition and the Residents' Board meeting demonstrate the benefits that spaces of participatory democracy provide in enabling
collaborative and contentious relationships between favelas, private actors,
and the state. However, it is also important to recognize the distinctions between democratic spaces in areas under threat by violent political actors
and in more peaceful spaces, where residents can attend meetings with the
state and the private sector without the overwhelming fear of being struck
by a stray bullet or being spied on by those involved in violent clientelism. In
Cidade de Deus, the simple act of traveling to meetings involved significant
risk due to frequent police operations in the streets. Meetings of both the
Community Coalition and the Residents' Board were often cancelled at the
last minute when a shootout broke out, and occasionally participants were
caught in a shootout on their way to or from the meetings. This created stress
for both CDD residents as well as outsiders less accustomed to facing these
risks in their everyday lives. Often, this meant that only those state and private actors most committed to direct engagement with favela activists were
willing to attend meetings, thereby excluding other potential allies.

Activists themselves were forced to navigate a tension between their
partnerships with social service branches of the state and the constant risk
of violence created by the state's security branch. In order to sustain their
partnerships with allies in the state, activists also had to overlook the perverse, albeit indirect, ties between their allies and the police. In conflict zones,
participatory democracy requires participants to be willing to face personal
risks, continually adapt to challenges, and accept the violence undergirding
the power of state officials. Favela activists nearly always held the short end of
the stick in these participatory spaces, which, for many people I got to know,
created significant psychological burdens from both constant fear and the
moral dilemmas they had to continually navigate.

Additionally, few studies of participatory democracy discuss the fear
among activists of the strong possibility of co-optation by local armed actors.
In conflict zones, where violent governance is pervasive, activists struggle to
keep these spaces safe for actual debate. In these cases, participatory democracy hinges on a tight policing of borders and the exclusion of outsiders who
could potentially be embedded in dangerous and corrupt political networks.
The Residents' Board adopted a number of strategies to protect their space
from the influence of violent politics. For one, they were cautious about

which politicians they associated with and avoided affiliation with party politics. They also repeated over and over that they were not representatives of Cidade de Deus. Isis, one of the board members, explained this logic to me:

> You have to include in your research project that the Board doesn't represent the entire Cidade de Deus. We are a piece of Cidade de Deus . . . and by virtue of this the Institute also only represents a piece . . . Because here [in Cidade de Deus] we have associations and organizations that don't share our methodology, the proposition of the Board, because we are non-partisan. We don't talk about party politics, we don't represent a political party. We are an open forum that goes after public policies. Here we don't speak in the name of Secretary this-and-such. He [the Secretary] can even be our friend, our partner at different moments, but we aren't going to say, "Oh, [we are with] so-and-so." We leave that really clear, it's in our statute. We are non-partisan, [in case] some of the Residents' Associations wear the shirt of a political party, and then it gets difficult, you know? And that's why we say that we aren't Cidade de Deus, we only represent a piece of Cidade de Deus.

As Isis's description suggests, the board's eagerness to reject any claim to representation of the neighborhood was strategic: they did not want to be confused with local political groups party politics, or Residents' Associations. While board members made many direct claims on the mayor, city council members, state deputies, and secretaries at the state and federal levels, they refused to engage in local politics or to campaign for specific political parties. Engagement with government actors at the local level would not only have brought board members into close contact with violent actors and likely required they engage in dangerous partnerships with them, it would also have eroded their legitimacy. Despite their best efforts to steer clear of these networks, the board was not entirely immune from these issues. Geovana explained to me the risk of infiltration by the gang:

> The Board doesn't have the ability to prevent anyone from attending [the meetings]. But a meeting is completely different when you have someone like that [i.e., widely known to have ties to the drug trade] . . . If there is something more serious [to discuss], you aren't going to talk about it, understand? And a resident goes to a meeting like that, and there's a guy that has ties to the drug trade, the resident enters mute and leaves in silence, he

doesn't speak, he doesn't say anything. And besides that, he looks at all of us and says . . . "What do these people (i.e., the Board) want? They are talking about rights and healthcare and they are sitting down with people who represent the interests of the drug trade." That hurts us . . . He looks at us and says, "It's all flour from the same bag, they must not want any real change if they are sitting with the drug trade."

The constant threat of being co-opted by the gang—or being perceived by other CDD residents in this way—required that the board safeguard entry to their meetings as closely as possible. One strategy had been to only allow "juridical" people—those who represented formal CBOs—to be voting members. This allowed the board to thoroughly vet people for potential ties to gangs or corrupt politicians before they were afforded a seat at the table. There was a technocratic logic to this approach as well: those with "expertise" in managing the social development of the neighborhood were deemed most adept at representing the neighborhood's interests with municipal and state organs and private investors. The board's decision to only allow "juridical" people helped to prevent members of the drug trade from co-opting meetings and delegitimizing their work, although it also limited broader participation and inclusion among other residents.

Solange also kept close tabs on who she invited to the Community Coalition. She had begun by inviting those people and organizations she already knew and trusted, and gradually the group had expanded to include those trusted by her colleagues. It was a growing, but nonetheless closed circle of friends and friends of friends. While there was always the possibility that someone affiliated with the drug trade might join the group, the members kept close watch on who they invited and who participated. By keeping the meetings private, rather than publicizing them to the neighborhood, the Community Coalition managed to keep out unwanted participants and perhaps some potential allies as well. Ironically, the democratic spaces that activists helped to construct were also zones of exclusion. They relied on a tight control over who could enter. In a context of corrupt and violent governance, participatory democracy could only be maintained through restrictive gatekeeping and exclusionary decision-making. Ultimately, both the Residents' Board and the Community Coalition sacrificed resources and representativeness for security and legitimacy. Actually existing democracies are never without internal contradictions, and the politics of non-violence in Cidade de Deus is no exception.

These closures help us think differently about what democracy looks like in favelas and other areas of extreme violence. Within the tightly guarded spaces of participatory democracy, residents could make demands for social services and civil rights directly to government administrators and elected officials. In this case, political democracy was replaced by "strong democracy," characterized by active engagement by ordinary citizens in discussion and organizing around local, everyday issues in dialogue with the state (Barber 2003). Thus, democracy has not disappeared in conflict zones; it has instead been reconfigured to adapt to the constraints of entrenched clientelism and dangerous politics within the neighborhood. Within the favela, this manifests in controlled spaces for dialogue and claims-making. As I show in the next section, strong democracy has also transcended favela boundaries, inserting Cidade de Deus—and its social and political concerns—into the city's urban political arena.

Transcending Boundaries

As I briefly mentioned in the conclusion of Chapter 3, Natalia announced her candidacy for city council at the end of Art Talk's crowded monthly Open Mic in April 2016, six months before the municipal election in October. It had been a fun, energizing event. Between 40 and 50 people had been in attendance, including many local artists as well as poets and songwriters from neighboring middle-class areas and other favelas who had become regular participants in CDD's cultural scene. After the last poet had spoken, Natalia took the mic and declared her plan to run for office. Although more than 20 CDD residents decided to run for city council that year, most of the activists I knew were fearful of electoral politics and its capacity to create undesired connections to dangerous networks. Natalia was fearless and determined, however, and was willing to take the risk for the reward of having what she perceived as a legitimate voice in government. Natalia smiled at her audience awkwardly, defending her decision to run: Democracy needed to be strengthened. The favela needed to be represented in government. It was critical for women to have a voice in the political system. As she spoke, the bar transitioned from a site of cultural production to one of political action. And Natalia transformed from a poet into a candidate. It would be the beginning of a long, arduous, and ultimately unsuccessful bid for public office. Yet, Natalia's campaign also played an important role in inserting the favela into the city's mainstream political spaces and bringing the center to the periphery.

A few months after her announcement, I became a volunteer on Natalia's campaign. It was a bare-bones operation. Her campaign headquarters were on the main avenue that cut through Cidade de Deus, in an açaí store that the owner shut down for a month for Natalia's campaign. The leftist political party under which she was running[1] had provided her with a few volunteers who appeared to be in their late 20s, and many of her colleagues from Art Talk—some from CDD and some from outside—also pitched in. Among her most dedicated volunteers was Catalina, one of Natalia's close friends from her time at a prestigious private university, which Natalia had attended a few years earlier on a full scholarship.

While many candidates opt to campaign across multiple neighborhoods to expand their support base, Natalia decided to focus on Cidade de Deus, where she thought she had a better chance of gaining support. Natalia convinced a friend to drive his van around the neighborhood carrying a large sound speaker that replayed an announcement and some songs informing residents of Natalia's candidacy and asking for their vote. Meanwhile, a handful of volunteers and I walked around the neighborhood handing out flyers and speaking to passersby. We did the best we could with the few resources we had, but Natalia was frustrated with the political party under which she was running and the little support it had provided her. Their volunteers spent more time sleeping than campaigning, she told me, and the flyers printed by the party with Natalia's name and photo only arrived three days before the election.

Natalia did not win. While several residents I spoke with about the campaign blamed her loss on her lack of charisma, there were much larger structural issues at play. For one, her own party had failed to properly support her campaign. An even larger obstacle was the electoral system itself, which has been antagonistic to the election of favela residents. In Rio de Janeiros, candidates are elected based on representational voting by political party, rather than by neighborhood or district, meaning that candidates must gain votes from residents from the same political party across multiple neighborhoods in order to be competitive (Gelape 2018). Given how few favela residents have the resources or visibility to obtain support outside their neighborhood, few are successful. The only favela resident elected to city council that year was Marielle Franco, a Black sociologist and human rights activist from the large Maré favela complex. Favela activists across Rio de Janeiro viewed her election as a victory for favelas—and it was. In order to win, however, Marielle had secured votes from dozens of neighborhoods in the wealthy Zona Sul and downtown areas as well. In an interview with newspaper *O Globo*, Marielle explained: "I didn't want to be a candidate only of Maré. The problems of Maré are reproduced across the entire city. For this reason, I traveled across all of Rio" (Soares 2016). Thus, even when favela residents do win a seat, they must advocate for issues that transcend the favela.

While Natalia was disappointed that she did not win, she had established herself as a fierce and eloquent candidate. She strengthened relationships with members of her party and other left-leaning political parties in power at City Hall and positioned herself as an important political figure in Cidade de Deus. Her legitimacy and connections to the city's progressive political parties became vital networks of mobilization six weeks after the election, when a police helicopter went down in Cidade de Deus during an operation. All four military police officers in the helicopter died. Immediately, rumors spread that CDD's drug traffickers had shot down the helicopter. Police operations in CDD continued throughout the night. The following morning, seven young, dark-skinned men were found assassinated, their bodies tossed into the swamp, presumably killed by the police as payback for the downed helicopter. Several were naked, and some had limbs or organs cut off. According to the human rights newspaper *The New Democracy*, police posted a selfie a few days later on a police-focused Facebook page celebrating the execution. The photo featured eight police officers standing in what appeared to be a swamp with a young man held between them on his knees, later recognized as one of the victims (Antônio 2016).

The day after the crash, State Secretary for Public Security Roberto Sá reported that no bullet holes had been found in the helicopter. Later reports would confirm that the helicopter crashed due to mechanical malfunction. State neglect, not CDD's drug traffickers, had killed the police officers. Nevertheless, a state judge proceeded to order a "collective search warrant," allowing the police to search any house in CDD deemed to be "of interest" in the investigation. She justified it by claiming that "In exceptional times, exceptional measures are also required in order to restore public order" (OABRJ 2016). Soon after, residents began sharing pictures across social media groups of their doors broken down and furniture destroyed by the police.

Natalia and other local activists organized a street protest, in which hundreds of residents took to the streets, holding signs demanding their right to peace and security and decrying the mandate by the judge. Natalia also spoke with several leaders in the city's progressive political parties, the press, and various human rights networks with which she was involved, providing them with information about the killings and home invasions. In response, the State of Rio de Janeiro's Public Defender's Office took on the case. Within two days, they succeeded in annulling the collective search and seizure order due to its violation of habeas corpus. Finally, the police stopped their searches and left the neighborhood, after days of terrorizing residents. Schools and business were able to reopen. The Public Defender's Office issued a statement about the case, noting how the nullification of the warrant would help to set a precedent against similar warrants in the future. According to the Justice Forum, which offers analysis of legal cases, "In addition to the practical and concrete effect that the declaration of nullity in the process will produce, the decision has an important symbolic effect to establish a precedent tending to form jurisprudence contrary to this invasive and generalized measure against residences in marginalized territories" (Fórum Justiça 2016).

The connections that Natalia and other local activists established with powerful urban political actors and social justice organizations have thus played an important role in fighting for the civil rights of CDD residents and in advocating for justice against state violence more generally.

Activists also build these ties through wide-reaching coalitions. In 2017, for instance, Leonardo helped to launch a new initiative that aimed to include favela youth in urban and national debates around drug policy. The initiative was a partnership between a research center in Rio de Janeiro State University and a group of young people from several favelas in Rio de Janeiro. Leonardo had played a key role in organizing the group, identifying its objectives, bringing in new members, and speaking about the initiative at events across the city. I attended the official launch in August 2017, at an arts center in the Maré complex, one of the city's largest favelas. There were at least 300 people at the event, mostly young and dark skinned. Leonardo was the MC, leading the audience through hip hop and poetry performances, a discussion about drugs, security, and favelas in Rio among Black academics and activists, and a reception. The event was recorded and streamed to an additional 1,000 viewers across Brazil.

While people mingled after the event, Leonardo beamed as he handed me the group's shiny new booklet. It contained information about the history of drug use and drug control across the globe, the types of drugs used and those most common in Brazil—highlighting that 50% of Brazilians reported using alcohol in the last 12 months—and explained the transformation of drug use into a social problem with criminal penalties. "In Brazil, between 2006 and 2008," it reads, "8 thousand people died per year due to drug use. But 96% of these deaths were caused by legal drugs, like alcohol and tobacco." Skipping ahead two pages, the brochure notes that "The majority of individuals incarcerated and killed in the war on drugs are young, Black, and residents of favelas and the periphery, demonstrating that this policy is selective." The brochure concludes by suggesting that this situation can only change with the decriminalization and regulation of drugs. Favela residents, it claims, "suffer from daily violence, our rights are restricted, and we lose opportunities. It is time for us to be included in the debate about drug policy in order to make our perspective heard."

The organization expanded in the following years. They have since organized national conferences, slam poetry events, a podcast, and a residency program for favela youth to debate and learn about drugs and violence in favelas. Although their organization is by and for favela youth, they have established partnerships with organizations in São Paulo and Bogotá, Colombia, and several universities across Rio de Janeiro. Through his participation in this organization and many other social and political campaigns before that, Leonardo was engaged in networks across the city and beyond.

Like Leonardo, other Cidade de Deus activists routinely crossed neighborhood boundaries to establish connections with urban actors in an attempt to gain resources, social capital, and knowledge they could use to help their neighborhood and promote favela rights more broadly. Maria Rita, Solange, Carmen, and many other CBO leaders regularly traveled to other favelas and to downtown business areas to meet with NGOs and public agencies who funded their projects. MC Claudinho, Luz, and other artists showcased their work in public venues, including art festivals, theaters, and other performance spaces. Many played organizing roles in the Literary Festival of the Urban Periphery (FLUPP), an annual event started in 2012 that brought together writers and artists from across Rio's favelas. The newspaper *Rio on Watch* (2016) describes FLUPP this way: "The idea of the 'periphery' in this festival extends beyond the geographical sense to include communities and identities that are marginalized in society. The themes of the activities varied from racism, homophobia and sexism, and legacies of colonialism, to self-empowerment and self-determination."

FLUPP festivals and planning meetings provided an important space for cultural activists in CDD to meet with other favela activists, discuss issues of urban inequality and rights, and construct collective identities around shared experiences of discrimination, violence, and poverty. Activists were engaged in other urban social and political networks as well. Leonardo, for instance, helped to campaign for Eduardão, a progressive city councilman from the Manguinhos favela running for re-election in 2016. Fernanda, a local social worker, had established connections to multiple large businesses across the city to establish school-to-work programs in order to help favela residents obtain employment. Carmen established a satellite CBO in another favela, using a similar model of ecological development and environmental justice as the CBO in Cidade de Deus. Most other activists I knew were similarly integrated in a diversity of groups, political parties, and social movements across the urban landscape.

As these examples demonstrate, favela activists are engaged in a wide variety of social and political organizations, movements, and spaces throughout the city. These include the formal political arena, where some activists have volunteered on campaigns for progressive candidates or, in the case of Natalia, have run for city council themselves. Many activists are affiliated with, or declare allegiance to, left-leaning political parties. Some activists work for the state as public employees, including as social workers, teachers and garbage collectors and in other professions, and many of them are members of labor unions. Activists also engage in an array of urban social movements, some of which were specific to favela interests (such as FLUPP) while others addressed broader issues related to racism, poverty, and urban inequality that affect favelas as well as other urban residents. Activists also have relationships with well-established urban NGOs and universities, which offer financial resources, staff or intern support, and capacity-building trainings to favela-based CBOs. All of these connections have embedded Cidade de Deus in the social and political fabric of the city and helped to channel resources, tactics, and tools into the favela.

Favelas and other poor urban neighborhoods are often defined by their material and symbolic exclusion from the city (Cardoso 2013; Fahlberg and Vicino 2015; Gonçalves 2013; Ventura 1994). Not only are the urban poor pushed out of desirable urban spaces and denied access to high-quality urban services, they are also barred from effective political participation. While favela activists have not been able to completely rewrite this process of exclusion, they push forcefully against it. By cultivating ties to powerful political arenas and movements across the city, favela activists combat isolation and invisibility. As Bautès, Dupont, and Landy (2013) have suggested, slum dweller movements have become increasingly complex, targeting a range of state and private actors across the city and often working with civil society organizations that mediate between the state and slums. This diversification of alliances facilitates movement by favela residents outward and movement of urban actors into the favela.

Notably, this movement between the favela and the city has an important effect: it allows activists to bypass local political institutions that have been co-opted by drug traffickers and go directly to city-wide political spaces to make demands for resources and rights. By taking political action outside the favela, activists can avoid making claims on neighborhood associations or the regional administration, both of which are widely perceived to be corrupt and ineffective. Instead, they organize through urban networks that fall outside the reach (or interests) of drug traffickers and where they have a greater likelihood of making change, however incremental, without significant threat to their lives or the integrity of their work.

From the Favela to the World

Cidade de Deus residents move not only around the city but across the country and the world. Cultural activists in particular are highly mobile, traveling to other states in Brazil to perform their poems and music or to attend conferences and seminars through various universities, collectives, and NGOs. Several artists I met had been invited to perform in Europe, and Natalia had spent one semester as an exchange student in North Carolina. Members of the Residents' Board had also taken a few trips outside the state of Rio de Janeiro, often to give invited talks about their successes in bringing new social development projects to Cidade de Deus. In one particularly important trip, for instance, the board lobbied a federal legislator to fund airfare for two board members to fly to Brasilia, the country's capital, shortly after Lula's election. According to Geovana, they then met with various federal ministries, including the ministries of health, housing and sports, and the Federal Bank (Caixa Econômica Federal) to ask that federal resources be invested in Cidade de Deus. They requested that the Ministry for Sports (Secretaria do Esporte) invest in a factory to make soccer balls in CDD in preparation for the 2007 Pan American games. They asked the Ministry for

Education (Secretaria da Educação) to build a secondary school in CDD and requested that the Federal Bank fund the construction of more public housing. As Geovana explained to me, board members had viewed this trip as essential when their many efforts to engage then-mayor Cesar Maia had been ignored. In an effort to improve their neighborhood, national, as well as international, travel has become a core strategy of favela activism.

In addition to demanding specific resources, activists also used these trips to strengthen the connections between favelas and transnational social movements. Rosangela's embeddedness in a global network of female activists provides a useful example. Rosangela was an avid poet and writer and often engaged with other writers on a range of websites. Through these connections, she had been invited to serve as a reporter for *World Alive*, a global social media platform that aims to "unite and empower women everywhere" through storytelling and facilitating connections between female change-makers across countries. Many of her stories were about community journalism and cultural events in Cidade de Deus. Her articles were often liked or commented on by women in Africa, Europe, and Latin America, and Rosangela had embraced these virtual relationships. In 2016, *World Alive* asked Rosangela to attend and write a story about the 13th International Forum of AWID (The Association for Women's Rights in Development), a four-day conference of over 2,000 women from across Latin America. The theme for the conference was "Feminist Futures: Constructing Collective Power in Promotion of Rights and Justice." The forum took place in Bahia, in northeastern Brazil. Rosangela animatedly reported her experiences to me after she returned. She had established several relationships with feminists at the conference, including the president of AWID, the founder of *World Alive*, a Capoeira Master who had founded capoeira schools in six other countries,[2] a labor rights organizer from São Paulo, and many feminist activists from Africa and other Latin American countries. When I asked Rosangela what she had taken from the event, she replied:

> I realized that I was born to be a reporter, that I like communication and that there is nothing in the world better than listening to people. And that World Alive values me and supports me in actions. Everything I learn with my friends and sisters from World Alive makes me realize how much we can contribute to the development of people. I feel embraced by the women of the world in the World Alive network.

Rosangela spoke about *World Alive* during most, if not all, of my visits to her home. According to the *World Alive* website, Rosangela has 167 followers and has impacted 1,804 readers since she joined in 2011. She wrote her articles in Portuguese and then posted them in English after running them through Google Translate, sometimes asking me to review the translations first. Her posts were about art and culture, urban violence, and resistance in Cidade de Deus. In 2018, she shared a post about her participation in the World Social Forum in Bahia, Brazil, where she had met activists from across the world advocating for anti-capitalist practices. The World Social Forum first met in 2001, in Porto Alegre, Brazil as a response—and resistance—to neoliberal globalization (De Sousa Santos 2008). It has since become a yearly, multi-day conference that brings together thousands of progressive activists from across the world. According to its charter:

> The World Social Forum is an open meeting place for reflective thinking, democratic debate of ideas, formulation of proposals, free exchange of experiences and interlinking for effective action, by groups and movements of civil society that are opposed to neo-liberalism and to domination of the world by capital and any form of imperialism, and are committed to building a planetary society directed towards fruitful relationships among humankind and between it and the Earth.

The World Social Forum enables activists from hundreds of countries to meet, exchange ideas, and form relationships and partnerships. While at the conference, Rosangela spoke on a panel on community-based communication platforms, sharing her own experiences helping to run *CDDSpeaks!* While Rosangela was at the forum, news of Marielle Franco's death was released. Below is an excerpt from Rosangela's post about the forum:

> I leave this encounter stirred in the streets against the picture of inequality painted in colors of misery because of the lack of public policies. It falls at night and my eyes see a waterfall when I learn that Marielle Franco, a councilwoman from Rio de Janeiro had been executed. She was a person who defended people, who fought for the guarantee of human rights . . .
>
> I spoke [at the Forum] about my indignation with the execution of Marielle Franco; the importance of giving visibility to the people of [Cidade de Deus]; the importance of [our partnership with a local university] in our learning; the importance of World Alive in my life and the respect with

which they deal in the capacity of each of the participants, I spoke of the pride and that I had been among the 20 women leaders of the world. That I was now a Changemaker, I did not know how to pronounce correctly, but that I am a Changemaker and that I am really just a woman who does, talks and wishes to be happy having protected the happy people around [me].

Now we are building a Communication Web in Brazil, just as we have our International World Alive Network. We are artisans in time, we are embroiderers of life and I love to be part of this movement.

Five women from four different countries—Spain, Canada, the United States, and Nigeria—replied to Rosangela's post with words of encouragement and solidarity. Many of her other posts also elicited responses and support from women across the world. Rosangela's participation in *World Alive* and the World Social Forum enabled her to remain connected to global networks of action "from below," wherein activists from both the Global North and the Global South could meet, dialogue, share information, and develop shared frames about human rights (Della Porta 2006). Rosangela brought these ideas back into CDD, sharing similar concepts and stories in the newspaper *CDDSpeaks!* and in her volunteer work at several CBOs.

Notably, despite the globality of Rosangela's networks, her post also demonstrates that her identity as a member of the Cidade de Deus community remained salient in these interactions. This was true of other favela activists, who made frequent reference to CDD and favelas more generally in their conversations, art, and speeches with activists from transnational movements. When an actor from CDD took a trip to multiple states, his photos on Facebook were followed by the caption #TheFavelaintheWorld, suggesting the salience of his identity as a favela resident during his interactions outside his community. Leonardo, Natalia, MC Claudinho, and many others similarly reaffirmed their status as favela residents by performing plays, songs, and poems about the favela, even when they were in other spaces. This emphasis on being *da favela* (from the favela) helped locate the favela as a political object. João Paulo, for instance, posted on Facebook: "Are you from the Left, the Right, or the Center? I am from and in the favela." In this way, the favela became parallel to, but distinct from, party politics and mainstream political ideologies, worthy of its own identity and set of demands.

The participation of favela activists in urban and transnational movements provided favela activists an opportunity to be part of national and global organizations and movements, while also allowing them to reaffirm the importance of their favela identity within these spaces. When Natalia was invited to attend a conference on human rights in Brussels in 2017, she posted the following caption below a photo of herself with a progressive representative from the British Parliament: "Conversation about the coup in Brazil, the organization of youth in favelas and fight for rights, connection in the perspective of cultural movements." She may have been in Europe, but she was there to defend her neighborhood.

Transnational Resistance

The relationship between the local and the global has become an object of great scholarly interest in recent years, in particular the relationship between indigenous and regional movements and transnational movements (Basu 2000; Guilherme 2019). As noted in Chapter 2, the rise of global communication networks have enabled a diversity of actors across the world to exchange ideas and views, thereby constructing an international public sphere that transcends national structures and identities (Castells 2008). Connections to international organizations and global movements serve multiple functions in strengthening favela activism. In addition to material contributions in the form of donations and payment for travel and work, they bolster favela activists' legitimacy and symbolic inclusion in the global public sphere. Scholarship on intellectual imperialism has shed light on the hierarchy of ideas and knowledge that is reinforced when certain ways of seeing and knowing are privileged over others (Connell 2007; Go 2016; Yuval-Davis 2012). Favela residents, particularly Black residents and those who have not obtained higher education degrees, are frequently positioned at the bottom of this hierarchy, as their views of the world are considered lacking or "backwards" by urban society (Alatas 2000). The solidarity and praise that favela activists receive from allies in other countries helps to combat this subordination of ideologies. By co-producing knowledge—through plays, films, research papers, and news articles—international actors lend legitimacy to activists' beliefs and experiences. These partnerships also render favela activists legible to the outside world, as affiliation with well-known organizations, especially those in Europe and the United States, provides favela activists legitimacy in the eyes of international and local actors who may be quick to dismiss favela activists—especially those without college degrees or lengthy resumés—as unworthy of funding or other types of support.

The globalization of favela activism is also symbolically constitutive of a transnational movement against the drug trade and the global War on Drugs. While CDD activists have not, on their own, organized in sufficient force to make a significant impact on militarized policing in poor, gang-controlled neighborhoods across North, Central, and South America, they are part of multiple movements that are taking on these issues either directly or indirectly. The Black Lives Matter movement and many other transnational racial justice movements expanding across the Americas have become powerful advocates against police violence in Black neighborhoods, and most CDD activists were either affiliated with racial justice movements or spoke out against police violence in their own organizations. They also participated in transnational feminist movements like *World Alive*. Many of these organizations speak out against archaic beliefs about violent hyper-masculinity, which gives meaning to the territorial battles between the police and drug traffickers. By fighting for gender equality, non-violence, and transformative masculinities (Borde, Page, and Moura 2020), feminist organizations provide symbolic resistance to the gendered power of armed conflict. While much work remains ahead for these groups before significant changes will take place in the policing of poor Black neighborhoods, favela activists' ties to transnational social movements provide them entry into organized resistance against urban violence without requiring that they directly confront the drug traffickers in their own neighborhood. These ties have proved crucial to resisting the socio-political isolation of the favela and to providing activists with essential financial resources, human capital through outside volunteers, political leverage, and training on activist discourses and repertoires of action. Through their engagement, favela activists also become producers of global social movements. As Millie Thayer (2009:6) has argued, "Social movements do not *have* relationships, they *are* relationships: a set of always shifting interactions with a variety of allies and interlocutors, whether individuals, organizations, discourses or other social structures." Favela activists have become global political actors creating and transforming transnational social movements.

Unequal Collaborations

Despite the importance of favela activists' ties to urban and transnational networks, Cidade de Deus activists occupy a subordinate social and economic location relative to many urban and transnational allies that they can neither escape nor reverse. These inequities operate along a number of lines, including race, class, gender, language, education, and national origin. They also operate at the neighborhood level, in that the practices necessary to remain operational within a favela context also retrench their marginalization in mainstream urban institutions.

One of the most persistent reproducers of inequality between the city and the favela has been national funding practices, some of which became visible in the Residents' Board meeting, but that impact all CBOs in the neighborhood. For instance, there was often a mismatch between the types of grants and private funding that CBOs could access and what they needed to maintain a well-functioning organization. Eloise, a professor at one of Rio's public universities who was helping the Residents' Board through the restructuring process, described some of these problems to me:

> The profile [of Cidade de Deus organizations] is sometimes technically good for organizing and popular mobilization, but not necessarily for grant applications, or for accounting, for managing resources . . . You have to be trained in this, you know . . . What happened in this agency gets repeated in most organizations. They have some money, like LAMSA[3] offers to fund a project, like a sporting activity for youth, or Capoeira. And the funding is for one year. Sometimes it gets renewed, great. But if at the end of the year it's not renewed, who is going to pay the teacher? Who is going to pay for the snacks? The physical space? Maintenance?

The grants provided to favelas were often small and temporary. They rarely covered salaries for staff members or costs for overhead expenses, such as rent or electricity, although these were the most essential costs for keeping operations running. Solange and Maria Rita were constantly worried about how they would fund their activities when their six-month or one-year grants ran out. On many occasions I stayed up late at night with Maria Rita as she puzzled over the exact wording of a grant Youth Promise had received, trying to figure out how to redistribute funds to cover the costs of their basic necessities. Maria Rita was often exasperated at being forced to spend, for instance, R$1,000 (approximately USD$300) on backpacks for the children when what she really needed was to give the cook her monthly stipend. In their quest to avoid any illegal practices, Maria Rita and Solange toiled over ways to abide by what often felt like arbitrary clauses of their agreements with funders. Following these rules came at great cost to their volunteers and to their own mental well-being. Solange and Maria Rita both had college degrees, however, and exceptional skills in organizational management. They knew how to balance complex budgets and apply for more substantial private and state grants. However, as our community-wide survey found, one-third of CDD adults have not completed primary school and only 7% have taken college courses. Most CBO leaders I met did not have a high level of formal training, and their organizations did not have the internal infrastructure needed to get even small, short-term grants, much less the larger federal grants that could cover overhead expenses. Many operated entirely with volunteers and donated space and materials.

The challenges of obtaining funding have made CBOs heavily reliant on external NGOs, most of which are based in Rio's downtown area. I visited several of these and interviewed their directors and staff members. These NGOs were often well-funded, at times receiving grants worth several million reals from the federal or municipal government or international institutions, such as Oxfam International, the Ford Foundation, Open Society, USAID, and various branches of the United Nations. They also were funded by private for-profit companies and received individual donations from citizens in the United States or Europe. In contrast to favela CBOs, which were largely run by Black women, many of the urban NGOs I visited had lighter-skinned men in main leadership positions. Urban NGOs sometimes provide their own services in favelas or for favela residents, including job training, youth activities, and dance and martial arts classes. They also frequently outsource this labor to favela-based CBOs, providing them small grants to offer services in the most dangerous areas of the city.

In his research on India's slums, Arjun Appadurai (2001:29–30) has argued that demands for urban resources are often "entangled in an immensely complicated web of slum rehabilitation projects, financing procedures, legislative precedents and administrative codes which are interpreted differently, enforced unevenly and whose actual delivery is almost always attended by an element of corruption." These webs of bureaucracy and sometimes tinged with corruption, have created challenges for favela-based CBOs, who must engage in constant decision-making about which resources and partnerships to accept and which to decline. In Cidade de Deus, activists struggled with these decisions and did not always agree on which partnerships to embrace. Solange tended toward a more collaborative approach, accepting most offers for funding from outsiders, provided they did not come from a political actor believed to have ties to gangs. She often bemoaned the emotional labor that was required to preserve these ties, thanking her volunteers and donors vociferously both in person and on social media, and silently putting up with incompetence in their execution of their duties and (sometimes unreasonable) demands for how she spend the funds they had donated.

Youth Promise was heavily dependent on these external "partners," though Solange was often frustrated by her powerlessness to challenge her funders or sever ties with some of these organizations. For example, in 2015 I accompanied Solange and a group of children and Youth Promise staff to the Communications Hub, a well-established NGO that had given Youth Promise over a dozen computers and funded some of their computer classes and Maria Rita's salary. It was the celebration of Communications Hub's 20-year anniversary and was held in one of their sites, a large open gymnasium in another favela. They had bused in participants from CBOs in other favelas as well who had received donations and funding from them. We sat in the gymnasium for over an hour before we were finally served snacks. Claudette, the lawyer who volunteered regularly at Youth Promise, called it "the snack of the poor," as it consisted of coffee and crackers with ham and cheese rather than more substantial food.

An hour later, Gilmar, the founder and president of Communications Hub came on stage, a tall, light-skinned, middle-aged man. After showing us a professionally made (and likely very costly) video of his organization's many accomplishments, he spent the next 20 minutes detailing his life story, the moments of inspiration that had led him to create Communications Hub, and all of the awards and accolades he had received for his work at the organization. Thanks to the success of his organization, Gilmar had been hired at a prominent international NGO based in the United States and had moved to the United States for the new job. As he concluded his speech, he noted that all this success was owed to "us," (i.e., the people in the audience from the many CBOs that had received Communications Hub funds), though he said little about how these CBOs had contributed to his success. I was bemused by his ability to use the celebration an opportunity for barely disguised self-glorification. After the event, I watched as Gilmar came over to greet Solange. She had shaken his hand and given him a large smile as she thanked him for the organization's continued support.

In the car ride home, Solange rolled her eyes and complained that Gilmar had ridden to success on the coattails of her hard work and the work of many other favela organizations, though he took all the credit and received all the awards. I wondered how many other large NGOs I had toured had similarly benefited from the low-cost partnerships they had with informal organizations in favelas. Despite Solange's antipathy toward Gilmar, she had little choice but to maintain a good relationship with him and the other staff at Communications Hub. The little money she received was critical to her ability to continue to offer services and to pay Maria Rita's stipend. In many respects, Solange's relationship to Gilmar reflects "the multiple and hybrid cultures of action followed by social actors, [where] slum dwellers often play a very restricted role or are underrepresented, including in wider political stakes" (Bautès et al. 2013:370–71). Their partnership allowed for a greater diversity of actors and funding streams in their shared efforts to promote the interests of favela residents, but continued to hold Youth Promise hostage to a collaboration that overwhelmingly benefited non-slum dwellers.

Large, urban-based NGOs that fund favela-based CBOs are often the international face of the favela. The leaders of these NGOs have college degrees and formal education in business or non-profit management. The NGO leaders I met tended to be lighter skinned and often male. They had similar class, race, and gender profiles as politicians, CEOs, and leaders of international NGOs, which has surely facilitated relationships between these organizations and paved the way for large donations to these NGOs. Thanks to this funding, these organizations have been able to invest substantial funds into professional videos, websites, and flyers that make them more legible to international funders and the broader English-speaking population. For instance, one of the first urban NGOs I visited was VivaRio, a large organization that refers to itself as a "social enterprise." It was founded in 1993 to address urban violence through a host of development projects in various favelas across the city. I was welcomed by several staff members and handed a large magazine-sized booklet of their services and successes, with colorful professional photos of favela residents scattered throughout the thick pages. It must have cost them quite a bit to produce the booklet, and I have no doubt that it enabled them to better communicate and forge ties with their international donors. Their website is also professionally designed and available in English and Portuguese. VivaRio has been incredibly successful in securing large national and international grants. When I met with them, they were working on a partnership with the UPP program to provide trainings to the police on how to properly interact with favela residents, along with many other projects on healthcare, education, employment, and more. While urban-based NGOs do share much-needed funding with favela-based CBOs, relations between them remains radically imbalanced. Meanwhile, favela activists continue to do the challenging, dangerous, and intensive work on the ground, remaining invisible to the international funding community and dependent on external allies who reap many rewards from their work.

These tensions sometimes became manifest in relationships with global movements as well. Leonardo, for instance, was frequently frustrated with the broader Black movement. Leonardo's racial justice work often connected him—both in person and through social media—with activists from Black Lives Matter and other global racial justice movements. However, he sometimes felt frustrated by the focus of his colleagues' demands and discourses, particularly among those in international academic circles. According to Leonardo:

> I was tired of the young Black movement, because I was a little disenchanted, because I did not recognize myself there . . . I think the fact that I heard a lot of these racial issues talked about in and about the favela, I got tired of hearing these questions spoken by the [Black] academics. They do not talk about favela issues, they talk about racial issues, but not about the favela. Sometimes they talk about racial issues that people in the favela have already solved. We've already learned how to get along with white people . . . sometimes my own brother is white, my mother is white, the woman on whose breast I nursed was white, so we realize that we need to work together in the favela; I can't be excluding people just because they are lighter skinned. So the favela has solved some of the issues that academics talk about.

While Leonardo understood the role of race in promoting social exclusion, he was primarily concerned with its impact on segregated poverty and the practical solutions he embraced that required unity within the favela, rather than antagonism based on racial difference. It was also a reminder that favela residents occupy a unique and subordinate location within the global racial justice movement, as well as in feminist and other movements.

Favela activists did not always submit to these unequal ties, however. The Residents' Board was notorious for turning down offers of funding and resources from politicians and even NGOs if they would not benefit the favela sufficiently. Carmen, the founder of the Environment League, explained some of the reasons she might turn down offers for partnerships:

We're always thinking about who these partners are. Is this partner going to use Environment League logo? In the T-shirts, in everything they publish? Are they? . . . People say: "Ah, but you work with the environment, can't you partner with anyone?" No, we cannot. We will partner with those who do not harm the environment . . . Because being big is very easy, the problem is keeping with our ethics and values, so we prefer to stay small, staying within our ethics and values. Sometimes we don't have the money to buy sugar, or a snack, but that's not the idea. Our goal is to be an institution that strengthens human values in young people and in the people who pass through here . . . If someone comes here and I know that he is not a nice guy to be able to partner, I will not partner with him so he can use me, use my name, use the name of the institution and use Cidade de Deus.

As Carmen explains, she selected partners whose practices fit within the values of the Environment League and who would not take advantage of their partnership for their own personal gain. Carmen was willing to say no, even if it meant having little or no money with which to sustain her movement, in order to protect her organization from ties with unethical and predatory institutions. Carmen and other board members had become strict gatekeepers, trying to keep out preying NGOs whenever possible. They similarly held me to a high standard. Several members of the Residents' Board interrogated my motives when I asked them for interviews and for permission to observe their meetings: "What are you going to do with our stories? How is this going to help the community?" they asked. I explained that I was using a Participatory Action Research approach and would involve residents in making decisions about the project and create data to support the needs of the community. They remained distrustful. "How do we know you will keep your word?" Even after acquiescing to interviews, Carmen and Geovana continued to question my motives and commitment to participatory research. Finally, several years into the project I felt I had earned their trust after consulting with them on the project numerous times and co-leading the community-wide, PAR-based survey project.

While I found their questioning to be incredibly effective at holding me accountable to promoting participation and action in my research, many other partners found it exhausting and eventually gave up their collaborations. For instance, Simone, the director of ABT who had funded the board's restructuring process, eventually pulled their funding, leaving the two new staff without jobs. Off and on, the electricity was shut off at the Residents' Board for lack of funds to pay even its most basic costs. Sadly, the board provided a cautionary tale to other activists: they would be left with no funds and no means to support their families if they refused the crumbs their allies sent their way.

These inequities were not limited to the relationship between CBOs and NGOs. Natalia and Jordana had both felt sidelined by the progressive political movements with which they were involved. Natalia, as noted earlier, had felt abandoned by her party when they did so little to support her candidacy. Jordana, a student who had started a Vlog on favelas, often complained that progressive student groups and other young leftist activists overlooked their privileged position as white middle-class urban residents. A frequent complaint was that these young activists claimed to be progressive but refused to set foot in a favela, out of a combination of fear and thinly veiled racism. While collaborations based on shared racial and political identities enabled favela activists to engage in urban and transnational movements, they were unable to escape the unique dynamics of poverty and segregated violence that distinguished them from their allies and positioned them in a highly unequal and more vulnerable location.

Elizabeth Friedman (1999:358) refers to the unequal relations between transnational networks and national women's movements as "transnationalism reversed," wherein "domestic conditions combine with global opportunities in ways that may be detrimental as well as productive for national women's movements." This has been especially pervasive in countries like Bangladesh, where the heavy reliance of indigenous women's groups on international western NGOs has forced local organizations to construct a "victim-to-survivor-to-activist trajectory," which does not always fit with what individual women desire of their own lives (Chowdhury 2011). In Rio de Janeiro, where national and urban resources are more robust, favela activists have become enmeshed in multiple layers of dependency with both urban and transnational NGOs. Thus, inequities operate not only along the global axis (i.e., between the Global North and the Global South) but also along more local networks differentiated based on geography, class, and race.

These inequities were pronounced in my own engagement in CDD. When I co-founded the Building Together Research Collective, a partnership between CDD residents and formally trained researchers, our main objective was to level the playing field between researchers and favela residents in the production of knowledge. Despite my best efforts to send funds to the favela by paying residents for their participation in the project, to provide safe spaces for "dialogical reflexivity" (Yuval-Davis 2012), and to democratize each step of the project, the benefits were not evenly distributed. My status as a white professor in an American university differentially positioned me and the rest of the team. Funding for residents' work was reliant on my grant-writing skills, institutional access, and professional timeline. There were many months in which I did not have the time or bandwidth to search for more funds or lead a new project, and our team dispersed to engage in our own (unequally paid) activities. The visibility of the project was also bolstered by my access to a well-resourced English-speaking community. When favela activists and their allies occupy different social locations and operate within unequal social forces, inequities will continue to permeate these groups, even when external allies have good intentions.

This does not mean that favela activists are powerless. Writing about the position of rural Brazilian women within transnational feminist movements, Milly Thayer (2009:7) contends that this feminist counter-public was a "hybrid space in which participants were linked both by relations of power and bonds of solidarity." Brazilian women could decide which discourses, resources, and allies to embrace and which to resist. Similarly, Cidade de Deus activists do not enter these ties blindly or without their own resources. The "favela" has become such a potent symbol across the world that international NGOs gain much status and respect from the global community when they partner with favelas. After the release of the movie *City of God* in 2002, Cidade de Deus became a particularly coveted site of engagement, as NGOs located in the United States and Europe desired to portray themselves as permeating the "dangerous" urban frontier. Isabella, Solange, Carmen, and many others were sought out *because* CDD was known for violence, and these offers increased dramatically after the release of the movie. Recognizing the cultural capital their partners could derive from marketing these partnerships, they leveraged this to obtain more resources and set clear expectations about their boundaries and needs.

Conclusion

Arjun Appadurai (2001) argues that India's grassroots movements help to create "deep democracy" by working with transnational movements to co-construct new ideas and practices that not only reinvigorate and reshape the local environment but engender new forms of resistance and regulation of everyday life. Similarly, favela activists have become active members of urban and transnational networks, which not only helps to bring outside resources and knowledge into the favela but also allows favela-based knowledge and actors to travel outside of these segregated spaces and into Rio de Janeiro and the world. Through this work, favela activists resist the segregation of poor urban neighborhoods and join forces with myriad social movements fighting for gender and urban equality, racial justice, and non-violence.

Partnerships beyond the neighborhood are an essential strategy in this conflict activism, as they allow activists to find allies and resources outside the domain of violent governance. In CDD, municipal and national state actors who do not have close ties to drug traffickers in Cidade de Deus, as well as political parties and urban and transnational social movements, provide political and social spaces in which activists can make demands and create connective threads to groups without a high risk of becoming embroiled in local corruption schemes. By constructing participatory democratic spaces within Cidade de Deus and political ties outside the neighborhood, activists mobilize under and above violent governance, thereby resisting violence without directly challenging its perpetrators.

These partnerships have enabled favela activists to channel valuable resources into favelas while also inserting Cidade de Deus into urban and transnational political spaces. However, their location in these communities is not without its problems and has often resulted in favela activists occupying a subordinate role relative to their allies. Membership in identity politics offers favela activists an avenue for connection with movements across the globe, though segregated poverty remains central to their struggle for rights, belonging, and power even within the very movements that claim to speak for them.

Conclusion

Seek and Ye Shall Find

Looking for Non-Violence in Conflict Zones

Sonia, Not the Cross

On October 19, 2016, Sonia—the co-founder of the community-based news-paper *CDDSpeaks!*—died. She had been one of Cidade de Deus's fiercest and most well-loved activists. Her death was as tragic as it was symbolic. She was only 50 years old. She died of a heart attack after being caught in a shootout on her way to a meeting for *CDDSpeaks!*. Rosangela had found her on the side-walk leaning against the door at Youth Promise, too paralyzed by the gun fire around her to get her key into the lock. Miraculously, Rosangela got Sonia to the local emergency room, but after two days of anxiety-driven heart attacks and poor medical care, her heart finally gave out. It had taken her family two more days to find space to bury her at the local cemetery, two miles outside of Cidade de Deus. I learned of her death alongside dozens of other activists shortly after I finished presenting some of my research findings to the group. For two hours that morning, I had met with an attentive and engaged group I had invited to hear and offer feedback on my analyses of their activism. I had wondered why Sonia and Rosangela had not been there, since they had both RSVP'd. After my presentation, we huddled in a circle and started an an-imated discussion about the many challenges of activism under fire. An hour into the conversation, my participants' phones began beeping with messages from Rosangela and family members announcing Sonia's death. Someone fi-nally broke the news aloud. We sat in silence trying to process what we had just heard as tears streamed down our faces.

Two days later, the crowd of mourners gathered at the entrance to the cem-etery. Standing next to Maria Rita and many others who were familiar to me, I looked up the steep hill we would need to climb, past hundreds of crypts and white crosses, to arrive at Sonia's burial site. In the sweltering heat, it seemed unbearable. We began to hike up the central walkway behind Sonia's son and other male family members who were carrying her coffin. Over 100

Activism under Fire. Anjuli Fahlberg, Oxford University Press. © Oxford University Press 2023.
DOI: 10.1093/oso/9780197519325.003.0007

of her friends, family members, and fellow activists had come from across the city. What Sonia had lacked for in wealth she made up for in community.

As Maria Rita and I panted our way to the top, we examined the tombstones around us. There was a distinctive class dynamic to the layout of the cemetery: large, colorful marble crypts adorned the bottom near the entrance, while plain white crosses with numbers haphazardly drawn on them were laid in rows nearer the top. "Even in death there is inequality between the rich and the poor," Maria Rita commented as I pointed out the landscape. "The rich get the vaults, and the poor have to compete for space all the way at the top." Not knowing which burial site awaited Sonia, I said a silent prayer that she would not be buried beneath one of the plain white crosses: she deserved to be remembered for her effervescence, not her poverty. My prayer was not answered. As we reached the very top of the hill, her family lowered her coffin next to a grave in the poor people's section, between hundreds of other white crosses.

Once everyone had gathered around Sonia's coffin, people began to shout out words that represented Sonia's mark in the world. "Happiness!" someone shouted. "Present!" we all replied. "Poetry!" shouted another. "Present!" we chimed. The descriptions continued: "Large smile!" "Present!" "Fight!" "Present!" "Family!" "Present!" "Warrior!" "Present!" We recited a prayer and sung as we watched the cemetery staff lay her body in the ground and cover it in dirt. Once the grave was filled, people laid enormous wreaths of flowers over the earth, as well as a sash with the words *CDDSpeaks!*. A cement cross was tucked into the soil. One of the cemetery staff read the four-digit number on her cross for her family to write down so they could locate her burial site. It was the only thing distinguishing her from the thousands of other people buried there. In death, Sonia had become a number. To be rendered nameless and dateless in death was the final act of violence against Rio's poor (Figure C.1).

Shortly after we returned home from the funeral, Rio's police forces descended onto Cidade de Deus by the dozen in search of a penitentiary officer who had disappeared that morning. Presumably, he had been kidnapped and was being held hostage by drug traffickers in Cidade de Deus. We huddled at home listening to the shootouts, watching videos of tires and garbage cans burning that residents were sharing on social media. Reports circulated that the police had set some shacks ablaze and were breaking down doors searching for the missing officer. When a street vendor was shot by the police, residents began barricading and looting streets in protest.

Figure C.1 The cemetery where Sonia is buried
Photo by the author.

By the afternoon, news spread that the officer had been rescued. The major news channel *Record* sent a reporter to the scene. The four-minute report is captioned: "Director is freed after kidnapping from Cidade de Deus." It shows images of the barricades and burning tires, of shirtless dark-skinned men the reporter referred to as "suspects" running from the police, and of dozens of armored vehicles preparing to enter the neighborhood—all of this *after* the officer had been found and brought to safety. A substantial portion of the newscast focused on the impact of the commotion on traffic flow of the main rotary nearby, offering viewers tips on which roads to avoid.[1] Needless to say, no one was interested in reporting Sonia's death, much less her life.

There is no shortage of news reports or studies about violence, but these make little space for people like Sonia and other activists in areas known to us as "dangerous." Yet Sonia's story is the one that must be told, lest she and other activists become invisibile or forgotten. They cannot be known merely as victims of violence in life or numbers on a cross in death. As reporters and filmmakers display burning tires, police raids, and Black suspects, we must mobilize to tell another story, of the non-violent organizing that occurs in Rio's peripheries and in other areas of conflict. We must balance the narrative. Nay, we must shift the narrative. As long as poor militarized neighborhoods are viewed only, or primarily, as spaces of violence, they will continue to be treated as such: society will fear them, and this fear will continue to motivate aggressive policing, mass incarceration, and the criminalization of poverty.

This does not mean we pretend there is no violence in these spaces, but that we focus our attention on the other things, on the "good things" that enable residents to survive, to keep the neighborhood afloat, and to help the world move in the direction of peace and justice even in the face of danger. To do this, we must start with a new set of questions other than those usually asked of these neighborhoods. The first of these is to ask residents themselves what stories they wish to be told about them. While some may respond that they wish the world knew more about the tragedies they suffer, I suspect most residents in dangerous neighborhoods recognize that there is no shortage of reports about violence. They know what the media—and researchers— say about them and what is missing from these reports. They know which narratives are still waiting to be told, and they know these narratives better than any outsider, however well read, ever will.

The second question we must focus on is what *else* people are doing, besides perpetrating or being victimized by violence. We must ask not only how people are surviving, but how they are doing this collectively. Which tactics are people using to build and support their community? What external resources exist to support these efforts, and how are people capitalizing on them? What are the gendered dynamics of local governance, and what roles have women taken up? How do racial or ethnic dynamics bring people together and promote collective action, even across armed and non-armed residents? And finally, what is the role of researchers as allies in this fight? How can we support activists while minimizing inequities within the social movements and academic discussions we are a part of? Surely there are many other important questions waiting to be asked. Yet they all begin with a basic assumption: that there is much more to areas of conflict than what we have been told.

* * *

One year later, I attended another Art Talk Open Mic event and sparked up a conversation with Sonia's two sisters, whom I had only briefly met at Sonia's wake. Neither of them had been especially engaged in social mobilization before then. "That was always Sonia's thing," they told me. I mentioned how much I missed Sonia's bright, welcoming smile. "You know," one of her sisters said, "we never saw that side of Sonia. But after she died, everyone from all these movements she was part of started telling us about this bright smile of hers. We had no idea how happy it made her to be part of all of this, and how much she mattered to these groups." For the next hour, the three of us huddled in a corner sipping *caipirinhas* as we exchanged stories of Sonia. They told me they had started a small CBO a few months earlier in honor of their sister to "transform our sadness into culture." Since then, they had turned their street into a "cultural corridor," bringing artists and poets to perform, showing movies, and welcoming discussion about culture among local residents and neighborhood children on Sunday afternoons. They had also organized field trips to take children and their parents to museums in Rio's downtown area. "Many people feel like they aren't good enough to go to these places," they had explained. "They worry that they don't have the right clothes, that they will be discriminated against, that they'll say or do the wrong thing. We wanted to show them that they have just as much right to be in these spaces as anyone else, and that they could do it!" The two sisters beamed, proud that they had found a way to make their sister's death meaningful. In a neighborhood frequently charged with reproducing the cycle of violence between generations, activists were reproducing what I think of as the *cycle of non-violence*, or the inter-generational transmission of values and practices committed to decreasing violence and promoting social justice.

Sonia's death took a heavy toll on CDD's activists, who not only mourned the loss of their friend for many years but were regularly reminded of the constant risks they faced by living and working in such a dangerous environment. Despite this, the fight for equality and justice endures in Cidade de Deus. The possibility of death and the certainty of suffering pose challenges to mobilization efforts and the individual well-being of local activists, but these are also the very elements that inspire their struggle. Favela activists fight along multiple fronts, not only for residents' everyday needs but also against much larger historical and global forces that hurt favelas and other poor communities across the world. Racism, colonialism, militarized policing, the war on drugs, urban inequality, harmful economic policies, and gang violence are but a few of the forces that conspire to keep favela residents in subordinate social locations. Long-term change will require radical global transformations that favela activists cannot enact on their own. In the meantime, they make do with what little they have. "The strategy now is to resist," Geovana told me in our last interview. "We must continue to do small things, but not abandon it. Do small things to keep the flame alive."

Conflict activism in CDD is not big and bold. It does not seek public attention or the international spotlight. It is humble, small, and easily misrecognized as apolitical, as survival, or as women doing women's work. If we are to locate activism in areas of extreme violence, we must think differently. While the literature on the politics of urban violence has contributed important insights into the negotiations of power between armed, corrupt, masculinized political groups, this is only half of the story. We must now start telling the other half. To do this, we must look beyond the dynamics of violent governance we've spent decades studying. Politics, in these studies, is composed of webs of dangerous and illicit ties between drug traffickers, police officers, paramilitary troops, politicians, and businessmen. This book demonstrates, however, that these are not the networks or spaces that favela activists inhabit. Those who wish to find non-violent activism must look under, beyond, and around violent governance. And they must begin with the women. In other words, we will not find non-violent politics in the spaces we think of as political, for these are the very spaces that armed actors co-opt first. Non-violence in conflict zones must be creative, innovative, and diffuse; scholars of non-violence will need to be the same.

Those of us accustomed to studying social movements will need a new lens as well. Favela activists rarely protest in the streets or start trendy hashtags, and when they do, these are small groups that are often ignored by the press. We will not hear about them on the BBC or read about them in the Washington Post. They are not organized into powerful, visible NGOs, and they do not mobilize to take down regimes or transnational corporations. To survive, they must disperse. CBO leaders must remain inconspicuous and poor to avoid the suspicion of residents or co-optation by violent actors. However, favela activists are nonetheless embedded in local governance, urban politics, and transnational movements. They distribute resources and advocate for community needs. They are members of political parties and partners with urban actors. And they are spokespeople against racism and for gender equality, among many other issues. To find them, we must look, sadly, to the very bottom layers of the movements we study and support, to those who often lack the resources to afford regular internet access, a fancy website, bus fare to join downtown street protests or airfare to participate in international conferences.

This does not mean activists in areas of conflict should be overlooked in social movement studies. To the contrary: conflict activism has learned the skills to survive in the most hostile of terrains. They *are* the experts in keeping movements alive. As national democracy continues to dwindle across the globe and urbanized political violence threatens to undo democratic spaces, conflict activism may become more the rule than the exception. We should not be surprised if people increasingly turn to a patchwork approach that emphasizes participation without structure, claims-making without visibility, politics without leadership. This strategy may not topple regimes or change national policies on its own, but it stands a solid chance of improving the lives of the communities most hit by violence and inequality, preserving a seat in urban governance, and contributing people and ideas to broader and bigger movements.

Conflict activism can also offer important lessons about the limits of "academic" knowledge. The subordination of favela activists in broader spheres of political claims-making affords them a unique and valuable lens into not only the experiences of marginalization but also the construction of knowledge and practice about how to make change. They are the "outsiders within" social movements, contributing perspectives that can challenge and enrich the theories and concepts being developed in progressive ivory towers. If I have learned anything from my years of research and relationships in Cidade de Deus, it is that the best ideas emerge when we all work together, when each individual—Maria Rita, Leonardo, Natalia, Sonia, me, and so many others with their own unique positionalities—work collectively to co-create knowledge. If we truly desire to understand non-violence in areas of conflict, our first step must be to ask residents not only for their stories but also for their perspectives, theories, and analyses. And then we must invite them to the table, to co-collect data, co-analyze and co-publish research, and we must encourage, support, and fund those who wish to become published authors in their own right.

Cidade de Deus in Context

Although Cidade de Deus has been the focus of this book, favela activism is widespread in other large and medium-sized favelas. The Complexo da Maré and the Complexo do Alemão, which house several favelas each, have dozens, if not hundreds, of community-based organizations, artists' collectives, community newspapers, and much more. Favela activism extends across the city, and many activists are connected to each other. Leonardo and Natalia spent as much time traveling between favelas and across urban spaces as they did in Cidade de Deus. There are now dozens of organizations, conferences, events, and forums related to favela rights and racial justice, which help bring

activists from across favelas together. *Catalytic Communities*, and its offshoot
Rede Favela Sustentável, play important roles in organizing service providers
across favelas. Meanwhile, the newspaper *Rio on Watch* and the favela-based
digital newspaper *Voz das Comunidades* (*Voices from the Communities*)
provides critical journalism that shares many stories about service, cultural,
and mobilization work in favelas. Many organizations have also emerged in
response to the killing of former city councilwoman and racial justice activist Marielle Franco, including the Instituto Marielle Franco, which was
created by Marielle's family with the mission of "inspiring, connecting and
empowering black women, LGBTQIA + and peripheral women to continue
moving the structures of society toward a more just and egalitarian world."[2]
The online *Dicionário das Favelas Marielle Franco* (the Favela Dictionary
Marielle Franco) is another great example of how favela activists and their
allies are collaborating to create spaces for the sharing, institutionalization,
and valuing of knowledge from favelas. Many other collectives, initiatives
and organizations could be cited here as well.

   However, opportunities for such visible forms of activism may be more
constrained in territories governed by more dominant and centrally organized drug lords or vigilante groups. Since dynamics of "armed territorial
control" vary across neighborhoods and cities (Moncada 2016:3), the spaces
for non-violent activism will vary along with these. As the work of Enrique
Desmond Arias (2017) demonstrates, in many of Latin America's dangerous
neighborhoods local drug lords play a central role in the provision of social
services. In neighborhoods governed by the *milicia*, there appear to be fewer
opportunities for autonomous political organization. Dozens of politicians,
including Rio de Janeiro's former Governor Pezão, have been arrested and
imprisoned for bribery schemes connected to the *milicia*. While further research is required, it would not be a stretch to assume that leadership in local
governance may be more dangerous for activists in territories controlled by
paramilitary groups than those controlled by drug traffickers.

   This book has provided a "deep dive" into the lifeworld of Cidade de Deus's
activist efforts. More studies are needed to examine the extent to which the
strategies of survival and resistance of conflict activism in CDD operate in
other favelas, in gang territories across the Americas, and in conflict zones
throughout the world. As Arias (2017) has argued in the case of Latin
America's gang territories, the possibilities for an autonomous civil sphere
depend in large part on the political ambitions of local violent actors. Surely
there will be differences between neighborhoods and across countries, and

even in the same location, adaptations will need to be made as the dynamics of politics, violence, and resources shift.

The Future of Favela Activism

On January 1, 2019, far-right president Jair Bolsonaro took office after winning the popular vote by a wide margin against Worker's Party candidate Fernando Haddad. Bolsonaro rose to power on a platform of hate against the LBGTQ community, indigenous groups, the "ideological left," and "criminals in favelas." A rock settled in my stomach and in the stomachs of my colleagues in Cidade de Deus, who feared the persecutions that might come next. Brazil's 20-year dictatorship was a recent memory, and one that many conservative Brazilians still remember with nostalgia. Dozens of progressive politicians and activists began to flee the country, while others courageously issued public statements condemning Bolsonaro and his new policies. The rest of us waited to see what would happen next.

On the same day, Bolsonaro's political ally Wilson Witzel became the new governor of Rio de Janeiro. In the first year of his tenure, more favela residents were killed by the police than in the 20 previous years. I received near-daily messages and videos from my friends in Cidade de Deus of police raids down their streets, including a particularly horrific video of a father whose baby had died because a police blockade prevented him from driving his son to the emergency room after he had fallen gravely ill. Meanwhile, Governor Witzel issued a not-so-subtle threat of sending missiles into CDD to deal with what he termed the "no-good criminals" living there. These changes sparked many difficult questions: Would these politicians usher in a new era of political repression and force activism to reconfigure once again? Would activists need to worry not only about local drug traffickers and corrupt police and politicians but also new, dictatorial laws and official state persecutions? Would activists be persecuted? Should I even move forward with this book?

I returned to Cidade de Deus in 2019 and again in 2020—just before the start of the pandemic—to find out the answers to these questions, and to ask my main participants if they wanted me to continue with the book. They did. While police violence had persisted and Bolsonaro's rhetoric had remained antagonistic to the left, the regime had not directly targeted favela activists. And activists wanted their story told. In any event, they had spent years, if not decades, learning how to organize under political repression. If anyone was equipped to survive in this new era, it was them. For the most part, their work continued under Bolsonaro's rule, though under conditions of more shootouts and less funding. However, I made a decision to stop collecting data on specific examples of activism under Bolsonaro to minimize any threats to their safety under the new and unpredictable regime. And, as I detail in the Appendix, I have meticulously excluded any details that might put activists at risk. Some stories are best left untold.

The broader questions remained: What does the future hold? How will activism in Cidade de Deus change to adapt to new political waves? Will it ever become a larger, more robust and well-organized social movement in its own right? While I cannot definitively answer these questions, my participants gave me their takes in our book workshops. According to Geovana, activism in Cidade de Deus has gone through many phases. When local drug traffickers assert greater control over local political institutions, she explained, the "collective forces" of activism withdraw and instead focus on partnerships outside of Cidade de Deus, with universities and urban social movements. For Geovana, this centrifugal movement was not a bad thing:

> This is a way of survival; it is a wise way of survival. Because it is fueling itself and taking the concrete base of [knowledge] it has learned in the community to the outside. But still the base is the territory (i.e., the neighborhood). So the institutions exist, even if they don't have a collective connection, it's a very important form of resistance because it's a means of survival.

In other words, by cultivating local forms of knowledge and organizing practices, as well as allies outside the neighborhood, activists can alternate between a focus on the neighborhood or more participation in external movements as political opportunities shift. Political realities and violent alliances are never static: built into the very foundations of conflict activism is the ability to adapt. Activism that is directly connected to the needs of a neighborhood may be, in many respects, more sustainable than large-scale political or social movements that are more easily subdued by shifting global and national forces. Leonardo echoed this sentiment: "I am in three-hundred thousand favelas, and even when I'm there, I'm there as Cidade de Deus." His hyperbolic point suggests at once that he was malleable and movable—his activism was not confined to CDD—but that his identity and loyalty were firmly rooted in CDD and could be activated to make change wherever he went.

Many social movement studies suggest that movements become more powerful when they are large, united, and well organized, when they can cohere around a shared set of frames and identities and work toward a clear set of demands. In our workshops, I asked my participants if they thought that someday Cidade de Deus's collectives might unite with each other and with other favela-based collectives to form a cohesive favela movement. No one thought this would happen. Maria Rita offered a poignant analysis, which captured the spirit of what many others noted as well.

> [Technology] left us much more connected, but I don't see these movements, with so many different nuances and some that are more political than the others, I don't see a unification, you know, I see a connection. Maybe in our work [we can have] an intersectoral collaboration. But one unified movement, I find that kind of difficult.

As Maria Rita explains, there are too many differences between collectives for there to be unity between them. As I described in Chapter 2, it is this diversity that makes them effective at obtaining resources from across the spectrum of political opportunities and cultivating ties to a range of urban and international movements. This fragmentation allows activists to mobilize without threatening drug lords. But these differences are also what make it so difficult to merge with other collectives. As Rosangela put it, "I think this union for me is unattainable . . . because each place has its individuality, has its independence, has its culture, has its history, it was formed in a [particular] way." Diversity and dispersion are critical to the survival of conflict activism while at the same time limiting their unification.

This was not a bad thing, however. As Maria Rita noted, many connections are created across favelas and movements that aid in the sharing of knowledge and resources. Leonardo referred to this as "social technology," or teaching collectives in other places how to engage in activism—in theater, journalism, service provision, grassroots organizing—to promote urban equality and social justice. Leonardo continued: "We can't erase [our differences] to be just one thing, because erasing doesn't make sense to unify anything. But it makes sense for us to respect each part, to integrate and promote integration between them." Through partnerships, collectives could remain independent and autonomous, subvert the watchful eye of drug lords, and continue to fight for a variety of needs and rights, even while learning from each other and sharing resources, people, and knowledge.

This is not to say that all favela activists will keep away from more traditional, formal political tactics. Some favela residents have followed in the footsteps of Marielle Franco, taking enormous risks to their personal safety in order to run for city council or state legislature on a human rights platform. Tainá de Paula, an urban activist, architect, and Black woman from the Loteamento favela in Rio's West Zone, was elected to Rio de Janeiro's city council in 2020 as a representative of the Worker's Party. On the same day, another Black woman, Thais Ferreira, was also elected to city council. In Niterói, a city just next door to Rio de Janeiro, Verônica Lima, another Black woman, was elected to city council. Running on a platform of racial, gender, and economic justice, they will be champions for many of the issues that impact favelas. It remains to be seen whether they will find enough allies in government to pass progressive legislation. There is another important question we must also consider: "Who is going to look after each of the women elected in each state of this country?" asked Anielle Franco, Marielle's sister, in an interview a few days after these women were elected (Cícero and Pina 2020). As human rights activists dare to insert themselves into Brazil's political institutions, will favela activists be able to make demands for meaningful urban change without being threatened or killed? And will they find enough support to pass meaningful legislation?

Regardless of what happens in city halls and political parties, I have little doubt that Maria Rita and Solange will continue to get up each day and struggle to keep Youth Promise afloat. Carmen will continue speaking out for social development in Cidade de Deus, Leonardo will continue organizing for Black rights, and Natalia will continue planning cultural events across the city. This is the *trabalho de formiguinha*, or the "work of ants" that constitutes the backbone of favela activism. It is structured to persist, even when government offices are unsafe and ineffective for addressing urban inequality and insecurity. Whatever direction national politics moves in, I believe the everyday, ordinary work of favela activism will remain.

In the meantime, the rest of us have work to do: we must re-write our collective imaginaries about favelas and other conflict zones. From time to time, my work has brought me into conversation with reporters seeking data for their articles about shootouts and violence in Cidade de Deus. In one particular conversation, I asked a reporter if he would be willing to write a story about non-violent activism instead of the shootouts. He replied: "I'd love to, Anjuli. But since our magazine works with a dynamic of covering hot topics, it's difficult to go in that direction. On the flip side, if you know of any interesting news there or in other communities, let me know and I'll do my best to take advantage of that. I'd love to talk about the good things too." Violence is hot; activism is not. Even well-meaning reporters are unable to write about the good things because there is so much demand for stories of brutality.

What we choose to talk about and how we choose to talk about people in conditions of extreme violence has a direct and powerful effect on the stories the media shares. These, in turn, impact favela residents' opportunities to secure employment, walk through shopping malls without being followed, be treated with civility by police officers, make friends or romantic ties outside the favela, and, ultimately, be treated as urban citizens rather than criminals. While the forms and consequences of violence do need to be understood and discussed, we ultimately do the urban poor a disservice by becoming consumers of violence. We may have little direct control over Brazil's broken political system or the global issues sparked by the War on Drugs, but a good place to start is by rethinking the way we talk, read, study, and write about conflict zones. Let us focus less on violence and more on non-violence. Let us remember Sonia's activism, not her cross.

Ethnographic Reflections

Participatory Action Research in Areas of Violence

"This book is a book where Cidade de Deus has the chance to have a relationship with the academy in a much more horizontal way," noted Leonardo in our book workshop after reading a first draft of the manuscript. I had invited Leonardo and nine of my other core participants to read a translated draft of the book and offer their feedback. It is common in academia for scholars to invite fellow professors to read the draft of a book and provide suggestions on how to strengthen it. It is far less common to invite research participants to read and comment on the book written about them while it is still in the making. For this book I did both, hosting one workshop with five formal scholars in the field and two additional workshops with Cidade de Deus residents. All ideas were treated as valuable, and many were incorporated into the final draft. This was one of several strategies I employed to create a more equal and reciprocal relationship between the academy and a neighborhood harmed by not only physical and structural violence but also by epistemic violence, or the subordination of favela residents' perspectives based on the belief that their knowledge is inferior to that constructed by formally trained scholars (Alatas 2000; Castro Gomez 2019).

While this book has helped situate conflict activism in urban and transnational hierarchies of power, this Appendix discusses how I have tried to reduce the unequal relationship between the academy and some of its most marginalized research participants by using Participatory Action Research, or PAR. PAR is not a method per se, but an approach to how researchers engage with and think about our research participants, particularly those in less powerful social locations. PAR advocates for leveling the playing field between formal researchers and participants through more collaborative research practices. It is based on three overarching principles: (1) the inclusion of research participants in each stage of the research process, from forming questions, and collecting data to analyzing and publishing findings; (2) intentional dialogues that aim at co-learning and the co-production of ideas; and (3) social or political actions intended to improve the well-being of the research community (Fine and Torre 2021; Wallerstein et al. 2017). I attempted to implement a PAR model alongside a complex terrain of violent governance, which at times made PAR more challenging but also more necessary. I hope this reflection is helpful to people who study conflict zones and other marginalized populations, who may also be wondering how to co-create knowledge with participants and level an epistemic playing field that is so skewed against those we study. As I discovered, collecting data in a conflict zone is hard; trying to do this through a more democratic approach is even harder. No single scholar can entirely evade power hierarchies or external pressures imposed by a Western academic system, nor fully ensure the safety of ourselves or our participants. But in small, thoughtful, and collaborative ways we can help level relations, promote inclusion and safety, advocate for change, and creatively move beyond old assumptions about what constitutes "good" research in areas of violence and conflict.

Ethical Moments

In my first interview with Sonia, she subtly reminded me of my social location as an outside researcher studying a marginalized neighborhood. I had arrived at her house in search of an interview, and she had graciously agreed and invited me to sit on the couch next to her. On the wall behind us hung a black and white photograph of her deceased mother, adorned in a white *baiana* dress with a white turban wrapped around her head, the type worn by priestesses in the Afro-Brazilian Umbanda religion. Sonia answered my questions with precision and thoughtfulness, while also inserting a critique of academics.

Sonia recounted an exchange she'd recently had with a Brazilian academic who had wanted to conduct a study on Cidade de Deus with his team of students. "Why is it," she had confronted him, "that in most cases we are seen only as *objects* of study, and not as its protagonists? . . . Look, we're tired of doing interviews. People do a monograph, they do a master's thesis, they do a doctoral thesis, and then we do not see anything about it. We don't know if it worked out, if it didn't . . . 'No, but with me it's going to be different,' [they say], and we're like, 'Is it really going to be different?' " Sonia's comments pointed to a significant problem in academia: outside researchers often turn marginalized groups into data, rarely share their findings with participants or involve them in the analysis, and do little to help participants or their communities. I promised her I would do better: I would share my findings with her, and I would find ways to help the community. Behind her polite smile was a tired disbelief.

Sonia's pointed comments were a reminder that my research would be filled with what Marilys Guillemin and Lynn Gillam (2004:262) refer to as "ethically important moments," those that alert us to the potential impact of our research and our presence on our participants. Try as we might, it is not possible for an ethnographer to be a "fly on the wall": our presence is known and felt, even after we are gone. As our participants allow us into their lives, tell us their stories, introduce us to their friends and family members, and ultimately give us permission to tell the world about who they are and what they do, ethnography opens a Pandora's box of practical and ethical challenges. In neighborhoods like Cidade de Deus, where poverty and racial discrimination intersect with the constant threat of violence, the likelihood of doing harm is even further exacerbated.

I left our interview a bit shaken by her candor, but grateful for what I took as a challenge. I would find a way to include my participants in the research and make my presence beneficial in some way. But along the way, I also stumbled on dozens of dilemmas around my research, writing, and attempts to do something to help the community. Some of these dilemmas are common among ethnographers of conflict zones, and others emerged from my attempt to apply the principles of PAR as much as possible. They emerged in tandem, and I describe several here.

Entering the Field

When I first entered Cidade de Deus in 2014—when most of it was still "pacified" by the UPP police—the serene streets belied my internal anxiety, induced almost entirely from what I had heard, read, and watched about Cidade de Deus. While the roots of urban ethnography place great value on "unbiased" observations by external researchers who, presumably, come into a new community with an open mind, I had already been tainted by Cidade de Deus's reputation. Frankly, it was that reputation that had drawn me to it: there is an allure to researching areas well known for violence. I had prepared for my trip by reading news reports, studies, some local history, and many ethnographies about other "ghettos" and "slums," which informed me about what types of questions and theories were deemed interesting to my field. This required scholarly preparation did exactly the opposite of cleaning my slate: it filled me with pre-determined images, questions, and beliefs about what was "worth" my attention. On top of that, I had applied for and received a small stipend from my department to cover the costs of the trip. In the application, I had proposed a set of theories and questions I would study. An academic narrative, constructed by courses, colleagues, assumptions, and scholars I had never met, had begun to emerge before I'd even set foot in CDD. This was my first lesson about fieldwork: there is no unbiased scholar. These biases are perhaps even more pronounced in areas of conflict, where journalists, filmmakers, tourists, and others help construct particular narratives and perspectives about these sites that often emphasize violence over other elements.

In order to gain a more holistic understanding of CDD and make my presence useful to the community, I began fieldwork as a volunteer at Youth Promise. I had done some simple work for Solange, the director of Youth Promise, over email in the months before my trip. Once I arrived, I did whatever was needed, from teaching a class when a teacher was absent to helping write a grant to sweeping the floors. It wasn't much, but it felt like something. I gave what I had to give. Volunteering in these various capacities was also my attempt at trying to level power relations with residents, to demonstrate that I was willing to take a backseat, not be the leader, and to resist whatever urge I had to be a "white savior" in this community.

I hadn't realized this at the time, but being a member of Youth Promise became critical to my research in two ways. For one, it gave me a home base. Since I did not know other residents and it would have been unsafe to approach strangers on the street, Youth Promise gave me a place where I could go every day and still be in the community. At the time, I was staying with a childhood friend in a neighborhood nearby, so having a reason to enter CDD every day was crucial in my early days. I quickly got to know the other staff and volunteers, and many of them graced me with my first interviews. Youth Promise was a hub of activity. Solange was constantly meeting with staff from various CBOs, private funders, state administrators, and many others. Rosangela, a family friend from CDD with whom I had first entered the neighborhood, introduced me to another CBO, the Center for Dona Otávia, and convinced her ex-husband, a lifelong Cidade de Deus resident, to introduce me to some of his friends and work colleagues, who allowed me to interview them. Through a multi-entry snowball sampling, these participants introduced me to others, invited me to church, parties, meetings, and their homes. Soon, my network began to grow. It helped that I was fluent in Portuguese, had lived in Rio de Janeiro during my childhood, and loved Brazilian food and culture. My enthusiasm for their lives and desire to get to know them surely helped too, as did the sociability and friendliness for which Brazilians are well known. I also suspect that my status as a white American both evoked prestige and applied pressure on people to treat me well. While I'm sure my early participants withheld many important details about their stories, they were kind, welcoming, and helpful. Over the following years, I gradually built up trust and rapport with my key participants and was welcomed into their more private lives and thoughts.

My affiliation with Youth Promise also allowed me to enter the neighborhood without provoking any notable suspicion from local gang leaders. Although drug traffickers had not yet returned to the streets in 2014, it was widely believed that they had eyes and ears everywhere. Surely they knew of my presence and would have sent someone to question me if they suspected I was a journalist or undercover police agent. But these same eyes and ears would have seen me walking in and out of Youth Promise, helping to herd children onto buses for our field trips and chatting with Maria Rita in the streets about computer programs for kids. Thanks to Youth Promise, I arrived as a "teacher" and received de facto protection from this status. I was never questioned by drug gangs or the police.

It was also at Youth Promise that I became close friends with Maria Rita, who invited me to live with her, her sister Esther, and Esther's sons on my third trip, and every visit thereafter. Fieldwork became much easier and more interesting then. Esther took me anywhere I wanted to go and introduced me to everyone she knew. She helped me understand the everyday workings of the neighborhood and the impact of urban exclusion on its residents. Maria Rita, who was well connected to the activist community, put me in touch with other activists and groups, got me invited to meetings, and connected me to Facebook pages and WhatsApp groups. Many other participants introduced me to new people and graciously answered my barrage of questions. Whenever I was back in the United States, I maintained regular contact with them, and they often sent me videos or news stories of relevant events and their take on them. As I watched meetings being streamed live on Facebook or followed lengthy discussions unfolding about security or funding issues on WhatsApp groups, I often had the feeling of being in the "spaces of flows," both present and absent at the same time.

New Project, Same Goal

As I became more embedded in the neighborhood, I looked for additional ways to promote the values of PAR. Volunteering at Youth Promise enabled me to do many of these informally. However, by my third year in the field, I was so busy conducting interviews and attending events that I had less time to volunteer at Youth Promise. This created an ethical dilemma: should I prioritize research or action? As I discovered, one of the main challenges of PAR is time. There are only 24 hours in a day, and fieldwork on its own is incredibly time-consuming and exhausting, making it hard to engage in more action-oriented activities.

I resolved this challenge by transitioning to a different way to "give" to the community: by collecting data that activists and other residents could use to in grant applications and advocacy campaigns. I decided to put my research skills to good use, gathering data through a PAR approach that could become a resource for local activists. I was fortunate enough to have access to a generous seed grant from Northeastern University—under the supervision of (and with great support from) two faculty, Thomas Vicino and Dietmar Offenhuber—to fund the project. As it turns out, PAR is also expensive. Funding is essential to pay local participants for their labor.

Every element of the project was based on the principles of PAR. First, I asked a well-known and well-liked resident to serve as co-leader of the project, and we met regularly to determine what data to collect and how to ensure the process was as democratic and participatory as possible. The last census had been conducted in 2010, but this data was limited and often did not reflect what residents believed was most relevant or important.

A few organizations had collected some data in some areas near the main avenue, but the neighborhood had become increasingly hostile and dangerous to outside scholars, making it difficult for outsiders to do research deeper inside the neighborhood, where people tended to be worse off. We asked residents what they wanted us to study. Through several focus groups, residents told us what issues were most urgent and relevant to them. My co-leader and I used this information to construct a survey that was subsequently revised by dozens of residents. Residents also helped collect the data. We aimed to collect data that would promote broader social change, giving activists data they could use to apply for grants or to lobby for more resources.

We hired and trained a team of residents to interview participants. Their knowledge of the neighborhood was essential to revising the final questionnaire and determining the best ways to approach residents who might think we worked for the government and responding to inquiries from drug traffickers about what we were doing. Our team's local knowledge helped us connect with residents as safely as possible, allowing us to interview a sample numbering 989 participants. Once the data was collected, we hired a graphic designer from Cidade de Deus to make a simple, colorful brochure with some of the main findings. Our team handed out 3,000 of these brochures to residents in the streets in an effort to "give back" the data. It was the first time, to our knowledge, that any researcher had shared their findings with the neighborhood. The data analysis was also collective: we presented our findings in several meetings so residents could offer explanations for the results and suggest dissemination strategies. I partnered with another local resident to help write up the report, and then published a co-authored journal article with my partners from CDD (see Fahlberg et al. 2020). In 2019, we created a website, established a team of local resident-scholars, and began planning new projects. Shortly after the pandemic hit Cidade de Deus, our team organized and led two additional research projects through a PAR model.[1] Each project incorporated the ideas of dozens of residents throughout and has allowed team members to gain first-hand training and experience on how to collect data by and for their neighborhood.[2]

Negotiating Safety

Safety was a significant concern while I was in the field. There are several things one must worry about in a gang territory. One was the risk of being threatened or killed by drug traffickers if they perceived me as a threat to them. I believe my success at avoiding them was due partly to strategy, partly to luck, and partly to the help of a lot of people who taught me the social norms of the neighborhood. In addition to volunteering at Youth Promise, I decided early on not to interview drug traffickers or police officers, which may have limited the breadth of perspectives on conflict activism but also helped keep my project out of their watchful gaze and avoided unnecessary exposure. I also heeded every bit of advice offered by Maria Rita, Esther, and other participants. They told me which streets to go down at which times, recruited people to walk with me to parts of the neighborhood where I was not known to drug traffickers, and helped me figure out what questions I could ask safely. Ironically, they worried more about my safety when ventured into Rio's bustling downtown, where I was almost guaranteed to be pick-pocketed, than in my forays around Cidade de Deus. In fact, the only "crime" I ever suffered during my fieldwork was when my watch was stolen right off my wrist in the packed all-women's metro wagon.

Not all risks were avoidable, however. Walking anywhere in Cidade de Deus meant constantly passing right next to heavily armed drug traffickers and being far from the doors of Esther's home, where we could more easily hide from shootouts. I had learned to keep my eyes down, to never look drug traffickers in the eye, and to not scroll or take pictures on my cell phone while in sight of a gang member, in case they might suspect I was snitching to the police. There had been many close calls, however. On one occasion, I was nearly run over by a drug trafficker on a motorcycle who stopped only inches away from me as a cross the street. On another occasion, I barely made it out of CDD and to the airport in time for a flight when a massive policing operation shut down the neighborhood. It was also common for armored police vehicles to drive by on my walks around the neighborhood, often slowly and so close I could have reached out my arm and touched these vehicles of war. Each time, the experience sent chills down my spine as I anticipated a shootout. Whenever I was near police officers, I avoided their gaze and crossed the road. Beyond a few cat calls, the police never interacted with me or stopped to question me. And I, like all residents, had learned to duck or run the other way whenever I heard shots being fired. While I was always doing my best to avoid risks, no resident or ethnographer could avoid a stray bullet. I was lucky, but every year, many were not.

Given the possibility that I might be accosted and questioned, I remained fearful and vigilant about what I wrote down in any notes I carried with me. I wrote only minimal notes of any meetings or conversations that bordered on discussions about the drug trade, fearing that a drug trafficker might pull me over on my walk home and ask to read my notebooks. I wrote most of my notes at night, in the safety of Esther's living room, on my computer, which I kept stored safely at her home. I was also careful about asking questions on my recorder, which drug traffickers might confiscate and listen to. If some of the details in some stories are sparse, it is because I deemed it unsafe to write them down or record them, though I tried my best to recreate them later.

In my everyday work, however, I was often just as worried about how to manage my relationships with non-armed men. As an ethnographer, I exuded friendly curiosity about the lives of everyone I met. This was sometimes misread as romantic interest by men, even men many years (or decades) older than me. Some asked me out, and a few became angry when I politely declined. I often worried about accepting a car ride, going for a walk, or going into homes with male participants alone, both for my personal safety and for the possibility that others might interpret this as an inappropriate relationship. On one night, when I had stayed late at Camilla's house, her neighbor offered me a ride home on his motorcycle. It seemed safer than making the 10-minute walk back to Esther's house by myself, but only slightly. The motorcycle ride home had felt like a scene from *The Fast and the Furious* as we flew past pedestrians, between moving cars, and through parties in the street. He got me home safely, though in the following days he started to follow me on social media and asked me several times to go out on a date. Fortunately, he never retaliated when I refused, but I began to keep my distance from him—and from my friend's home— after that.

On another occasion, a male activist, well liked by many of my participants and whom I had met on several occasions, offered to give me a tour of his neighborhood, a favela on the other side of the city. I journeyed out there alone, meeting him on the beach near the entrance to his community, only to spend the first hour watching him bathe in the ocean in his speedo, followed by an interview he insisted we hold at a bar on the beach, while he remained nearly naked. We then walked to his home, into a windy favela where I knew no one and had no idea how to get out. Once in his house, he proceeded to undress, shower, and stretch slowly and provocatively in his underwear in the small living room while I stared out a window, petrified of what he might try to do next. Finally, he got dressed and gave me the tour of his neighborhood, but it was among the more terrifying experiences I had in the field. If he had decided to hurt me, there was little I could have done. I later found out that he had placed other women in similarly uncomfortable situations. Unfortunately, female ethnographers often deal with these overlapping forms of insecurity and violence (Hanson and Richards 2019). I share these experiences in part to remind my readers that, although there is much focus on the violence perpetuated by gangs and police in conflict zones, ordinary men, and even activists, can also pose a threat to women's safety.

While I was often concerned about my own safety in the field, I became increasingly concerned with my participants' safety when I started writing up my findings. I worried about whether the contents of this book might create tensions with drug traffickers or corrupt politicians, particularly since favela activism survives partly by not drawing attention to itself. How might exposing it impact my participants and other activists? I was also concerned that, in the process of constructing my own analysis of their lives and actions, I might erase or misrepresent their own understanding of themselves. Could I tell their story without erasing their narrative? I turn to these questions next.

Creating Knowledge: A Negotiated Narrative

Writing is said to be a lonely process: the lone author sits for months or years at home or in their office analyzing the data, diagramming their ideas, writing and rewriting their theories until they become a coherent whole. In reality, however, no idea emerges in a vacuum. All ideas are produced from and in relation to other ideas. Reading scholarly literature, participating in courses and conversations with peers, seeking mentorship from advisors, and struggling through the critique of anonymous reviewers give us the conceptual tools to figure out what we want to say. As we write, there are hundreds of cooks in our mental kitchen. In the spirit of PAR, I decided to add a few more cooks to mine: my participants. My writing has become a product of what I call a *negotiated narrative*, an account constructed in conversation with not only academic mentors and the scholarly literature but my participants as well. As I describe in this section, I have developed myriad ways to include my participants' perspectives, concerns, and questions in my thinking and writing process. While ultimately this book was written by me, it was enriched by a collective and inclusive process.

Not all will take well to the inclusion of participants in the construction of theory and revision of the manuscript. The social sciences were founded on the premise that data is only "good" or accurate if it is collected systematically and objectively—if it is devoid of the subjects' perspectives (Comte 1868). Presumably, the unbiased external observer can see things the subjects themselves cannot. There is certainly merit to this: we are all a bit blind to our own patterns and behaviors, especially the less savory ones we'd rather pretend did not exist. Outsiders, especially those trained with a sociological imagination, may be better positioned to see certain attributes of a community than insiders committed to a more normative view of themselves. Furthermore, those with training in the social sciences, who have read many other studies and theories, have possession of a great toolkit of concepts and theories they can employ to make sense of the phenomena they are studying.

While there is value to this epistemological approach, this perspective has also created systemic inequities in the production of knowledge, thanks to our colonial history and its current manifestations. In the hands of early anthropologists, ethnography emerged as a product of empire, a practice that often reified stereotypes about the "primitive Other" and provided useful information to more easily conquer, colonize, and, in some cases, annihilate indigenous tribes (Go 2016). While sociological research may no longer be conducted with the aim of conquering all objects of ethnographic study,[3] most well-funded universities and researchers remain in the Global North and are populated by scholars trained in Western theories and policies. Thanks to inequalities that give some groups more access to higher education than others, many of these scholars are white and from middle- and upper-class backgrounds. Meanwhile, ethnography, and urban ethnography in particular, continues to be fascinated with poor communities of color in and outside the United States. This helps to create epistemic disequilibrium, with many more books written about the cycles of poverty and violence in these neighborhoods than accounts of the good things people do there. This in turn reinforces the view of poor neighborhoods as sites of racialized criminality. When race and class inequities in academia merge with the objectification of participants, social science ultimately reproduces colonial narratives and practices.

Recognizing these challenges, many critical scholars have called for reflexivity, or a critical assessment of the impact of one's race, class, gender, etc., on subjects. "There . . . should be feminist research that is rigorously self-aware and therefore humble about the partiality of its ethnographic vision and its capacity to represent self and other," writes Judith Stacey in her seminal reflection on feminist ethnography (1988:26). Meanwhile, Victor Rios (2015) calls for reflexivity in the ethnographer's social location and the impacts of "white space" on our participants and data. While there is certainly a moral imperative in the practice of self-reflexivity in ethnographic research, I found the actual practice of it quite challenging. I knew I was white and privileged in many ways, but I did not know how this affected my participants without a lot of guesswork and reliance on assumptions. Perhaps more importantly, I wondered if identifying the impact of my positionality on my participants was sufficient. Does awareness of one's role in the reproduction of epistemic violence do enough to address it? Frankly, I do not think it does.

In my experience, PAR does a much better job of this: it seeks to reverse these dynamics by transforming participants from objects to subjects, making them producers of knowledge rather than just its data points. While I cannot change my whiteness or alter most of my other identity markers, I can invite those who are more distant from the centers of power to create knowledge *with* me. I can learn from them, and I can incorporate their ideas into my research and writing. I can ask them how my positionality has affected them and what I can do to address it, transforming self-reflexivity into *dialogical* reflexivity (Yuval-Davis 2012). And this was what I did. It took years of building relationships and trust and finding many opportunities to invite favela residents to critique and contribute to my research. As I mentioned in the Introduction, I asked participants what stories they wanted told, and I turned my research in that direction. Throughout my years of data collection and analysis, I presented my findings to my participants multiple times, both formally and informally, soliciting their feedback and ideas. I presented several conference-style presentations to groups of anywhere from 15 to 25 CDD residents, which were followed by collective discussion and analysis. I also shared my ideas with several participants over coffee or while sitting in the back of an Uber, giving them a chance to engage in the same types of conversations about my work I might have with an academic colleague.

Once I completed a first draft of my manuscript, I shared a translated copy with my key participants and asked them to respond with their opinions, critiques, and comments. I then held two book workshops with my participants from Cidade de Deus. I did not automatically incorporate every suggestion, but I took the comments of my participants as seriously as I did those of my academic advisors. Each had their own unique perspectives based on their differing social locations, training, and lived experiences. Each had something valuable to contribute. Like all scholarship, it was a team effort, but my team included marginalized research subjects, not just formal scholars.

The workshops with my participants were an overwhelmingly positive experience for me and, I believe, for the participants. Each lasted two hours and were held on Zoom—in the middle of the global pandemic. Activists were excited that my book told their story, which they believed had been largely ignored by scholars more interested in violence and suffering. They appreciated how I had tied all the pieces together, connecting local experiences of mistreatment and resistance to global and national forms of structural inequality and racism. Maria Rita reported: "I was very excited about the connection you made between politics, economics and the historical basis of building the favelas and going to Brazil itself, it was very interesting . . . It was one of the best books about favelas that I've read." Activists were also interested in how I theorized the tactics they deployed to remain safe, alive, and distant from the drug trade. According to Geovana, "what I found interesting [in the book] was to observe that even without us sitting down, agreeing to have a meeting and a strategy, most of the institutions, groups or collectives of Cidade de Deus have a great concern in keeping the distance between both the police and the drug trade, and have a very big concern about implications of this approach."

Activists also appreciated that my writing style was accessible, that the book was written in a manner that favela residents would be able to read and understand. For Rosangela, who had a post-graduate degree and had read many academic texts, one of her main observations was that "It will be a book that anyone can read and understand." Others talked about what they had learned from reading the book. Jefferson noted that he hadn't fully appreciated the role that non-activists like Esther played in supporting activists and creating a supportive environment in which activism was possible. Geovana was interested in the diversity of clusters of social change the book documented. According to Rosangela, she could see this diversity but also noticed how even activists with different approaches to politics were just as dedicated to Cidade de Deus as she was: "I saw myself in the other; how other people were also working for the emotional interests [of the community], for the interests of local development."

Participants also had several recommendations for how to improve the first draft of the manuscript, which I have since incorporated into the book. Leonardo noted that a more explicit explanation of race and colorism in Brazil would be important to contextualize Brazilian racial identities to a US audience. Geovana, Jefferson, and Carmen felt that Chapter 1 needed more content on the history of activism. They had spent years collecting documents about their work, but these were burned in a fire several years ago and there are now few official records of their work. I believe they viewed this book as a place to document and protect this history. Several activists were also upset about references to *assistencialismo* in Chapter 2, which they viewed as a pejorative term that did not reflect their emphasis on social justice and structural change. Geovana felt that my argument about the gendered division of governing labor needed a bit more nuance, given the leadership of men in non-violent activism before the consolidation of power under drug gangs. The final draft of the book includes many of these changes, as well as the excellent suggestions provided by my academic reviewers.

I asked my participants if any of them worried about whether the book could endanger them in any way. Participants believed that what I chose to share would not jeopardize their well-being, even if their identities were discovered. Jefferson, however, worried about the long-term consequences of exposing what he called the "central nervous system" of favela activism to the public, and specifically to Brazilian and US policymakers who might use this information to more severely police favelas. I acknowledged that historically ethnographic research had been used by states to dominate indigenous communities and that it was difficult to predict who might read the book and how this information might be used. Given this, I asked my participants if they wanted me to move forward with publishing the book. Jefferson himself believed it was worth the risk, stating that "I believe that this [book] can serve as a reference for us to be able to advance further in the fight to improve the quality of life of the poor population of the whole world." Jefferson and others hoped that this detailed narrative of their work could serve as a guidebook to activists in other countries also trying to mobilize under conditions of extreme violence. Ultimately, they did not see the "exposure" of their work as a major risk. Rosangela noted:

> Only those who are there [in Cidade de Deus] will truly know [how it's done], so no matter how much you explain it, it will give people a sense of what is experienced, but you are not giving the recipe of how to do it, right? To truly know how to do this work, you have to ally with Carmen, with Dona Otávia, even if she's dead it's important, right? And with Sonia and Jefferson. So it is these personalities all together that can move a pebble out of the way. That stuff you only learn in the everyday, only by living it.

While none of us can predict how this book will impact favela activists, I take comfort in knowing that this publication was based on an informed and collective decision-making process. Those most affected by it were offered multiple opportunities to revise or veto the project; I share it with you with their consent, approval, and hope that it might, as my participants suggest, be helpful to people organizing in other areas of conflict and violence.

The Benefits of PAR

The democratic approach of PAR has both a justice logic and a scholarly logic. According to Colombian sociologist Orland Fals Borda (1991:3), "This experiential methodology implies the acquisition of serious and reliable knowledge upon which to construct power, or countervailing power, for the poor, oppressed and exploited groups and social classes—the grassroots—and for their authentic organizations and movements." By prioritizing the views and perspectives of marginalized participants, PAR helps to promote the epistemic subjectivity of those typically excluded from knowledge production in the academy. It also emphasizes the production of data and theories that address social inequality and that promote the needs of the research community. It helps to balance the scales so severely distorted by neocolonialism.

This approach also contributes to theory by adding a diversity of ideas from different viewpoints. The very people who lack the financial resources and social networks needed to get into a graduate program and become the formal producers of knowledge have, by virtue of this exclusion, an ability to see things that the academic cannot. Their distance from the epistemic centers of power, the places where formal knowledge is made, provides them a view unfiltered and unmolded by canons and mentors (Narayan 1998). This is not to say their views are in fact free of constraint. In the same way social scientists produce knowledge that will help us get jobs, grants, and the praise of our colleagues, marginalized populations produce knowledge that might help bring more government aid, more allies, more empathy from the broader society, and more justice. Since it is not possible to produce objective knowledge, I have based my arguments on a dialogue between diverse perspectives.

In truth, every story is a negotiated narrative between the things we have been raised to believe, our subjective interpretations of reality, our colleagues and mentors, and the many possible outcomes we hope to achieve or avoid. By inviting marginalized participants to the negotiating table, we allow them to sit side by side with, to talk about and to challenge, the things we have learned from decades of pre-conceived beliefs, the news, our books, our advisors, and our future (or current) employers. For both ethical and epistemological purposes, our research subjects deserve to be part of constructing the narrative, to participate in making the questions and analyzing the findings. They should also share in the benefits of the story, whether by being allowed (and trained) to use the data themselves, receive dividends from book royalties, share in the acclaim or status, or be invited to give talks in universities. They must be both producers and beneficiaries of knowledge. Otherwise, we risk reproducing some of the racist and neocolonial forces many of us seek to dismantle.

Maneuvering Common Dilemmas

Practically, I also faced a number of dilemmas as I decided what to write. The first was whether to disclose the real name of my field site or give it a pseudonym. I consulted with several other favela scholars faced with this decision, and all of them told me I had no choice: Cidade de Deus has so many specificities, it would be impossible to provide any real history without making it immediately clear which favela I was writing about. My colleagues believed it would be unethical to hide these contextual details, or to present Cidade de Deus as if it were similar to other favelas. In fact, each favela has a unique history and political logic. To give it a pseudonym and hide its constitutive details would be to falsely attempt to claim that my findings could be generalized to other favelas. While I do believe many of my findings around conflict activism can and do carry to other sites, this must be empirically investigated.

Naming Cidade de Deus was not a decision made lightly, however, for it has removed many layers of anonymity between my readers and my participants. This was another reason I asked my participants to read and approve the manuscript. That I was writing about non-criminal, non-violent activism has helped to minimize some risks from the state's security apparatus, but not all threats. I was also strategic about what to share and what to leave out. I witnessed or heard many stories about violence, corruption, and conflicts between activists that would have provided compelling evidence to support my arguments and make this a more dramatic book. Some stories I decided not to tell in order to avoid perpetuating the "pornography of violence," or the tendency for writers to whet their audience's appetite by enticing them with gory stories of brutality (Bourgois 2001). Others I left out because I feared that armed actors might retaliate against a participant (or me) if they read the account and discovered the person's identity. I also did not recount all of the conflicts I witnessed between activists because they were not central to my arguments and could have exacerbated tensions between participants. While some may view these choices as "watering down" or over-simplifying the narrative, I think of it as a strategic choice to include the evidence needed to back up my claims, but no more than necessary. Even with my participants' consent, these stories were never truly mine to tell. Rigorous scholarship is important but, so are my participants' rights to privacy, safety, and dignity. I believe that, with careful reflection and open dialogue, both can be honored. While there is much we can learn from my participants' stories, their fate is to co-exist with this book. Their legacy lives on through it, even if in pseudonyms. I hope it is a legacy that brings them reflection, interest, pride, and new ways to think about their work, not shame or fear.

Thinking Back, Looking Forward

In my second visit to Cidade de Deus, I presented my preliminary findings about residents' perceptions of the UPP police, a topic I originally planned to be the subject of this book, but which I decided to publish as an article so I could focus more of my time researching activism instead. I invited the participants I had interviewed in my first year, along with several others I had formed relationships with, including Sonia, to the presentation. She was unable to make it, so the following day I went to her house with my computer, sat in her living room, and walked through the presentation with her. We talked for over two hours, pausing in between slides so she could add comments and information. I left with more ideas, a better understanding of the situation, and a feeling that Sonia was beginning to trust me. A year later, while I sat at an Art Talk open mic listening to the speaker, Sonia snuck up behind me and enveloped me in a bear hug. I had not seen her in several months, and it was a joyful reunion. I hoped it meant that she saw me as an ally doing my best to keep my promises to her.

Sonia died before she could review the manuscript for this book. I am left now wondering what she would have made of it all, what questions she would have asked, what critiques she would have offered, and what she would have added. Her absence is a warning: for those of us working with vulnerable populations, there is an urgency to ask our participants what they want and what they think before it is too late. These questions must be asked when we are first starting our projects, when we are in the throes of constructing our ideas, and when we are adding to, fixing, amending, and improving our arguments. There is a whole other layer of knowledge we can learn from them, and there is much we can do to support the needs of vulnerable populations. If we can put aside the imperial project of positivist, detached, and "unbiased" research, great partnerships are possible. We may not be able to change our social locations, but there is much we can do to honor different ways of knowing and to give our participants something in return. These are small steps, but I believe they move us in the right direction.

Notes

Introduction

1. Although the term favela is often used pejoratively due to the many negative stereotypes attached to these areas, in recent years it has been reclaimed as a political word by activists and other residents who point to the shared experiences of poverty, urban exclusion, racism, and other forms of discrimination people in these spaces must endure and combat. In this book, I use favela in the spirit of the latter definition and in line with how my participants use it.

2. Throughout the book, the racial category "Black" is capitalized to recognize the shared identity, community, and experiences of marginalization faced by those perceived as belonging to this racial identity. "White" is presented in lower-case given that in Brazil and many other countries whites remain the majority and are not necessarily a community united by shared experiences of discrimination.

3. There are many other useful definitions of activism, some of which consider movements that include violence in their toolkit.

4. Cidade de Deus is recognized by the municipal government as a neighborhood, or "bairro" while also qualifying as a "favela" or, what are legally termed "subnormal agglomerations." According to IBGE, subnormal agglomerations are those that possess "a set consisting of at least fifty-one housing units (shacks, houses . . .) lacking most essential public services, occupying or having occupied, until recently, land owned by others (public or private) and being arranged, in general, in a disorderly and dense way." However, as Jaílson de Souza e Silva (2012) notes, "favelas" are also defined by their relation to the city, including a lack of formal investments by the state, sociospatial stigma and racism, the auto-construction of homes, high rates of poverty and informality, low rates of education and employment, and low state sovereignty over the area.

5. Participants were remunerated for their work in reviewing the book manuscript.

6. The possibility of a united favela-based social movement is a question I explore in the book's conclusion.

7. This space is also shared with religious leaders and institutions, in particular Evangelical Christian and Catholic churches that have a strong presence in Rio's favelas and across Brazil.

Chapter 1

1. Zona Sul is Rio de Janeiro's wealthiest area.

2. The boundary from the community was drawn by my team of 16 residents from across the neighborhood in preparation for conducting our community-based survey in 2017. We also consulted with other residents about any boundaries around which my team felt ambivalent, demonstrating that even among residents there is disagreement about exactly where Cidade de Deus begins and ends.

3. Our team decided to survey this region, but only those who considered themselves CDD residents were asked to participate in the study.

4. Cidade de Deus's residents hold a variety of attitudes toward homosexuality and nontraditional gender presentations. In the city of Rio de Janeiro, it is illegal to discriminate against a person based on their sexual orientation, and a number of resources exist to promote the well-being of the LGBTQ community. However, many people in Cidade de Deus and across Brazil, particularly the country's growing Evangelical Christian community, continue to view homosexuality and gender nonconformity as a sin. Bullying and violence against members of the LGBTQ community remain pervasive in CDD and throughout the country.

5. Those who do move out of Cidade de Deus often end up in other favelas due to the high cost of living in safer neighborhoods. One woman I met, who managed to move out of CDD with her mother, told me she considered herself a refugee, having been forcibly displaced from CDD due to the violence there.

6. Rates of poverty and unemployment swelled in 2020 thanks to the COVID-19 pandemic and the ensuing lockdown and economic recession.

7. One hundred and two people did not answer this question, possibly because they were too embarrassed to report that they did not complete primary school. Given this, the actual rate may be closer to 45% of adults who had not completed primary school.

8. Rates of unemployment and poverty were even more staggering during the pandemic. See Fahlberg et al. (2021) for more recent data.

9. In the late 1800s, the Canudos community, under the leadership of radical Christian leader Antônio Conselheiro, began attracting thousands of peasants seeking to escape the tyranny of rural oligarchs. In 1893, the community declared its refusal to pay taxes, and the government began a massive media campaign to (mis)label Canudos residents as fanatical monarchists threatening to overthrow the new Brazilian republic. With widespread support, the state launched several failed attempts to kill Conselheiro and take over the community. On the fourth attempt, the state sent in 8,000 troops, who murdered 15,000 Canudos residents, including thousands of women and children, and set the town on fire.

10. Add note about this program.

Chapter 2

1. Here the term "communities" refers to other favelas.

2. LAMSA operates the Yellow Line, one of the city's largest expressways that cuts directly through Cidade de Deus.

3. It was located only a few doors down from the UPP headquarters, and the robbery became yet another symbol of the UPP's weakening power in the territory.

4. In Rio, the municipal government oversees the implementation and administration of preschools and elementary schools, while the state government oversees secondary education.

5. Ironically, the main branch of Farmanguinhos was situated on the outskirts of Cidade de Deus and directly in front of one of the area's most precarious informal settlements. This location, however, also prompted its staff to take special interest in the development of Cidade de Deus.

6. In the original quote, Carmen uses the term *ele*, literally translated as "he." However, in Portuguese, *ele* is often intended to designate a third party (without emphasis on male gender). To honor this sentiment, I have translated this as "we" instead.

7. Approximately USD$15,000 in 2011.

Chapter 3

1. In contrast to the United States and Central America, where gangs frequently operate like "brotherhoods," in which there is an initiation and a promise of loyalty to the group, gang membership in Rio de Janeiro is based on a looser structure and motivated primarily by economic gain, rather than allegiance to a "family." In Cidade de Deus, all drug traffickers were members of the Comando Vermelho, or CV, drug faction.

2. "Tia" and "Tio" mean "Aunt" and "Uncle" respectively and are terms of endearment and respect used by children when speaking to adults.

3. The ear lobes get smoothed from being rubbed on the tatami by opponents. Marial arts is a very common activity among Cidade de Deus's residents, and several were sponsored to live and compete in Europe and the United States.

Chapter 4

1. Police also were killed in these operations, but at one-twentieth the rate of civilians. In 2016, 925 civilians were killed by the police (Mello 2017). In the same year, 146 police were killed, though over 100 of them were not on duty at the time of their death (AFP 2017).

2. Innocence is a label attached to people widely known by friends and family, and the broader community, to have no direct involvement with drug gangs.

3. This is the main refrain of a famous funk song written by Cidade de Deus residents MC Cidinho & Doca in the 1990s and which has become the "anthem" for favelas across Brazil ever since.

4. The BOPE is the Battallion for Special Ops, similar to a SWAT team. It is housed within the state's military police forces. The Choque, also run by the military police, is a unit "specially instructed and trained for urban and rural counterguerrilla missions," according to the BPChoque's Facebook page. The CORE is the tactical policing unit for the state's civil police force.

5. As the reader might notice, I have adopted a similar strategy in the narrative of this book.

6. Note that I did not collect data on perpetration of interpersonal violence, so it is not possible to identify how many of those who professed commitment to not harming others in fact followed this edict. In fact, it is possible that some of the men and women I met may have at some point engaged in intimate partner violence, sexual assault, or child abuse, among other violent actions.

7. Even more dangerous than being labeled a researcher in a favela is being viewed as a journalist. I was warned dozens of times to make it clear that I was not a journalist to any stranger or drug trafficker who might question my reason for being there.

8. The remaining pages contained a mix of religious institutions and commercial entitites (i.e., pizza shops, car washes, etc.).

9. Lava Jato, or Car Wash, was the largest money laundering scheme in Brazilian history ever to be prosecuted, which resulted in the arrest of former President Lula and dozens of other politicians and businessmen, many from the leftist Worker's Party.

10. Translation by author. Given the poetic nature of the original song and its references to metaphors and slang whose literal translation would not reflect its intention, the translation attempted to reflect the meaning of the song.

Chapter 5

1. The name of the party is not listed in an effort to maintain Natalia's confidentiality.

2. Capoeira is a popular activity that combines dance and martial arts and is derived from African cultures.

3. LAMSA is a private dealership contracted by the city of Rio de Janeiro to maintain the Yellow Line, a 17.4km highway that cuts directly through Cidade de Deus and connects dozens of neighborhoods to the city center. LAMSA has provided a number of grants to local CBOs to promote social development.

Chapter 6

1. https://recordtv.r7.com/cidade-alerta-rj/videos/diretor-e-liberato-apos-sequestro-na-cidade-de-deus-18022020.

2. https://www.institutomariellefranco.org/.

Appendix

1. For more details, visit our website www.construindojuntos.com.
2. All team members were fully remunerated for their labor.
3. There has also been extensive scholarship into the role of contemporary research in perpetuating state control over vulnerable populations.

Bibliography

Abelson, Miriam J. 2014. "Dangerous Privilege: Trans Men, Masculinities, and Changing Perceptions of Safety." *Sociological Forum* 29(3):549–70. doi: 10.1111/socf.12103.

Addie, Jean-Paul D. 2022. "The Times of Splintering Urbanism." *Journal of Urban Technology* 29(1):109–16. doi: 10.1080/10630732.2021.2001716.

AFP. 2017. "Rio Registra 100 Policiais Mortos Em 2017—ISTOÉ Independente." *ISTOÉ Independente*, August 26.

Aguiar, Pedro. 2021. "Breve História da Internet no Brasil." Pp. 293–306 in *Apostila de História dos Meios de Comunicação*. IACS/UFF.

Alatas, Syed Hussein. 2000. "Intellectual Imperialism: Definition, Traits, and Problems." *Asian Journal of Social Science* 28(1):23–45. doi: 10.1163/030382400X00154.

Albarracín, Juan, and Nicholas Barnes. 2020. "Criminal Violence in Latin America." *Latin American Research Review* 55(2):397–406. doi: 10.25222/larr.975.

Almeida, Silvio. 2019. *Racismo Estrutural*. São Paulo, SP: Pólen Produção Editorial LTDA.

Alvarez, Sonia E. 1990. *Engendering Democracy in Brazil: Women's Movements in Transition Politics*. Princeton, NJ: Princeton University Press.

Alves, Jaime Amparo. 2019. "Refusing to Be Governed: Urban Policing, Gang Violence, and the Politics of Evilness in an Afro-Colombian Shantytown." *PoLAR: Political and Legal Anthropology Review* 42(1):21–36. doi: https://doi.org/10.1111/plar.12276.

Alves, Maria Helena Moreira, and Philip Evanson. 2011. *Living in the Crossfire: Favela Residents, Drug Dealers, and Police Violence in Rio de Janeiro*. Philadelphia, PA: Temple University Press.

Alves, Mário Aquino, and Natália Massaco Koga. 2006. "Brazilian Nonprofit Organizations and the New Legal Framework: An Institutional Perspective." *Revista de Administração Contemporânea* 10(SPE):213–34. doi: 10.1590/S1415-65552006000500011.

Amaral, Fernanda. 2019. "Representatividade, Estereótipo, Identidade e Democracia as Margens da Cidade." *Revista Eletrônica de Ciências Sociais* (30):18.

Amaral, Fernanda. 2021. *Voices from the Favelas: Media Activism and Counter-Narratives from Below*. Washington, DC: Rowman & Littlefield.

Amnesty International. 2015. *You Killed My Son: Homicides by Military Police in the City of Rio de Janeiro*. Rio de Janeiro: Anistia Internacional Brasil.

Ana, Fabiana Lemos Sant'. 2019. "O Negro na Cidade: Quilombos, Favelas e Cidadania." *ENANPEGE: A Geografia Brasileira na Ciência-Mundo* XIII:13.

Anderson, Ashley. 2021. "'Networked' Revolutions? ICTs and Protest Mobilization in Non-Democratic Regimes." *Political Research Quarterly* 74(4):1037–51. doi: 10.1177/1065912920958071.

Antônio, João. 2016. "Chacina na Cidade de Deus é guerra contra o povo." *A Nova Democracia*, December.

Appadurai, Arjun. 2001. "Deep Democracy: Urban Governmentality and the Horizon of Politics." *Environment and Urbanization* 13(2):23–43. doi: 10.1177/095624780101300203.

Arabindoo, Pushpa. 2011. "Rhetoric of the 'Slum': Rethinking Urban Poverty." *City* 15(6):636–46. doi: 10.1080/13604813.2011.609002.

Arbatli, Ekim. 2017. "Introduction: Non-Western Social Movements and Participatory Democracy in the Age of Transnationalism." Pp. 1–9 in *Non-Western Social Movements and Participatory Democracy: Protest in the Age of Transnationalism, Societies and Political Orders in Transition*, edited by E. Arbatli and D. Rosenberg. Cham: Springer International Publishing.

Arias, Enrique Desmond. 2006a. *Drugs & Democracy in Rio de Janeiro: Trafficking, Social Networks, & Public Security*. Chapel Hill: University of North Carolina Press.

Arias, Enrique Desmond. 2006b. "Trouble En Route: Drug Trafficking and Clientelism in Rio de Janeiro Shantytowns." *Qualitative Sociology* 29(4):427–45. doi: 10.1007/s11133-006-9033-x.

Arias, Enrique Desmond. 2017. *Criminal Enterprises and Governance in Latin America and the Caribbean*. Cambridge, UK: Cambridge University Press.

Atuesta, Laura H., and Yuri Soares. 2016. "Urban Upgrading in Rio de Janeiro: Evidence from the Favela-Bairro Programme." *Urban Studies*. doi: 10.1177/0042098016669290.

Auyero, Javier. 2001. *Poor People's Politics: Peronist Survival Networks and the Legacy of Evita*. Durham, NC: Duke University Press.

Auyero, Javier, and Claudio Benzecry. 2017. "The Practical Logic of Political Domination: Conceptualizing the Clientelist Habitus." *Sociological Theory* 35(3):179–99.

Auyero, Javier, and María Fernanda Berti. 2015. *In Harm's Way: The Dynamics of Urban Violence*. Princeton, NJ: Princeton University Press.

Auyero, Javier, Philippe Bourgois, and Nancy Scheper-Hughes. 2015. *Violence at the Urban Margins*. New York: Oxford University Press.

Auyero, Javier, Agustín Burbano de Lara, and María Fernanda Berti. 2014. "Violence and the State at the Urban Margins." *Journal of Contemporary Ethnography* 43(1):94–116. doi: 10.1177/0891241613494809.

Baird, Adam. 2018. "Becoming the 'Baddest': Masculine Trajectories of Gang Violence in Medellín." *Journal of Latin American Studies* 50(1):183–210. doi: 10.1017/S0022216X17000761.

Baiocchi, Gianpaolo. 2005. *Militants and Citizens: The Politics of Participatory Democracy in Porto Alegre*. Redwood City, CA: Stanford University Press.

Baiocchi, Gianpaolo, Patrick Heller, Marcelo Kunrath Silva, and Marcelo Silva. 2011. *Bootstrapping Democracy: Transforming Local Governance and Civil Society in Brazil*. Redwood City, CA: Stanford University Press.

Baldez, Lisa. 2002. *Why Women Protest: Women's Movements in Chile*. Cambridge, UK: Cambridge University Press.

Barber, Benjamin R. 2003. *Strong Democracy: Participatory Politics for a New Age*. Cambridge, UK: University of California Press.

Barbosa, Jorge Luiz. 2017. "A Favela na Política Cultural do Rio de Janeiro." P. 13 in *Políticas Culturais: Conjunturas e Territorialidades, Centro de Memória, Documentação e Referência*, edited by Lia Calabre e Deborah Rebello Lima. São Paulo, BR: Itaú Cultural.

Barbosa, Jorge Luiz, and Caio Gonçalves Dias. 2013. *Solos culturais*. Observatório das Favelas. Edited by Jorge Luiz Barbosa and Caio Gonçalves Dias. Rio de Janeiro, BR: Observatório das Favelas.

Barbosa, Valéria. 2012. *Os Grandes Mestres Guardiões Da Cidade de Deus: Fazedores de Destinos*. São Paulo: Casa do Novo Autor Editora.

Barcellos, Christovam, and Alba Zaluar. 2014. "Homicídios e Disputas Territoriais Nas Favelas Do Rio de Janeiro." *Revista de Saúde Pública* 48(1):94–102. doi: 10.1590/S0034-8910.2014048004822.

Barnes, Nicholas. 2017. "Criminal Politics: An Integrated Approach to the Study of Organized Crime, Politics, and Violence." *Perspectives on Politics* 15(4):967–87. doi: 10.1017/S1537592717002110.

Basu, Amrita. 2000. "Globalization of the Local/Localization of the Global Mapping Transnational Women's Movements." *Meridians* 1(1):68–84.

Bautès, Nicolas, Véronique Dupont, and Frédéric Landy. 2013. "Acting from the Slums: Questioning Social Movement and Resistance." Pp. 363–408 in *Megacity Slums: Social Exclusion, Space and Urban Policies in Brazil and India*, edited by M.-C. Saglio-Yatzimirsky and F. Landry. London: Imperial College Press.

Bay-Meyer, Kelly. 2013. "Do Ortega's Citizen Power Councils Empower the Poor in Nicaragua? Benefits and Costs of Local Democracy." *Polity* 45(3):393–421. doi: 10.1057/pol.2013.10.

Bayat, Asef. 2013. *Life as Politics: How Ordinary People Change the Middle East.* 2nd edition. Redwood City, CA: Stanford University Press.

Beall, Jo, Owen Crankshaw, and Susan Parnell. 2014. *Uniting a Divided City: Governance and Social Exclusion in Johannesburg.* New York: Routledge.

Beall, Jo, Tom Goodfellow, and Dennis Rodgers. 2013. "Cities and Conflict in Fragile States in the Developing World." *Urban Studies* 50(15):3065–83. doi: 10.1177/0042098013487775.

Bejarano, Cynthia L. 2002. "Las Super Madres de Latino America: Transforming Motherhood by Challenging Violence in Mexico, Argentina, and El Salvador." *Frontiers: A Journal of Women Studies* 23(1):126–50. doi: 10.1353/fro.2002.0002.

Benford, Robert D., and David A. Snow. 2000. "Framing Processes and Social Movements: An Overview and Assessment." *Annual Review of Sociology* 26:611–39.

Berry, Marie E. 2018. *War, Women, and Power: From Violence to Mobilization in Rwanda and Bosnia-Herzegovina.* Cambridge, UK: Cambridge University Press.

Bherer, Laurence, Pascale Dufour, and Françoise Montambeault. 2016. "The Participatory Democracy Turn: An Introduction." *Journal of Civil Society* 12(3):225–30. doi: 10.1080/17448689.2016.1216383.

Borde, Elis, Victoria Page, and Tatiana Moura. 2020. "Masculinities and Nonviolence in Contexts of Chronic Urban Violence." *International Development Planning Review; Liverpool* 42(1):73–91. doi: http://dx.doi.org/10.3828/idpr.2019.28.

Bourdieu, Pierre, and Loic Wacquant. 2004. "Symbolic Violence." Pp. 272–75 in *Violence in War and Peace: An Anthology*, edited by N. Scheper-Hughes and P. I. Bourgois. Oxford, UK: Blackwell Publishing.

Bourgois, Philippe. 2001. "The Power of Violence in War and Peace: Post-Cold War Lessons from El Salvador." *Ethnography* 2(1):5–34. doi: 10.1177/14661380122230803.

Bourgois, Philippe. 2003. *In Search of Respect: Selling Crack in El Barrio.* Cambridge, UK: Cambridge University Press.

Briceño-León, Roberto. 2005. "Urban Violence and Public Health in Latin America: A Sociological Explanatory Framework." *Cadernos de Saúde Pública* 21(6):1629–48.

Burawoy, M. 2012. "The Roots of Domination: Beyond Bourdieu and Gramsci." *Sociology* 46(2):187–206. doi: 10.1177/0038038511422725.

Burgos, Marcelo Baumann. 2005. "Cidade, Territórios e Cidadania." *DADOS—Revista de Ciencias Sociais* 48(1):189–222.

Calabre, Lia. 2014. "Política Cultural em tempos de democracia: a Era Lula." *Revista do Instituto de Estudos Brasileiros* (58):137–56. doi: 10.11606/issn.2316-901X. v0i58p137-156.

Caldeira, Teresa P. R., and James Holston. 1999. "Democracy and Violence in Brazil." *Comparative Studies in Society and History* 41(04):691–729.

Cano, Ignacio, Doriam Borges, and Eduardo Ribeiro. 2012. *O Impacto Das Unidades de Polícia Pacificadora (UPPs) No Rio de Janeiro.* Rio de Janeiro, BR: Fórum Brasileiro de Segurança Pública.

Cardoso, Marcus. 2013. "A dimensão simbólica dos conflitos: moradores de favela e polícia." *Anuário Antropológico* (I):167–90. doi: 10.4000/aa.392.

Carril, Lourdes. 2006. *Quilombo, favela e periferia: a longa busca da cidadania.* São Paulo, BR: Annablume.

Carvalho, José Murilo de. 2001. *Cidadania no Brasil: o longo caminho.* Rio de Janeiro, BR: Civilização Brasileira.

Castells, Manuel. 1983. *The City and the Grassroots: A Cross-Cultural Theory of Urban Social Movements.* Oakland, CA: University of California Press.

Castells, Manuel. 2008. "The New Public Sphere: Global Civil Society, Communication Networks, and Global Governance." *The ANNALS of the American Academy of Political and Social Science* 616(1):78–93. doi: 10.1177/0002716207311877.

Castro Gomez, Santiago. 2019. "The Social Sciences, Epistemic Violence, and the 'Invention of the Other.'" Pp. 211–27 in *Unbecoming Modern: Colonialism, Modernity, and Colonial Modernities,* edited by Saurabh Dube, Ishita Banerjee-Dube. New York: Routledge.

Cazarré, Marieta. 2016. "Mulheres representam 13% das vereadoras e 12% das prefeitas de todo o país." *Agência Brasil,* March 20.

Chasteen, John Charles. 2016. *Born in Blood and Fire: A Concise History of Latin America.* 4th edition. New York: W. W. Norton & Company.

Chenoweth, Erica, and Kathleen Gallagher Cunningham. 2013. "Understanding Nonviolent Resistance: An Introduction." *Journal of Peace Research* 50(3):271–76. doi: 10.1177/0022343313480381.

Chowdhury, Elora Halim. 2011. *Transnationalism Reversed: Women Organizing against Gendered Violence in Bangladesh.* New York: SUNY Press.

Chua, Lynette J. 2012. "Pragmatic Resistance, Law, and Social Movements in Authoritarian States: The Case of Gay Collective Action in Singapore." *Law & Society Review; Amherst* 46(4):713–48.

Cícero, José, and Rute Pina. 2020. "Mulheres negras eleitas: 'e agora, quem cuida delas?'" *Pública,* November 24.

Clair, Matthew, and Jeffrey S. Denis. 2015. *Sociology of Racism.* International Encyclopedia of the Social and Behavioral Sciences, 2nd edition. 19:857–63.

Cockburn, Cynthia. 2004. "The Continuum of Violence: A Gender Perspective of War and Peace." Pp. 24–44 in *Sites of violence: gender and conflict zones,* edited by W. M. Giles and J. Hyndman. Berkeley: University of California Press.

Collins, Patricia Hill. 1986. "Learning from the Outsider Within: The Sociological Significance of Black Feminist Thought." *Social Problems* 33(6):s14–32. doi: 10.2307/800672.

Connell, Raewyn. 2007. "The Northern Theory of Globalization." *Sociological Theory* 25(4):368–85. doi: 10.1111/j.1467-9558.2007.00314.x.

Comitê Comunitário de Cidade de Deus. 2014. *Favela É Cidade: Plano De Inclusão Socioeconômica*. Rio de Janeiro, BR: INAE.

Comte, Auguste. 1868. *The Positive Philosophy of Auguste Comte*. New York: W. Gowans.

Córdova, Abby. 2019. "Living in Gang-Controlled Neighborhoods: Impacts on Electoral and Nonelectoral Participation in El Salvador." *Latin American Research Review* 54(1):201. doi: 10.25222/larr.387.

Cornwall, Andrea, and Vera Schatten Coelho. 2007. *Spaces for Change?: The Politics of Citizen Participation in New Democratic Arenas*. London: Zed Books.

Coutinho da Silva, Rachel, and Thaisa Comeli. 2018. "Vidas Que Importam: Por Uma Agenda de Cidadania e de NãoViolência Nas Favelas Cariocas." *Venanparq*.

Custódio, Leonardo. 2017. *Favela Media Activism: Counterpublics for Human Rights in Brazil*. Lanham, MD: Lexington Books.

Dantas, Rosimery Cruz de Oliveira, Rosielly Cruz de Oliveira Dantas, and Symara Abrantes Albuquerque de Oliveira Cabral. 2020. "Violência policial: dor, cor e lugar." *Revista Interdisciplinar em Violência e Saúde* 3(2).

da Silva Porto, Maria Célia. 2005. "Estado Assistencialista e 'Questão Social' No Brasil Pós-Constituinte." *II Jornada Internacional de Politicas Públicas*.

Davis, Diane. 2010. "Irregular Armed Forces, Shifting Patterns of Commitment, and Fragmented Sovereignty in the Developing World." *Theory and Society* 39(3–4):397–413. doi: 10.1007/s11186-010-9112-6.

Davis, Diane E., and Nora Libertun de Duren. 2011. "Introduction: Identity Conflicts in the Urban Realm." Pp. 1–14 in *Cities and Sovereignty: Identity Politics in Urban Spaces*, edited by D. E. Davis and N. L. de Duren. Indiana University Press.

de Sousa, José Nilton. 2003. "A Exclusão Pela Urbanização Favela: Governo e Conflito Na Cidade Do Rio de Janeiro." *GEOgrafia Ano* V(10):1–19.

de Souza, Marcelo Lopes. 2005. "Urban Planning in an Age of Fear: The Case of Rio de Janeiro." *International Development Planning Review* 27(1):1–19.

De Sousa Santos, Boaventura. 2008. "The World Social Forum and the Global Left." *Politics & Society* 36(2):247–70. doi: 10.1177/0032329208316571.

Déa, Ariane Dalla. 2012. "Representations of Resistance in Latin American Art." *Latin American Perspectives* 39(3):5–9. doi: 10.1177/0094582X11436103.

Deckard, Faith, and Javier Auyero. 2022. "Poor People's Survival Strategies: Two Decades of Research in the Americas." *Annual Review of Sociology* 48. doi: 10.1146/annurev-soc-031021-034449.

Della Porta, Donatella. 2006. *Globalization from Below: Transnational Activists and Protest Networks*. Minneapolis, MN: University of Minnesota Press.

Diamint, Rut. 2015. "A New Militarism in Latin America." *Journal of Democracy* 26(4):155–68. doi: 10.1353/jod.2015.0066.

Diego Rivera Hernández, Raúl. 2017. "Making Absence Visible: The Caravan of Central American Mothers in Search of Disappeared Migrants." *Latin American Perspectives* 44(5):108–26. doi: 10.1177/0094582X17706905.

Dueñas, Gabriela Polit. 2019. *Unwanted Witnesses: Journalists and Conflict in Contemporary Latin America*. 1st edition. Pittsburgh, PA: University of Pittsburgh Press.

Duncombe, Stephen. 2007. "(From) Cultural Resistance to Community Development." *Community Development Journal* 42(4):490–500. doi: 10.1093/cdj/bsm039.

Duran-Martinez, Angelica. 2018. *The Politics of Drug Violence: Criminals, Cops and Politicians in Colombia and Mexico*. Unabridged edition. New York: Oxford University Press.

Elsner, Jas. 2001. "Cultural Resistance and the Visual Image: The Case of Dura Europos." *Classical Philology* 96:269–304.

Escóssia, Fernanda da. 2003. "Rio Contrata ONGs Para Serviços Em Favelas." *Folha de São Paulo*, November 17.

Fahlberg, Anjuli. 2018. "'It Was Totally Different than What We Had Before': Perceptions of Urban Militarism under Rio de Janeiro's Pacifying Policing Units." *Qualitative Sociology Special Issue on Ethnographies of Insecurity.* 41:303–24.

Fahlberg, Anjuli N. 2019. "Uneven Development and the Making of Rio de Janeiro." Pp. 173–83 in *The Routledge Companion to the Suburbs*, edited by B. Hanlon and T. Vicino. New York: Routledge.

Fahlberg, Anjuli, Viviane Potiguara, and Ricardo Fernandes. 2020. "Pelos Olhos Da Comunidade: Cidade de Deus e Suas Necessidades, Capacidades e Desafios." *Coletivo de Pesquisa Construindo Juntos.* doi: 10.13140/RG.2.2.15031.47528.

Fahlberg, Anjuli, and Thomas Vicino. 2015. "Breaking the City: Militarization and Segregation in Rio de Janeiro." *Habitat International* 54(1):10–17.

Fahlberg, Anjuli, Thomas J. Vicino, Ricardo Fernandes, and Viviane Potiguara. 2020. "Confronting Chronic Shocks: Social Resilience in Rio de Janeiro's Poor Neighborhoods." *Cities* 99:102623. doi: 10.1016/j.cities.2020.102623.

Fals-Borda, Orlando, and Mohammad Anisur Rahman. 1991. *Action and Knowledge: Breaking the Monopoly with Participatory Action Research.* New York: Rowman & Littlefield Publishers.

Fernandes, Sujatha. 2007. "Barrio Women and Popular Politics in Chávez's Venezuela." *Latin American Politics and Society* 49(3):97–127.

Filgueiras, Luiz. 2006. "O Neoliberalismo No Brasil: Estrutura, Dinâmica e Ajuste Do Modelo Econômico." Pp. 179–206 in *Neoliberalismo y sectores dominantes: tendencias globales y experiencias nacionales, Colección Grupos de trabajo*, edited by E. M. Basualdo and E. O. Arceo. Ciudad de Buenos Aires: Consejo Latinoamerica de Ciencias Sociales.

Filho, Antônio Sérgio Maia de Carvalho and Juliana Barreto da Silva. 2020. "Colorismo: Entendendo a Diversidade Étnico-Racial e a Discriminação Brasileira." *Mostra de Extensão IFF—UENF—UFF—UFRRJ 12*: 1–2.

Fine, Michelle, and María Elena Torre. 2021. *Essentials of Critical Participatory Action Research.* 1st edition. Washington, DC: American Psychological Association.

Fine, Michelle, María Elena Torre, Austin Gerhard Oswald, and Shéár Avory. 2021. "Critical Participatory Action Research: Methods and Praxis for Intersectional Knowledge Production." *Journal of Counseling Psychology* 68(3):344–56. doi: 10.1037/cou0000445.

Fischer, Brodwyn M. 2008. *A Poverty of Rights: Citizenship and Inequality in Twentieth-Century Rio de Janeiro.* Redwood City, CA: Stanford University Press.

Fishman, Robert M., and David W. Everson. 2016. "Mechanisms of Social Movement Success: Conversation, Displacement and Disruption." *Revista Internacional de Sociología* 74(4):e045. doi: 10.3989/ris.2016.74.4.045.

Fleury, Sonia Maria, and Carlos Eduardo Santos Pinho. 2018. "Authoritarian Governments and the Corrosion of the Social Protection Network in Brazil." *Revista Katálysis* 21(1):29–42. doi: 10.1590/1982-02592018v21n1p14.

FolhaPress. 2015. "Moradores Do Alemão Fazem Nova Manifestação Após Morte de Menino | O TEMPO." *Jornal O Tempo*, April 4.

Fórum Justiça. 2016. "Habeas Corpus contra Busca e Apreensão Coletiva na Favela Cidade de Deus." Casoteca de Litigância Estratégica em Direitos Humanos. Retrieved

April   23,   2021   (https://casoteca.forumjustica.com.br/caso/habeas-corpus-contra-busca-e-apreensao-coletiva-na-favela-cidade-de-deus/).

França, Wellington. 2019. "Associativismo de Base Comunitária Na Cidade de Deus—O Movimento -." *Dicionário de Favelas Marielle Franco.* https://wikifavelas.com.br/index.php/Associativismo_de_base_comunit%C3%A1ria_na_Cidade_de_Deus_%E2%80%93_O_Movimento.

Franco, Marielle. 2014. "UPP—A Redução da Favela a Três Letras: Uma Análise da Política de Segurança Pública do Estado do Rio de Janeiro." *Universidade Federal Fluminense,* Master's thesis, Niterói, RJ.

Fraser, Nancy. 1990. "Rethinking the Public Sphere: A Contribution to the Critique of Actually Existing Democracy." *Social Text* (25/26):56. doi: 10.2307/466240.

Freedom House. 2018. "Freedom in the World 2018: Brazil." Retrieved September 25, 2020 (https://freedomhouse.org/country/brazil/freedom-world/2018).

Freedom House. 2022. *Freedom in the World 2022: The Global Expansion of Authoritarian Rule.* Washington, DC: Freedom House.

Freeman, James. 2012. "Neoliberal Accumulation Strategies and the Visible Hand of Police Pacification in Rio de Janeiro." *Revista de Estudos Universitários* 38(1): 95–126.

Friedman, Elisabeth J. 1999. "The Effects of 'Transnationalism Reversed' in Venezuela: Assessing the Impact of UN Global Conferences on the Women's Movement." *International Feminist Journal of Politics* 1(3):357–81. doi: 10.1080/146167499359790.

Friedman, Elisabeth. 2009. "Re(Gion)Alizing Women's Human Rights in Latin America." *Politics & Gender* 5:349–75. doi: 10.1017/S1743923X09990171.

Fujii, Lee Ann. 2011. *Killing Neighbors: Webs of Violence in Rwanda.* 1st edition. Ithaca, NY: Cornell University Press.

Fundação Getúlio Vargas. 2009. *Banco Nacional de Habitação.* Rio de Janeiro, BR: Centro de Pesquisa e Documentação de História Contemporânea do Brasil.

Fung, Archon. 2009. *Empowered Participation: Reinventing Urban Democracy.* Princeton, NJ: Princeton University Press.

Gallo-Cruz, Selina. 2020. *Political Invisibility and Mobilization: Women against State Violence in Argentina, Yugoslavia, and Liberia.* 1st edition. New York: Routledge.

Galtung, Johan. 1969. "Violence, Peace, and Peace Research." *Journal of Peace Research* 6(3):167–91.

Gamson, William. 2015. "Defining Movement 'Success.'" P. 445 in *The Social Movements Reader: Cases and Concepts,* edited by J. Goodwin and J. M. Jasper. Hoboken, NJ: John Wiley & Sons.

Gay, Robert. 1993. *Popular Organization and Democracy in Rio De Janeiro: A Tale of Two Favelas.* Philadelphia: Temple University Press.

Gay, Robert. 2012. "Clientelism, Democracy, and Violence in Rio de Janeiro." Pp. 81–98 in *Clientelism in Everyday Latin American Politics,* edited by T. Hilgers. New York: Palgrave Macmillan US.

Gelape, Lucas. 2018. "Representação Territorial e Marielle Franco." *Medium,* March 21.

Gideon, Jasmine. 2018. "Gendering Activism, Exile and Wellbeing: Chilean Exiles in the UK." *Gender, Place & Culture* 25(2):228–47. doi: 10.1080/0966369X.2018.1428534.

Glenn, Evelyn Nakano. 2011. "Constructing Citizenship: Exclusion, Subordination, and Resistance." *American Sociological Review* 76(1):1–24. doi: 10.1177/0003122411398443.

Go, Julian. 2016. *Postcolonial Thought and Social Theory.* New York: Oxford University Press.

Gohn, Maria da Gloria. 2013. "Sociedade Civil No Brasil: Movimentos Sociais e ONGs." *Revista Meta: Avaliação* 5(14):238–53.

Gohn, Maria da Glória. 2014. *Movimentos sociais e redes de mobilizações civis no Brasil contemporâneo*. Petrópolis, RJ: Editora Vozes Limitada.

Goldstein, Donna M. 2003. *Laughter Out of Place: Race, Class, Violence, and Sexuality in a Rio Shantytown*. Oakland, CA: University of California Press.

Gomes, Nilma Lino. 2019. *O movimento negro educador: Saberes construídos nas lutas por emancipação*. Petrópolis, RJ: Editora Vozes Limitada.

Gonçalves, Rafael Soares. 2013. "A política, o direito e as favelas do Rio de Janeiro: um breve olhar histórico." *URBANA: Revista Eletrônica do Centro Interdisciplinar de Estudos sobre a Cidade* 1(1). doi: 10.20396/urbana.v1i1.8635115.

Gonzales, Lélia. 2018. *Lélia Gonzalez: Primavera Para as Rosas Negras*. União dos Coletivos Pan Africanistas.

Gordon, Daanika. 2022. *Policing the Racial Divide: Urban Growth Politics and the Remaking of Segregation*. New York: New York University Press.

Governo do Rio de Janeiro. 2014. "UPP—Unidade de Polícia Pacificadora." Retrieved March 10, 2015 (http://www.upprj.com/).

Graham, Jessica Lynn. 2019. *Shifting the Meaning of Democracy: Race, Politics, and Culture in the United States and Brazil*. Oakland, CA: University of California Press.

Graham, Stephen. 2011. *Cities Under Siege: The New Military Urbanism*. London; New York: Verso.

Graham, Stephen, and Simon Marvin. 2001. *Splintering Urbanism: Networked Infrastructures, Technological Mobilities and the Urban Condition*. London: Psychology Press.

Guilherme, Manuela. 2019. "Glocal Languages beyond Post-Colonialism: The Metaphorical North and South in the Geographical North and South." Pp. 42–64 in *Glocal Languages and Critical Intercultural Awareness*, edited by M. Guilherme and L. M. T. M. de Souza. Routledge.

Guillemin, Marilys, and Lynn Gillam. 2004. "Ethics, Reflexivity, and 'Ethically Important Moments' in Research." *Qualitative Inquiry* 10(2):261–80. doi: 10.1177/1077800403262360.

Gupta, Akhil. 2012. *Red Tape: Bureaucracy, Structural Violence, and Poverty in India*. Durham, NC: Duke University Press.

Hall, Peter A., and Michèle Lamont, eds. 2013. *Social Resilience in the Neoliberal Era*. Cambridge: Cambridge University Press.

Hanchard, Michael. 2006. *Party/Politics: Horizons in Black Political Thought*. Oxford, New York: Oxford University Press.

Hanson, Rebecca, and Patricia Richards. 2019. *Harassed: Gender, Bodies, and Ethnographic Research*. 1st edition. Oakland: University of California Press.

Harvey, David. 2005. *A Brief History of Neoliberalism*. Oxford; New York: Oxford University Press.

Harvey, David. 2012. *Rebel Cities: From the Right to the City to the Urban Revolution*. London: Verso Books.

Harvey, David. 2015. "The Right to the City." Pp. 281–89 in *The City Reader*, edited by R. T. LeGates and F. Stout. Routledge.

Hasić, Jasmin, Dženeta Karabegović, and Bisera Turković. 2020. "Locally Embedded Civil Society Organizations and Public Diplomacy: The Advocacy Roles of the 'Mothers of

Srebrenica' in Promoting a Culture of Remembrance." *Studies of Transition States and Societies* 13(1):21–35.

Henry, Laura, and Elizabeth Plantan. 2022. "Activism in Exile: How Russian Environmentalists Maintain Voice after Exit." *Post-Soviet Affairs* 38(4):274–92. doi: 10.1080/1060586X.2021.2002629.

Holston, James. 2008. *Insurgent Citizenship: Disjunctions of Democracy and Modernity in Brazil.* Princeton, NJ: Princeton University Press.

Hufty, Marc. 2011. "Investigating Policy Processes: The Governance Analytical Framework (GAF)." Pp. 165–84 in *Research for Sustainable Development: Foundations, Experiences, and Perspectives*, edited by U. Weismann and H. Hurni. Rochester, NY: Geographica Bernensia.

Human Rights Foundation. 2022. "In Pursuit of Freedom: A Collection of Global Protest Art." *Art in Protest.* Retrieved August 1, 2022 (https://artinprotest.viewingrooms.com/in-pursuit-of-freedom#belarus).

Hunt, Kate. 2019. "Twitter, Social Movements, and Claiming Allies in Abortion Debates." *Journal of Information Technology & Politics* 16(4):394–410. doi: 10.1080/19331681.2019.1659901.

Hunt, Stacey. 2009. "Rethinking State, Civil Society and Citizen Participation: The Case of the Colombian Paramilitaries." *Behemoth* 2(1):64–87.

Husain, Saima. 2009. "On the Long Road to Demilitarization and Professionalization of the Police in Brazil." Pp. 47–77 in *Policing Insecurity: Police Reform, Security, and Human Rights in Latin America.* Washington, DC: Lexington Books.

Inclán, María. 2018. "Latin America, a Continent in Movement but Where To? A Review of Social Movements' Studies in the Region." *Annual Review of Sociology* 44(1):535–51. doi: 10.1146/annurev-soc-073117-041043.

Instituto Millenium. 2012. "O Historiador Marco A. Villa Critica o Assistencialismo Eleitoreiro: 'Sob o Controle Dos Vereadores o Centro Social Transforma-Se Numa Espécie de Escritório Eleitoral.'" *Instituto Millenium.* Retrieved December 27, 2017 (https://www.institutomillenium.org.br/divulgacao/entrevistas/o-historiador-marco-antonio-critica-assistencialismo-nas-eleies-sob-controle-dos-vereadores-centro-soc ial-se-transforma-numa-espcie-de-escritrio-eleitoral/).

Isin, Engin Fahri. 2002. *Being Political: Genealogies of Citizenship.* Minneapolis, MN: University of Minnesota Press.

Jovchelovitch, Sandra, and Jacqueline Priego-Hernandez. 2013. "Sociabilidades Subterrâneas: Identidade, Cultura e Resistência Em Favelas Do Rio de Janeiro." Retrieved October 21, 2017 (http://www.unesco.org/new/en/brasilia/).

Keck, Margaret E., and Kathryn Sikkink. 1998. *Activists beyond Borders: Advocacy Networks in International Politics.* 1st edition. Ithaca, NY: Cornell University Press.

King, Anthony. 2021. *Urban Warfare in the Twenty-First Century.* 1st edition. Cambridge, UK; Medford, MA: Polity.

Kinzo, Maria D'alva G. 2001. "A Democratização Brasileira: Um Balanço Do Processo Político Desde a Transição." *São Paulo Em Perspectiva* 15(4):3–12. doi: 10.1590/S0102-88392001000400002.

Konaev, Margarita. 2019. *The Future of Urban Warfare in the Age of Megacities.* Paris: Études de l'Ifri.

Kongkirati, Prajak. 2016. "Thailand's Failed 2014 Election: The Anti-Election Movement, Violence and Democratic Breakdown." *Journal of Contemporary Asia* 46(3):467–85. doi: 10.1080/00472336.2016.1166259.

Krause, Jana. 2018. *Resilient Communities: Non-Violence and Civilian Agency in Communal War*. Cambridge, UK: Cambridge University Press.

Krook, Mona Lena, and Juliana Restrepo Sanín. 2016. "Gender and Political Violence in Latin America. Concepts, Debates and Solutions." *Política y Gobierno* 23(1):127–62.

Larkins, Erika Mary Robb. 2015. *The Spectacular Favela: Violence in Modern Brazil*. Oakland, CA: University of California Press.

Lasswell, Harold D. 2018. *Politics: Who Gets What, When, How*. Auckland, NZ: Pickle Partners Publishing.

Lawson, Erica S. 2018. "Bereaved Black Mothers and Maternal Activism in the Racial State." *Feminist Studies* 44(3):713–35. doi: 10.15767/feministstudies.44.3.0713.

Leeds, Elizabeth. 1996. "Cocaine and Parallel Polities in the Brazilian Urban Periphery: Constraints on Local-Level Democratization." *Latin American Research Review* 31(3):47–83.

Lefebvre, Henri, and Michael J. Enders. 1976. "Reflections on the Politics of Space." *Antipode* 8(2):30–37. doi: 10.1111/j.1467-8330.1976.tb00636.x.

Leite, Ilka Boaventura. 2000. "Os Quilombos No Brasil: Questões Conceituais e Normativas." *Etnográfica* 4(2):333–54.

Lessing, Benjamin. 2017. *Making Peace in Drug Wars: Crackdowns and Cartels in Latin America*. Cambridge: Cambridge University Press.

Ley, Sandra. 2018. "To Vote or Not to Vote: How Criminal Violence Shapes Electoral Participation." *Journal of Conflict Resolution* 62(9):1963–90. doi: 10.1177/0022002717708600.

Lopes, Adriana Carvalho, and Adriana Facina. 2012. "Cidade Do Funk: Expressões Da Diáspora Negra Nas Favelas Cariocas." *Revista Do Arquivo Geral Da Cidade Do Rio de Janeiro* 6:193–206.

Lourenço, Natália, and João Paulo dos Santos. 2011. "Assistencialismo versus Emancipação: O Papel Do Terceiro Setor Na Sociedade Atual." *Revista Saber Acadêmico* (12):10–14.

Loveman, Mara. 1998. "High-Risk Collective Action: Defending Human Rights in Chile, Uruguay, and Argentina." *American Journal of Sociology* 104(2):477–25.

MacKinnon, Catharine A. 1994. "Rape, Genocide, and Women's Human Rights." *Harvard Women's Law Journal* 17:5–16.

Magalhães, Luiz. 2018. "Prefeitura do Rio deixou de usar empréstimos para concluir obras." *O Globo*, June 21.

Magaloni, Beatriz, Edgar Franco-Vivanco, and Vanessa Melo. 2020. "Killing in the Slums: Social Order, Criminal Governance, and Police Violence in Rio de Janeiro." *American Political Science Review* 114(2):552–72. doi: 10.1017/S0003055419000856.

Marcelino, Jonathan da Silva. 2013. "A Força Do Lugar: Das Lutas Comunitárias Ao Comitê Comunitário. A Trajetória de R-Êxistencia Do Bairro Cidade de Deus Na Urbe Carioca." Universidade de São Paulo, São Paulo.

Marques Junior, Joilson Santana. 2020. "O 'equívoco' como morte negra, ou como 'naturalizar' balas racializadas." *Revista Katálysis* 23(2):366–74. doi: 10.1590/1982-02592020v23n2p366.

Massey, Douglas S., and Nancy A. Denton. 1993. *American Apartheid: Segregation and the Making of the Underclass*. Cambridge, MA: Harvard University Press.

Mattos, Geísa. 2017. "Flagrantes de racismo: imagens da violência policial e as conexões entre o ativismo no Brasil e nos Estados Unidos138." *Revista de Ciências Sociais* 2(33):185–217.

Mayer, Margit. 2013. "Against and beyond the Crisis: The Role of Urban Social Movements." *Geographies* 22:67–72.

Mazurana, Dyan E., Khristopher Carlson, and Sanam Naraghi Anderlini. 2004. *From Combat to Community: Women and Girls of Sierra Leone*. Washington, DC: Hunt Alternatives Fund.

McAdam, Doug, Sidney Tarrow, and Charles Tilly. 2001. *Dynamics of Contention*. Cambridge, UK: Cambridge University Press.

McCann, Bryan. 2014. *Hard Times in the Marvelous City: From Dictatorship to Democracy in the Favelas of Rio de Janeiro*. Durham, NC: Duke University Press.

McFarlane, Colin. 2012. "Rethinking Informality: Politics, Crisis, and the City." *Planning Theory & Practice* 13(1):89–108. doi: 10.1080/14649357.2012.649951.

Meirelles, Renato, and Celso Athayde. 2016. *Um país chamado favela: A maior pesquisa já feita sobre a favela brasileira*. Rio de Janeiro, BR: Editora Gente Liv e Edit Ltd.

Mello, Daniel. 2017. "Mortes Causadas Por Policiais Crescem 25,8% Em 2016." *Agência Brasil*, October 30.

Mello, Edir. 2010. "Luz, câmera, ação: Cidade de Deus entre histórias e memórias." Doctorate in Social Sciences, Universidade do Estado do Rio de Janeiro, Rio de Janeiro.

Menés, Lara Gil. 2020. "Introducción: Resistiendo a La Guerra, Construyendo Paz." Pp. 2–4 in *Resistimos a la Guerra: Cuaderno sobre Mujeres y Ejercícios de Construcción de Paz*, edited by Paz con Dignidad and Corporación Con-Vivamos. Madrid, SP: Ayuntamiento de Madrid.

Meyer, D. S., and D. C. Minkoff. 2004. "Conceptualizing Political Opportunity." *Social Forces* 82(4):1457–92. doi: 10.1353/sof.2004.0082.

Mina, An Xiao. 2019. *Memes to Movements: How the World's Most Viral Media Is Changing Social Protest and Power*. Boston, MA: Beacon Press.

Misse, Michel, Carolina Christoph Grillo, and Natasha Elbas Neri. 2015. "Letalidade policial e indiferença legal: A apuração judiciária dos 'autos de resistência' no Rio de Janeiro (2001–2011)." *DILEMAS: Revista de Estudos de Conflito e Controle Social* 1(29):43–71.

Mohanty, Chandra Talpade. 2013. "Transnational Feminist Crossings: On Neoliberalism and Radical Critique." *Signs* 38(4):967–91. doi: 10.1086/669576.

Molenaar, Fransje. 2017. "Power Short-Circuited: Social Movement Organisation under Cartel Rule in Rural Guatemala." *Journal of Latin American Studies; Cambridge* 49(4):829–54. doi: 10.1017/S0022216X17000062.

Moncada, Eduardo. 2016. *Cities, Business, and the Politics of Urban Violence in Latin America*. Stanford, CA: Stanford University Press.

Moncada, Eduardo. 2013. "The Politics of Urban Violence: Challenges for Development in the Global South." *Studies in Comparative International Development* 48(3):217–39. doi: 10.1007/s12116-013-9133-z.

Montambeault, Françoise. 2015. *The Politics of Local Participatory Democracy in Latin America: Institutions, Actors, and Interactions*. Redwood City, CA: Stanford University Press.

Moser, C. O. N. 2004. "Urban Violence and Insecurity: An Introductory Roadmap." *Environment and Urbanization* 16(2):3–16. doi: 10.1177/095624780401600220.

Moss, Dana. 2014. "Repression, Response, and Contained Escalation under Liberalized Authoritarianism in Jordan." *Mobilization: An International Quarterly* 19(3):261–86. doi: 10.17813/maiq.19.3.q508v72264766u92.

Moss, Dana. 2022. *The Arab Spring Abroad: Diaspora Activism against Authoritarian Regimes.* Cambridge, UK: Cambridge University Press.

Murillo, M. Victoria, Virginia Oliveros, and Rodrigo Zarazaga. 2021. "The Most Vulnerable Poor: Clientelism among Slum Dwellers." *Studies in Comparative International Development* 56(3):343–63. doi: 10.1007/s12116-021-09324-x.

Narayan, Uma. 2003. "The Project of Feminist Epistemology: Perspectives from a Nonwestern Feminist." Pp. 308–17 in *Feminist Theory Reader:Local and Global Perspectives,* edited by Carole R. McCann and Seung-Kyung Kim. London, UK: Routledge.

Nascimento, Abdias. 2016. *O Genocídio do Negro Brasileiro: Processo de um Racismo Mascarado.* São Paulo, BR: Editora Perspectiva S.A.

Nascimento, Jorge Luiz do. 2019. "Violência policial, racismo e resistência: notas a partir da MPB." *Contexto—Revista do Programa de Pós-Graduação em Letras da UFES* (35). doi: 10.47456/contexto.v%vi%i.23023.

Nemer, David. 2022. *Technology of the Oppressed: Inequity and the Digital Mundane in Favelas of Brazil.* Cambridge, MA: MIT Press.

Neto, Antônio Ludogero da Silva, and Rodrigo de Lima Nunes. 2012. "Traçado Urbano e Criminalidade Carioca: Aspectos Históricos da Favelização do Rio De Janeiro." *Espaço Aberto* 2(1):39–54.

Netto, José Paulo. 2016. *Pequena história da ditadura brasileira (1964-1985).* São Paulo, BR: Cortez Editora.

Nichter, Simeon. 2018. *Votes for Survival: Relational Clientelism in Latin America.* Cambridge, UK: Cambridge University Press.

Nojeim, Michael J. 2004. *Gandhi and King: The Power of Nonviolent Resistance.* Westport, CT: Greenwood Publishing Group.

Nunes, Nilza Rogeria de Andrade. 2021. "Mulher de favela: interseccionalidades e territorialidades/Favela woman: intersectionalities and territories." *Em Pauta* 19(47):103–21. doi: 10.12957/rep.2021.56073.

Nunes, Nilza, and Anne-Marie Veillette. 2022. "Mulheres de Favelas e o Outro Feminismo Popular / Women from Favelas and (the Other) Popular Feminism." *Revista Estudos Feministas* 30. doi: 10.1590/1806-9584-2022v30n175556.

OABRJ. 2016. "Juíza do RJ autoriza busca e apreensão coletiva na Cidade de Deus." *OABRJ,* November 22.

O'Donnell, Guillermo. 1993. "On the State, Democratization and Some Conceptual Problems: A Latin American View with Glances at Some Postcommunist Countries." *World Development* 21(8):1355–69.

Oliveira, Fabiana Luci de, and Izabel Saenger Nuñez. 2014. "A Vida nas Favelas." Pp. 25–60 in *Cidadania, justiça e "pacificação" em favelas cariocas, Centro de Justiça e Sociedade,* edited by F. L. de Oliveira. Rio de Janeiro, RJ, Brasil: FGV Editora.

Ong, Aihwa. 2006. *Neoliberalism as Exception: Mutations in Citizenship and Sovereignty.* 1st edition. Durham NC: Duke University Press.

Pailey, Robtel Neajai. 2020. "De-Centring the 'White Gaze' of Development." *Development and Change* 51(3):729–45. doi: 10.1111/dech.12550.

Paiva, Gabriel. 2007. "Cabral Defende o Aborto Para Reduzir Crimes." *O Globo,* October 25.

Paley, Dawn. 2014. *Drug War Capitalism.* Chico, CA: AK Press.

Park, Robert E., Ernest W. Burgess, and Roderick Duncan McKenzie. 1984. *The City.* Chicago, IL: University of Chicago Press.

Paschel, Tianna S. 2016. *Becoming Black Political Subjects: Movements and Ethno-Racial Rights in Colombia and Brazil*. Princeton, NJ: Princeton University Press.

Pearce, Jenny, Rosemary McGee, and Joanna Wheeler. 2011. "Violence, Security and Democracy: Perverse Interfaces and Their Implications for States and Citizens in the Global South." *IDS Working Papers* 2011(357):01–37.

Penglase, Benjamin. 2008. "The Bastard Child of the Dictatorship: The Comando Vermelho and the Birth of 'Narco-Culture' in Rio de Janeiro." *Luso-Brazilian Review* 45(1):118–45. doi: 10.1353/lbr.0.0001.

Penglase, R. Ben. 2014. *Living with Insecurity in a Brazilian Favela: Urban Violence and Daily Life*. New Brunswick, NJ: Rutgers University Press.

Pereira, Luiz Antonio. 2008. "O Programa Favela-Bairro: Dois Estudos de Caso." Universidade Federal, Fluminense.

Perlman, Janice E. 1979. *The Myth of Marginality: Urban Poverty and Politics in Rio de Janeiro*. Oakland, CA: University of California Press.

Perlman, Janice. 2010. *Favela: Four Decades of Living on the Edge in Rio de Janeiro*. New York: Oxford University Press.

Perry, Keisha-Khan Y. 2013. *Black Women against the Land Grab: The Fight for Racial Justice in Brazil*. Minneapolis, MN: University of Minnesota Press.

Pfeiffer, Cláudia Ribeiro. 2010. "Plano Para o Desenvolvimento Comuniitáriio Em Ciidade de Deus: Updated in 2010." Comitê Comunitário da Cidade de Deus.

Pfeiffer, Cláudia Ribeiro. 2014. "Desenvolvimento no território a partir da colaboração público-privado: possibilidades." Pp. 69–86 in *Política pública, rede social e território*, edited by T. T. C. Egler and H. M. Tavares. Rio de Janeiro, RJ: Letra Capital Editora LTDA.

Piven, Frances Fox, and Richard Cloward. 2012. *Poor People's Movements: Why They Succeed, How They Fail*. New York: Knopf Doubleday Publishing Group.

Platonow, Vladimir. 2015. "Manifestantes e PMs se enfrentam em protesto por sumiço de Amarildo no Rio." *UOL Cotidiano*, July 22.

Porta, Donatella della, and Mario Diani. 2009. *Social Movements: An Introduction*. Malden, MA: Blackwell Publishing.

Portela, Jacob A. S. 2017. *Diagnóstico Cidade de Deus*. Rio de Janeiro: Núcleo de Gestão Social/Farmanguinhos.

Quijano, Aníbal. 2000. "Coloniality of Power and Eurocentrism in Latin America." *International Sociology* 15(2):215–32. doi: 10.1177/0268580900015002005.

Quijano, Aníbal. 2005. "Colonialidade do poder, eurocentrismo e América Latina." Pp. 107–30 in *A colonialidade do saber: eurocentrismo e ciências sociais Perspectivas latino-americanas*, edited by E. Lander. Buenos Aires: CLASCO.

Raimundo, Valdenice José. 2016. "A Resistência das Dandaras Contemporâneas: As Formas Informais de Organização das Mulheres Negras Moradoras de Áreas Segregadas." *Caderno Espaço Feminino* 29(1).

Ramos, Silvia. 2015. "Violência e Polícia: O Que Aconteceu Com o Rio de Janeiro." Pp. 122–142 in *Uma agenda para o Rio de Janeiro: estratégias e políticas públicas para o desenvolvimento socioeconômico*, edited by M. Osorio, L. M. De Melo, M. H. Versiani, and M. L. Wernek. Rio de Janeiro: Editora FGV.

Reed, T. V. 2019. *The Art of Protest: Culture and Activism from the Civil Rights Movement to the Streets of Seattle*. 2nd edition. Minneapolis, MN: University of Minnesota Press.

Ribeiro, Luiz Cesar, and Edward Telles. 2011. "Rio de Janeiro: Emerging Dualization in a Historically Unequal City." Pp. 78–94 in *Globalizing Cities: A New Spatial Order?*, edited by P. Marcuse and R. V. Kempen. Malden, MA: Blackwell Publishing.

Ricci, Ruda. 2014. *Nas Ruas—A Outra Política Que Emergiu Em Junho de 2013.* Belo Horizonte, MG: Editora Letramento.

Rio on Watch. 2016. "FLUPP Literary Festival for Rio's Favelas Returns for Fifth Edition in City of God." *RioOnWatch*, November 21.

Rios, Victor M. 2011. *Punished: Policing the Lives of Black and Latino Boys.* New York: NYU Press.

Rios, Victor M. 2015. "Decolonizing the White Space in Urban Ethnography." *City & Community* 14(3):258–61. doi: 10.1111/cico.12122.

Rocha, Adair. 2005. *Cidade cerzida: a costura da cidadania no morro Santa Marta.* Rio de Janeiro, RJ: Museu da República Editora.

Rodgers, Dennis. 2009. "Slum Wars of the 21st Century: Gangs, Mano Dura and the New Urban Geography of Conflict in Central America." *Development & Change* 40(5):949–76. doi: 10.1111/j.1467-7660.2009.01590.x.

Rodrigues, Thiago. 2016. "Narcotráfico, Militarização e Pacificações: Novas Securitizações No Brasil." Pp. 55–88 in *Visões do Sul: crise e transformações do sistema internacional—Volume 2 | Laboratório Editorial*, edited by R. D. Passos and A. Fuccille. Marília/São Paulo: Oficina Universitária/Cultura Acadêmica/FAPESP.

Rodrigues, Thiago, Fernando Brancoli, Mariana Kalil, and Rio de Janeiro National University. 2018. "Brazil, Pacification and Major Events: Forging an 'Ambience of Security' in Rio." *Revista de Estudios En Seguridad Internacional* 4(1):87–105. doi: 10.18847/1.7.6.

Romero, Simon. 2014. "Rio's Race to Future Intersects Slave Past." *The New York Times*, March 8.

Roth, Cassia, and Ellen Dubois. 2020. "Feminism, Frogs and Fascism: The Transnational Activism of Brazil's Bertha Lutz." *Gender & History* 32(1):208–26. doi: 10.1111/1468-0424.12461.

Ruediger, Marco Aurélio. 2013. "The Rise and Fall of Brazil's Public Security Program: PRONASCI." *Police Practice and Research* 14(4):280–94. doi: 10.1080/15614263.2013.816488.

Santana, Marco Aurélio, and Ricardo Medeiros Pimenta. 2009. "Public History and Militant Identities: Brazilian Unions and the Quest for Memory." *International Labor and Working-Class History* 76(1):65–81. doi: 10.1017/S0147547909990093.

Santiago, Vinícius, Marta Fernández, Vinícius Santiago, and Marta Fernández. 2017. "From the Backstage of War: The Struggle of Mothers in the Favelas of Rio de Janeiro." *Contexto Internacional* 39(1):35–52. doi: 10.1590/s0102-8529.2017390100002.

Santos, Boaventura de Sousa. 2015. *Epistemologies of the South: Justice against Epistemicide.* New York: Routledge.

Sassen, Saskia. 2002. "The Repositioning of Citizenship: Emergent Subjects and Spaces for Politics." *Berkeley Journal of Sociology* 46:4–26.

Savell, Stephanie. 2015. "'I'm Not a Leader': Cynicism and Good Citizenship in a Brazilian Favela." *PoLAR: Political and Legal Anthropology Review* 38(2):300–317. doi: 10.1111/plar.12112.

Savell, Stephanie. 2016. "Performing Humanitarian Militarism: Public Security and the Military in Brazil." *Focaal* 2016(75):59–72. doi: 10.3167/fcl.2016.750105.

Scott, James C. 1987. *Weapons of the Weak: Everyday Forms of Peasant Resistance*. Reprint edition. Princeton, NJ: Yale University Press.

Seeliger, Leanne, and Ivan Turok. 2014. "Averting a Downward Spiral: Building Resilience in Informal Urban Settlements through Adaptive Governance." *Environment and Urbanization* 26(1):184–99. doi: 10.1177/0956247813516240.

Sharp, Gene. 1959. "The Meanings of Non-Violence: A Typology (Revised)." *Journal of Conflict Resolution* 3(1):41–64. doi: 10.1177/002200275900300104.

Sharp, Gene. 2013. *How Nonviolent Struggle Works*. East Boston, MA: The Albert Einstein Foundation.

Sheridan, Mary Beth, and Mariana Zuñiga. 2019. "Maduro's Muscle: Politically Backed Motorcycle Gangs Known as 'Colectivos' Are the Enforcers for Venezuela's Authoritarian Leader." *Washington Post*, March 13. https://www.washingtonpost.com/world/the_americas/maduros-muscle-politically-backed-motorcycle-gangs-known-as-colectivos-are-the-enforcers-for-venezuelas-authoritarian-leader/2019/03/13/2242068c-4452-11e9-94ab-d2dda3c0df52_story.html. Accessed June 22, 2020.

Silva, Gerardo. 2013. "ReFavela (notas sobre a definição de favela)." *Lugar Comum: Estudo de Mídia, Cultura e Democracia* (39):7.

Silva, Luiz Antônio Machado da. 2008. "Introdução." Pp. 13–26 in *Vida sob cerco: violência e rotina nas favelas do Rio de Janeiro*, edited by Luiz Antônio Machado da Silva. Nova Fronteira.

Smith, Barbara Ellen. 2016. "Across Races and Nations: Social Justice Organizing in the Transnational South." Pp. 235–56 in *Latinos in the New South: Transformations of Place*, edited by O. Furuseth and H. Smith. Routledge.

Smith, Nicholas Rush. 2019. *Contradictions of Democracy: Vigilantism and Rights in Post-Apartheid South Africa*. New York: Oxford University Press.

Soares, Rafael. 2016. "Moradores de Favelas Não Conseguem Se Eleger Vereadores No Rio; Candidata Do PSOL é Exceção." *O Globo Extra*, October 7.

Sonoda, Katerine. 2012. "'Liderança Muito Perigosa': Relatos de Líderes Comunitários Vítimas Da Violência Urbana No Rio de Janeiro." *Revista EPOS* 3(2):1–21.

Sousa, Miguel Alves de. 2019. "'Sou Feia, Mas tô na Moda': O Funk como Canal de Transmissão da Voz Feminina Negra Periférica." *Humanidades & Inovação* 6(16):146–55.

Souza, Altamir da Silva. 2010. "Caderno: Cidade de Deus." In *Pesquisa Nas Favelas Com Unidades de Policia Pacificadora Da Cidade Do Rio de Janeiro*. Instituto de Estudos de Trabalho e Sociedade. Master's thesis, Rio de Janeiro, RJ.

Souza e Silva, Jaílson de. 2012. "O que é favela, afinal?" *Prefeitura do Rio de Janeiro, Conselho Estratégico de Informações da Cidade*: 8–12.

Souza, Pe Ney de. 2006. "Ação Católica, militância leiga no Brasil: Méritos e Limites." *Revista de Cultura Teológica* (55):39–59. doi: 10.19176/rct.v0i55.15033.

Souza, Renata. 2020. *Cria da favela: Resistência à militarização da vida*. São Paulo, BR: Boitempo Editorial.

Stacey, Judith. 1988. "Can There Be a Feminist Ethnography?" *Women's Studies International Forum* 11(1):21–27. doi: 10.1016/0277-5395(88)90004-0.

Staudt, Kathleen. 2009. *Violence and Activism at the Border: Gender, Fear, and Everyday Life in Ciudad Juarez*. Austin, TX: University of Texas Press.

Staudt, Kathleen, and Zulma Y. Méndez. 2015. *Courage, Resistance, and Women in Ciudad Juárez: Challenges to Militarization*. Austin, TX: University of Texas Press.

Stefani, Silvia. 2021. "Building Mistrust: 'Minha Casa Minha Vida' and Its Political Effects in Rio de Janeiro." *Bulletin of Latin American Research*. doi: 10.1111/blar.13261.

Stephen, Lynn. 2010. *Women and Social Movements in Latin America: Power from Below.* Austin, TX: University of Texas Press.

Stuart, Forrest. 2020. "Code of the Tweet: Urban Gang Violence in the Social Media Age." *Social Problems* 67(2):191–207. doi: 10.1093/socpro/spz010.

Tarlau, Rebecca. 2021. *Occupying Schools, Occupying Land: How the Landless Workers Movement Transformed Brazilian Education.* Reprint edition. S.l.: New York: Oxford University Press.

Tarrow, Sidney. 1996. "Social Movements in Contentious Politics: A Review Article." *American Political Science Review* 90(4):874–83. doi: 10.2307/2945851.

TCMRJ. 2008. "O Repasse Do Dinheiro Público a Organizações Não-Governamentais." *Tribunal de Contas do Município do Rio de Janeiro* (39).

Thayer, Millie. 2009. *Making Transnational Feminism: Rural Women, NGO Activists, and Northern Donors in Brazil.* 1st edition. New York: Routledge.

Theoharis, Jeanne, and Komozi Woodard. 2009. *Want to Start a Revolution?: Radical Women in the Black Freedom Struggle.* New York: NYU Press.

Theron, Linda Carol, and Adam Theron. 2013. "Positive Adjustment to Poverty: How Family Communities Encourage Resilience in Traditional African Contexts." *Culture & Psychology* 19(3):391–413. doi: 10.1177/1354067X13489318.

Tilly, Charles. 2003. *The Politics of Collective Violence.* Cambridge, UK: Cambridge University Press.

Torres, Ana Carolina, and Fábio Guimarães. 2014. "Menino Morto Em Tiroteio Na Cidade de Deus Queria Ser Jogador de Futebol; 'Estava Doido Com a Copa', Diz Tia." *Globo Extra*, June 17.

Urani, André. 2008. *Trilhas Para o Rio—Do Reconhecimento Da Queda À Reinvenção Do Futuro.* Rio de Janeiro, BR: Elsevier.

Valla, V. 1981. *Para Uma Formulação de Um Teoria de Educação Estra-Escolar No Brasil: Ideologia, Educação e as Favelas Do Rio de Janeiro: 1880-1980.* Rio de Janeiro: FINEP/IESAE/FGV.

Valladares, Licia do Prado. 2005. *A invenção da favela: do mito de origem a favela.* Rio de Janeiro: FGV.

Vargas, J. H. C. 2006. "When a Favela Dared to Become a Gated Condominium: The Politics of Race and Urban Space in Rio de Janeiro." *Latin American Perspectives* 33(4):49–81. doi: 10.1177/0094582X06289892.

Vargas, Joao H. Costa. 2010. *Never Meant to Survive: Genocide and Utopias in Black Diaspora Communities.* Lanham, MD: Rowman & Littlefield.

Veillette, Anne-Marie. 2021. "Racialized Popular Feminism: A Decolonial Analysis of Women's Struggle with Police Violence in Rio de Janeiro's Favelas." *Latin American Perspectives* 48(4):87–104. doi: 10.1177/0094582X211015324.

Veillette, Anne-Marie, and Priscyll Anctil Avoine. 2019. "Women's Resistance in Violent Settings: Infrapolitical Strategies in Brazil and Colombia." Pp. 53–67 in *Re-writing Women as Victims.* New York: Routledge.

Ventura, Zuenir. 1994. *Cidade Partida.* Rio de Janeiro, RJ: Editora Companhia das Letras.

Vianna, Adriana, and Juliana Farias. 2011. "The Mothers' War: Pain and Politics in Situations of Institutional Violence." *Cadernos Pagu* (37):79–116. doi: 10.1590/S0104-83332011000200004.

Vicino, Thomas J., and Anjuli Fahlberg. 2017. "The Politics of Contested Urban Space: The 2013 Protest Movement in Brazil." *Journal of Urban Affairs* 39(7):1001–16. doi: 10.1080/07352166.2017.1323545.

Vogt, Wendy A. 2018. *Lives in Transit: Violence and Intimacy on the Migrant Journey.* Oakland, CA: University of California Press.

Wacquant, Loïc. 2009. *Punishing the Poor: The Neoliberal Government of Social Insecurity.* Durham, NC: Duke University Press.

Wade, Peter. 2009. *Race and Sex in Latin America.* New York: Pluto Press.

Wahman, Michael, and Edward Goldring. 2020. "Pre-Election Violence and Territorial Control: Political Dominance and Subnational Election Violence in Polarized African Electoral Systems." *Journal of Peace Research* 57(1):93–110. doi: 10.1177/0022343319884990.

Wallerstein, Nina, Bonnie Duran, John Oetzel, and Meredith Minkler. 2017. *Community-Based Participatory Research for Health: Advancing Social and Health Equity.* 3rd edition. Hoboken, NJ: Jossey-Bass.

Weinstein, Liza. 2014. *The Durable Slum: Dharavi and the Right to Stay Put in Globalizing Mumbai.* Minneapolis: University of Minnesota Press.

Wilde, Matt. 2017. "Contested Spaces: The Communal Councils and Participatory Democracy in Chávez's Venezuela." *Latin American Perspectives* 44(1):140–58. doi: 10.1177/0094582X16658257.

Willis, Graham Denyer. 2015. *The Killing Consensus: Police, Organized Crime, and the Regulation of Life and Death in Urban Brazil.* Oakland, CA: University of California Press.

Wilson, William Julius. 1999. *The Bridge over the Racial Divide: Rising Inequality and Coalition Politics.* Berkeley, CA: University of California Press.

Williamson, Sue. 2010. *Resistance Art in South Africa.* Cape Town, SA: Juta and Company Ltd.

Winton, A. 2004. "Urban Violence: A Guide to the Literature." *Environment and Urbanization* 16(2):165–84. doi: 10.1177/095624780401600208.

Wolford, Wendy. 2010. "Participatory Democracy by Default: Land Reform, Social Movements and the State in Brazil." *The Journal of Peasant Studies* 37(1):91–109. doi: 10.1080/03066150903498770.

Yanitsky, Oleg. 2010. *Yanitsky O.N. (2010) Russian Environmentalism. The Yanitsky Reader.* Moscow: TAUS.

Young, Amber, Lisen Selander, and Emmanuelle Vaast. 2019. "Digital Organizing for Social Impact: Current Insights and Future Research Avenues on Collective Action, Social Movements, and Digital Technologies." *Information and Organization* 29(3):100257. doi: 10.1016/j.infoandorg.2019.100257.

Young, Iris Marion. 2000. *Inclusion and Democracy.* Oxford; New York: Oxford University Press.

Yuval-Davis, Nira. 2012. "Dialogical Epistemology—An Intersectional Resistance to the 'Oppression Olympics.'" *Gender & Society* 26(1):46–54. doi: 10.1177/0891243211427701.

Zaluar, Alba. 1994. *Condominio Do Diabo.* Rio de Janeiro: Editora Revan.

Zaluar, Alba. 2004. *Integração perversa: pobreza e tráfico de drogas.* Rio de Janeiro, RJ: FGV Editora.

Zaluar, Alba. 2010. "Youth, Drug Traffic and Hypermasculinity in Rio de Janeiro." *VIBRANT-Vibrant Virtual Brazilian Anthropology* 7(2):7–27.

Zaluar, Alba, and Marcos Alvito. 1998. *Um século de favela*. Rio de Janeiro, RJ: FGV Editora.

Zubillaga, Verónica, Manuel Llorens, and John Souto. 2019. "Micropolitics in a Caracas Barrio: The Political Survival Strategies of Mothers in a Context of Armed Violence." *Latin American Research Review* 54(2):429–43. doi: 10.25222/larr.196.

Zulver, Julia Margaret. 2022. *High-Risk Feminism in Colombia: Women's Mobilization in Violent Contexts*. New Brunswick, NJ: Rutgers University Press.

Index

For the benefit of digital users, indexed terms that span two pages (e.g., 52–53) may, on occasion, appear on only one of those pages.

Figures are indicated by *f* following the page number

Action Aid, 124
Alliance for Progress, 59
Amaral, Fernanda, 17
Amefricanidade, 192–93
AP da PM neighborhood (Cidade de Deus), 38
Appadurai, Arjun, 226–27, 232–33
Argentina, 133, 173–74
Arias, Enrique Desmond, 118–19, 137, 241–42
Art in the Park events, 125–26
Art Talk
    anti-racism and, 104
    grants won by, 107–8
    LGBTQ rights and, 104
    meetings following Rouseff impeachment (2016) organized by, 2–4, 102–4
    open mic format at meetings of, 2, 77
    space for protest against violence at, 175
    visual art showcased at, 104
assistencialismo (charity), 64–65, 92–93, 95, 255–56
Association for a Better Tomorrow (ABT), 205–7
Association for Women's Rights in Development (AWID), 220
Athayde, Celso, 17, 196

Badolato, Giuseppe, 59–60
Baird, Adam, 120
bandido social category (criminals), 167–68
Bank of Brazil, 90
Barbosa, Jorge, 174

Barbosa, Valéria, 33, 61–62
Barnes, Nicholas, 136–37
Battalion for Special Policing Operations (BOPE), 73, 119–20, 157–59
Bayat, Asef, 11–12
Bejarano, Cynthia, 173–74
Beltrame, Mariano, 71–72
Berry, Marie, 134–35, 138
Blackness. *See also* racism
    Amefricanidade and, 192–93
    Black Lives Matter movement and, 224, 229
    Black Movement and, 189, 229
    Black women's role in feminized nonviolent politics and, 26–27, 131–32, 189–93
    Brazilian racial categories and, 31–32, 189
    education and, 186–89
    intersectional perspectives on, 189–90, 192–93
    nonviolent collective organizing and the culture of, 182–86
Bolsa Familia (Family Purse) welfare program, 83–85, 203–4
Bolsonaro, Jair, 20, 242–43
Bosnia, 138
Bourgois, Philippe, 62–63
Brasilia (Brazil), 58
Brazilian Development Bank, 90
Brito, Rosalina, 59–60
Brizola, Leonel, 69–70, 78, 83
Business Forum of Rio, 95–96, 97–98

Cabral, Sérgio, 14–15, 71–72, 100, 179

Caldeira, Theresa, 199
Canudos War (1896-97), 54, 260n.9
Canuto, Lucas, 152–53
Cardoso, Henrique, 81, 83, 89, 106–7
Cardoso, Marcos, 159
Castells, Manuel, 86, 99
Castelo Branco, Humberto, 58–59
Catalytic Communities, 240–41
Catholic Church, 57, 61–62, 79–
    80, 186–87
CDD Connects Facebook page
    community-based organization
        networks and, 88, 113, 165
    crime stories on, 152, 165
    cultural opportunities and resources
        publicized by, 125–26
    "doing good" stories on, 165–66
    organizing for political change on, 124–
        25, 157
    political campaign information barred
        from, 113–14
    searches for missing people and, 125
Center Dona Otávia, 87, 91–92, 249
Center for Racial Justice, 87, 187
Centros Integrados de Educação Pública
    (CIEPS, Integrated Centers of Public
    Education), 69–70
Chenoweth, Erica, 166–67
Children's Institute, 202–3
China, 6–7, 173–74
Chua, Lynette, 7
Cidade de Deus (CDD)
    AP da PM neighborhood in, 38
    City of God movie and, 13–14, 70–71,
        175, 232
    clientelism in, 61–62, 118–19
    communal ties in, 43–44, 46–47, 59–60
    community-based newspapers
        in, 175–79
    conflict activism and, 23–30, 68
    cultural production in, 173–80, 180f,
        181f, 182f
    drug trade in, 3, 15–16, 18–19, 33–34,
        35–36, 37–38, 46, 62, 65–67, 71–74,
        116–17, 118–19, 121–22, 149–51,
        243, 250, 252
    education levels in, 225–26
    epistemic disequilibrium in, 16–17

"favelization" of, 58–62
flood (1996) in, 70, 100, 123
gang territories in, 45–46, 48–50, 62–65,
    67–68, 121–22, 138
healthcare in, 20–21, 47–48, 47f, 51–52,
    64–65, 84, 234
infrastructure conditions in, 39, 44, 50,
    51f, 59–62, 70, 84, 117–18, 124–25,
    138, 146
local economy of, 42, 44–45
maps of, 14f, 15f, 36f, 37f
naming of, 58–59
neighborhood associations in, 64–65,
    67–68, 76, 120–21
neoliberal proposals outsourcing of
    public services in, 91
patchwork politics and, 7–8, 28–29
photos of, 13f, 40f, 41f, 42f, 43f, 45f, 51f
police in, 35–36, 45–46, 48–50, 67,
    71–74, 119–20, 215–16, 235–36,
    242, 252
population growth in, 60–61
poverty levels in, 13–14, 42
public works projects in, 71, 74, 84,
    123, 219–20
racial demographics of, 13–14, 39
Regional Administration in, 36–37, 121
religious practices in, 39
schools in, 42–43, 48–50, 71,
    146, 219–20
self-made shacks in, 39–41, 41f, 59–
    60, 61
sexual violence and gender-based
    violence in, 62, 63–64
soccer in, 16, 61–62, 118, 122
Social Development Plan (2010) of,
    97, 99–100
social service agencies in, 42–43, 61–
    62, 87–88
social welfare programs in, 84
strategies to avoid co-optation by drug
    gangs in, 136–40
structural violence and, 50–52
sub-neighborhoods of, 37f, 39
Cidinho, 172–73
CIEP Luiz Carlos Prestes, 176
City Council elections (Rio de Janeiro,
    2016), 113, 147–48, 213–15, 218, 231

City Council elections (Rio de Janeiro, 2020), 245
City of God (movie), 13–14, 70–71, 175, 232
civil rights
  constitution of 1988 and, 81–82
  gang neighborhoods and, 9–10
  police searches and, 215–16
  racism in the denial of, 81–82
  structural violence and, 52, 70
  Vargas era and, 56
clientelism
  in Cidade de Deus, 61–62, 118–19
  democracy eroded through, 11, 81–82, 118, 120–21
  drug gangs' role in, 10, 23–24, 118–19
  masculine politics of violence and, 118–19, 120, 134–35
  politicagem and, 113–14
  soccer and, 118, 119, 122
  Vargas era and, 56–57
  women's role as political brokers and, 120
Cloward, Richard, 29
Cockburn, Cynthia, 131–32
Cold War, 66
Coletivo de Pesquisa Construindo Juntos (Building Together Research Collective), 22–23, 231–32
Collor, Fernando, 81
Colombia, 120, 133–34
colorism, 31, 255–56
Comando Vermelho (CV, "Red Command" drug gang)
  community-based organizations' coexistence with, 138
  favelas as operating bases of, 65–67, 73–74
  former prisoners as members of, 65–66
  informal community rules enforced by, 139
  local officials' relations with, 136–37
  neighborhood associations and local politicians co-opted by, 67, 120–21
  origins of, 65–66
  police conflict with, 66–67
  rival gangs of, 65–66
  War on Drug policies and, 66

Comeli, Thaisa, 25–26, 159–60
Communications Hub, 227–28
Communist Party, 57, 64–65
community-based organizations (CBOs). *See also* nongovernmental organizations (NGOs); *specific organizations*
  anti-racism and, 35, 187–89, 238, 240–41
  assistencialismo (charity) approach rejected at, 95
  clientelism rejected by, 126
  community militancy and, 95–102
  conflicts within, 111–12, 127
  corruption at, 127
  cultural politics and, 78, 102–9, 130–31
  drug traffickers' interactions with, 128–29, 135, 138
  feminized nonviolent politics model and, 122–23, 130–31, 134–35
  formal registration process for, 91–92
  fragmented sovereignty as an opportunity for, 137–39
  neoliberal proposals regarding outsourcing of public services and, 90
  participatory democracy cultivated by, 199–209
  police meetings with, 170
  resource challenges at, 91, 142–44
  state allies of, 201–4
  strategies to avoid co-optation by drug gangs at, 114–15, 126, 141–46, 239
  transformative assistance and, 87–95
  transnational networks and, 219–33
Community Coalition, 196–98, 202, 203–4, 210, 212
Complexo da Maré (Rio de Janeiro), 240–41
Complexo do Alemão (Rio de Janeiro), 240–41
conflict activism. *See also* nonviolent collective organizing
  in Cidade de Deus, 23–30, 68
  consent and support of local residents for, 27
  definition of, 6
  disguised forms of protest and, 6–7, 173–74

conflict activism (*cont.*)
  exile movements and, 6–7
  feminization of, 7–8, 26–27
  high-risk oppositional politics and, 6
  infrapolitics and, 12
  limits of academic knowledge and, 240
  nongovernmental organizations
    and, 29–30
  patchwork politics and, 7–8, 28–30
  pragamatic resistance and, 7
  sphere of nonviolent politics
    established by, 24
  violent activism and, 6
Constitution of Brazil (1988), 72–73, 81–
    82, 163–64
corruption
  artwork addressing, 179–80
  Collor Administration and, 81–82
  community-based organizations
    and, 127
  da Silva administration and, 81–82
  democracy threatened by, 162–63
  Lava Jato investigation and, 108–9,
    179, 262n.9
  masculine politics of violence and, 120
  mensalão political scandal (2005)
    and, 179–80
  neighborhood-level forms of, 5
  one-party systems and, 5
  police engagement in, 15–16, 26, 73,
    116, 119, 163–64
  politicians' engagement in, 26, 81–82,
    142–43, 161–62, 163f
  protests against, 161–62
  public works projects and, 71
  Regional Administration and, 121
Council of Residents of Cidade de Deus
    (COMOCID), 64–65, 67–68
Coutinho da Silva, Rachel, 25–26, 159–60
Cunningham, Kathleen Gallagher, 166–67

da Silva, Luiz Inácio ("Lula")
  election to presidency (2002) of,
    81, 83–84
  government investment in cultural
    programs under, 106–7
  imprisonment for fraud (2017)
    of, 81–82

political activism under dictatorship
    by, 79–80
  social welfare programs supported
    by, 83–85
  Workers' Party and, 79–80
Davis, Diane, 137
democracy. *See also* elections;
    participatory democracy
  Brazil's expansion after 1985 of, 67,
    80–81, 199
  clientelism as a threat to, 11, 81–82,
    118, 120–21
  constitution (1988) and, 81, 163–64
  corruption as a threat to, 162–63
  decentralization of power in Brazil
    under, 107
  disjunctive democracy and, 81–82,
    162–63, 199
  free speech and assembly rights
    under, 162–64
  global declines in, 239–40
  Latin America's expansion after 1980 of,
    8–9, 80, 199
  racial democracy ideology and, 53–54
  urban violence as a threat to, 199–
    200, 239–40
desaparecidos ("the
    disappeared"), 173–74
Diani, Mario, 23
Dicionário das Favelas Marielle Franco
    (The Favela Dictionary Marielle
    Franco), 240–41
Dilma. *See* Rousseff, Dilma
Disque Denuncia, 222
Doca, 172–73
Dona Iracema, 147
dos Santos, João Paulo, 92–93
drug trade. *See also* gangs
  Black drug traffickers and, 27
  in Cidade de Deus, 3, 15–16, 18–19,
    33–34, 35–36, 37–38, 46, 62, 65–67,
    71–74, 116–17, 118–19, 121–22, 149–
    51, 243, 250, 252
  City of God movie and, 13–14, 70–71
  Comando Vermelho and, 65–67, 69,
    73–74, 120–21, 136–39
  community-based organizations'
    coexitsence with, 128–29, 135, 138

drug legalization proposals and,
150, 216–17
masculine politics of violence and,
7–8, 115–16, 119, 120, 121–22,
126, 131–32
oppositional culture in, 12, 62–63
performative violence against
community leaders and, 9–10, 67–68
politicians' ties to, 113–14
sympathy for murdered members
of, 158–59
Unidade de Policia Pacifcadora's
"pacification" campaigns and, 71–72,
159, 248–49
War on Drugs policies and, 2–3, 9, 66–
67, 150, 224, 238, 246
women's involvement in, 115

educador (educator) social category, 23–
24, 168–69, 172
elections
gangs and decreased levels of
participation in, 10–11
municipal elections (2016) and, 113,
147–48, 213–15, 218, 231
municipal elections (2020) and, 245
presidential elections (1985)
and, 80–81
state government elections (1982) and,
69–70, 80–81, 83
Vargas era and, 56–57
El Salvador, 173–74
embedded resistance, 151, 180–81, 194–95
Entrepreneurial Forum of Rio, 71
Environment League, 96, 169–70, 229–30
epistemic disequilibrium, 16–17, 254
Escóssia, Fernanda da, 89–90
Espaço Urbano Seguro (Safe Urban
Spaces), 84

Facebook. See also CDD Connects
Facebook page
artistic and cultural networks on, 109
cultural production showcased on, 173
global civil society networks on, 86
virtual ethnography practiced on, 19–
20, 38, 250
Fals Borda, Orlando, 256

Federal Bank (Caixa Econômica Federal),
84–85, 219–20
Federal University of Rio de Janeiro, 108
feminized nonviolent politics
art collectives and, 130–31
Black women and, 26–27, 131–
32, 189–93
community-based organizations and,
122–23, 130–31, 134–35
coordination of citizens' relationshp
with the state and, 126, 138–39, 139f
emotional toll of, 135
feminist organizing and, 148, 224, 232
fragmented sovereignty as opportunity
for, 137–39
masculine politics of violence's
hegemony over, 115, 135
men's participation in community-
based organizations and,
131, 135–36
protests against police and, 159
self-defense classes and, 190–91
"the superexploited" and, 26–27
transnational networks and, 220–22
women's role as caretakers in violent
conflicts and, 133
women's social role as mothers
and, 132–34
Fernandes, Sujatha, 132–33
Ferreira, Thais, 245
First of May Rendezvous (Encontro), 68
Fischer, Brodwyn, 47–48, 55
França, Wellington, 91
Franco, Anielle, 245
Franco, Marielle
community-based organization
established in honor of, 240–41
election to City Council (2016) of, 147–
48, 214–15
murder of, 17, 147–48, 162–63, 221–22
progressive policies promoted
by, 147–48
Freire, Paulo, 169–71
Friedman, Elizabeth, 231
Fuji, Lee Ann, 127
Fundação Leão XIII, 57, 65, 76

Galtung, Johan, 50–51, 166

gangs. *See also* drug trade; gang territories
activists' strategies to resist co-optation
by, 114–15, 126, 141–46, 239
clientelism and, 10, 23–24, 118–19
electoral participation suppressed
by, 10–11
informal community rules enforced
by, 139
oppositional culture in, 12
police's violent conflict with, 1, 9, 15–16,
26, 34, 35–36, 45–46, 66–67, 72–74,
116, 119, 136–37, 138, 149–50,
154, 215–16
politicians' alliances with, 114–
15, 118–19
services provided to communities by,
63, 116–17, 121–22, 139–40, 241
structural violence as factor influencing,
25, 157, 160–61
symbolic violence by, 63
gang territories
in Cidade de Deus, 45–46, 48–50, 62–
65, 67–68, 121–22, 138
civil rights eroded in, 9–10
fragmented sovereignty in, 10, 136–40
infrapolitics in, 12
neighborhood associations co-opted in,
10–11, 30, 67–68, 120–21
performative violence against
community leaders in, 9–10, 67–68
political activism suppressed in, 67–68
politics of survival in, 11–12
sexual violence and gender-based
violence in, 62, 63–64, 67–68
Gay, Robert, 11
gender-based violence, 25, 26–27, 63–
64, 133–34
gendered division of governing labor.
See feminized nonviolent politics;
masculine politics of violence
Gillam, Lynn, 248
Girl Power group, 190–91
Global South, 17, 69, 222, 231
Gohn, Gloria, 88–89
Gonzalez, Lélia, 53
Goulart, João, 58
Grotten, Julio, 61–62
Growth Acceleration Program (PAC), 84

Guillemin, Marilys, 248

Haddad, Fernando, 242
Hamilton Land Municipal Health
Center, 64–65
Harvey, David, 89
Holston, James, 199
House of Rights, 176
Hufty, Mark, 122–23

information communication technologies
(ICTs), 78, 86, 109
infrapolitics, 12
Institute for a Better Neighborhood, 205
Instituto Marielle Franco, 240–41
Inter-American Development
Bank, 83, 90
International Literary Congress of Paraty
(FLIP), 176
International Literary Festival, 178
Isin, Engin, 52

Jacarepaguá region (Brazil), 59

Karatê neighborhood, 37, 39–41, 116, 152
Kennedy, John F., 59
Kinzo, Mary, 80–81
Kubitschek, Juscelino, 58

Lacerda, Carlos, 59
LAN Houses (internet cafés), 85–86
Lava Jato corruption investigation, 108–9,
179, 262n.9
Law of Social Quotas (2012), 108
Lawson, Erica, 133
LGBTQ populations
Bolsonaro's campaigns against, 242
Brazilian attitudes regarding, 260n.4
cultural and artistic activism and, 76,
103–4, 106–7
democracy's expansion in Latin
America and, 8–9
Instituto Marielle Franco and, 240–41
municipal elections (2016) and, 147
transgender men and, 136
Lima, Verônica, 245
Lins, Paulo, 70–71
literacy, 29, 53–54, 56–57, 97–98, 169

Literary Congress for Favelas (FLUPP), 176, 217–18
Lourenço, Natália, 92–93
Lula. *See* da Silva, Luiz Inácio ("Lula")

Machado da Silva, Luiz Antonio, 11
Madres de la Plaza de Mayo (Argentina), 133
Maia, Cesar, 70–71, 89–90, 95–96, 219–20
masculine politics of violence
    clientelism and, 118–19, 120, 134–35
    coordination of citizens' relationshp with the state and, 126, 138–39, 139*f*
    drug trade and, 7–8, 115–16, 119, 120, 121–22, 126, 131–32
    hegemony over feminized nonviolence organizing of, 115, 135
    the military and, 53
    office-holding politicans and, 3, 120, 131–32
    police and, 7–8, 53, 119–20
    race and, 120
    reward structure in, 116, 135
    vulnerability of participants in, 135
McCann, Bryan, 69–70
MC Claudinho, 178–80, 184–85, 217, 222
McFarlane, Colin, 92
Meirelles, Fernando, 70–71
Meirelles, Renato, 196
Mello, Edir Figueiredo de, 60–61
Mendes, João de, 144–45
mensalão political scandal (2005), 179–80
Mexico, 5, 64, 133–34, 173–74
milicia. See police
Mina, An Xiao, 6–7, 173–74
Minha Casa Minha Vida (My Home My Life, public housing program), 85
Ministério das Cidades (Ministry of Cities), 84–85
Ministry for Education (Secretaria da Educação), 219–20
Ministry for Sports (Secretaria do Esporte), 219–20
miscegenation, 31
Moncada, Eduardo, 9–10
Montambeault, Françoise, 204
Morro da Providência (Providence Hill), 54

Moser, Caroline, 160–61
Municipal Secretariat for the Development of Economic Solidarity, 97–98, 124
murals, 125–26, 173, 180*f*, 182*f*

National Bank, 204, 209
National Foundation for the Arts (Funarte), 106–7
National Housing Bank (BNH), 58–59, 60
neoliberalism, 83, 89–91, 92–93, 99, 106–7
Neves, Tancredo, 80–81
nongovernmental organizations (NGOs). *See also* community-based organizations (CBOs); *specific organizations*
    assistencialismo (charity) approach at, 92–93
    conflict activism and, 29–30
    feminized nonviolent politics model and, 134–35
    foundation grants for, 91, 226
    funding to community-based organizations from, 227–29, 230–31
    increased opportunities following democratization of Brazil for, 88–89
    neighborhood association partnerships with, 64–65
    neoliberal proposals regarding outsourcing of public services and, 90
    Nonprofit Law of 1999 and, 88–89
    online networks among, 85–86
    Worker's Party initiatives funding, 86–87
Nonprofit Law of 1999, 88–89
nonviolent collective organizing. *See also* conflict activism
    anti-racism and, 151–52, 180–89
    art's role in, 173–75
    Bolsonaro regime as threat to, 20, 242–43
    community-based newspapers and, 175–79
    community militancy and, 78, 95–102
    consent and support of local communities and, 27
    cultural politics and, 78, 102–9
    educador social category and, 168–69
    mutual aid activities and, 164, 167

nonviolent collective organizing (*cont*)
online activism and, 155–58, 156*f*, 161, 162*f*
peaceful marches following killings and, 152–53
protests and, 153–55, 155*f*, 159, 161–63
resource matrix "milking" and, 79
structural violence as a focus of, 159–60, 161, 163–64
transformative assistance and, 78, 87–95
Nunes, Nilza Rogéria, 192–93

Observatório das Favelas, 107
O'Donnell, Guillermo, 199
Oliveiras, Pablo, 149
Olympic Games (2016), 71–72, 100, 108–9, 172–73

Paley, Dawn, 66
pardo (mixed-race), 31–32, 39, 182–83, 186, 189
Participatory Action Research (PAR)
in areas of violence, 247–48
dialogical reflexivity and, 23, 231–32
origins of, 21–22
participants' involvement in decisions about research in, 21–22, 230, 247–48, 250–51, 253–57
safety issues and, 251–53
participatory democracy
community-based organizations and, 199–209
definition of, 200
personal risks involved in, 210, 238, 245
stategies to avoid co-optation by violent actors and, 210–13
Pastoral das Favelas, 187
patchwork politics, 7–8, 28–30, 109–12
Paula, Tainá de, 245
Pavão-Pavãozinho favela, 159
Pechincha neighborhood, 38
Penglase, Ben, 65–66, 167–68
Pereira Passos, Francisco, 55
Perlman, Janice, 11, 55–56, 208–9, 223
Perry, Keisha-Kahn, 26–27, 131–32, 182–83
Petrobras, 107–9
Pezão, Luiz Fernando, 241

Piven, Frances Fox, 29
police. *See also* Unidade de Policia Pacificadora
brutality by, 5, 25, 28–29, 104, 172, 215–16
in Cidade de Deus, 35–36, 45–46, 48–50, 67, 71–74, 119–20, 215–16, 235–36, 242, 252
community meetings with, 170
corruption among, 15–16, 26, 73, 116, 119, 163–64
gangs' violent conflicts with, 1, 9, 15–16, 26, 34, 35–36, 45–46, 66–67, 72–74, 116, 119, 136–37, 138, 149–50, 154, 215–16
helicopter crash in Cidade de Deus (2016) and, 215
masculine politics of violence and, 7–8, 53, 119–20
national police force in nineteenth century and, 53
protests against, 153–55, 155*f*, 159
racism of, 2–3, 9, 45–46, 53–54, 57, 72–73, 81–82, 181–82, 184–85, 199, 224
undercover police and, 46, 118
political upcycling, 27, 151–52, 193–95
Porta, Donatella della, 18–19
Program Favela-Bairro, 83
proibidão funk music, 173
projetos (informal collectives), 87, 95, 110
PRONASCI prison reform, 84
Public Interest Civil Organizations (OSCIPS), 88–89

Quijano, Aníbal, 181–82
quilombos (runaway slave communities), 53, 191

racism
colonial era in Brazil and, 53–54, 188–89, 194–95
community-based organizations' efforts to combat, 35, 187–89, 238, 240–41
constitution of 1988's addressing of, 81
definition of, 31
favelas in Brazilian political culture and, 38, 57
intellectual imperialism and, 223

police and, 2–3, 9, 45–46, 53–54, 57, 72–73, 81–82, 181–82, 184–85, 199, 224
racial categories in Brazil and, 30–32, 182–83, 186, 255–56
in Rio's mainstream urban spaces, 44, 50–51, 62–63
segregation and, 1, 25, 59
sexual violence and, 64
slavery's legacies and, 59, 181–82
structural violence and, 27, 31, 50–51, 52, 59
symbolic violence and, 25
in the United States, 31
voting rights and, 53–54
Raimundo, Valdenice, 192
Reagan, Ronald, 66, 150
Rede de Comunidades e Movimentos contra a Violência (Network of Communities and Movements against Violence), 159
Rede Favela Sustentável, 240–41
Regional Administration (submunicipal branch of government), 36–37, 121, 124–25, 219
Residents' Board
community bank opened by, 124
community meetings organized by, 101
community militancy model of organizing and, 99–100
feminized nonviolent politics model and, 122–23, 130–31, 134
grants awarded to, 97–98, 124, 205
lobbying and advocacy for delivery of services by, 101–2, 123–25, 134
origins of, 95–98
participatory democracy at, 204–9
partnerships of, 124
secondary education opportunities organized by, 98
Social Development Plan of Cidade de Deus and, 97, 99–100
strategies to avoid co-optation at, 144, 210–12, 230
transnational networks and, 219–20
resource matrix, 79
Restaurante Cidadão, 43f
Ribeiro, Darcy, 69–70
Rio+ 20 forum, 176

Rio de Janeiro. *See also specific neighborhoods*
capital of Brazil moved (1960) from, 58
drug trade's overall impact on, 11, 65–66
elections (1982) in, 83
elections (2016) in, 113, 147–48, 213–15, 218, 231
elections (2020) in, 245
history of informal settlements in and around, 54–56
map of, 15f
Master Plan (1992) of, 83
neoliberal proposals regarding outsourcing of public services in, 89–90
Olympic Games (2016) in, 71–72, 100
party-based political system in, 214–15
racial demographics of, 57
recession (2015-16) in, 73, 85, 108–9
rural migration to, 54
slavery's legacy in, 53
social benefits for low-income families in, 83–84
urban planning and investment in, 55, 59, 69, 71, 83
World Cup tournament (2014) in, 71–72, 100
Rio Estado Digital program, 85–86
Rio on Watch newspaper, 240–41
Rios, Victor, 254
Rocinha favela, 137
Rodrigues, Thiago, 66
Rousseff, Dilma
impeachment of, 2–4, 74, 82, 85, 103, 106–7, 191
social welfare programs supported by, 2, 84–85
Rwanda, 127, 138

Sá, Roberto, 215
Salvador (Brazil), 182–83
Sarney, José, 80–81
Scott, James, 12, 51–52
Secretariat for Identity and Cultural Diversity (SID), 107
Secretariat for Public Security, 222
Senior Center (Cidade de Deus), 87

SESI Cidadania, 87–88
sexual violence, 62, 63–64, 67–68, 164–65
Sharp, Gene, 164–65
shootouts
  buildings damaged in, 39, 45f, 146
  bystanders threatened by, 1, 34, 45–46,
    152–53, 155–57, 156f, 234
  ceasefires and, 73–74, 116
  civil society disrupted by, 116–17,
    137, 210
  deaths in, 152–53
  educational opportunities disrupted by,
    48–50, 146, 157
  peaceful marches following, 152–53
  psychological damage from, 157–58
Sierra Leone, 133–34
Silva, Gerardo, 61
Silva, Rafaela, 172–73
Simone, Nina, 185
slavery
  Brazil's abolition (1888) of, 54
  education regarding, 186–87, 189
  historical legacies of, 15–16, 59, 193
  miscegenation and sexual
    violence in, 31
  quilombos and, 53, 191
  slave trade before 1866 and, 53
Soares, Luiz Eduardo, 71, 95–96
soccer, 16, 61–62, 118, 119, 122
South Africa, 106, 199–200
Souza, Renata, 17
SpeakCDD! community newspaper,
  22, 175–76
Stacey, Judith, 254
State Company for Housing
  (COHAB), 58–59
structural violence
  civil rights denied in, 52, 70
  drug laws and, 25
  economic inequality and, 25, 160–61
  gang violence as symptom of, 25,
    157, 160–61
  healthcare and, 51–52
  natural disasters and, 70
  nonviolent collective organizing
    against, 159–60, 161, 163–64
  overpolicing and, 160–61
  racism and, 27, 31, 50–51, 52, 59

segregation and, 25, 59
  unequal life changes and, 50–51
Stuart, Forest, 19–20
the superexploited, 26–27, 192
symbolic violence, 12, 25, 50–52, 63

Tarrow, Sydney, 23
Teen Connection, 87–88
Temer, Michel, 82, 85, 108–9, 191
Território da Paz (Territory of Peace), 84
Thayer, Milly, 224, 232
trabalhador social category
  (workers), 167–69

Unidade de Policia Pacificadora (UPP;
  Pacifying Policing Units)
  anti-drug "pacification" campaigns of,
    71–72, 159, 248–49
  corruption among, 73
  Disque Denuncia and, 222
  funding cuts for, 73–74
  killings by, 159
  popular opinion regarding, 72–73
  precincts established by, 71–72, 141f
  racism of, 72–73
  UPP Social programs and, 72–74, 87–
    88, 100–1, 202–3
Unidade de Pronto Atendimento (UPA,
  emergency rooms), 47–48, 84
United Nations, 95–96, 176, 186, 226
United Nations Educational, Scientific,
  and Cultural Organization
  (UNESCO), 97–98, 124
United States
  Alliance for Progress program and, 59
  anti-Communist political and military
    interventions in Latin America by, 58
  Mexico's border with, 64
  neocolonialism and, 25
  racism in, 31
  War on Drugs and, 9, 66, 150
Urban Social Center (Centros Sociais
  Urbanos), 65

Valladares, Licia, 55–56
Vargas, Getúlio, 56–58
Veillette, Anne-Marie, 192–93
Venezuela, 132–34, 200–1

Vila Kennedy housing complex, 59
VivaRio, 228–29
Vogt, Wendy, 64
Voz das Comunidades newspapers, 240–41

Wade, Peter, 53
War on Drugs, 9, 66–67, 150, 224, 238, 246
Weinstein, Liza, 38
West Zone (Rio de Janeiro), 44, 59
WhatsApp message groups, 19–20, 86,
    109, 196, 250
Witzel, Wilson, 14–15, 242
Worker's Party
    emergence during Brazilian
        dictatorship of, 64–65, 79–81
    expansion of social and political rights
        under, 199
    Lava Jato corruption investigation
        and, 108–9
    mensalão political scandal (2005), 179–80
    nongovernmental organizations funded
        via initiatives by, 86–87
    Rouseff impeachment and, 2
    state elections (1982) and, 80–81
World Bank, 71, 90
World Cup tournament (2014), 71–72,
    100, 161–62

World Pulse social media platform, 220–
    22, 224
World Social Forum, 221–22

Yanitsky, Oleg, 6–7
Yellow Line highway, 68
Youth Promise
    anti-racism and, 187–89
    author's research and volunteer work
        at, 18–19, 22, 46, 129–30, 203–
        4, 249–50
    educational programing at, 87, 170–72
    feminized nonviolent organizing model
        and, 130–31
    fundraising and resource challenges at,
        91, 142–44
    nongovernmental organizations'
        relationships with, 227–28
    radio station organized by, 123
    social media presence of, 130
    space for alternative forms of
        masculinity at, 136
Youth Recreation Center, 100

Zaluar, Alba, 61–63
Zona Sul district (Rio de Janeiro), 33, 105,
    214–15